date

elephone

Visit the *Introduction to Political Concepts* Companion Website at **www.pearsoned.co.uk/hoffman** to find valuable **student** learning material including:

• Case studies
• Student guide to studying Political Theory
• Links to relevant sites on the web

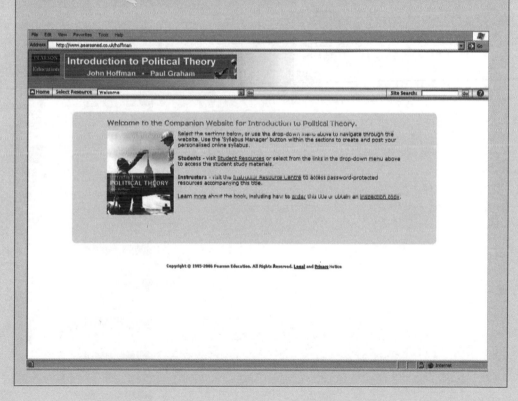

PEARSON
Education

We work with leading authors to develop the strongest educational materials in politics, bringing cutting-edge thinking and best learning practice to a global market.

Under a range of well-known imprints, including Longman, we craft high quality print and electronic publications which help readers to understand and apply their content, whether studying or at work.

To find out more about the complete range of our publishing, please visit us on the World Wide Web at: www.pearsoned.co.uk

Introduction to Political Concepts

John Hoffman
University of Leicester

Paul Graham
University of Glasgow

PEARSON
Longman

Harlow, England • London • New York • Boston • San Francisco • Toronto • Sydney • Singapore • Hong Kong
Tokyo • Seoul • Taipei • New Delhi • Cape Town • Madrid • Mexico City • Amsterdam • Munich • Paris • Milan

Pearson Education Limited
Edinburgh Gate
Harlow
Essex CM20 2JE
England

and Associated Companies throughout the world

Visit us on the World Wide Web at:
www.pearsoned.co.uk

First published in Great Britain in 2006

ISBN-13: 978-1-4058-2438-5
ISBN-10: 1-4058-2438-7

British Library Cataloguing-in-Publication Data
A catalogue record for this book is available from the British Library

Library of Congress Cataloging-in-Publication Data
Hoffman, John, 1944–
    Introduction to political concepts / John Hoffman, Paul Graham.
      p.   cm.
    Includes bibliographical references and index.
    ISBN-13: 978-1-4058-2438-5 (pbk. : alk. paper)
    ISBN 10: 1-4058-2438-7 (pbk. : alk. paper)
    1. Political science.   I. Graham, Paul.   II. Title.

  JA66.H64 2006
  320—dc22

                                                              2005057755

10 9 8 7 6 5 4 3 2 1
10 09 08 07 06

Typeset in Sabon 10/12 by 59

Printed by Ashford Colour Press Ltd., Gosport

The publisher's policy is to use paper manufactured from sustainable forests.

Brief Contents

Contents

Part 2 New Concepts

Supporting resources
Visit **www.pearsoned.co.uk/hoffman** to find valuable online resources

Companion Website for students
• Case studies
• Student guide to studying Political Theory
• Links to relevant sites on the web

For instructors
• Original theory text extracts
• Multiple choice questions for the original theory text extracts
• Instructor guide with teaching ideas for tutorials and case studies from the main book

Also: The Companion Website provides the following features:

• Search tool to help locate specific items of content
• E-mail results and profile tools to send results of quizzes to instructors
• Online help and support to assist with website usage and troubleshooting

For more information please contact your local Pearson Education sales representative or visit **www.pearsoned.co.uk/hoffman**

Guide to Features

How To Read Boxes

Ideas and Perspectives Boxes

Influences and Impact Boxes

Guided Tour

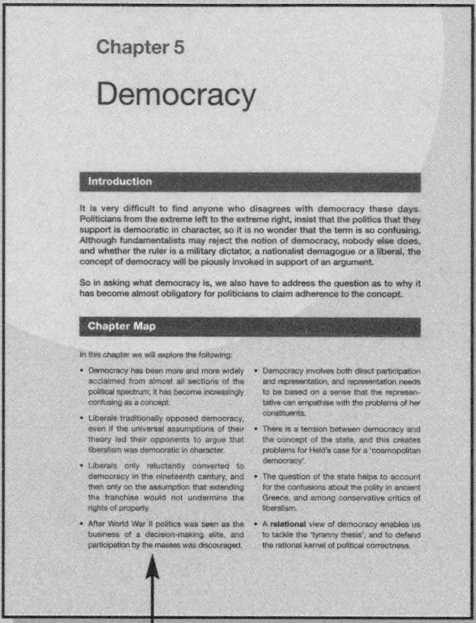

Chapter 5

Democracy

Introduction

It is very difficult to find anyone who disagrees with democracy these days. Politicians from the extreme left to the extreme right, insist that the politics that they support is democratic in character, so it is no wonder that the term is so confusing. Although fundamentalists may reject the notion of democracy, nobody else does, and whether the ruler is a military dictator, a nationalist demagogue or a liberal, the concept of democracy will be piously invoked in support of an argument.

So in asking what democracy is, we also have to address the question as to why it has become almost obligatory for politicians to claim adherence to the concept.

Chapter Map

In this chapter we will explore the following:

- Democracy has been more and more widely acclaimed from almost all sections of the political spectrum; it has become increasingly confusing as a concept.
- Liberals traditionally opposed democracy, even if the universal assumptions of their theory led their opponents to argue that liberalism was democratic in character.
- Liberals only reluctantly converted to democracy in the nineteenth century, and then only on the assumption that extending the franchise would not undermine the rights of property.
- After World War II politics was seen as the business of a decision-making elite, and participation by the masses was discouraged.
- Democracy involves both direct participation and representation, and representation needs to be based on a sense that the representative can empathise with the problems of her constituents.
- There is a tension between democracy and the concept of the state, and this creates problems for Held's case for a 'cosmopolitan democracy'.
- The question of the state helps to account for the confusions about the polity in ancient Greece, and among conservative critics of liberalism.
- A **relational** view of democracy enables us to tackle the 'tyranny thesis', and to defend the rational kernel of political correctness.

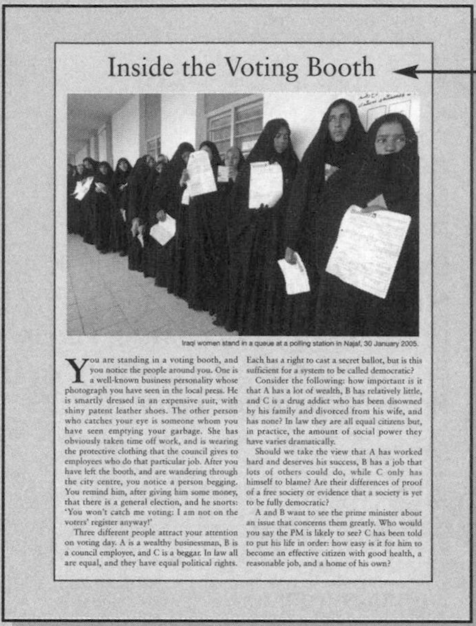

Inside the Voting Booth

Iraqi women stand in a queue at a polling station in Najaf, 30 January 2005.

You are standing in a voting booth, and you notice the people around you. One is a well-known business personality whose photograph you have seen in the local press. He is smartly dressed in an expensive suit, with shiny patent leather shoes. The other person who catches your eye is someone whom you have seen emptying your garbage. She has obviously taken time off work, and is wearing the protective clothing that the council gives to employees who do that particular job. After you have left the booth, and are wandering through the city centre, you notice a person begging. You remind him, after giving him some money, that there is a general election, and he snorts: 'You won't catch me voting: I am not on the voters' register anyway!'

Three different people attract your attention on voting day. A is a wealthy businessman, B is a council employee, and C is a beggar. In law all are equal, and they have equal political rights. Each has a right to cast a secret ballot, but is this sufficient for a system to be called democratic?

Consider the following: how important is it that A has a lot of wealth, B has relatively little, and C is a drug addict who has been disowned by his family and divorced from his wife, and has none? In law they are all equal citizens but, in practice, the amount of social power they have varies dramatically.

Should we take the view that A has worked hard and deserves his success, B has a job that lots of others could do, while C only has himself to blame? Are their differences of proof of a free society or evidence that a society is yet to be fully democratic?

A and B want to see the prime minister about an issue that concerns them greatly. Who would you say the PM is likely to see? C has been told to put his life in order: how easy is it for him to become an effective citizen with good health, a reasonable job, and a home of his own?

Test cases focus on interesting and contentious real-life examples and are accompanied by questions to challenge your own views.

The **Introductions** concisely set the scene at the start of each chapter and **Chapter Maps** summarise the key points that will be covered.

The lives and achievements of the most important theorists are fully covered in **Biography** boxes throughout the text.

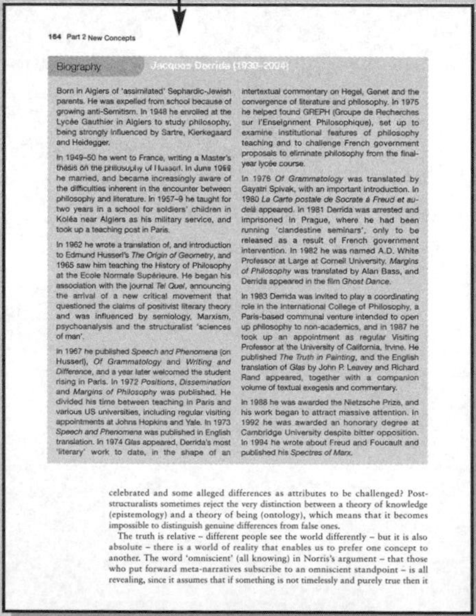

164 Part 2 New Concepts

Biography Jacques Derrida (1930–2004)

Born in Algiers of 'assimilated' Sephardic-Jewish parents. He was expelled from school because of growing anti-Semitism. In 1948 he enrolled at the Lycée Gauthier in Algiers to study philosophy, being strongly influenced by Sartre, Kierkegaard and Heidegger.

In 1949–50 he went to France, writing a Master's thesis on the philosophy of Husserl. In June 1956 he married, and became increasingly aware of the difficulties inherent in the encounter between philosophy and literature. In 1957–9 he taught for two years in a school for soldiers' children in Koléa near Algiers as his military service, and took up a teaching post in Paris.

In 1962 he wrote a translation of, and introduction to Edmund Husserl's *The Origin of Geometry*, and 1965 saw him teaching the History of Philosophy at the Ecole Normale Supérieure. He began his association with the journal *Tel Quel*, announcing the arrival of a new critical movement that questioned the claims of positivist literary theory and was influenced by semiology, Marxism, psychoanalysis and the structuralist 'sciences of man'.

In 1967 he published *Speech and Phenomena* (on Husserl), *Of Grammatology* and *Writing and Difference*, and a year later welcomed the student rising in Paris. In 1972 *Positions*, *Dissemination* and *Margins of Philosophy* was published. He divided his time between teaching in Paris and various US universities, including regular visiting appointments at Johns Hopkins and Yale. In 1973 *Speech and Phenomena* was published in English translation. In 1974 *Glas* appeared, Derrida's most 'literary' work to date, in the shape of an intertextual commentary on Hegel, Genet and the convergence of literature and philosophy. In 1975 he helped found GREPH (Groupe de Recherches sur l'Enseignment Philosophique), set up to examine institutional features of philosophy teaching and to challenge French government proposals to eliminate philosophy from the final-year lycée course.

In 1976 *Of Grammatology* was translated by Gayatri Spivak, with an important introduction. In 1980 *La Carte postale de Socrate à Freud et au-delà* appeared. In 1981 Derrida was arrested and imprisoned in Prague, where he had been running 'clandestine seminars', only to be released as a result of French government intervention. In 1982 he was named A.D. White Professor at Large at Cornell University. *Margins of Philosophy* was translated by Alan Bass, and Derrida appeared in the film *Ghost Dance*.

In 1983 Derrida was invited to play a coordinating role in the International College of Philosophy, a Paris-based communal venture intended to open up philosophy to non-academics, and in 1987 he took up an appointment as regular Visiting Professor at the University of California, Irvine. He published *The Truth in Painting*, and the English translation of *Glas* by John P. Leavey and Richard Rand appeared, together with a companion volume of textual exegesis and commentary.

In 1988 he was awarded the Nietzsche Prize, and his work began to attract massive attention. In 1992 he was awarded an honorary degree at Cambridge University despite bitter opposition. In 1994 he wrote about Freud and Foucault and published his *Spectres of Marx*.

celebrated and some alleged differences as attributes to be challenged? Post-structuralists sometimes reject the very distinction between a theory of knowledge (epistemology) and a theory of being (ontology), which means that it becomes impossible to distinguish genuine differences from false ones.

The truth is relative – different people see the world differently – but it is also absolute – there is a world of reality that enables us to prefer one concept to another. The word 'omniscient' (all knowing) in Norris's argument – that those who put forward meta-narratives subscribe to an omniscient standpoint – is all revealing, since it assumes that if something is not timelessly and purely true then it

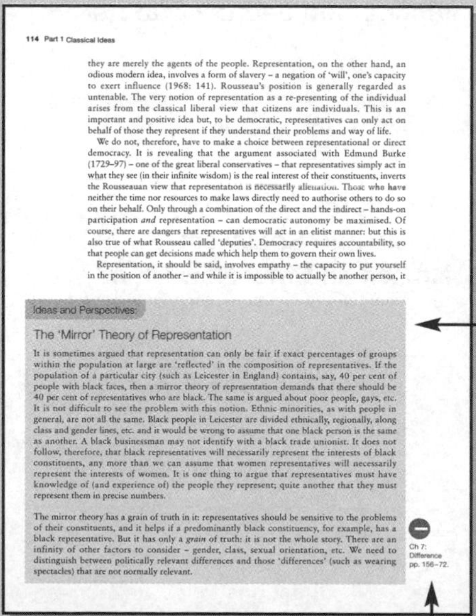

114 Part 1 Classical Ideas

they are merely the agents of the people. Representation, on the other hand, an odious modern idea, involves a form of slavery – a negation of 'will', one's capacity to exert influence (1968: 141). Rousseau's position is generally regarded as untenable. The very notion of representation as a re-presenting of the individual arises from the classical liberal view that citizens are individuals. This is an important and positive idea but, to be democratic, representatives can only act on behalf of those they represent if they understand their problems and way of life.

We do not, therefore, have to make a choice between representational or direct democracy. It is revealing that the argument associated with Edmund Burke (1729–97) – one of the great liberal conservatives – that representatives simply act in what they see (in their infinite wisdom) is the real interest of their constituents, inverts the Rousseauan view that representation is necessarily alienation. Those who have neither the time nor resources to make laws directly need to authorise others to do so on their behalf. Only through a combination of the direct and the indirect – hands-on participation *and* representation – can democratic autonomy be maximised. Of course, there are dangers that representatives will act in an elitist manner: but this is also true of what Rousseau called 'deputies'. Democracy requires accountability, so that people can get decisions made which help them to govern their own lives.

Representation, it should be said, involves empathy – the capacity to put yourself in the position of another – and while it is impossible to actually be another person, it

Ideas and Perspectives:

The 'Mirror' Theory of Representation

It is sometimes argued that representation can only be fair if exact percentages of groups within the population at large are 'reflected' in the composition of representatives. If the population of a particular city (such as Leicester in England) contains, say, 40 per cent of people with black faces, then a mirror theory of representation demands that there should be 40 per cent of representatives who are black. The same is argued about poor people, gays, etc. It is not difficult to see the problem with this notion. Ethnic minorities, as with people in general, are not all the same. Black people in Leicester are divided ethnically, regionally, along class and gender lines, etc. and it would be wrong to assume that one black person is the same as another. A black businessman may not identify with a black trade unionist. It does not follow, therefore, that black representatives will necessarily represent the interests of black constituents, any more than we can assume that women representatives will necessarily represent the interests of women. It is one thing to argue that representatives must have knowledge of (and experience of) the people they represent; quite another that they must represent them in precise numbers.

The mirror theory has a grain of truth in it: representatives should be sensitive to the problems of their constituents, and it helps if a predominantly black constituency, for example, has a black representative. But it has only a *grain* of truth: it is not the whole story. There are an infinity of other factors to consider – gender, class, sexual orientation, etc. We need to distinguish between politically relevant differences and those 'differences' (such as wearing spectacles) that are not normally relevant.

Ch 7: Difference pp. 156–72.

Ideas and Perspectives boxes focus on detailed issues.

Margin **cross references** emphasise the linkages between thinkers and ideas throughout the book.

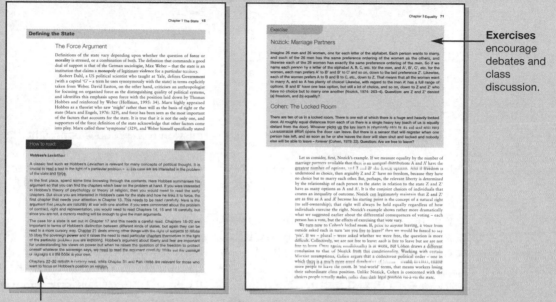

How To Read boxes analyse key political texts and identify core points.

Summaries pull together the fundamental concepts presented in the chapter

Each chapter is supported by a detailed **bibliography** giving full details of all cited references and a **further reading** list directing you to more printed resources.

Weblinks lists in each chapter provide online sources for independent study

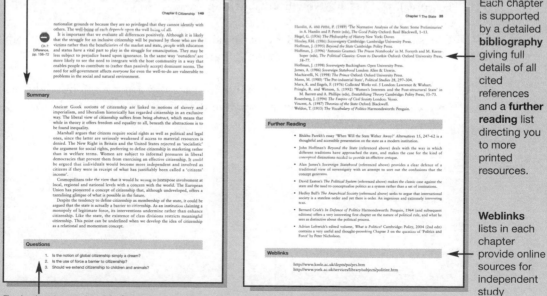

Each chapter ends with **Questions** to test your understanding of the topics covered, reflect on the theories presented and to formulate your own opinions.

Exercises encourage debates and class discussion.

Publisher's Acknowledgements

We are grateful to the following for their permission to reproduce copyright material:

Figures 3.2, 3.3 and 3.4 reprinted by permission of Sage Publications Ltd. from Laver, M. (1997) *Private Desires, Political Actions*, Copyright © Sage, 1997.

Photographs: p13 (©CORBIS), p16 (AKG Images), p17 (©Bettmann/CORBIS), p37 (Rex Features), p39 (©CORBIS), p59 (©Charles Gupton Photography/CORBIS), p81 (©Getty/Tim Boyle), p83 (Harvard News Office/Jane Reed), p90 (Harvard News Office/Jane Reed), p96 (Joseph Raz), p103 (©Faleh Kheiber/Reuters/CORBIS), p106 (©Bettmann/CORBIS), p108 (©Classic Image/Alamy), p127 (Rex Features), p131 (©CORBIS), p140 (Popperfoto), p157 (Empics), p160 (Rex Features/SIPA Press), p175 (Punchstock/Brand X), p199 (Empics), p203 (©Rune Hellestad/CORBIS), p213 (Rex Features/Everett Collection), p225 (Rex Features), p247 (©Ira Nowinski/CORBIS).

Glossary extracts reprinted by permission of Sage Publications Ltd from John Hoffman, *Citizen Beyond the State*, © John Hoffman, 2004.

In some instances we have been unable to trace the owners of copyright material, and we would appreciate any information that would enable us to do so.

Authors' Acknowledgements

We are very grateful for the help received from Morten Fuglevand and David Cox of Pearson Education. David Cox read and commented on drafts with great enthusiasm and acumen and was an endless source of lively and interesting ideas. Morten and David's commitment to the book has been inspiring and sustaining. The anonymous referees made invaluable, if at times painful, observations and have played an important part in improving the quality of the book.

John Hoffman

I would like to thank the publishers of the *Cambridge Dictionary of Sociology*, Cambridge University Press, for permission to draw upon entries submitted to this project. I am also very grateful to Edinburgh University Press for permission to use material that has also been submitted to a *Political Glossary* dealing with political theory, and to Sage Publications Ltd., who have kindly allowed me to draw upon my work *Citizenship Beyond the State* that appeared last year.

I have been supported by my partner, Rowan Roenisch, and my son, Fred and daughter, Frieda. All three have encouraged me in the project.

Paul Graham

OneWorld Books kindly granted permission to draw upon material from *Rawls* (forthcoming).

I would like to express my gratitude to my parents, Douglas and Heather Graham, for their support and encouragement, and to my colleagues in the Department of Politics at Glasgow University, for providing a stimulating intellectual environment in which to work.

About the Authors

John Hoffman has taught in the Department of Politics, University of Leicester since 1970. He is currently Emeritus Professor of Political Theory, having retired at the end of September 2005. He has written widely on Marxism, feminism and Political Theory, with his most recent book being *Citizenship beyond the State*, published by Sage in 2004. He is currently working on John Gray and the problem of utopia.

Paul Graham is a Lecturer in Political Theory at Glasgow University. He teaches and researches in German and Anglo-American political thought, with a special focus on multiculturalism, human autonomy and rationality, freedom, and distributive justice.

Introduction

Students of politics often believe that politics can be studied without theory. They take the view that we can focus upon the facts without worrying about general ideas. In everyday life, however, we are guided by notions of right and wrong, justice and injustice, so that everything we do is informed by concepts. Politicians are similarly guided. It is not a question of *whether* political animals follow theory, but a question of *which* theory or concept is supported when they present policies and undertake actions. We can argue as to whether the British prime minister or the US president acts according to the right political concepts, but it is undeniable that their actions are linked to theory. Humans in general cannot act without ideas: indeed it is a defining property of human activity that we can only act when we have ideas in our head as to what we should do.

In discussing ideas about the state or democracy or freedom in this book, we are talking about ideas or concepts or theories – we use the terms interchangeably – that guide and inform political action. The state is particularly important in Part 1 and readers should tackle this topic at an early stage. It is a great pity that theory is sometimes presented as though it inhabits a world of its own: as though it can be discussed and analysed in ways that are not explicitly linked to practical questions and political activity. This is, indeed, something this book seeks to address.

Theory as Abstraction

We accept that all theory by definition involves abstraction. The very words we use involve a 'standing back' from specific things so that we can *abstract* from them something that they have in common. To identify a chair, to use a rather corny example, one needs to abstract the quality of 'chairness' from a whole range of objects, all of which differ in some detail from every other. Take another example. The word 'dog' refers both to particular dogs and dogs in general. If we define a dog as a mammal with four legs, it could be said that a dog is the same as an elephant. So our definition is too abstract. We need to make it more particularistic. A dog is a four-legged mammal with fur. But does this mean that all dogs are poodles? Such a view is *too* particularistic: we need to argue that 'dogness' is more abstract than just being a poodle.

The point is that we are abstracting all the time, whether we like it or not! This is the only way to understand. Thus, in an analysis of the recent war in Iraq, we might use a whole host of abstractions to make sense of what we see: 'war', 'violence', 'law', 'armies', the elusive 'weapons of mass destruction' etc. Particular things are injected with a conceptual dimension, so that references to 'democracy' or 'terrorism' (for example) reflect interpretations as well as physical events.

Political theory, however, seems rather more abstract than say an analysis of the Iraq war, because it considers the notion, for example, of 'violence' beyond any particular instance, asking what violence is in every circumstance that we can imagine. This apparent remoteness from specific instances creates a trap and gives rise to a pejorative use of the term 'abstract'. For thousands of years theorists have believed that the abstraction is somehow independent of reality, or even worse, that it creates reality. Because we cannot act without ideas, the illusion arises that ideas are more important than, and are even independent of, objects. We can, therefore, talk about democracy or the state, for example, without worrying about particular states or specific kinds of democracies. Understandably students may find it bewildering to be asked 'what is power?' or 'what is democracy?' without this being related to, for example, the power which Mao Zedong exerted over the Chinese people before he died in 1976 or the question of whether the inequalities of wealth in contemporary Britain have a negative impact upon the democratic quality of its political institutions.

We believe that this link between theory and recognisable political realities is essential to an understanding and appreciation of the subject. What gives concepts and theories a bad name is that they are all too often presented abstractly (in the pejorative sense). Thinkers may forget that our thoughts come from our experience with objects in the world around us, and they assume that political thought can be discussed as though it is independent of political realities. It is true that a person who is destitute and asking for money in the street is not necessarily conscious of whether he is acting with freedom and what this concept means; but it is equally true that a theorist talking about the question of freedom may not feel the need to relate the concept of freedom to the question of social destitution. It is this act of 'abstraction' that makes many students feel that theory is a waste of time and is unrelated to the world of realities. What we are trying to do in this book is to show that general ideas can help rather than hinder us in getting to grips with particular political events.

The Distinction between Facts and Values

One of the common arguments that aggravates theory's abstractness (unless otherwise stated, we will use the term 'abstraction' in its pejorative sense), arises when people say that theory is *either* empirical *or* it is normative. In fact, it is always both. Facts and values interpenetrate, so that it is impossible to have one without the other.

Are facts the same as values? To answer this, we turn to a concrete example. It is a fact that in Western liberal societies fewer and fewer people are bothering to vote. George Bush was elected in 2000 in a situation in which only about half of the electorate turned out to vote. This fact has an implicit evaluative significance, because historically, democracy has implied participation, and this fact suggests either that Western liberal societies are minimally democratic, or that the notion of democracy has to be revised. The implicitly evaluative dimension of this fact is evidenced in the way it is challenged, or at least approached. It might be said that low voter participation is only true of *some* Western liberal societies (the United States in particular), and it might be said that voting is not the only form of political participation that counts – people can participate by joining single-issue organisations such as Greenpeace or Amnesty International.

The point about facts is that they are generally agreed upon, and can be verified in ways that are not particularly controversial. They are accepted much more widely than explicit value judgements. Evaluation, on the other hand, refers to the relationships that are only implicit in the fact. Thus the interpretation of the fact that fewer and fewer people in Western liberal societies vote raises the question of why. Does the reason for this arise from a relationship with poverty, lack of self-esteem, education, disillusionment, or is it the product of a relationship to satisfaction? The explanation embodies the evaluative content of the fact much more explicitly, since the explanation offered has obvious policy implications. If the reason for apathy is poverty, etc., then this has very different implications for action than an argument that people do not vote because they are basically satisfied with what politicians are doing in their name.

Therefore we would argue that although facts and values are not the same, they are inherently linked. In our view it is relationships which create values, so that the more explicit and far-reaching these relationships the more obviously evaluative is the factual judgement. The fact that the earth goes round the sun is not really controversial in today's world, but it was explosively controversial in the medieval world, because the notion that the earth was the centre of the universe was crucial to a statically hierarchical world outlook.

The idea that facts and even ideas can be value free ignores the linkage between the two. Not only is this empiricist view (as it is usually called) logically unsustainable, but it is another reason why students may find theory boring. The more you relate political ideas to political realities (in the sense of everyday controversies), the more lively and interesting they become. David Hume (1711–76) argued famously that it would be quite rational to prefer the destruction of the whole world to the scratching of my finger (1972: 157), but we would contest this scepticism. Reason implies the development of humans, and this is why political theory matters. Of course, what constitutes the well-being of people is complex and controversial, but a well-argued case for why the world should be preserved and its inhabitants flourish is crucial for raising the level of everyday politics.

The Problem with the Contestability Thesis

As we see it, all theories and concepts are contestable, by which we merely mean that they are part of an ongoing controversy (Hoffman, 1988). Thus, democracy is contestable because some identify democracy with liberal parliamentary systems that already exist such as the British or French or Indian systems, while others argue that democracy implies a high level of participation so that a society is not democratic if large numbers are not involved in the process of government.

But there is a more specialist use of the notion of '**contestability**' associated in particular with a famous essay by Gallie (1955: 188–93). Gallie argued, first, that only some political concepts are contestable (democracy was his favoured example), and that when concepts are essentially contestable we have no way of resolving the respective methods of competing arguments. We can note the rival justifications offered (they are mere emotional outpourings), but we cannot evaluate them in terms of a principle that commands general agreement.

But this implies that evaluation is only possible on matters about which we all agree. Such an argument stems from a misunderstanding of the nature of politics. For politics arises from the fact that we all have different interests and ideas, and the more explicit the difference between us is, the more explicit the politics. It therefore follows that a political concept is always controversial and it cannot command general agreement. Where an issue ceases to be controversial, it is not political. In this case differences are so slight that conflict is not really generated. Let us assume that chattel slavery – the owning of people as property – is a state of affairs which is so widely deplored that no one will defend it. Slavery as such ceases to be a political issue, and what becomes controversial is whether patriarchal attitudes towards women involve a condoning of slavery, or the power of employers to hire and fire labour gives them powers akin to a slave-owner. We think that it is too optimistic to assume that outright slavery is a thing of the past, but it is used here merely as an example to make a point.

All political concepts are inherently contestable, since disagreement over the meaning of a concept is what makes it political. But does it follow that because there is disagreement we have no way of knowing what is true and what is false? It is crucial not to imagine that the truth has to be timeless and above historical circumstance. But this rejection of ahistorical, timeless truth does not mean that the truth is purely relative. A relativist, for example, might argue that one person's terrorist is another person's freedom fighter. But this would make an 'objective' definition of terrorism (to pursue our example) impossible.

To argue that something is true is not to banish all doubt. If something is true, this does not mean that it is not also false. It simply means that *on balance* one proposition is more true or less false than another. To argue otherwise is to assume that a phenomenon has to be one thing or another. Philosophers call this a 'dualistic' approach. By dualism is meant an unbridgeable chasm, so that in our example, a dualist would assume that unless a statement is timelessly true, it is absolutely false. In fact, to say that the statement 'George W. Bush is a good president' is *both* true and false. Even his most fervent admirers would admit (we hope!) that he is deficient in some regards, and even his fiercest critics ought to concede that he has some positive qualities.

Take the question of freedom, as another example. What is freedom for Plato (427–347 BC) differs from what freedom is for Rousseau (1712–78), and freedom for Rousseau differs from what we in the twenty-first century normally mean by freedom. So there is an element of relativity: historical circumstances certainly affect the character of the argument. But we can only compare and contrast different concepts of freedom if we have an absolute idea as to what freedom is. The absolute notion of freedom refers to some kind of absence of constraint, but this absolute idea can only be expressed in one historical context rather than another, and it is this context that gives an absolute idea its relativity. As a consequence, there is *both* continuity (the absolute) *and* change (the relative).

There is a distinction between the absolute and the relative, but not a dualism, for we cannot have one without the other. The same is true of the distinction between the general and the particular, and the subjective and the objective. In our arguments in this book we strive to make our ideas as true as possible – i.e. we seek to make them objective, accurate reflections of the external world – but because they are moulded by *us*, and we live in a particular historical context, an element of subjectivity necessarily comes in.

What we think of freedom today will necessarily be refined by the events of tomorrow. We are only now becoming aware of how, for example, sexual orientation affects the question of freedom, and there is understandable concern about increasing freedom for people with disabilities. Health, physical and mental, also affects freedom, and all we can say is that our conception of freedom will inevitably alter in the future. But the change that will take place is not without its continuity with past concepts. Freedom is still an absolute concept, although it can only be identified in relative form.

The contestability thesis must, in our view, be able to address not merely the controversial character of political concepts, but how and why we can prefer some definitions in relation to others. Otherwise the thesis becomes bogged down in a relativism that merely notes disagreements, but has no way to defend preferences. A belief that the recent elections in Iraq will advance democracy is not an arbitrary assertion: it is the argument which can be defended (or challenged) with evidence and information to establish how much truth it contains.

Structure of the Book

In our view, a work on political theory should address itself to the kind of issues that politicians and the media themselves raise, and which are part and parcel of public debate. In the first part of this work we seek to investigate the classical concepts. These are the ones that readers are likely to be more familiar with, if they have already read some political thought, and they represent the 'staple diet' of courses on political theory. This is our justification for dealing with these concepts first. We aim to explain even the older ideas as clearly as possible so that those who have had no contact with political theory at all will not feel disadvantaged.

Of course, the fact that these concepts are traditional does not mean that our treatment of them will be traditional. We seek to make them as interesting and contentious as possible, so that readers will be stimulated to think about the ideas in a new and more refreshing way. We aim to combine both exposition and argument to enable readers to get a reasonable idea of the terrain covered by the concept, and to develop a position on the concept, often in opposition to the one we adopt. The fact that this work is written by two people means that differences will manifest themselves in the way that ideas and ideologies are analysed.

The ideas that we deal with are interlinked so that, for example, the argument about the state (and its problematic character) has a direct bearing on democracy. It is impossible to discuss the issue of citizenship without, for instance, understanding the argument about justice. Of course, it is always possible to choose to present ideas differently. In some texts, for example, 'sovereignty' is dealt with as a separate topic. In making sense of ideas and ideologies, it is crucial to say something about the key thinkers and the key texts. Our biography boxes seek to show the background and wider interests of key thinkers, and the exercises will try to emphasise why the ideas in the chapter are so relevant to understanding significant events. We have tried to make political theory challenging and enjoyable, and to deal with more detailed issues in special sections entitled 'Ideas and Perspectives'. The use of arrows is intended to cross-reference both thinkers and ideas so as to emphasise linkages between them.

In Part 2 we look at some of the contemporary concepts – such as difference, victimhood, human rights and terrorism – where the problems that these concepts address have either developed recently or have been given a new urgency by contemporary events. Sometimes it is difficult to decide what to include as an idea. Is terrorism an ideology or a concept? We have treated it as a concept, because it raises sufficient thorny conceptual problems to be treated as an idea.

Thus the outline of the book is as shown in the box.

Part 1 – Classical Ideas (state, freedom, equality, justice, democracy, citizenship)

Part 2 – New Concepts (difference, human rights, civil disobedience, terrorism, victimhood)

It might be thought that the newer ideas relate more specifically to political controversies, and of course it is true that recent debates have raised these questions acutely. But the classical ideas have not lost their relevance. Think of the debate about smoking, for example. Arguments about whether to ban smoking in public places revolve around contradictory interpretations of freedom.

All the ideas, whether contemporary or classical, are treated in ways that relate them to ongoing controversies, and show why an understanding of theory is crucial to an understanding of political issues.

Questions

1. Is it possible to devise political concepts that have no normative implications, and are thus value free in character?
2. Can one make a statement about politics without theorising at the same time?
3. Should political theory embrace or seek to avoid controversy?
4. Do teachers of political theory make practical political judgements?
5. Is the use of logic and the resort to factual evidence ethically neutral?

References

Gallie, W. (1955) 'Essentially Contested Concepts' *Proceedings of the Aristotelian Society,*
     56, 167–98.
Hoffman, J. (1988) *State, Power and Democracy* Brighton: Wheatsheaf.
Hume, D. (1972) *A Treatise of Human Nature* Books 2 & 3 London: Fontana/Collins.

Part 1

Classical Ideas

As indicated in the *Introduction* the structure of the book is as shown in the box.

> **Part 1**   **Classical Ideas** (Ch. 1 state, Ch. 2 freedom, Ch. 3 equality,
> Ch. 4 justice, Ch. 5 democracy, Ch. 6 citizenship)
>
> **Part 2**   **New Concepts** (Ch. 7 difference, Ch. 8 human rights,
> Ch. 9 civil disobedience, Ch. 10 terrorism, Ch. 11 victimhood)

In introducing the concepts of the state, freedom, equality, justice, democracy and citizenship here, we need to find an idea that underpins them all, and indeed, politics in general. In our view, this is *power*.

We are always talking about power. Do ordinary people have any? Do prime ministers and presidents have too much? Do people decline to vote because they feel they have no power? The question of power inevitably merges into the question of authority. Is might right? Are those who have power entitled to exercise it? When we raise questions such as these we are in fact asking whether power is the same as, or different from, authority. No one can really dispute the fact that after Operation Iraqi Freedom in Iraq, the United States has power, or considerable power, in Iraq, but does that mean that it is entitled to exercise this power? The critics of US policy would argue that it lacks authority. Does this mean that it will be frustrated in its exercise of power?

It is not difficult to see that when we talk about power and its relation to authority we are also implicitly raising issues that have a direct bearing on the classical concepts of Part 1.

The Link with Other Concepts

The definition of the state which we will adopt is that of the famous German sociologist Max Weber (1864–1920), who defined the state as an institution claiming a monopoly of legitimate force. How does the notion of 'legitimate force' connect to the notion of power? Is the use of force the same as power? We will try to argue that while the two ideas sound similar, in fact power requires compliance, whereas force does not. Of course, it is easy to think of examples where the two come very close to one another. In the proverbial case of the person with a gun who demands your money or life, you have a 'choice' in a technical sense, but the 'power' exercised involves a threat of credible force, so that in reality your choice is illusory. In this case we would prefer to speak of coercion rather than power.

One of the most frequently debated topics is the question of whether force can be legitimate, and by legitimacy we mean force that has been authorised and limited. Clearly a soldier or a member of the police can use force, and usually this force has been authorised by parliament and, therefore, ultimately by those who can vote and hold parliament accountable. Does this make the force legitimate and, thus, an act blessed by authority? And if the act of state force is authoritative, in whose eyes does it have authority? Those who are subject to this force (let us say protesters in a demonstration that is deemed to get out of hand), or those who are not part of the demonstration and approve of the action of the police? These are difficult questions, and we introduce them here in order to show why in a discussion of the state it is important to involve questions of power and its relation to authority.

Consider the question of freedom or liberty. We usually think of a person being free if she can exercise power, thus changing herself and her surroundings. But if freedom is defined 'negatively', it may simply mean that you are free when no one deliberately interferes with you. Being free in this case is merely being left alone, not actually exercising power. On the other hand, if freedom is defined 'positively', it relates to a person's capacity to do something, so that, for example, freedom of speech is concerned with the power of a person to speak his mind, not the restrictions that may be placed on someone's right to do so. When does a person's freedom become an act of power that should be accepted or tolerated, and when should it be curbed? Clearly, a person who had no power at all could not (say) smoke, but should smoking be banned from public places on the grounds that it is a form of power that is harmful? It is impossible to discuss these issues and the famous argument raised by the British liberal thinker John Stuart Mill (1806–73) without having some kind of idea about power and authority and that is what Chapter 2 of this book sets out to do.

Equality and justice rest upon ideas of 'rightness'. Some people see a conflict between equality and freedom on the grounds that redistributing wealth through high taxation prevents individuals from being rewarded according to their merits. The state has too much power and the **individual** too little. This, it is argued, undermines the authority of the state: people pay their taxes because they have to, not because they want to. Egalitarians, on the other hand, link equality with justice, and argue that everyone should be treated equally. We should aim to spread power so that one person or group cannot tell another individual or group what to do, and governments should implement policies that move in this direction. People have the same rights, and therefore exercise similar power. Bill Gates, the billionaire owner of Microsoft, has rather more power than Josephine Bloggs who cleans his office or Willhelm Peter who removes some of the 4 million emails that Bill Gates receives every day. Is this just? Equality and justice rely, as we have already commented, upon the question of rightness, and can it be right that some individuals have so much more power than others?

Indeed, one definition of democracy is the 'power of the people'. Historically, the objection to democracy was precisely that the wrong kind of person would exercise power, and nineteenth-century liberals such as Lord Macaulay feared that democracy would enable the poor to plunder the rich. On the other hand, left-wing critics of liberal democracy complain that the right to vote does not in itself give a person power to influence the course of events and that material resources must be available to people if they are to exercise power. The authority of liberal democracy rests upon equal rights rather than equal power so that the notion of power is indissolubly tied to debates about democracy.

The same is true with the concept of citizenship. Being a **citizen** gives you power. But does it give you enough? Is the housewife a citizen? She may have the right to vote and stand for parliament, but at the same time she may feel compelled to do what her husband tells her, and have limited power over her own life. Nancy Hartsock, a US academic, wrote a book entitled *Money, Sex and Power* (1985). Yet one of the most central questions in the debate about citizenship is whether the unequal distribution of resources distort the power that people exercise. Are we already citizens or can we only become citizens if resources are more evenly spread both within and between societies? It is not difficult to see why the question of **power**, how we define it, identify it and analyse it is central to this (as to other) classical political ideas.

Power and Authority: an Indissoluble Link?

Power, as defined here, is a social concept. By this we mean that power is concerned with human relations and not with the mere movement of inanimate objects.

Power and authority are often contrasted. The police have power (power comes from the barrel of a gun, the former Chinese leader Mao Zedong is supposed to have said) whereas the late Queen Mother in Britain had authority (she inspired love and warmth – at least among some). A simple definition to start with would be to argue that power involves dominating someone or some group, telling them what to do, whereas authority is concerned with the rightness of an action. A person has to be pressured into complying with power, whereas they will obey authority in a voluntary way.

Alas, things are not so simple, because power and authority always seem to go together. This problem particularly bothers Jean-Jacques Rousseau, the great French eighteenth-century thinker (1712–78). On the one hand, might can never be transformed into right, since 'force is a physical power; I do not see how its effects could produce morality' (Rousseau, 1968: 52). On the other hand, Rousseau famously insists that people must obey the **law**. The social contract would be worthless unless it could ensure that those who refuse to abide by the general will must be constrained to do so. Dissenters must, in that most celebrated of phrases, be 'forced to be free' (1968: 64).

Power and authority contradict each other, and yet there is an indissoluble link between them.

Our problem can be presented as shown in the diagram.

Power implies	Authority implies
constraint	consent
force	morality
subordination	will
dependence	autonomy

This is the problem of the 'two levels'. Power and authority appear to exclude one another, but they are never found apart.

Does a Broad View of Politics Help?

It might be argued that the problem of power and its relationship to authority is not a serious one. All we need to do is point to a state that rests purely on power, and one that rests solely upon authority, and the problem is solved!

But April Carter in her *Authority and Democracy* concedes that in the political sphere, 'authority rarely exists in its pure form', and she says that even a constitutional government acting with great liberalism would still lack 'pure authority' since, as she puts it, such a government 'relies ultimately upon coercion' (1979: 41; 33). Political authority (defined in statist terms) is paradoxical – a contradiction in terms – since no state, however benevolent, can wholly abstain from the use of force. Pure authority turns out to be a pure abstraction, at least as far as politics is concerned, and Carter demonstrates that rigorous definition and common sense cannot avoid the problem of paradox. Power and authority may be mutually exclusive, but it seems impossible to effect a clean divorce.

This is why Barbara Goodwin in her *Using Political Ideas* (1997) argues that the attempt to distinguish rigorously between power and authority is 'doomed to failure. In any normal political situation, and in every state institution, they co-exist and support each other' (1997: 314). It might be objected that politics is far broader than the state, and involves social relations between individuals. Surely here, at least, we can find a sharp separation between power and authority.

Taylor, who is interested in anthropological material on stateless societies, argues that a society without any form of coercion is 'conceivable' (1982: 25), and the New Left theorist, C.B. Macpherson (1911–87), takes the view that in a simple market model in which every household has *enough* either to produce goods and services for itself or to exchange with others, then we have an example of cooperation without coercion – or in our terminology, authority without power. But it could be objected that the market mechanism constrains and, Marx argues, under capitalism, 'the dull compulsion of economic relations' subordinates the labourer to the capitalist (1970: 737). Even the independent producers of commodities suffer what Marx calls 'the coercion exerted by the presence of their mutual interests' (1970: 356).

But what about social examples that not only avoid the state, but do not involve the market either? What of the relationship between parent and child, teacher and student, doctor and patient? Are these not spheres in which we *can* (although do not always) witness the kind of respect that is essential for authority but which excludes power? However, J.S. Mill raises a problem that calls this analysis into question. In *On Liberty* Mill champions the right of the individual to think and act freely. In his argument he contrasts the physical force of the state to what he calls 'the moral coercion of public opinion' (1974: 68). Morality itself is seen as constraining, and we would contend that the very notion of a **relationship** subverts the idea that power and authority can be spliced apart. If all relationships are governed by norms (i.e. morality) of some kind, how then can any relationships be free from pressures of a constraining kind?

Negative and Positive Power

We have assumed that power and authority are contrasting concepts. But a distinction is often made between power as a negative and power as a positive concept. This, as we will see, has important implications for the concept of authority.

Power is negative in the sense that it relates to my ability to get you to do things that you would not otherwise do. The negative view of power is associated with the liberal tradition, and centres around the capacity of the individual to act freely and take responsibility for their actions. It is a notion deeply rooted in our culture and, in our view, forms a necessary part of any analysis of power. People who exercise power can and should be punished (or helped) when they exercise this power in ways that harm others or, indeed, irreversibly harm themselves. By this latter point, we mean a situation in which people cannot change their minds because, as with serious self-abuse, or taking addictive drugs, it is too late! This notion emphasises the differences between people and their conflict of interests. Each individual is separate, and we are all capable of exercising negative power.

In contrast, power is deemed *positive* when it is expressed as empowerment. Empowerment occurs when one person helps ('empowers') themselves or another, or when a group or community enables people to develop. Contrary to what people may think, the notion of power as negative is a modern one, while the ancients took the view that power was always expressed positively within communities. The idea of power being exercised to strengthen our relations with others is a very old one.

Positive power is seen as the ability to do things by the discovery of our own strength – a capacity – a power *to* – as opposed to negative power that is seen as a power *over* – a domination. The conventional view sees power in negative terms, linked to the state, and force or the threat of force. Elshtain distinguishes between *potestas* – which relates to control, supremacy, domination, and *potential* – which relates to ability, efficacy and potency, especially that which is 'unofficial and sinister' (Elshtain, 1992: 117).

However we distinguish them, it is impossible to separate negative and positive power in an empirical sense. It is clear from Lukes's (2005) commentary that positive power broadly corresponds to what has sometimes been called authority, and negative power expresses the conventional view of power. Defining power in a way that separates out logically the negative from the positive does not resolve the power/authority problem and, like power and authority, negative and positive power always go together. It is impossible to think of a relationship in which one exists without the other.

Negative and Positive Power as a Relationship

The reason why negative and positive power cannot be divorced is that all relationships contain both. It is true that earlier notions of power were predominantly positive in character, but the problem, historically, is that this power has in practice been repressively hierarchical: the power of fathers, of lords, of priests, of kings. Positive power has been exercised in the past by people who claim (somewhat implausibly) to be acting on behalf of everyone else – men acting on behalf of women and children, lords for their serfs, priests for parishioners, sovereigns for subjects.

As liberals rightly object, 'negative power' is smuggled in through the back door. The holders of positive power see themselves as chastising others for their own good. The master may imagine that he is acting in the slave's interests – but when the slave is thought of as an individual, then things seem rather different! Power must be both positive and negative. It is important that we do not reject the individual focus of negative power, but seek to build upon it. We must come up with the proposition that if I am to exercise power as an individual, then I must allow you to exercise power as an individual. In other words, to sustain negative power, it must be exercised in terms of a *relationship* – or positively – so that I exercise power in a way that enables you to exercise power.

Power implies mutuality – but it can only be mutual if it is both positive and negative. If it is positive 'on its own', as it were, it stresses unity at the expense of separation, the community at the expense of the individual, so that (as liberals suspect), it becomes oppressive and hypocritical. Positive power exercised 'on its own' is as one-sided as negative power when the latter is conceived in an abstract manner, because when negative power is exercised on its own separation is expressed at the expense of unity. One individual exercises power in a way that prevents another from doing the same.

If the notion of 'negative' power is crucial for a person's freedom and individuality, it is not enough. 'On its own', it presents power in what is sometimes called a 'zero sum game', i.e. I have power because you do not. I exercise power *over* you – if I win, you lose. I am separate from you, and therefore my power differentiates me from you. Normally when people think of power they think of power in negative terms.

Why is this notion a problem? It assumes – as its classical liberal roots reveal – that individuals can exist in complete isolation from other individuals, whereas in fact, as any parent can tell you, we only acquire our sense of individuality (and thus separateness) in conjunction with others. Logically, if each person is to exercise power, then this negative power must take account of the right of each individual to be the same as everyone else. In other words, power can only be consistently 'negative' if it also has a social, positive and what we want to call a 'relational' attribute.

Three-dimensional Power and the Problem of Power and Authority

Lukes argues that power can be divided into three dimensions. The one-dimensional view identifies power as decision making, the two-dimensional view argues that power can be exercised beyond the decision-making forum as in a situation where certain issues are excluded from an agenda and people feel that their interests are not being met. Three-dimensional power arises when people express preferences that are at variance with their interests: they support a system through a consciousness that is 'false'.

Lukes's argument is that the first dimension is highly superficial. He is sharply critical of Dahl's defence of power as decision making in *Who Governs* (1961) on the grounds that those taking decisions may not exercise decisive power at all. The second dimension is an improvement but still confines itself to observable activity: we have to be able to show that groups outside the decision-making forum are consciously exercising power, while three-dimensional power is deemed the most subtle of all. People do not protest precisely because they are victims of a power system that creates a phoney consensus, and those exercising power (such as the media or educational system) may do so unintentionally. An example of three-dimensional power could be taken to be the Great Leap Forward in China that was supported by many who believed that through their heroic will-power the arrival of a communist society would be hastened. They certainly did not want the famine that followed.

But how can Lukes prove the existence of a 'latent' conflict, a potential event and a non-existing decision? How can he demonstrate an exercise of power when nothing takes place? The gulf between interests and preferences can, it seems, be demonstrated if it can be shown that with more information people's preferences would have changed, and that interests only come into line with preferences when no further unit of information would cause any further change. Lukes has indicated that at least under some circumstances (for example where partial information leads to people in the town of Gary, Indiana not campaigning for an air pollution ordinance), power can be exercised which *appears* authoritative. Power and authority seem to go together but in fact the authority is an illusion. Power is being exercised all along.

But has this really resolved the power/authority problem? It certainly points to the way in which unintended circumstances pressure people to do things they otherwise would not have done. But the fact is that the separation remains because when power is expressed in a situation without observable conflict the authority is simply a propagandist illusion – an idealised mystification of the reality of power. Indeed, Lukes seems to be saying that where people are fully informed, there is authority; where information is blocked even unintentionally, there is power. The problem is still not resolved.

Accounting for the 'Indissoluble Link'

Long after liberals rejected the notion of a state of nature in which individuals live in splendid isolation from one another, they continue to write as though individuals can be conceived in the absence of relationships through which they in fact discover their identity.

Constraint is unavoidable since no agent can exist except through a structure: these structures are both natural and social. You have to obey the laws of gravity and you have relationships with your family and friends whether you like it or not. Constraint should not be confused with force, although classical liberals and anarchists use the terms as though they were synonyms. Although we know of many societies that were or (in the case of international society) are stateless in character, we know of no society in which there is an absence of constraint. Consensus arises when people can 'change places' and show empathy with one another's point of view, and this necessarily involves constraining pressures. Force, on the other hand, disrupts consensus and relationships, since when force is used the other party ceases to be a person, and becomes a 'thing'.

To see how this translates into the argument about power and authority, the chart as shown can be drawn up.

Power	Authority
Necessity	Freedom
Circumstances	Rational consciousness
Negative power	Positive power
Pressure	Will
Constraint	Autonomy

All relationships involve constraints (power) and entitlements (authority). Remove one side of the power/authority equation, and the other crumbles. Take two diametrically opposed examples by way of illustration. In a master/slave relationship, power is obvious and manifest. Not only are there constraints, but there is also a threat of credible force. But at the same time unless slaves (however reluctantly or under whatever duress) 'acknowledge' or 'accept' their slavery, then the relationship between them and their masters is impossible, and they will die or escape. Relationships are mutual: being a slave obviously limits your freedom, but so too does *having* one, even if, in one case, the constraint causes pain and in the other, pleasure. To put the point *in extremis*: slave owners who simply kill their slaves or fail to keep them in service destroy the basis of their own power. Even the slave, in other words, makes some input in this most repressive of relationships, and it is this input that gives the relationship its (minimally) authoritative character. In this case, we would want to say that slave owners exercise 'much' power and 'little' authority.

Let us turn to a relationship at the other end of the political spectrum, that between doctor and patient (or if you prefer, between teacher/pupil; priest/ parishioner, etc.). In this case, it seems that only authority exists, and there is no power. People normally go to the doctor because they want to, and if they accept the advice offered it is because there is a communication of a persuasive or potentially persuasive kind. Authority predominates, but power also exists. Doctors communicate with their patients by pointing to constraints. If the advice they offer is not taken, highly unpleasant circumstances will follow! In these circumstances a person may have as much or as little freedom to choose as in a situation where they are threatened with force, since what choice does a chronically ill person have when told of the need for a dangerous operation, if the alternative is a swift and certain death? In this case, we have a relationship in which there is 'much' authority, but there is by no means a complete absence of power.

What has to be excluded from power and authority is the use of force itself, since this makes compliance impossible and is therefore a violation not merely of authority, but of power as well. Obviously the more authority predominates, the better, but even a purely consensual relationship involves some element of constraint.

Let us conclude by giving an example of a member of the police seeking to persuade football supporters who have been unable to obtain tickets to go home. Initially, mild pressures would be invoked: 'it would be a good idea not to hang around but to go home'. If this does not work something stronger might be tried, such as: 'I would like you to go home – it would be silly not to'. If this does not work, a command follows: 'I am ordering you to go home'. Then – a threat: 'if you don't go home, I will arrest you' and Black Marias around the corner are indicated. If the police authority has to actually seize the protester, then force is used and both power and authority have failed. But the point is that even in the most authoritative statement, power is also implied, and in the sternest expression of power, authority is also present. The two always go together, and unless they are linked, no relationship is possible.

There is therefore a difference between what are conventionally called democratic and authoritarian states. The latter rely far more upon power and the former have much more authority. But the two concepts always go together, even though they are different, and it is a sobering thought that for those subject to force neither power nor authority can be said to exist.

Power is not merely a crucial but the central concept of politics. It underpins, as we have tried to show, the other ideas that are elaborated in Part 1 and hence it deserves a separate (and fairly extended) treatment of its own by way of prefacing this section of the book.

References

Bock and James (eds)(1992) *Beyond Equality and Difference* London and New York: Routledge.

Carter, A. (1979) *Authority and Democracy* London: Routledge & Kegan Paul.

Dahl, R. (1961) *Who Governs?* New Haven: Yale University.

Elshtain, J. (1992) 'The Power and Powerlessness of Women' in G. Bock and S. James (eds), *Beyond Equality and Difference* London and New York: Routledge.

Goodwin, B. (1997) *Using Political Ideas* 4th edn Chichester and New York, *et al*.: John Wiley and Sons.

Hartsock, N. (1985) *Money, Sex and Power* Boston, Mass.: Northeastern University Press.

Hobbes, T. (1968) *The Leviathan* Harmondsworth: Penguin.

Hoffman, J. (1988) *State, Power and Democracy* Brighton: Wheatsheaf.

Lukes, S. (2005) *Power: A Radical View* 2nd edn Basingstoke: Palgrave.

Marx, K. (1970) *Capital* vol. 1 London: Lawrence & Wishart.

Mill, J.S. (1974) *On Liberty* Harmondsworth: Penguin.

Rousseau, J.–J. (1968) *The Social Contract* Harmondsworth: Penguin.

Taylor, M. (1982) *Community, Anarchy and Liberty* Cambridge: Cambridge University Press.

Chapter 1

The State

Introduction

If you asked the average person to identify the state, they might look at you in astonishment, and say that they were not aware of living under a state, unless by that you meant the 'government'. Indeed, some writers have spoken of Britain and the USA as stateless societies, although this is to confuse what people think about the state, and what the state really is. In tackling this question, we shall also try to deal with the problem: does the state really exist?

Chapter Map

In this chapter we will explore:

- The history of the concept of the state so as to decide whether the state is purely modern.

- Various definitions of the state, and our own definition.

- The link between the state and conventional notions of sovereignty.

- The argument that holds that it is possible to look beyond the state, provided certain conceptual distinctions are put in place.

Changing States: Hitler's Rise to Power

Adolf Hitler salutes a huge crowd of Hitler youth, Nuremberg, Germany ca. 1930s.

With the end of World War I in sight, the Weimar Republic was established and soon things began to deteriorate. War reparations, totalling £6.6 billion, had completely crippled the economy. France and Belgium occupied the Ruhr in response to alleged defaults in Germany's repayments. A general strike was called across the entire country.

It was in this climate that a group of right-wing ex-army officers attempted to seize power in Munich. One of the ringleaders, Adolf Hitler, was imprisoned and, on his release, the Nazis began a programme of violence towards the left, calculated to drive the bourgeoisie towards Nazism. In the 1928 elections the party won 800,000 votes.

Wealthy Germans, fearing for their lives and property if the Communists gained power, began to donate generously to the Nazis. The Wall Street Crash of 1929 had a further disastrous effect on the German economy, and within a year the price of a loaf of bread jumped from 163 marks to 200,000,000,000 marks.

As a result of such upheaval, extreme political polarisation between the right and left occurred. The presidential elections of 1932 saw the Nazi Party gain 13.5 million votes. A decision was taken to appoint Hitler as the Chancellor of Germany. The Cabinet believed that the Nazis would soon be revealed as unequal to the task of government, and hoped that Hitler would be easily controlled by the non-Nazis in the Cabinet, and their extreme views tempered.

This decision proved to be a fatal error. In just over a year Hitler became the undisputed dictator of Germany, ruling over a fascist state astonishing in its ruthless totalitarianism and violent anti-Semitism.

Germany in the inter-war years is a real laboratory for identifying and conceptualising politics and the state, as it changed from a liberal to a fascist state with amazing speed. In light of the article above, consider:

- How inevitable was World War II, and how could the state have worked to prevent it?
- Your thoughts on the question of whether or not Nazism is distinctively German. Compare those characteristics associated with a fascist regime to issues such as high unemployment, inflation and humiliation after war that could occur in any society.

How Modern is the Concept of the State?

The question of what the **state** is is linked to the question of when the state emerges historically. T.H. Green (a nineteenth-century British political philosopher) believed that states have always existed, since families and tribes require an ideal of what is right, and right is the basis of the state (1941). Hegel (who was a nineteenth-century German philosopher) took the view that tribal societies had neither states nor history. Lacking reason, they cannot be understood (1956: 61).

More common, however, is the argument that the state is a modern institution since its 'forms' are as important as its 'content'. The state, in one account, is defined in terms of five attributes (Dunleavy and O'Leary, 1987: 2).

1. **A public institution separated from the private activities of society** In ancient Greek **society**, the polis (wrongly called, Dunleavy and O'Leary argue, the city state) did not separate the **individual** from the state, and in a feudal society kings and their vassals were bound by oaths of loyalty that were both public and private. Certain sections of society, such as the clergy, had special immunities and privileges, so that there was no sharp separation between members of society, on the one hand, and the polity on the other.

2. **The existence of sovereignty in unitary form** In a feudal society, for example, the clergy, the nobility, the particular 'estates' and 'guilds' (merchants, craftsmen, artisans, etc.) had their particular courts and rules, so that the only loyalty which went beyond local attachments was to the Universal Church, and in Europe this was divided between pope and emperor. **Laws** confirmed customs and social values – they were not made by a particular body that had a united '**will**'.

3. **The application of laws to all who live in a particular society** In the ancient Greek polis, protection was only extended to citizens, not slaves, and even a stranger required patronage from a **citizen** to claim this protection. Under feudalism, protection required loyalty to a particular lord. It did not arise from living in a territory, and the ruling political system could not administer all the inhabitants.

4. **The recruitment of personnel according to bureaucratic as opposed to patrimonial criteria** Whereas the state selects people for an office according to impersonal attributes, earlier polities mixed the office holder with the job, so that offices belonged to particular individuals and could be handed to relatives or friends at the discretion of the office holder. Imagine the vice-chancellor of a university deciding to name his or her own successor!

5. **The capacity to extract revenue (tax) from a subject population** In **pre-modern** polities, problems of transport and communication meant that this was limited, and rural communities in particular were left to their own devices.

The argument is that only the state is sovereign, separate from society, can protect all who dwell within its clearly demarcated boundaries, recruits personnel according to bureaucratic criteria and can tax effectively. These are seen not merely as the features of a modern state, but of the state itself. We will later challenge this argument but it is very widely held.

Defining the State

The Force Argument

Definitions of the state vary depending upon whether the question of **force** or **morality** is stressed, or a combination of both. The definition that commands a good deal of support is that of the German sociologist, Max Weber – that the state is an institution that claims a **monopoly** of legitimate **violence** for a particular territory.

Robert Dahl, a US political scientist who taught at Yale, defines **Government** (with a capital 'G' – a term he uses synonymously with the state) in terms explicitly taken from Weber. David Easton, on the other hand, criticises an anthropologist for focusing on organised force as the distinguishing quality of political systems, and identifies this emphasis upon force with the position laid down by Thomas Hobbes and reinforced by Weber (Hoffman, 1995: 34). Marx highly appraised Hobbes as a theorist who saw 'might' rather than will as the basis of right or the state (Marx and Engels, 1976: 329), and force has been seen as the most important of the factors that accounts for the state. It is true that it is not the only one, and supporters of the force definition of the state acknowledge that other factors come into play. Marx called these 'symptoms' (329), and Weber himself specifically stated

How to read:

Hobbes's *Leviathan*

A classic text such as Hobbes's *Leviathan* is relevant for many concepts of political thought. It is crucial to read a text in the light of a particular problem – in this case we are interested in the problem of the state and force.

In the first place, spend some time browsing through the contents. Here Hobbes summarises his argument so that you can find the chapters which bear on the problem at hand. If you were interested in Hobbes's theory of psychology or theory of religion, then you would need to read the early chapters. But since you are interested in Hobbes's case for the state and how he links it to force, the first chapter that needs your attention is Chapter 13. This needs to be read carefully. Here is the argument that people are naturally at war with one another. If you were concerned about the problem of contract, right and representation, you would need to read Chapters 14, 15 and 16 carefully, but since you are not, a cursory reading will be enough to give the main arguments.

The case for a state is set out in Chapter 17 and this needs a careful read. Chapters 18–20 are important in terms of Hobbes's distinction between different kinds of states, but again they can be read in a more cursory way. Chapter 21 deals among other things with the right of subjects to refuse to obey the sovereign **power** and it raises the need to read particular chapters themselves in the light of the particular problem you are exploring. Hobbes's argument about liberty and fear are important for understanding his views on power but when he raises the question of the freedom to protect oneself whatever the sovereign says, we need to read the argument carefully. Write out the passage or highlight it if the book is your own.

Chapters 22–30 require a cursory read, while Chapter 31 and Part Three are relevant for those who want to focus on Hobbes's position on religion.

German economist and sociologist. Born in Saxony of a prosperous middle-class family. Weber initially studied the history of commercial law at the University of Heidelberg. Here he took a chair in political economy in 1897 and co-founded the first sociological journal, *Archiv für Sozialwissenschaft und Sozialpolitik (Journal for Social Science and Politics)* (1903). Weber was variously a lawyer, historian, economist, philosopher, political scientist and sociologist!

A personal breakdown in 1898 led to his withdrawal from teaching. He continued writing. He was initially concerned with the impact of capitalism on the agricultural estates east of the Elbe, and this led to a wider study of capitalism and its relation to the Protestant religion, *The Protestant Ethic and the Rise of Capitalism* (1904–5). Here he argued that the impulse to accumulate far beyond the needs of personal consumption was grounded in the 'worldly asceticism' of reformed Christianity, and this ethic led the believer to demonstrate salvation through the accumulation of wealth.

Weber became interested in exploring modern Western rationalism, and he argued that only in modern societies has the conscious linkage of ends to means become central to a goal-maximising calculation. Reason was crucial to the scientific assumption that the world could be subject to human control. Whereas legitimacy (or the entitlement to rule) was based upon hereditary lords or monarchs in traditional societies, in the modern world legitimacy is rooted in a rationalised administration ruled by professionals, who are selected according to merit.

Although he took repressive hierarchy for granted, he was concerned about restricting bureaucracy through energetic political leaders who had been elected. He was a member of the German Social Democratic Party, a member of the German delegation to the Armistice settlement following World War I and one of the authors of the Weimar Constitution that existed until the Nazis came to power.

that force is not the only attribute of the state. Indeed his definition makes it clear that the force of the state has to be 'legitimate', monopolised and focused on a particular territory. Nevertheless, as Weber himself says, force is a 'means specific to the state' (Gerth and Wright Mills, 1991: 78; 134).

The other factors are important but secondary. Force is central to the state, its most essential attribute.

The Centrality of Will

Those who see morality or right as the heart of the state are often called 'idealists' because they consider 'ideas' rather than material entities to be central to reality. Hegel, perhaps the most famous of the idealist thinkers, described the state as the realisation of morality – the 'Divine Idea as it exists on Earth' (1956: 34).

T.H. Green argued that singling out what he called 'supreme coercive power' as the essential attribute of the state undermines the important role that morality plays in securing a community's interests (1941: 121). Green acknowledges the role of Jean-Jacques Rousseau, an eighteenth-century French writer, in arguing that morality, **right** and duty form the basis of the state. Green does not deny that what he calls 'supreme coercive power' is involved in the state, but crucial to the state are the moral ends for which this power is exercised. This led Green's editor to sum up his argument with the dictum 'will, not force, is the basis of the state' (Hoffman, 1995: 218–19).

More recently, writers such as Hamlin and Pettit have argued that the state is best defined in terms of a system of rules which embody a system of rights – this is crucial to what they call a 'normative analysis of the state' (1989: 2).

The State as a Mixture of Will and Force

Others argue that the state does not have a 'basis' or central attribute, but is a 'mixture' of both force and morality. It is wrong to regard one of these as more important than the other.

Antonio Gramsci, an Italian Marxist, traced this view of the state back to Machiavelli's *The Prince*. Machiavelli, writing in the sixteenth century, declared that there are two means of fighting: 'one according to the laws, the other with force; the first way is proper to man, the second to beasts', but because, Machiavelli argued,

Biography

Georg Wilhelm Frederich Hegel (1770–1831)

Born in Stuttgart. He studied philosophy and classics at the University of Tübingen, and became a private tutor in Berne and then in Frankfurt.

His first work (only published posthumously) was *The Spirit of Christianity and Its Fate*, but in 1801 he returned to the study of philosophy at the University of Jena. In 1806 he completed a very serious systematic study of philosophy entitled *Phenomenology of the Mind* – just in time to flee Jena from the approaching French armies. In 1816 he became a professor at the University of Heidelberg, and in 1817 *The Encyclopaedia of the Philosophical Sciences* followed. Two years later he became a professor at the University of Berlin, where he remained until his death in 1831.

In 1821 he published his major political work, *Philosophy of Right*. In this Hegel argued that while society consists of laws which are necessary for the good life, man (and by 'man' Hegel means biological men!) also possesses a free conscience. It is necessary to balance the need for a legal order and a realm of responsible personal freedom. The danger is that one tendency will prevail over another, so that the state will be either a legal tyranny or an anarchy of human wilfulness. Hegel took modern constitutional monarchy as it evolved out of the French Revolution and the French Restoration as the state form most likely to realise freedom.

After his death his lecture notes were compiled into a number of publications: *Philosophy of Religion* (1832), *History of Philosophy* (1833–36), *Philosophy of Fine Art* (1835–38), and *Philosophy of History* (1837).

Antonio Gramsci (1891–1937)

Born in Sardinia. He had a physical deformity (he was hunchbacked) and his father was imprisoned for corruption. Despite a wretched childhood, he won a scholarship to the University of Turin. Here he specialised in linguistics and fell under the influence of the Hegelian, Benedetto Croce. Gramsci joined the Italian Socialist Party in 1913, supported the Russian Revolution (which he saw as a triumph of the 'will' over circumstances) and in a socialist weekly, the *Ordine Nuovo* (New Order), he championed the factory council movement.

After World War I he opposed what he saw as the passivity of the Socialist Party and became a founding member of the Italian Communist Party. In 1924 he became its general secretary and was elected to parliament. However, this did not protect him from being tried and sent to prison during Mussolini's rule.

Here he wrote his magnum opus the *Prison Notebooks* (1929–35), which dealt with a wide range of topics from the theatre to the state. He considered classical Marxist theory too deterministic and concentrated a good deal on moral and intellectual factors in politics. He regarded Bolshevik strategy as inappropriate for conditions in the West and argued the case for what he called 'a war of position' that would take full account of cultural as well as economic circumstances.

He was released from prison in 1937, as a result of an international campaign, but in extremely poor health and died shortly afterwards.

the first is often not sufficient, 'it becomes necessary to have recourse to the second' (1998: 58). The state was seen as analogous to the mythical creature, the centaur, which was half-human and half-beast. Gramsci embraced this argument. The state is linked to force, but equally important is law, morality and right (1971: 170). The state in this argument has a dual character, and although Gramsci subscribed to the Marxist argument that the state would wither away, he argues that what disappears is force, and an 'ethical state' remains (Hoffman, 1996: 72).

It has become very common to contend that theories which argue that the essential property of the state is either morality or force are 'essentialist' or 'reductionist'. By this is meant an approach that highlights one factor as being crucially relevant. Just as it is wrong to ignore the part of the state which imposes force upon those who will not voluntarily comply with the law, so it is wrong to downgrade the 'civilising' aspects of the state – the aspects of the state which regulate people's lives in ways that make them healthier and happier. The notion of a 'welfare state' captures this amalgam, since it is argued that the state is *both* negative and positive – a mixture of force and 'will'. Your local hospital is part of the National Health Service and funded from taxes that people *have* to pay. But the staff there are trained to help you with healthcare. The hospital is part of a state that is both negative and positive in its role.

Force and the Modernity Argument

Those who stress the centrality of force argue that the state is far older than the 'modernists' assume. It is true that earlier states are different from modern ones and lack the features described by Dunleavy and O'Leary. Force is regarded as the defining attribute of the state. Feudal and ancient polities may have been more partisan and less effective than the modern state, but they were states nevertheless. They sought to impose supreme power over their subjects. We come back to Weber's definition of the state as an institution that claims a monopoly of legitimate force for a particular territory. Does this mean that only the modern state is really a state, or do all post-tribal polities act in this way (albeit less efficiently and more chaotically), and therefore deserve to be called states as well?

Proponents of the force argument contend that differences in 'form' should not be allowed to exclude similarities. Once we argue that only modern states can be called states, we ignore the problem of defining totalitarian states (such as Iraq under Saddam Hussein). Are they not states because they are corrupt and violate in all sorts of ways bureaucratic criteria for recruiting functionaries and the **public/private** distinction as elaborated above?

The danger with the 'modernist argument' (as we call it) is twofold. It assumes that states have to be liberal in character, and that modern states live up to the forms which are prescribed for them. But even liberal states that consider themselves democratic do not always practise what they preach, and are plagued with corruption (think of the role played by money in the election process in the United States) so that criteria for appointments are violated and the rule of law is breached. Is the Italian state not a 'real' state, for example, because it fails to live up to the 'ideals' of the state? If it is not a state, then what is it? It would be much better to identify states in terms of the supreme force that they exercise (albeit in different ways) over subjects. Weber's definition applies to all (post-tribal) polities for roughly the last 5,000 years.

Exercise

List the features that make the state modern.

Are these features enough to bolster the argument that the modern state is the state, and that earlier polities should not be called states at all?

T.H. Green called the Tsarist state a state by courtesy (1941: 137). Would you call the following states?

- Iraq under Saddam Hussein

- (contemporary) Yugoslavia

- apartheid South Africa

- the United States

- Afghanistan.

Make two columns, one headed 'Difference in Degree', the other 'Difference in Kind'. Now list the features that differentiate modern states from pre-modern states, or the state from earlier (but post-tribal) polities under what you see as the appropriate column.

The Argument against the Concept of the State

Three bodies of argument contend that the state is not a suitable concept for political theory, since it is impossible to define it. The state has been described as one of the most problematic concepts in **politics** (Vincent, 1987: 3) and it has been seen as so problematic as to defy definition at all.

The Behaviouralist Argument

The first group to subscribe to what might be called the 'indefinability thesis' was developed by political scientists who worked in the United States in the 1960s but whose influence was not confined to that country alone. It extended throughout Europe. This group is generally known as the *behaviouralists.*

The founding father of behaviouralism is considered to be Arthur Bentley, who argued that the state was afflicted with what he called in 1908 'soul stuff' – an abstract and mystical belief that the state somehow represents the 'whole' of a community. Much better, Bentley argued, to adopt a process view of politics that contends that the state is no more than one government among many (1967: 263).

The term 'behaviour' coined by the behaviouralists was intended to capture the fact that humans, like animals, *behave*, and hence the approach denied that human society is different in kind from animal society or the activity of other elements in nature. This led to a view that the study of politics was like a **natural** science, and behaviouralists argued that as a science, it must not make value judgements. Just as biologists would not describe a queen bee as 'reactionary' or 'autocratic', so the political scientist must abstain from judgements in analysing the material she studies. Behaviouralists believe that a 'science' of politics should not defend particular values, and instead should draw up testable hypotheses by objectively studying political 'behaviour'.

The Argument of David Easton

A leading figure of the behavioural political scientists was David Easton, who examined the theoretical credentials of the state in his *Political System* (1953, 2nd edn 1971). He argues that the state is a hopelessly ambiguous term. Political scientists cannot agree on what the state is or when it arose. Some define the state in terms of its morality, others see it as an instrument of exploitation. Some regard it as an aspect of society, others as a synonym for government, while still others identify it as a unique and separate association that stands apart from social institutions such as churches and trade unions. Some point to its **sovereignty**, others to its limited power.

What makes the state so contentious, Easton argues, is that the term is imbued with strong mythical qualities, serving as an ideological vehicle for propagating national sovereignty against cosmopolitan and local powers. Given this degree of contention and controversy, there is no point, Easton argues, in adding a 'definition of my own' (1971: 106–15). If political theory is to be scientific, then it must be clear, and clarity requires that we abstain from using the concept of the state altogether.

For around three decades after World War II the state, conceptually at any rate, appeared in the words of one writer to have 'withered away' (Mann, 1980: 296). Yet in 1981 Easton commented that a concept which 'many of us thought had been polished off a quarter of a century ago, has now risen from the grave to haunt us once again' (1981: 303). What had brought the state back into political science? Easton noted the following:

- the revival of interest in **Marxism**, which places the state at the heart of politics;
- a conservative yearning for stability and authority; a rediscovery of the importance of the **market** so that the state is important as an institution to be avoided;
- a study of policy which found the state to be a convenient tool of analysis.

Easton is however still convinced that the state is not a viable concept in political science. He recalls the numerous definitions that he had noted in 1953, and argues that 'irresolvable ambiguities' have continued to proliferate since then. To make his point, he engages in a hard hitting and witty analysis of the work of a Greek Marxist, Nicos Poulantzas (who was much influenced by the French theorist, Louis Althusser). Poulantzas, Easton tell us, concludes after much detailed and almost impenetrable analysis that the state is an 'indecipherable mystery'. The state is 'the eternally elusive Pimpernel of Poulantzas's theory' – an 'undefined and undefinable essence' (1981: 308). All this confirms Easton's view that the concept of the state is obscure, empty and hopelessly ambiguous. It should be abandoned by political science.

David Easton's Concept of the Political System

If the concept of the state should be pushed to one side by political theorists, what do we put in its place? Easton argues that at the heart of our study of politics lies, not the idea of the state, but rather the concept of the political system. This Easton defines as 'the authoritative allocation of values for society as a whole' (1971: 134). Politics, he contends, is far better defined in this way. Such a definition avoids the ambiguity of the state concept, but at the same time it is not so broad that it considers all social activity to be political. After all, a political system refers to the allocation of values for society *as a whole*. It therefore confines the term 'political' to public matters, so that, as far as Easton is concerned, the pursuit of power which may take place in trade unions, churches, families and so on is not part of politics itself.

The notion of a political system makes it possible to differentiate sharply the political from the social. It also resolves historical problems that afflict the concept of the state. Whereas the state only arose in the seventeenth century (in Easton's view), the concept of the political system can embrace politics as a process existing not only in medieval and ancient times, but in tribal societies that had no significant concentrations of power at all. Once we free politics from the state we can also talk about a political system existing at the international level, authoritatively allocating values for the global community.

In his later work, Easton contends that a political system can persist through change so that one could argue that a system continues to allocate values authoritatively while its structures change dramatically. Thus it could be said, for example, that a political system persisted in Germany while the imperial order fell to the Weimar Republic, which yielded to the Nazi regime that was replaced by a very different order after World War II (1965: 83).

Easton's concept of the political system is, he claims, superior to the concept of the state. The latter is ambiguous, limited and ideological. Even though Robert Dahl is critical (as we will see) of Easton's particular definition, he too prefers to speak of a 'political system' that can exist at many levels, and which he defines as any persistent pattern of human relationships involving, to a significant extent, control, influence, power or **authority** (1976: 3).

The Linguistic and Radical Argument

The **linguistic analysts** were a philosophical school fashionable in the 1950s and 1960s in Britain and the United States. Their doyen, T.D. Weldon, wrote an extremely influential book called *The Vocabulary of Politics* in 1953 in which he argued that analysts are only competent to tackle what linguistic analysts called 'second order' problems. This referred to the words politicians use, and not the realities to which these words are supposed to refer. The concept of the state is (Weldon argued) a hopelessly muddled term, frequently invested with dangerously misleading mystical overtones. Practical political activists use it but it is an unphilosophical 'first order' term that has imported into political theory its confusions from the world of practice. Whereas we all know (as citizens) that the United States and Switzerland are states whereas Surrey and the United Nations are not, the term has no interest for political philosophers (1953: 47–9).

We refer to the radical argument as one that is in favour of radical **democracy** and sees the concept of the state as a barrier to this end. Why conceive of politics in statist terms when we want people at all levels of society to participate in running their own affairs? Radicals come in many forms. Some see the term guilty of a kind of monopolisation of politics, so that political activity outside the state is downgraded. Others argue that the term is so complex that it is fruitless to try and define it. Richard Ashley, a postmodernist or post-structuralist in international relations, takes the view that it is impossible to 'decide what the state is' (1988: 249), while Pringle and Watson quote the words of the French postmodernist, Michel Foucault, that 'to place the state above or outside society is to focus on a homogeneity which is not there' (1992: 55). The state, says Foucault, is 'a mythical abstraction whose importance is a lot more limited than many of us think' (Hoffman, 1995: 162). Pringle and Watson, for their part, find the state too erratic and disconnected to evoke as an entity (1992: 63), while a feminist, Judith Allen, takes the view that the state is too abstract, unitary and unspecific to be of use in addressing the disaggregated, diverse, specific or local sites which require feminist attention (Allen, 1990: 22).

The radicals agree with the linguistic analysts and the behaviouralists that the concept of the state should be abandoned. Their particular argument is that the notion discourages participation and involvement at local levels and in social institutions, and is therefore an unhelpful term.

Behaviouralism

Not to be confused with behaviourism – a psychological theory – **behaviouralism** developed in the United States after World War II as an intellectual concept that stressed precision, systems theory and pure science. The idea is that all living things behave in regular ways and it is possible to see them as adjusting to their environment as a result of the inputs they receive and the outputs they produce. Generalisations can be made that can be verified through methods that have no ethical implications. Theory must be scientific in the sense that no values are involved, and the social sciences do not involve any special approaches which are not relevant to the natural sciences. Indeed, the notion of behaviour makes it possible to examine all living things since the human will express itself in regularities that can be scientifically investigated. The behavioural 'revolution' (as its supporters called it) reached its height in the 1960s but was accused of taking the politics out of politics by its critics, who felt that the methods of natural science were not appropriate to the social sciences, and that the notion anyway that science could be value free is naive and superficial.

Problems with the Argument against the State

Many of the points that the critics of the concept of the state make are useful. It is certainly odd to identify politics with the state and, therefore, to take the view that families, tribes, voluntary organisations from cricket clubs to churches and universities, and international institutions are not political because the state is either not involved at all, or at least directly at any rate, in running their affairs.

But it does not follow from this that we cannot define the state, or that the state is not an important concept and institution for political scientists to study. Indeed we will argue that it is impossible to ignore the state, and that unless one can contend that the state no longer exists it can and must be defined.

The Argument of David Easton

At no point does Easton suggest that the state does not exist, and Dahl, his fellow behaviouralist, speaks explicitly of the state as 'the Government' (1976: 10). In a more recent book, Easton identifies with those who argue that the state has never really been left out (1990: 299n).

Nevertheless, we must consider Easton's argument that the concept of the political system is a much clearer and more flexible idea than the concept of the state. Easton's notion might seem ingenious but in fact it has serious difficulties of its own. Easton's argument is that, when we define a political system as the authoritative allocation of values for society as a whole, we can say that the **conflict** within a tribe which leads to secession of one of its clans is 'exactly similar' to conflicts between states in international institutions (1971: 111). But what is the meaning of 'society as a whole'?

Easton defines society as a 'special kind of human grouping' in which people develop 'a sense of belonging together' (1971: 135). When secession occurs within a tribe or war between states takes place, there would seem to be the absence, not the presence, of that sense of belonging together which Easton defines as a society. To say that tribes and international orders that involved warring states are 'genuine societies' (1971: 141) seems to empty the term society of any content. The same problem afflicts his argument that a political system can persist through change even though (in the case of Germany, for example) the authorities and the regimes not only change drastically, but are divided until 1991 into two warring halves. The political system appears to be a shadowy abstraction that could only perish if all popular participants were physically obliterated. It could be argued that Easton's 'political system' seems no less mysterious than Poulantzas's elusive state.

In later definitions, Easton speaks of the political system not as a 'something' that authoritatively allocates values for society as a whole, but as that which takes decisions 'considered binding by most members of society, most of the time' (1990: 3). But this does not solve his problem. Indeed, in an early review of *The Political System*, Dahl raises the problem of Easton's definition, by asking how many have to obey before an 'allocation' is deemed binding. Criminals, as Dahl points out, do not believe that criminal statutes must be obeyed (Hoffman, 1995: 28). The point is a good one, and it is not answered by saying that most of the members of society, most of the time have to consider allocations binding. What happens if the order is an authoritarian one in which relatively few people support the regime? Moreover, what counts as genuine support as opposed to compliance based upon fear? Think of 'popular support' in Nazi Germany, Stalinist Russia or in Saddam Hussein's Iraq. How useful is it to say that people considered the allocations binding? This is a real problem, and what it shows is that Easton has not done away with the ambiguities and elusiveness that characterise the state.

Indeed it has been argued that Easton can only bring his political system down to earth by making it synonymous with the state, so that we can give some kind of empirical purchase to the notion of society as a whole. And once we return to the state, then the problem of ambiguity and abstractness remain. The substitution of the political system for the state has not solved any of the problems that led Easton to reject the concept of the state in the first place.

The Question of Existence

Moreover, Easton's argument suffers from the same difficulty that confronts all who argue that the state cannot be defined. We have to ask: does the state exist? None of the critics of the concept of the state suggest that the state as a real-life institution has disappeared. Easton tries to adopt a sceptical position to the effect that political life has no 'natural' coherence so that we could, for argument's sake, construct a political system out of the relationship between a duckbilled platypus and the ace of spades. But he does insist that a conceptually 'interesting' idea must have 'empirical status' (1965: 33; 44), and this seems to suggest that there must be something in the world out there which corresponds to the political system. Such an institution is the state.

Neither behaviouralists, nor linguistic theorists or radicals argue that the state does not exist. If states do exist, then the challenge is surely to define them. Weber's notion of the state as an institution that claims a monopoly of legitimate force for a particular territory is a useful definition: as we see it, it is rather silly to talk about the state and then deny that it can be defined.

Force and Statelessness

The value of highlighting force as the central attribute of the state is that it focuses upon a practice that is extraordinary: the use of force to tackle conflicts of interest. It is true that states defined in a Weberian way have been around for some 5,000 years, but humans have been in existence for much longer, and therefore an extremely interesting question arises. How did people secure order and resolve disputes before they had an institution claiming a monopoly of legitimate force?

Most anthropologists would dispute Green's argument that states have always existed. They argue that in tribal societies, political leaders rely upon moral pressures – ancestor cults, supernatural sanctions, the threat of exclusion – to maintain social cohesion and discipline. Although many of these sanctions would strike us today as being archaic and unworkable, the point about them is that they demonstrate that people can live without a state.

International relations writers have also become aware of how international society regulates the activities of states themselves, without a super or world state to secure order. Moral and economic pressures have to be used to enforce international law, and as the recent conflict in Iraq has demonstrated, there is nothing to prevent states from interpreting international law in conflicting ways.

The Distinction between Force and Constraint, State and Government

When we define the state in terms of force, we are naturally curious about the political mechanisms in societies without a state. But to understand how order is maintained in societies without institutions claiming a monopoly of legitimate force, we need to make two distinctions that are not usually made in political theory.

The first is the distinction between force, on the one hand, and **constraint**, on the other, and the second (which we will come to later) is the distinction between state and government. If stateless societies exert discipline without having an apparatus that can impose force, how do we characterise this discipline? In our view, it is necessary to distinguish between force and constraint. The two are invariably lumped together, particularly by classical liberal writers who often use the terms force and constraint synonymously. Yet the two are very different.

Force imposes physical **harm**, and it should be remembered that mental illnesses such as depression create physical pain so that causing depression counts as force. **Coercion** we take to be a credible threat of force: a two-year-old with a plastic gun cannot be said to coerce because the force 'threatened' is not credible. Thus, in the standard example of 'your money or your life' demand, what causes you to comply is the knowledge that force will be used against you if you do not.

It is true that coercion can be defined in a much broader way. Here coercion is seen not as the threat of force, but moral and social pressures that compel a person to do something that they otherwise would not have done. It is better, however, to describe these pressures as 'constraints': constraints certainly cause you to do something you would not otherwise have done, but these pressures do not involve force or the credible threat of force. Constraint may involve pressures that are unintentional and informal.

Take the following example. You become religious and your agnostic and atheist friends no longer want to have coffee with you. You are cycling on a windy day and find that you have to pedal considerably harder. Constraints can be natural or social and, when moral judgements are made about a person's behaviour, these constraints are 'concentrated' in ways that are often unpleasant. But the point about these constraints, whatever form they take, is that they are impossible to avoid in a society. They do not undermine our capacity for choice. On the contrary, they are conditions that make choice both possible and necessary.

This distinction between force and constraint translates into the second distinction we want to discuss, that between state and government. The latter two are not the same, even though in state-centred societies it may be very difficult to disentangle them. The term 'governance' is often used but the argument is better expressed if we stick to the older term. Government, it could be argued, involves resolving conflicts of interest through sanctions that may be unpleasant but do not involve force. Families, schools, clubs and voluntary societies govern themselves with rules that pressure people into compliance but they do not use force. States, on the other hand, do use force. It is true that states do not always act as states. In other words, they may in particular areas act 'governmentally', as we have defined it: in these areas they can be said to constrain, rather than resort to force. Of course in real-life institutions in state-centred societies these two dimensions are invariably mixed up. The NHS in Britain is a good example of an institution that is mostly governmental in that its rules do not have force attached to them, but rely upon social pressures – naming and shaming, embarrassing and using verbal sanctions – to enforce them. On the other hand, it cannot be said that the state (strictly defined) does not play a role as well. After all, the NHS is tax funded, and if people refuse to pay taxes they are likely to be subject to more than moral pressures to pay up!

The distinction between state and government is important, first because it explains how stateless societies have rules and regulations that make order possible, and why people conform or dissent through pressures which most of the time are non-statist in character. You may try to get to the doctor's on time – not because you are fearful of being arrested and put in prison but because it seems discourteous and improper not to do so. The distinction separates force (or violence) – the terms seem to boil down to the same thing in this context – from human nature, pointing to the fact that force comes into play only in situations in which moral and economic pressures do not work.

The Argument So Far...

- We have argued that the state is not just a modern institution even though the 'modern state' does have features that distinguish it from more traditional states.

State, Politics and Government

Is there a case for distinguishing between politics and the state? List all the things in your life that you would call 'political' and see whether it can be said that the state is directly involved.

The following is sometimes argued:

- the family is political
- the church is political
- sport is political
- relations between people are political.

Do you agree, and if so, what makes these institutions political?

How would you counter the argument that if 'everything is political, then nothing is political'?

Do you see government as a synonym for politics; is there a distinction between government and the state? List the institutions that have governments, starting with yourself (do you govern your own life?).

Consider the following institutions: are they inherently statist in character, or could they be run without the state?

- the National Health Service
- the prisons
- the Post Office
- the army and police.

- We have defended Max Weber's 'force argument'. Although force is not the only attribute of the state, it is the central attribute so that the state is distinguished from other social institutions because it uses 'legitimate force' to address conflicts of interest. The police, the army and the prisons are the distinctive attributes of the state.
- We have assumed that the state is an important concept in political theory. But there are those who argue that the state is too vague, elusive, divisive and ambiguous to merit attention. We have identified these critics as behaviouralists, linguistic analysts and radicals. Their arguments are rejected on the grounds that since states clearly exist in the real world it is important to try and define them, however difficult this task might be.
- States have not always existed. In fact throughout most of human history, people have resolved conflicts without relying upon a special institution that claims a monopoly of legitimate force. Even today states are (usually) bound by

international law and treaties even though there is no world state to maintain order. These facts make it important that we distinguish between constraints of a diplomatic kind (relying upon economic pressures, self-interest, ostracism, etc.) and force as such, just as we need to distinguish between the state and government.

State and Sovereignty

It is impossible to talk about the state without saying something about sovereignty. This is the aspect of the state that relates to its supreme and unchecked power. Hence sovereignty is commonly regarded as an attribute of states. But here agreement ends since some argue that only modern states are sovereign, others that all states are sovereign. Does claiming a *monopoly* of legitimate force mean that this monopoly endows the state with sovereignty?

Sovereignty as a Modern Concept

It is argued by Justin Rosenberg, for example, that sovereignty only arises when the state is sharply separated from society. His argument is that only under **capitalism** do we have a sharp divide between the public and the private, and this divide is necessary before we can speak of the *sovereign* state (1994: 87).

Rosenberg takes the view that sovereignty is a modern idea just as the state is a modern institution. F.H. Hinsley, on the other hand, argues that while the state can be broadly defined as a modern as well as an archaic institution, sovereignty cannot, since sovereignty requires a belief that absolute and illimitable power resides in the 'body politic' which constitutes a 'single personality' composed of rulers and ruled alike (1986: 125). This means effectively that rulers and ruled must be deemed 'citizens' – a modern concept. Even the celebrated theory of Jean Bodin's (*c.* 1529–96), that sovereignty as unconditional and unrestrained power is, for Hinsley, undermined by the assumption that the holder of sovereignty is limited by divine and natural law. With Hobbes, however, law in all its forms is the creation of the sovereign, so that there is no distinction to be made between sovereign and subject. The sovereign is simply the individual writ large.

In Hinsley's view, therefore, the state can take a pre-modern form but sovereignty cannot. This is also the position taken by Murray Forsyth in his entry on the state in *The Blackwell Encyclopaedia of Political Thought*.

Sovereignty as a Broad Concept

It is perfectly true that the concept of sovereignty was not known 'in its fullness' before the fifteenth and sixteenth centuries (Vincent, 1987: 32). Like the state, it was only explicitly formulated in the modern period, but that does not mean that it did not exist in earlier times. The Roman formulation – 'whatever pleases the prince has the force of law' – demonstrates not only that the notion of sovereignty existed in pre-modern periods, but that formulations such as these clearly influenced the modern conception. The idea that God rather than secular rulers exercised sovereignty still expressed the notion of absolute and illimitable power, and although sovereignty was more chaotic in pre-modern times, it clearly existed. One writer has spoken of the 'parcellised sovereignty' of the medieval period (Hoffman, 1998: 35–6) so that those who define the state broadly often define sovereignty broadly as well.

Alan James argues that states have always been sovereign, and that sovereignty is best defined as constitutional independence: a sovereign state is a state that is legally in control of its own destiny (1986: 53). Although he is preoccupied with states in the modern world, the notion of sovereignty applies to all states, whether ancient, medieval or modern.

Problems with the Theories of State Sovereignty

Those who assume that sovereignty is about the power of the state are mistaken. They take the view that the state is capable of exercising absolute power whereas it has been argued that in fact the state only claims this sovereign power, because others – terrorists, criminals, etc. – challenge it. In other words, the state claims something that it does and cannot have, so that the notion of the state as sovereign imports into the notion of sovereignty the problem of the state itself.

Difficulties with the Modernist Conception

The idea that sovereignty is purely modern confuses formulation with institution. It is true that sovereignty is only explicitly formulated by modern writers, but the notion of supreme power is inherent in the state.

The modernist notion misses the ironic part of Weber's definition: that a monopoly can be *claimed*, not because it exists, but precisely because it does not. The sovereign state claims an absolute power that it does not and cannot have. Unless criminals and terrorists also exercise some of this 'supremacy', it cannot be claimed. In other words, the notion of sovereignty merely brings into the open the problem that has existed all along. Like the state itself, the idea of state sovereignty has severe logical difficulties associated with it.

On the one hand, sovereignty is unitary in its scope. It is absolute and unlimited. In modern formulations, rulers and ruled are bonded together as citizens. On the other hand, there has to be a sharp **division** between the public and the private, the state and society, before modern sovereignty can be said to exist. There is a clear contradiction here since we can well ask, how can an institution have absolute power, and yet be clearly limited to a public sphere? Sovereignty allows the state to have a hand in everything – and yet we are told that it is confined to the public sphere and must not interfere in private matters! The formulation of **state sovereignty** in the modern period serves only to highlight its absurd and contradictory character.

It is true that in 'normal' times the sovereign character of the state is not obvious to the members of a liberal society. But if there is a crisis or emergency – as when war breaks out between states – the capacity of the state to penetrate into all aspects of life becomes plain. During World War II the British state told its citizens what they must plant in their back gardens, and today, for example, the state tells us through advertising about safe sex, that we should conduct the most private of activities with adequate protection. The British Cabinet even had a discussion in the early 1980s about the importance of parents teaching children how to manage their pocket money (*The Guardian*, 17 February 1983).

We are told that state sovereignty needs to be limited and restricted. Yet it is clear from the practice of state even in 'normal' times that sovereignty is seen as a power which can penetrate into the most private spheres of life.

The Broad View of State Sovereignty

Realists in international relations define sovereignty in terms of states, whether these states are ancient or modern. But it is not difficult to see that state sovereignty is a problematic concept, however the state is defined.

James's theory of state sovereignty is a case in point. James regards sovereignty as an attribute of any state, ancient or modern, and defines it as a state's legal claim to constitutional independence. Sovereignty, James argues, is a formal attribute: a state is sovereign no matter how much it may in practice be beholden to the will of other states. But his argument comes to grief over the question of identifying sovereignty in situations when it is explicitly contested.

James contends that sovereignty expresses a legal, not a physical reality. Yet this position is contradicted by the position he takes on Rhodesia (today, Zimbabwe). In 1965 Ian Smith, a right-wing white Rhodesian leader, announced a 'unilateral declaration of independence' to prevent Britain from pushing the country into some kind of majority rule. However, James argues that the Smith regime was a sovereign state, even though it came about in what he concedes was an unlawful manner. What is the basis for arguing that the Smith rebel regime was sovereign? Because, James tells us, it was able to keep its enemies at bay – to defend itself through force of arms.

This implies that it is not legality that ultimately counts but physical effectiveness. In another of James's examples, he argues that the country Biafra (which broke away from federal Nigeria in the late 1960s) did not become a sovereign state because it was defeated by the superior strength of the federal state of Nigeria (after a long and bloody civil war). James makes it clear that sovereignty is ultimately the capacity of a state to impose its will through force. But if this is what sovereignty is, then it suffers from the same problem that afflicts states in general: the problem of asserting a monopoly that it does not have. James speaks of sovereignty as a statist effectiveness that rests upon 'a significant congruence between the decisions of those who purport to rule and the actual behaviour of their alleged subjects' (Hoffman, 1998: 27–9). But this congruence, in the case of Smith's Rhodesia – a state that lasted only 14 years – was met with massive resistance from those who challenged this sovereignty and sought to achieve a sovereignty of their own.

In other words, the absolute and illimitable will is shared with wills that have a power of their own. State sovereignty is as illogical and problematic as the state itself.

Rescuing the Idea of Sovereignty

The idea of sovereignty is too important to be chewed to pieces by those who uncritically embrace the concept of the state. We will suggest a way in which the notion can be reinstated without the problems that inhere in the state.

The classical liberals saw individuals as sovereign, and they were right to do so. But the problem with classical liberals is that they assumed that individuals could enjoy their supreme power in complete isolation from one another, and indeed, for this reason, depicted individuals as living initially in a 'natural' condition outside of society. This assumption runs contrary to everything we know about individuals. The individual who has not been 'socialised' cannot speak or think, and certainly cannot identify herself as an individual! Individuals acquire their identity through their *relations* with others – they are social beings. Our life develops through an infinity of relationships – with parents, friends, teachers, and more abstractly, with people we read about or see and hear in the media.

Sovercignty is an attribute that individuals enjoy, and which enables us to govern our own lives. This definition frees sovereignty from the problems that blight it when it is linked to the state. Not only is the search for self-government developed in our relations with others, but it involves an infinite capacity to order our own lives. We aspire to sovereignty, but we never reach a situation in which we can say that no further progress towards sovereignty is possible. The fact that sovereignty is individual does not mean that it is not organisational, for individuals work in multiple associations at every level – the local, regional, national and global. Each of these helps us to develop our sovereignty – our capacity to govern our lives.

Ironically, therefore, the idea of state sovereignty gets in the way of individual sovereignty as we see from the way in which states often resist **human rights** on the grounds that they, states, should be entitled to treat their inhabitants as they see fit. The Chinese authorities object when their policies are criticised, and the US administration considers that it is entitled to continue incarcerating prisoners in Guantanamo Bay. But when we define sovereignty as self-government, we place the rights of humans above the power of the state, and argue that only by locating sovereignty in the individual can it become consistent and defensible as a concept.

Moving to a Stateless World

Why are most people so sceptical about the possibility of a world without the state? Part of the reason, it could be argued, is that people think of government as being the same as the state, but if we make a sharp distinction (as we have above) between government and the state, then it can be seen that a stateless society is not a society without government, but rather a society in which an institution claiming a monopoly of legitimate force becomes redundant. What prevents this from happening?

People, it seems to us, can settle their conflicts of interest through moral and social pressures where they have a common interest with their opponents: when they can, in other words, imagine what it is like to be 'the other'. This does not mean that people have to be the same in every regard. On the contrary, people are all different, and these **differences** are the source of conflict. But it does not follow that because people are different and have conflicting interests that they cannot negotiate and compromise in settling these conflicts. It is only when they cannot do this that force becomes inevitable, and even if this force begins outside the state, the state will soon be involved, since the state claims a monopoly of legitimate force, and is concerned (quite rightly) about the force of private individuals. We are not, therefore, suggesting that we should not have a state in situations where people resort to force to tackle their conflicts.

But instead of taking this force for granted, as though it was part and parcel of 'human nature' (as Hobbes does), it could be argued that force arises where people lack what we have called 'common interests'. Policies that cement and reinforce common interests help to make government work. There is a case for resorting to force where this is the only way of implementing policies that will strengthen common interests. The debate about the war in Iraq revolved around the question of whether the use of force, in the form of a war, was the only way to defeat Saddam Hussein's regime, and whether the use of force could lead to a democratic reconstruction of the country.

It is true that force can never really be legitimate since it necessarily deprives those whom it targets of their **freedom**. But it can be justifiably used if it is the only way to provide a breathing space for policies that will cement common interests. For example, it could prove impossible to involve residents in running their own lives on a rundown housing estate until force has been used to stop gangs from intimidating ordinary people.

In early tribal societies conflicts of interest *were* settled through moral and social pressures. This historical reality is a huge resource for pursuing the argument that it is possible to find ways of bringing about order that dispense altogether with the use of the state. Max Weber's definition has implications that he himself did not see. When he read that Leon Trotsky had said that 'every state is founded on force', he commented 'That indeed is right' (Gerth and Wright Mills, 1991: 78). But in making this endorsement, Weber had not committed himself to Trotsky's Marxist analysis of politics. In the same way, we find Weber's definition immensely useful, even though we see implications in the definition, of which Weber himself would not have approved.

Moreover, it is not only tribal societies in the dim and distant past that were stateless. It is now nearly three decades since Hedley Bull (1977) noted the 'awkward facts' confronting a state-centric view of the world. These awkward facts embrace the following:

- the increasing importance of international law as a body of rules that has no wider monopoly of legitimate force to impose it;
- the **globalisation** of the economy that makes the notion of autonomous state sovereignty peculiarly archaic; and
- a growing number of issues – Bull mentioned the environment in particular – which can only be settled through acknowledging the common interests of contending parties.

This is why Bull characterised the international order as an 'anarchical society', and it is clear that developments of the kind noted above mean that statist solutions are

Influences and Impact:

The State

The state is often identified with civilisation, and it is easy to see why the state has such a profound impact upon our thought. Conventional religion depicts God as a sovereign overlord, and classical political thinkers such as Hobbes and Rousseau assumed that without a conception of God no state would be possible. It is also very tempting to translate contemporary concerns into a frozen notion of human nature as though how people behave in, for example, Britain today, represents the nature of humankind. Moreover, where people do resort to force to tackle their conflicts, a world without the state makes a bad situation even worse, and it would hardly be an advantage to do away with the state, if the alternative was rule by warlords or the Mafia. But it is ultimately an illusion to think that we can do away with force by resorting to the state. For what could be called a 'statist' mentality assumes that violent people are inexplicably evil. We cannot understand them; we can only crush them. The statist mentality never asks the question 'why?'. Why are people so brutalised that they resort to force? Of course, it is no help to merely invert the idea that people are evil so that we consider them to be naturally 'good' instead. Pacifists naively suppose that brutalised people or states will respond to moral pressures in a purely moral way, and anarchists fail to see that in conditions where force can be dispensed with we still need government to regulate social affairs. Firmness and rules are actually undermined by the use of force, since force encourages us to ignore complexities and not try and imagine what it is like to be in the shoes of another. The fact that the state remains hugely influential in our lives does not mean that we should not start thinking about ways and means of living without it.

becoming ever more dangerous as a mode of resolving conflicts. The increasing degree of interdependence that characterises both domestic and international society makes the resort to force (the chosen and distinctive instrument of the state) increasingly counter-productive. The fact that criminal individuals, like criminal states, are also the beneficiaries of a technology of violence (whose sophistication escalates all the time) means that if we want a secure future it is vital that we learn how to settle differences without the use of force, i.e. in a stateless manner.

Summary

The state is seen by some theorists as a modern institution that has, as its identifying features, a sharp separation of the public from the private; a capacity to exercise sovereignty throughout its domain and protect all who live in its territory; an ability to organise its offices along bureaucratic rather than patrimonial lines; and to extract tax revenues from its population.

The state can be defined in a way that sees its central attribute as the exercise of legitimate force, as based upon morality, or a mixture of the two. When it is defined in a way that stresses the importance of force, then it can be argued that modern states are crucially different from pre-modern states, but like all states, they claim to exercise a monopoly of legitimate force.

Three bodies of argument contend that politics is best identified without using the concept of the state. Behaviouralists argue that the state as a concept is too ambiguous and ideological to be useful, and the notion of a political system is preferable; linguistic analysts see the idea of the state as a practical institution rather than a coherent philosophical concept, while radicals argue that the notion of the state gets in the way of a pluralist and participatory politics.

The problem, however, is that the state does not simply disappear simply because it is not defined. The contradictory nature of the institution can only be exposed if we define it, and the definition of the state as an institution claiming a monopoly of legitimate force makes it possible to underline the state's problematic character.

The contradictory character of the state also undermines the notion of state sovereignty. Sovereignty can only be coherently defined as the capacity of individuals to govern their own lives.

Questions

1. Do you agree with the argument that the state is essentially a modern institution?
2. What is the best way of defining the state?
3. Is it possible to differentiate government from the state, and if so, how?
4. Do you see the notion of state sovereignty as irrelevant in the contemporary world?
5. Why do people physically harm one another?

References

Allen, J. (1990) 'Does Feminism Need a Theory of the State?' in S. Watson (ed.), *Playing the State* London: Verso, 21–37.

Ashley, R. (1988) 'Untying the Sovereign State: a Double Reading of the Anarchy Problematique', *Millennium* 17(2), 227–62.

Bentley, A. (1967) *The Process of Government* Cambridge, Mass.: Belknap, Harvard University Press.

Bull, H. (1977) *The Anarchical Society* Basingstoke: Macmillan.

Dahl, R. (1976) *Modern Political Analysis* 3rd edn Englewood Cliffs, New Jersey: Prentice-Hall.

Dunleavy, P. and O'Leary, B. (1987) *Theories of the State* London and Basingstoke: Macmillan.

Easton, D. (1965) *A Framework for Political Analysis* Englewood Cliffs, New Jersey: Prentice-Hall.

Easton, D. (1971) *The Political System* 2nd edn New York: Alfred Knopf.

Easton, D. (1981) 'The Political System Besieged by the State', *Political Theory* 9, 203–56.

Easton, D. (1990) *An Analysis of Political Structure* New York and London: Routledge.

Gerth, H. and Wright Mills, C. (1991) *From Max Weber* London: Routledge.

Gramsci, A. (1971) *Selections from the Prison Notebooks* London: Lawrence & Wishart.

Green, T.H. (1941) *The Principles of Political Obligation* London, New York and Toronto: Longmans, Green & Co.

Hamlin, A. and Pettit, P. (1989) 'The Normative Analysis of the State: Some Preliminaries' in A. Hamlin and P. Pettit (eds), *The Good Polity* Oxford: Basil Blackwell, 1–13.

Hegel, G. (1956) *The Philosophy of History* New York: Dover.

Hinsley, F.H. (1986) *Sovereignty* Cambridge: Cambridge University Press.

Hoffman, J. (1995) *Beyond the State* Cambridge: Polity Press.

Hoffman, J. (1996) 'Antonio Gramsci: *The Prison Notebooks*' in M. Forsyth and M. Keens-Soper (eds), *The Political Classics: Green to Dworkin* Oxford: Oxford University Press, 58–77.

Hoffman, J. (1998) *Sovereignty* Buckingham: Open University Press.

James, A. (1986) *Sovereign Statehood* London: Allen & Unwin.

Machiavelli, N. (1998) *The Prince* Oxford: Oxford University Press.

Mann, M. (1980) 'The Pre-industrial State', *Political Studies* 28, 297–304.

Marx, K. and Engels, F. (1976) *Collected Works* vol. 5 London: Lawrence & Wishart.

Pringle, R. and Watson, S. (1992) 'Women's Interests and the Post-structural State' in M. Barrett and A. Phillips (eds), *Destabilizing Theory* Cambridge: Polity Press, 53–73.

Rosenberg, J. (1994) *The Empire of Civil Society* London: Verso.

Vincent, A. (1987) *Theories of the State* Oxford: Blackwell.

Weldon, T. (1953) *The Vocabulary of Politics* Harmondsworth: Penguin.

Further Reading

- Bhikhu Parekh's essay 'When Will the State Wither Away?' *Alternatives* 15, 247–62 is a thoughtful and accessible presentation on the state as a modern institution.

- John Hoffman's *Beyond the State* (referenced above) deals with the way in which different traditions have approached the state, and makes the case for the kind of conceptual distinctions needed to provide an effective critique.

- Alan James's *Sovereign Statehood* (referenced above) provides a clear defence of a traditional view of sovereignty with an attempt to sort out the confusions that the concept generates.

- David Easton's *The Political System* (referenced above) makes the classic case against the state and the need to conceptualise politics as a system rather than a set of institutions.

- Hedley Bull's *The Anarchical Society* (referenced above) seeks to argue that international society is a stateless order and yet there is order. An ingenious and extremely interesting text.

- Bernard Crick's *In Defence of Politics* Harmondsworth: Penguin, 1964 (and subsequent editions) offers a very interesting first chapter on the nature of political rule, and what he sees as distinctive about the political process.

- Adrian Leftwich's edited volume, *What is Politics?* Cambridge: Polity, 2004 (2nd edn) contains a very useful and thought-provoking Chapter 3 on the question of 'Politics and Force' by Peter Nicholson.

Weblinks

- http://www.keele.ac.uk/depts/po/prs.htm
- http://www.york.ac.uk/services/library/subjects/politint.htm

Chapter 2

Freedom

Introduction

Freedom is regarded by many as the pre-eminent political value, but what does it mean to be free? Do we have to justify freedom, or do it we take it as axiomatic that we should be free, and that it is *restrictions* on freedom which require justification? And what are those justifications? If we go into the street and survey people's attitudes to freedom, we might find that they favour the freedom to do things of which they approve, but are in favour of the state using its power to restrict freedom to do things that they dislike. Is there then a *principled* way to establish what we should be free to do? At the core of freedom is the idea of 'choice', but can we choose to do anything we want?

Chapter Map

In this chapter we will:

- Provide a working definition of freedom.

- Outline one of the most important contributions to the debate over freedom – the argument advanced by John Stuart Mill in his book *On Liberty*.

- Distinguish freedom of expression and freedom of action in Mill's argument.

- Use Mill's argument to provide a framework for a wider discussion of freedom and its limits.

- Illustrate arguments over freedom through the use of case studies, and, in particular, the proposed ban on smoking in enclosed public spaces.

Smoking in the Last Chance Saloon?

More and more cities, provinces and countries are adopting restrictions, and complete bans, on smoking in enclosed public places. Most attention has focused on bans in bars and restaurants. New York City and State, California State, the Republic of Ireland, New Zealand, Norway and Italy have already introduced such bans.

The policy adopted in Ireland has become the model for other countries. Technically the ban, which was introduced in March 2004, extends to all workplaces, and the protection of bar staff from the alleged effects of 'passive smoking' (environmental tobacco smoke – ETS) was advanced as one of the major reasons for its introduction. Owners of bars in which people are caught smoking are liable to be fined up to €3,000. Policing of bars is the responsibility of health inspectors. It is still possible to smoke outside a bar, and quite elaborate heated outdoor spaces have been created. A year after the ban it was estimated that there was a 94–97 per cent compliance rate from bars, and the ban commands a very high level of support among the Irish population, as judged by opinion poll research.

At the end of this chapter we will apply the arguments advanced through the course of the chapter to the smoking ban. But before tackling the rest of the chapter it would useful to consider your own reactions to the ban: how valid are the arguments listed above? Can you think of arguments against a smoking ban? Is it possible to develop a position midway between no significant regulation of smoking in enclosed public places and a complete ban? Alternatively, should the prohibition on smoking be extended to all public places, and even to private homes – in short, should the sale and use of tobacco be made illegal?

Freedom

The starting point for many, although not all, political theorists is what can be termed *the presumption in favour of freedom*. That is, we assume people ought to be free unless there are compelling reasons for restricting their freedom – much of the discussion of freedom focuses on the legitimate limits to freedom. In this chapter we use John Stuart Mill's defence of this presumption in his book *On Liberty*. But before considering Mill's argument we need a working definition of freedom, or **liberty**.*

Gerald MacCallum argues that 'freedom is . . . always *of* something (an agent or agents), *from* something, *to* do, not do, become, or not become something' (MacCallum, 1991: 102). Freedom is therefore a 'triadic' relationship – meaning, there are three parts to it: (a) the agent, or person, who is free (or 'unfree'); (b) the constraints, restrictions, interferences and barriers that make the agent free or unfree, and (c) what it is that the person is free to do, or not do. It is important that (c) means a person is free to do *or* not do something – that is, he has a *choice*: an inmate of a jail is not prevented from residing in that jail, but he has no choice whether or not he resides there. MacCallum's definition is useful, but it leaves open a couple of important issues. First, what is the source of (b)? Must it be another person (or persons) who constrains or restricts your action? Could the source of your unfreedom be yourself – that is, your own weaknesses and irrationality? Second, some things are trivial – is your freedom to watch inane daytime television as valuable as your freedom to study challenging poetry?

To cast some light on the first issue, a distinction is made between positive liberty and negative liberty. The distinction is credited to Sir Isaiah Berlin, who set it out in his famous essay 'Two Concepts of Liberty' (1991). Acknowledging that in the history of political thought there have been more than two concepts of freedom, Berlin maintains that these two have had the greatest influence, and the contrast between them throws into relief fundamental differences about the role of the state:

- *Negative liberty* is involved in the answer to the question: 'what is the area within which the subject – a person or group of persons – is or should be left to do or be what he is able to do or be, without interference by other persons?' (Berlin, 1991: 121–2)

- *Positive liberty* is involved in the answer to the question: 'what, or who, is the source of control or interference that can determine someone to do, or be, this rather than that?' (1991: 122).

So, negative liberty is about being left alone, whereas positive liberty is about being in control of one's life. For example, a person may be unfree to leave her home because she is under 'house arrest'; alternatively, she may be unfree to leave because she has a phobia that makes her fearful of leaving. In the first case, she is negatively unfree to leave, whereas in the second she is positively unfree. Of course, elements of both types of 'unfreedom' may be evident: she may be fearful about leaving her home because

---

*Some writers draw a distinction between 'freedom' and 'liberty', arguing that the latter denotes political or legal freedom, whereas the former encompasses a broader range of activities and states. We do not make this distinction. For stylistic reasons, which include the possibility of using adjectival forms of the noun, we prefer freedom, but nonetheless we use freedom and liberty interchangeably.

she suspects she is under surveillance and that she is at greater harm away from home. Perhaps she is slightly paranoid, but if that paranoia has been caused by actual past experience, then the source of the unfreedom, or 'control', is not straightforwardly internal or external. But even if we cannot determine the source of unfreedom we can still make an analytical distinction between such sources, and therefore also between positive and negative freedom. In passing, it should be noted that Berlin was very hostile to the concept of positive liberty. He thought it implied a belief in psychological sources of unfreedom concealed from the person who is deemed unfree – this belief forms the basis of a political theory in which people are 'forced to be free'. In the section on Harm to Self (p. 53) we suggest a way of understanding positive freedom that does not rely on a belief in hidden psychological drives.

In summary, we can say that freedom is a triadic relation that must involve choice. When analysing the nature of constraints – or 'unfreedom' – a valid distinction can be drawn between internal and external sources of constraint.

Mill's Defence of Freedom

Mill's essay *On Liberty* has been hugely influential in discussions of political freedom, especially in his native Britain. Although there is always a danger in applying the thought of a long-dead thinker to contemporary issues, nineteenth-century Britain is sufficiently close to the contemporary Western world for us to ask what Mill might have had to say on contemporary issues. Once the reader gets beyond the rather ponderous literary style, Mill's reflections – especially his concern with the tyranny of popular opinion – have a strikingly contemporary feel. Some of his arguments, such as his faith in human progress, appear very dated, but they are nonetheless provocative.

Biography — John Stuart Mill (1806–73)

The son of James Mill, an important utilitarian philosopher, J.S. Mill was infamously the subject of a rigorously rationalist educational experiment by his father. He learnt Greek at the age of three but suffered a mental breakdown when he was 21.

For the rest of his life he sought to reconcile the rather austere elements of his father's utilitarianism to a more romantic individualism. This becomes clear in his essay *On Liberty*, which was published in 1859. In addition to important contributions to mainstream areas of philosophy, alongside *On Liberty* he wrote a number of other important political works, the most significant of which are *Considerations on Representative Government* (1861) and *The Subjection of Women* (1869). The latter essay, which owes a great deal to his wife Harriet Taylor, argued ahead of its time for the social and political emancipation of women.

Unusually for a political thinker he practised politics, being Liberal Member of Parliament for Westminster from 1865 to 1868. While an MP he made an unsuccessful attempt to extend the vote to women.

How to read:

Mill's *On Liberty*

On Liberty is a relatively short text – about 120 pages in length. There are many editions of the text, and most editions combine *On Liberty* with other essays by Mill. Despite the brevity of the text Mill can be convoluted and long-winded, although this reflects a certain Victorian style of writing. *On Liberty* is organised into five chapters. Chapter 1 is introductory, but important: among other things it sets out the harm principle. Chapter 2 is concerned with freedom of expression, and Chapter 3 with freedom of action – although this is not obvious from the title 'Of Individuality, as One of the Elements of Well-Being'. The core of the argument is in Chapters 1–3; however, Chapter 5 is important in explaining how the harm principle may be applied (unfortunately, in the process Mill contradicts himself). One final point: it is worth bearing in mind that more than many other philosophical texts Mill's essay is directed at a wide audience.

After some initial remarks about the danger of the majority tyrannising minorities, Mill articulates what has become known as the *liberty principle* (or *harm principle*):

> the sole end for which mankind are warranted, individually or collectively, in interfering with the liberty of action of any of their number, is self-protection. [. . .] The only purpose for which power can be rightfully exercised over any member of a civilized community, against his will, is to prevent harm to others. His own good, either physical or moral, is not a sufficient warrant (Mill, 1991: 14).

Mill goes on to clarify to whom the harm principle applies. Excluded are those who have not yet developed their intellectual and moral capacities, that is, children. But also excluded from the scope of the principle are those who live in societies that lack the cultural and institutional conditions for the exercise of freedom. Mill, as with most nineteenth-century thinkers, adopted an evolutionary view of **culture**.

Underpinning the harm principle is a certain conception of what it means to live a properly human life, as distinct from a merely animal existence. To be human is to enjoy a sphere in which one is able to think, express ideas, and lead a lifestyle of one's own choosing. In developing his argument Mill introduces some important concepts:

- **Self-regarding and other-regarding actions** Some actions affect *directly* only the individual (self-regarding actions), whereas other actions have a direct effect on other people (other-regarding actions) (Mill: 16).
- **Direct and indirect effects** Mill acknowledges the adage that 'no man is an island', and that most actions have effects on others, however remote, or indirect, those effects may be (16). How we distinguish between direct and indirect effects is a problem to which we shall return.
- **Consent** You can permit another person to do something to you which in the absence of **consent** would be deemed direct harm and therefore prohibited. A good example is boxing – an activity that would, without consent, be physical assault (16).

Mill then sets out what he terms the 'appropriate region of human liberty'. It consists of:

- **The 'inward domain of consciousness'** This requires freedom of thought and feeling and an 'absolute freedom' of opinion on any subject. Mill concedes that expression of opinions may appear to extend beyond freedom of conscience because it affects other people, but he asserts that expression is 'almost of as much importance as the liberty of thought itself' and it rests on the 'same reasons' (16).

- **The 'liberty of tastes and pursuits'** We should be free to act on our beliefs, and pursue a 'plan of life' consistent with our individual character and desires, subject, of course, to the harm principle. Other people can think your lifestyle 'foolish, perverse, or wrong', but they should not interfere with it (17).

- **Freedom to associate with others** It follows from freedom of expression and action that people should be free to 'combine' with others. Obvious examples would be the formation of trade unions, professional associations, political parties and movements, as well as the development of more personal relationships (17).

To tackle Mill's argument we need to distinguish freedom of thought and expression, discussed in Chapter 2 of *On Liberty*, and freedom of action, discussed in Chapter 3.

Freedom of Thought and Expression

Even if a person finds himself alone in expressing an opinion he should, according to Mill, be free to express it: 'if all mankind, minus one, were of one opinion, and only one person were of the contrary opinion, mankind would no more be justified in silencing that one person, than he, if he had the power, would be justified in silencing mankind' (Mill: 21). Mill has a neat defence of this claim:

- If the opinion is true then by suppressing it humanity is deprived of the truth and will not progress. (Mill observes that it has often been the case that today's heterodoxy is tomorrow's orthodoxy; an example might be Charles Darwin's theory of evolution by natural selection – in fact, today there is insufficient criticism of Darwin's theory (21).)

- If the opinion is false then humanity again loses, because if the opinion is false it will be shown to be so, but its expression is useful, for it forces us to restate the reasons for our beliefs. A competition of ideas is healthy (Mill, 1991: 21).

- The truth is often 'eclectic' (52). This argument is frequently misunderstood. It can mean: (a) an opinion can be broken into a number of discrete claims, some of which are true and some false; (b) the conclusion of an argument might be correct and the premises sound, but the conclusion does not follow from the premises; (c) two conflicting arguments may require a third argument to resolve the conflict between them. What Mill did *not* mean by 'eclecticism' was that the truth is 'subjective'. Such a claim would undermine the fundamental basis of his defence of freedom of expression, which is that it is the means by which truth is advanced.

People who seek to suppress an opinion assume their own beliefs are infallible; they confuse *their* certainty with *absolute* certainty. Mill accepts that people must make decisions and act on them, and those decisions are based on beliefs. It would, for example, be irrational for you to jump off the edge of a cliff if that action were motivated by a belief that you could fly unaided; a rational person is guided by a belief in the law of gravity. However, Mill distinguishes between holding a belief to be certain, and not permitting others to refute it – people should be free to question the law of gravity, and this is consistent with the rest of us acting as if the law were true. (There is an issue about whether we should stop you acting on a false belief if that action has disastrous consequences for you; since this relates to freedom of action, we shall turn to it in the next section.)

Progress in knowledge and understanding, Mill argues, comes about not through experience alone, but also through discussion. This is interesting because it shows that Mill's defence of freedom of expression rests on the good consequences of permitting such freedom. This contrasts with an argument which asserts that individuals have rights 'to be left alone', and that freedom of expression is justified on the basis of those rights and not the social good generated by it.

Mill's defence of freedom of expression is paradoxical. While it is a good thing for people to express different and conflicting opinions, the basic justification is that truth is advanced in the competition of ideas. This assumes that there is a truth (or set of truths), and the pursuit of that truth sets an end for humankind. The implication is that as we progress false beliefs lose their power over us, and we increasingly come to hold the same true beliefs. What Mill fears is that as a result of this process the beneficial aspects of the expression of false beliefs will be lost: 'both teachers and learners go to sleep at their post, as soon as there is no enemy in the field' (48). This suggests a distinction between the prevalence of true beliefs, and how human beings hold those beliefs; it is essential that we understand the reasons for our beliefs, otherwise the belief becomes 'dead dogma'.

Finally, although there is a distinction between freedom of action and freedom of expression, the line between them is fuzzy: some forms of expression are very close to action. A person 'must not make himself a nuisance to other people' (1991: 55). And Mill goes on to argue that:

> an opinion that corn dealers* are starvers of the poor, or that private property is robbery, ought to be unmolested when simply circulated through the press, but may justly incur punishment when delivered orally to an excited mob assembled before the house of a corn dealer, or when handed about among the same mob in the form of a placard (1991: 55).

There is a close causal relationship here between speech and action.

Freedom of Action

In Chapter 3 of *On Liberty* Mill discusses freedom of action and lifestyle. While acknowledging that 'no one pretends that actions should be as free as opinions' (1991: 62) Mill claims the same reasons which show an opinion should be free

---

*One of the major debates of the nineteenth century was over free trade versus protectionism, especially in foodstuffs; corn dealers controlled the price of corn and kept it high, relative to its free trade price, and so were deeply unpopular people. If you want a contemporary example, take the case of people who have served sentences for sexual offences against children and who have been released into the community: publicising their names and addresses may encourage vigilante groups to track them down and harm them.

demonstrate that an individual should be free to put his opinions into practice, even if the action is foolish. The only constraint is that the agent should not harm others. Some doubts can be raised as to whether freedom of expression and freedom of action really do rest on the same arguments, but for the moment we will follow the course of Mill's argument.

In discussing freedom of action, Mill introduces a concept not used in the discussion of expression: *individuality*. He regards individuality as 'one of the principal ingredients of human happiness' (63), and so it is linked to the well-being of society. The development of individuality requires two things: freedom and a 'variety of situations' (64). Although children need to be guided by those who have had experience of life, adults must be free to develop their own lifestyle and values, and not be subject to *custom*. The word 'custom' can be defined as accumulated, shared and often 'taken-for-granted' experiences. Mill criticises custom:

- Experience may be too narrow, and wrongly interpreted.
- Other people's experiences may not be relevant to you, given *your* character and *your* experiences.
- The custom may be 'good', but to conform to it as custom 'does not educate or develop . . . any of the qualities which are the distinctive endowment of the human being' (65). People need to make choices, and following custom is an evasion of choice. Following custom is analogous to holding beliefs without understanding the reasons for those beliefs.

At the heart of the notion of individuality is *originality*. To be original is to bring something into the world; this need not be a creation out of nothing, and it is quite possible that other people have thought the same thoughts and performed the same actions. Nor indeed must an action be uninfluenced by others; what makes an action 'original' is that a person consciously sets himself against custom and thinks for himself. Originality is most likely to take a 'synthetic' form, that is, originality is demonstrated in the ability to produce something new through the synthesis of diverse experiences and reflections. It serves a social function, for it provides role models for those who, by character or inclination, may be more timid about thinking or acting in ways not supported by custom. Those who are 'original' are providing what Mill calls *experiments in living*, some of which may have bad, even disastrous, consequences, but taken together the existence of experiments is over time beneficial. The link between freedom of expression and freedom of action is clear: the original person is the 'one in a hundred' prepared to advance a heterodox belief, and the 'failed experiment' parallels the 'false belief'.

Mill rejects **paternalism** – that is, stopping people harming themselves. He does endorse what is sometimes called 'soft paternalism', but it is a matter of debate whether it really is paternalism: if a person starts to cross a footbridge, unaware that it is insecure and liable to collapse into the ravine below, then if we cannot communicate with him – perhaps we do not share a language – we can intervene (106–7). If, however, he knows the risk then we are *not* entitled to stop him. Paternalism is discussed further in the section on Criticisms and Developments.

It should be stressed that we do not have to approve of other people's behaviour. If a person manifests a 'lowness or depravation of taste' we are, Mill argues, justified in making him a 'subject of distaste, or . . . even of contempt' (85). What we are not justified in doing is interfering in his actions. There is a tension here between encouraging diversity of lifestyle as if it were an intrinsically good thing, but being free to disapprove of it. If diversity is to be *promoted* rather than merely *tolerated* then the state should not just protect people's freedom, but actually encourage a change in attitudes among the majority.

Criticisms and Developments

Mill's argument provides a useful framework for discussing the nature and limits of freedom. As we suggested at the beginning of this chapter many political theorists concerned with freedom presume freedom to be a good thing, and search for legitimate reasons for limiting it. Mill claims that only non-consensual harm to others can constitute a legitimate ground for limiting another person's freedom. But Mill may be wrong, and in the box below we present for consideration a number of additional 'freedom-limiting principles' alongside the non-consensual harm to others one.

Liberty-limiting principle:		Mill's view (YES: reason for restricting freedom; NO: not a reason)
Harm to others	Non-consensual	YES – only ground for restriction
	Consent	NO
Harm to self (paternalism)		NO (argument is closely tied to the consent-to-be-harmed argument)
Offensiveness		NO (but Mill is not consistent)
Harmless wrongdoing *or* badness (these two are not the same)		NO: harmless wrongdoing is a contradiction in terms

Using these four, or arguably five, principles we can both criticise Mill and consider alternative perspectives on freedom.

Harm to Others

We start with some general comments about Mill's harm principle, ignoring for the moment the distinction between consensual and non-consensual harm to others. The first, and rather obvious, objection to the harm principle is: what, in fact, constitutes harm? Surely, no man or woman is an island – are there any truly self-regarding actions?

Mill concedes that no person is an 'entirely isolated being' (88) and almost all actions have remote consequences. If by 'harm' we mean any 'bad' effect another person's action may have then few actions would be self-regarding and it would be difficult to use 'harm' as a criterion for restricting freedom at the same time as guaranteeing a significant sphere of freedom for the individual. Mill operates with a 'physicalist' rather than a 'psychological' definition of harm; if we were to expand the concept of harm beyond physical harm to the person (and his property) to include psychological harm then the private sphere in which a person would be free to act would be severely contracted.

Another kind of harm might be caused when a person sets a 'bad example': if Mill is going to appeal to the *good* consequences of 'experiments in living', he must surely accept that some experiments may also have *bad* consequences for other people. Part of Mill's response to this problem is to argue that you cannot have the benefits of freedom without also suffering the negative consequences. To try to determine what are good experiments in living and what are bad, and seek to restrict the latter is to prejudge what is good and bad, and it is precisely only in the competition of lifestyles that such a judgement can be made. The consequences of an action are always in the future, and so we cannot know those consequences *now* such that we can predict them.

The appeal to competing lifestyles is an important argument but it is quite different to a defence of freedom based on the possibility that many important actions are self-regarding and do not therefore 'harm' others. To save the harm principle Mill must clarify what can count as 'harm'. One option is to redefine harm as: having one's fundamental interests damaged such that one's life goes (significantly) less well than it would otherwise have gone. It could be added that in most circumstances the individual who is 'harmed' should judge what is, or is not, in her interests – this raises the issue of consent, which is discussed in the next section. Obviously, this needs to be elaborated, but the point is that the threshold for deeming an action 'harmful' is high; it cannot simply be an action which has negative effects on another person. This would rule out temporary discomfort caused by someone else's action: so, for example, if you feel a bit groggy after spending an evening in the bar breathing other people's smoke that cannot count as harm, but contracting cancer *is* harm. We might still want to attach some importance to temporary discomfort, but rather than call it harmful we call it offensive. If we do this then we need a different principle for judging something offensive – this principle is discussed in the section on Offensiveness.

Consent

Mill argues that people can consent to be harmed. Activities such as boxing or duelling, even though they carry the risk of considerable harm, and even death, must be free so long as the people concerned consented, and were capable of consent, where being 'capable' means being an adult. It might be objected that there is no necessary connection between harm and consent: if something is harmful to other people then we should be prevented from engaging in it.

p. 41

But consent is important for Mill because it connects up with the third area in the 'appropriate region of human liberty': freedom of association. If the state were justified in interfering in consensual, albeit harmful, activities between consenting adults then the space in which people could associate would be severely restricted. A legal case in England from the early 1990s is interesting. In 1990 a number of men were charged with 'assault occasioning actual bodily harm' (*R. v. Brown and Others* (1993); the arrest was codenamed 'Operation Spanner'). The men had engaged in a rather protracted session of sadomasochistic sexual activity, which, foolishly, they had videotaped. Their defence – that they all consented – was dismissed by the court. Unsurprisingly, the parallel of boxing was used as part of the defence: if two men can beat each other up, then why can they not get sexual pleasure from inflicting pain on each other? The judge argued that consent was a ground for 'harm' but it had to be backed up by a justification of the activity itself, and the following were legitimate: surgery; a 'properly conducted game or sport'; tattooing and ear-piercing. On sport, Foster's *Crown Law* (1792) was cited: boxing and wrestling are 'manly diversions, they intend to give strength, skill and activity, and may fit people for defence, public as well as personal, in time of need'. The court deemed that consent was a necessary *but insufficient* ground for the action, and that the intrinsic qualities of the action could justify a restriction on the action. We return to this argument in the section on Harmless Wrongdoing.

Harm to Self

The issue of consent brings us to the question of harm to self: in effect, consenting to be harmed amounts to harming oneself and raises the issue of whether the state ought to protect people against themselves. For example, having an 'age of consent' for various activities amounts to a judgement that a person – or group of people, such as children – are incapable of giving consent, or, at least, *informed* consent. Laws that protect people against themselves are 'paternalistic', although in everyday language advocates of paternalism avoid the term because of its pejorative overtones. The etymology of the word 'paternalism' suggests a parent–child relationship, and most people would accept that laws regarding children should be paternalistic – though in some cases children should be protected by the state against their parents – but it is more controversial when applied to adults and thus where it is the state that acts as the 'parent'.

A distinction is sometimes made between 'soft' and 'hard' paternalism: if someone does not understand that what he is doing is potentially harmful then a soft paternalist would argue that intervention is justified. A hard paternalist will say that even if a person knows what he is doing is harmful to himself intervention is justified. We have briefly discussed Mill's bridge example: you can stop a person crossing an unsafe bridge if you are sure he is unaware of the risks (soft paternalism), but you are not justified in stopping him if he is aware of the consequences. Of course, a soft paternalist must explain what is meant by 'understanding': does mental incapacity mean that some people cannot understand the implications of their actions? Mill only addresses indirectly the problem of adults who have been incapacitated by mental illness or have an inherited condition that renders them incapable of consent – he argues against extending the notion of 'child protection' to any adults (1991: 89–90).

Mill suggests that if society wants the benefits of 'experiments in living' then it must also accept the risks. The difficulty is that there are some activities so patently harmful that there would be no loss to society if the agent were protected against himself. And even if this were not true, the loss to the individual concerned is so great that *his* good must warrant interference. The argument touched on in the section on Harm to Others earlier regarding not being able to predict the consequences of our actions applies only to novel actions – human experience tells us that if you jump off a cliff you will plunge to your death. We can debate the laws of gravity, and that is part of freedom of *expression*, but our *actions* should be governed by the subjective, experience-based certainty of what will happen if we jump.

It is, of course, possible to argue that many activities contain a good which cannot be separated from the risks involved. Boxing, for example, carries a significant danger of brain damage, but certainly in the past – in Mill's time – boxing gave pride and discipline to many working-class men. Nonetheless, if we are concerned with the capacity for freedom then 'harm to self' must *on occasion* be a ground for state interference: if you engage in action which ends your future capacity for action, such as consenting to be killed and eaten, then we cannot justify that action on grounds of human freedom, because the act itself extinguishes the capacity for freedom. This is where positive liberty is important. Adapting slightly Berlin's distinction we could argue that positive freedom entails a long-term capacity for choice, and for that reason it is conceptually possible for you to be the source of your own unfreedom: your actions *now* may harm your *future* self.

p. 39

Offensiveness

The principles discussed so far have tended to be concerned with freedom of action; offensiveness relates as much to freedom of expression as to action, and so we begin with some problems with Mill's argument for freedom of expression. Mill assumes that expression, be it speaking, writing and publication, or visual media, always entails the communication of truth. The paradigm – or model – of communication for Mill is a propositional statement to which one assents or from

---

Exercise

Should the state intervene in the following situations (all people involved are consenting adults)?

(a) to require adults to wear seatbelts in cars;

(b) to prevent adults boxing;

(c) to prevent adults duelling;

(d) to prevent adults engaging in sadomasochistic sexual activities, where there is a danger of moderate physical harm;

(e) where a person has a painful, terminal illness, to prevent another person ending that life;

(f) to prevent an adult consenting to be killed in the context of a cannibalistic activity, where the person is fully aware of the consequences of consent.

Case (f) may seem extreme, but there was a recent case in Germany. The defendant in this case – Armin Meiwes – advertised on the internet for a man willing to be killed and eaten. Eventually he found a 'victim'. The prosecution accepted that from web traffic and other evidence the victim did 'consent' to be killed, and under German law they were required to seek a verdict of 'requested killing', which carries a lesser sentence than murder. Our concern is not with the interpretation of law, but with what the law should be: should a person be permitted to consent to be killed in this way?

which one can dissent: scientific 'truth claims', claims about, for example, the laws of gravity, are propositional statements. In effect, Mill views society as engaged in one gigantic university seminar. But there are plenty of examples where this is not the case. Think of abusive speech: the point here is not that all 'non-propositional' forms of expression are bad and should be banned, but that Mill provides an inadequate account of human expression. Above all, there seems to be no place in his theory for restricting freedom of expression on grounds that a certain expression might be offensive.

Joel Feinberg's (1985) list of offensive situations ('A Ride on the Bus' – see the exercise below) should be sufficient to convince us that offensiveness can sometimes be a ground for restricting freedom. Although Mill does not directly address the problem of offensiveness, implicit in his argument is the view that to say 'I find x offensive' is equivalent to saying 'I do not agree with x', and he rejects disagreement as a ground for limiting a person's freedom. The alternative is to say that the action is not offensive but harmful – perhaps 'psychologically harmful'. This would, however, severely restrict the sphere in which a person is free to act. Mill does appeal to the notion of 'public decency' to forbid things that harm the agent and are done in public:

Exercise

'A Ride on the Bus'

Joel Feinberg in his book *The Moral Limits of the Criminal Law* (Vol. 2: *Offense to Others*) asks the reader to imagine taking a ride on a bus, and at various stages another passenger, or group of passengers gets on, and proceeds to do various things that while not harmful are offensive. He presents 31 'stories' in six groups (10–13), and we have reproduced (in abridged form) one from each group (no offence is intended by reproducing them here!). Ask yourself whether the agent(s) should be free to engage in the action.

1. **Affront to the senses:** a passenger turns on a radio to maximum volume; the sounds emitted are mostly screeches, whistles and static, but occasionally rock music blares through.

2. **Disgust and revulsion:** a group get on the bus, and sitting next to you spread a tablecloth over their knees and proceed to eat a picnic of live insects, fish heads and pickled sex organs of lamb, veal and pork, smothered in garlic and onions. Their table manners leave almost everything to be desired.

3. **Shock to religious sensibility:** a youth gets on wearing a T-shirt with a cartoon of Christ on the cross, underneath which are the words 'Hang in there, baby!'

4. **Shame and embarrassment:** a passenger masturbates in his seat.

5. **Annoyance and boredom:** the passenger next to you is a friendly and garrulous bloke, who insists on engaging you in conversation despite your polite but firm requests that you be allowed to read your newspaper. There is nowhere else on the bus to sit.

6. **Fear (resentment, humiliation, anger):** a passenger sits near you wearing a black armband with a large swastika on it.

There are many acts which, being directly injurious only to the agents themselves, ought not to be legally interdicted, but which, if done publicly, are a violation of good manners, and coming thus within the category of offences against others, may rightfully be prohibited. Of this kind are offences against decency; on which it is unnecessary to dwell . . . (1991: 109).

It would, in fact, have been interesting to dwell a while on these activities, for Mill's argument is hardly consistent with the harm principle. Sex in public is not (normally) 'injurious' to the participants but most people, even if they themselves are not offended, would probably accept that it should be prohibited. The basic point is that Mill has no serious discussion of offensiveness.

Feinberg groups instances of offensiveness under six categories, but a simpler distinction would be that between immediate and mediated offence. *Immediate offence* is offence to the senses. Imagine the neighbours from hell: they party and play loud music all night; they have a rusting car in their front garden and pile up household refuse – which stinks – in the back garden. These things hit the senses – sight, sound, smell. *Mediated offence* is when a norm or value is violated: the swastika is only offensive if you associate it with Nazi Germany, and with the implication that the person wearing the armband sympathises with what happened in Nazi Germany (it is not offensive when, for example, it is found in decorations on buildings predating the 1930s – the swastika is an ancient South American symbol, and is also a Hindu symbol).

Cutting across the distinction between immediate and mediated offence is the question of intentionality: is an act offensive if it is unintended? It is quite possible that a person 'gives offence' without intending to do so – once it is realised that the 'offence' is unintended then it may cease to be offensive. Using these two pairs of distinctions there are four possible types of offensiveness, as shown in the next box.

(a) Intended immediate offence	**(b)** Intended mediated offence
(c) Unintended immediate offence	**(d)** Unintended mediated offence

If there are grounds for restricting freedom then it would not normally apply to (d). Some restriction – although it must be proportional – on immediate offence may be justified. Intended mediated offence is much more problematic. Take the case of Steve Gough, the so-called 'Naked Rambler'. Gough took seven months to walk naked – except for boots and a hat – from Land's End to John O'Groats, that is, from one end of Britain to the other. He was arrested 17 times and spent two brief terms in prison. He has a website on which he says he is engaged in a 'celebration of the human body and a campaign to enlighten the public, as well as the authorities that govern us, that the freedom to go naked in public is a basic human right' (www.nakedwalk.co.uk). Clearly, what he did was illegal, but the question is whether it should have been, and whether there ought to be a 'human right' to go naked in public. If what he did was offensive, then most likely it was mediated, rather than immediate, offence (it would be immediate offence if people found him physically repulsive).

The difficulty with mediated offence connects up with the last of the principles: harmless wrongdoing (and to the judgment in the Operation Spanner case). What offends us depends on our values, and in a pluralistic society people disagree about what is of value. The best approach may be to distinguish public and private, where 'public' need not be narrowly defined as 'behind closed doors' but is a space in which people might legitimately expect certain things to happen. For example, Germans are more tolerant of public nudity than the British and indeed have a whole movement based around it – *freie Körper Kultur* (FKK) – such that, weather permitting, there is widespread nakedness in German public parks. There is, therefore, a *legitimate expectation* that if you stroll through a German park you will come across naked people, but that tolerance would not be extended to a Gough-type character striding along the highways of that country. In this sense German parks, although public in an everyday sense, constitute a 'private space' in a philosophical sense.

Harmless Wrongdoing

This is the most difficult principle to grasp. In part, the difficulty lies in its formulation: if 'wrongness' is defined as 'that which is harmful' then harmless wrongdoing is a contradiction in terms. It may however be that a distinction is being made between, on the one hand, right/wrong, and, on the other, good/bad. In everyday speech, we use these pairs interchangeably, so right equals good, and wrong equals bad. But philosophers do make a distinction between (a) **rightness**, or that which is obligatory, and (b) **goodness**, or an end that we should pursue. For example, if we obey the law we are doing right – we are fulfilling our obligations – but 'doing right' tells us nothing about *why* we do right. We might obey the law from purely self-interested reasons, or we might obey it because we recognise that other people matter – they have interests just as we have interests. Goodness is a quality of character, whereas rightness is a quality of behaviour. For this reason, it would be better to use a different label to that of 'harmless wrongdoing'.

In Mill's lifetime a view was articulated – by James Fitzjames Stephen (Stephen, 1873) – that to permit an 'immoral' act is equivalent to allowing an act of treason to go unpunished: the good of **society** was at risk. This view was rearticulated in the 1960s by Patrick (Lord) Devlin (Devlin, 1965) in response to the recommendation of a commission (Wolfenden Commission, 1957) that laws on homosexuality should be liberalised. Devlin argued that there was a 'shared morality' and that permitting 'immoral acts' in private threatened that morality (1965: 13–14). There was a danger of social disintegration. At first sight, Devlin's argument appears simply to be the claim that no action is completely self-regarding, and, of course, we have discussed a revised Millian response, which is to suggest that fundamental interests must be at stake for an action to be deemed harmful. Devlin's argument is however a little more sophisticated: actions may not have discernible harmful effects, but cumulatively they erode social norms, and that erosion is *seriously* harmful. But this still seems to be concerned with harm. A number of objections have been raised to Devlin's argument (what has become termed the 'social cohesion thesis'): (a) He was wrong about homosexuality; (b) Is there really a shared morality? Don't people disagree about morality? (c) Even if there is a shared morality does permitting 'private immorality' undermine it?

What is worth reflecting on is whether there is something in Devlin's argument that cannot be captured in a debate dominated by the concept of harm. The problem with the concept of harm is that it always requires identifying harms to *particular* individuals or groups, whereas there may be a good which cannot be reduced to identifiable individuals or groups; this might be an image of society which guides people to behave in a certain way. We can call this a *free-floating good* because although it is the product of human experience it cannot be reduced to the interests of individuals, or even groups. It could be argued that no society will survive unless it pursues some goods and the protection and promotion of these goods provide the justification for restricting human freedom. (One could also argue that we have an obligation to future generations to reproduce these goods, that is, reproduce a particular kind of culture.) If certain things are objectively valuable then any rational mind, contrary to Mill's fallibility argument, will recognise them to be so. John Finnis, in his book *Natural Law and Natural Rights*, observes that almost all cultures, despite apparent differences between them, exhibit a commitment to certain goods. He cites anthropological research (although, unfortunately, fails to give any reference for that research), suggesting that almost all cultures value the following: human life and procreation; permanence in sexual relations; truth and its transmission; cooperation; obligation between individuals; justice between groups; friendship; property; play; respect for the dead (Finnis, 1980: 83–4).

pp. 45–6

Stephen, Devlin and Finnis would not reject the idea that people should have a sphere of freedom ('private sphere'), but would maintain that it is a function of the state to change human behaviour, and that law should reflect morality. This position is termed **legal moralism**. For example, Finnis has been a vocal critic of laws which treat homosexuals and heterosexuals equally, arguing that equal treatment implies that they are equally valid: a position he rejects, maintaining that homosexuality is contrary to natural law. There is a parallel between legal moralism and the judgment made in the Operation Spanner case. Recall that the judgment maintained that consent was a necessary *but not a sufficient* condition for permitting another person to harm you, for the activity in which you are engaged must have some intrinsic value. This suggests that the men involved in sadomasochism have to justify the practice of sadomasochism. Legal moralists would argue that such an activity cannot be justified: it is a sexual perversion – that is, a misdirection of the libido on to an inappropriate object.

The difficulty with legal moralism is that it assumes more than just a shared morality – it assumes a shared conception of what is *ultimately valuable*. Many defenders of freedom would agree that we need a shared morality – respecting other people, and not harming them without their consent, is a moral position. But such a morality leaves open many questions of what is truly valuable in life – individuals, it is argued, must find their own way to what is valuable. This does not mean that there are no objectively valuable ends, but simply that coercion, by definition, will not help us to get there: the state can stop people harming one another, but it cannot make people good.

Smoking Ban Reconsidered

We can now apply the framework discussed above to the case of the smoking ban. It should be stressed that this is a case study and that we could have selected many other examples – it is important that political theory raises *general* arguments applicable across *different* cases. In popular debate a common attitude to the smoking ban is: 'I'm not a smoker, so it doesn't bother me'. This is an inadequate basis for supporting the ban. Any ban must be supported by reasons that could be advanced by smokers and non-smokers alike – this is what we mean by a general argument.

To be fair to those engaged in popular debate, there is often an implicit recognition that reasons and principles are at stake that extend further than the smoking ban itself – when people get beyond the simple statement made above and actually engage in debate they use analogies. An opponent of a ban might say 'if you ban smoking, then why not ban the consumption of fatty foods'; a proponent of a ban might respond by pointing out that the analogy is false because there is no direct harm to others involved in the consumption of fatty foods. The point is that both proponent and opponent are attempting to apply general arguments to specific cases. Without necessarily realising it, they are engaging in political theory. So in the spirit of seeking general arguments that can be applied to the ban, let us apply the freedom-limiting principles discussed in Criticisms and Developments to the smoking ban (the last – Harmless Wrongdoing – is not really applicable to this case).

Harm to Others

We argued that Mill's harm principle needs to be revised so that harm is defined as serious harm, and suggested that the temporary discomfort of being in a smoky environment cannot constitute harm – although if you follow the popular discussion around the smoking ban the immediate discomfort from smoking is a common theme. If we do revise Mill's harm principle along the lines just suggested – that is, damage to a person's long-term interests – we still have a problem: your action in itself may not harm another person. If you go to a particular bar just once, and sit by the bar chain-smoking for a couple of hours, then your action will not kill the barman. Accepting for the purposes of the argument that passive smoking can kill, and that working long shifts in a bar puts a person in harm's way, then the barman will still contract cancer without your two-hour period of chain-smoking. The paradox is that if the barman comes into contact with thousands of people during his career *no single one of them* will be responsible for his death. This is Sorites Paradox: millions of grains of sand make a heap of sand, subtract a grain and you still have a pile, keep subtracting and you will end up without a pile, but no single grain makes the difference between a pile and no pile. So we have to make a second revision to the harm principle: your action (smoking in a bar) belongs to a set of actions (thousands of people smoking in that bar) which together cause harm.

Consent

This brings us to the second part of the harm to others principle: harm to others does not, for Mill, in itself constitute grounds for restricting freedom. Rather, it must be *non-consensual* harm to others that triggers a restriction. This is where debates about the effects of passive smoking slightly miss the point: we could agree that passive smoking is harmful, or, if we are not sure, we could adopt the 'precautionary principle' – we assume, until we have the evidence, that if smoking is harmful to the smoker, then sustained contact with cigarette smoke in an enclosed environment will be harmful to non-smokers. So let us just accept that passive smoking is harmful. That in itself does not justify a ban on smoking bars because non-smokers might consent to be harmed. That then shifts the debate to the meaning of consent: do low-paid bar staff consent? Maybe they have no meaningful option but to work in a bar or club. If so, an alternative to a complete ban would be a licensing scheme.

A variant on the 'we-don't-consent' argument is that a group of friends, consisting of smokers and non-smokers, have no choice but to go to smoking bars and clubs. Of course, the reverse would also be true if there were only smoke-free bars. But there is a deeper point: should the state be responsible for individual relationships? Is it really the role of the state to 'enable' non-smokers to go to a bar with smoker friends? Should the state be responsible for your social life? A more weighty objection to the consent argument is that it assumes that by entering a bar a non-smoker *intends* to be among smokers, rather than entering a building in which he knows he will have to *tolerate* smokers. If you go into a boxing ring you intend to participate in an activity in which harm is intrinsic to the activity – you do not intend to get brain damage, but such damage is part-and-parcel of boxing. To make the equivalent case for consent to go into a smoking pub, you would have to say that smoking is an intrinsic part of pub life – it goes with the 'craich' as the Irish (no longer) say.

Harm to Self

Much of the argument in favour of banning smoking is not just to prevent harm to others, but is a public health measure intended to reduce the number of smokers. For some anti-smoking campaigners this seems to be the main objective of a ban. If it were not an objective then licensing rather than banning would be the obvious policy to adopt. Is the aim of reducing the amount of smoking justified? Some points in favour:

(a) It is a relatively soft form of paternalism – making the sale or use of tobacco illegal would be the hard measure.

(b) Smokers, it is claimed, want to give up – the ban will help them.

(c) Even if smokers do not want to give up it is in their interests to stop smoking.

The last argument is the core paternalist one. The state is saying to smokers – we are doing this for your own good. There are several arguments against paternalism, some of which we have discussed in relation to Mill's argument. First, paternalist actions by the state rest on the assumption that the state knows better than the individual what is in her interests. Sometimes there are good grounds for believing this to be so, but more often the choices individuals make are part of a complex that are more immediately accessible to the individual – for example, smoking may be a means of relieving tension, or, despite its health and financial costs, simply a pleasurable activity. Second, there is a 'slippery slope' objection: if the state decides that smoking is bad for the individual and for that reason it should be banned, then why not ban other unhealthy habits or dangerous activities? Paternalistic intervention erodes the sphere in which individuals make choices, whether or not those choices are 'good'. Third, and possibly the most philosophically significant, paternalism implies that agents cannot be persuaded that an activity is harmful – if the *coercive* power of the state is employed to *prevent* people behaving in certain ways then this implies that a society cannot be rational.

Offensiveness

Some people find smoking offensive – could this be a ground for banning it? Most likely it is the immediate 'offensiveness' of smoking that would create the basis for banning it. If you look at comments made by 'ordinary people' some of them describe smoking as a 'disgusting habit'. One advocate of a complete smoking ban, commenting on the inadequacy of having demarcated smoking areas, likened bars with segregated smoking areas to a swimming pool in which one lane is reserved for people to urinate in. Presumably this analogy was intended to convey the problems of restricting the harmful effects of smoking to one area of a bar, but perhaps it also reveals his disgust at smoking.

Summary

We have explored both freedom of expression and action, using Mill's harm principle as the starting point. That principle is not as 'simple' as Mill suggests, and to address the complexities of freedom we have discussed further liberty-limiting principles: harm to self, offensiveness, 'harmless wrongdoing'. It is for the reader to assess the validity of these different principles, but it is clear that a discussion of freedom must at least address the charge that the harm principle is inadequate as an explanation of the limits of freedom. Freedom is certainly regarded as a 'positive' word and this may reflect an underlying belief not just of political theorists, but also 'ordinary people', that although freedom must on occasion be limited we assume freedom to be a good thing – there is a 'presumption in favour of freedom'.

Questions

1. If the protection of a person's interests is so important should the state permit a person to harm him- or herself?
2. If the protection of a person's interests is so important should the state permit a person to consent to be harmed by somebody else?

3. Should the fact that someone finds an expression or action offensive be a reason for banning that expression or action?

4. Are some activities 'intrinsically bad' and therefore can they justifiably be banned?

References

Berlin, I. (1991) 'Two Concepts of Liberty' in D. Miller (ed.), *Liberty* Oxford: Oxford University Press.

Devlin, P. (1965) *The Enforcement of Morals* London: Oxford University Press.

Feinberg, J. (1985) *The Moral Limits of the Criminal Law*, vol. 2: *Offense to Others* New York: Oxford University Press.

Finnis, J. (1980) *Natural Law and Natural Rights* Oxford: Clarendon Press.

MacCallum, G. (1991) 'Negative and Positive Freedom' in D. Miller (ed.), *Liberty* Oxford: Oxford University Press.

Mill, J.S. (1991) *On Liberty and Other Essays* (ed. John Gray) Oxford: Oxford University Press.

Further Reading

Apart from Mill's *On Liberty*, the best starting points for a further exploration of freedom are Tim Gray, *Freedom* (London: Macmillan, 1991), George Brenkert, *Political Freedom* (London: Routledge, 1991), and David Miller (ed.), *Liberty* (Oxford: Oxford University Press, 1991), which is a collection of important essays on freedom, and Alan Ryan (ed.), *The Idea of Freedom* (Oxford: Oxford University Press, 1979), again a collection of essays. Also useful, but arguing a line, is Richard Flathman, *The Philosophy and Politics of Freedom* (Chicago and London: University of Chicago Press, 1987). Matthew Kramer, *The Quality of Freedom* (Oxford: Oxford University Press, 2003), is far from introductory, but is interesting, especially as he stresses the measurability of freedom. Two books that explore 'autonomy', which is a concept cognate to freedom, are: Richard Lindley, *Autonomy* (Basingstoke: Macmillan, 1986) and Robert Young, *Personal Autonomy: Beyond Negative* and *Positive Liberty* (London: Croom Helm, 1985). Specifically on Mill, the following works are useful: John Gray, *Mill on Liberty: A Defence* (London: Routledge, 1996); Gerald Dworkin (ed.), *Mill's On Liberty: Critical Essays* (Lenham: Rowman & Littlefield, 1997); C.L. Ten, *Mill on Liberty* (Oxford: Clarendon Press, 1980); Nigel Warburton, *Freedom: An Introduction with Readings* (London and New York: Routledge, 2001). See also John Skorupski, *John Stuart Mill* (London: Routledge, 1989), and relevant essays in John Skorupski (ed.), *The Cambridge Companion to Mill* (Cambridge: Cambridge University Press, 1998).

Weblinks

- There are some interesting sites that attempt to 'measure' freedom in different countries. Obviously there are philosophical issues here, such as whether we can say one society is more free than another without making judgements about the value of different freedoms. The best-known site is http://www.freedomhouse.org/

- There are many libertarian sites. Although they define freedom in a controversial way their websites are interesting. You should take the test (the 'world's smallest political quiz') on this one: http://www.self-gov.org/

- There are a couple of good websites on John Stuart Mill: http://www.jsmill.com/ and http://www.utilitarianism.com/jsmill.htm

Chapter 3

Equality

Introduction

Equality is a fundamental political concept, but also a very complex one. While the core idea of equality is that people should be treated in the same way, there are many different principles of equality. To provide a coherent defence of equality requires putting the various principles in order of priority, and explaining what it is that is being equalised: is it income, or well-being, the capacity to acquire certain goods, or something else? Equality, or particular principles of equality, must then be reconciled with other political values, or principles, such as freedom and efficiency. For that reason, this chapter is primarily conceptual, in that it aims to set out a number of principles of equality, and explain the relationships between them. The discussion will necessarily refer back to Chapter 2 (Freedom), and forward to Chapter 4 (Justice).

Chapter Map

In this chapter we will:

- Provide, in summary form, a scheme setting out various principles of **equality**: formal equality, moral equality, equality before the law, equal liberty and equal access, material equality (**equality of opportunity**, equality of outcome and **affirmative action**).

- Discuss, in more detail, those principles.

- Consider the relationship between freedom and equality.

- Draw out the implications for theories of **justice** – these will be discussed in greater detail in Chapter 4.

What do People Deserve?

The chances are that anybody reading this book will either be on above-average income or be in the process of acquiring the skills that will generate such an income. Studies have shown that in Britain graduates earn, over a lifetime, 49 per cent more than people with only school-leaving qualifications (A levels and equivalent) and 209 per cent more than those without any qualifications (www.prospects.ac.uk). Precise percentages will vary, but studies from other European countries, and North America, reveal a similar picture. Do graduates *deserve* this advantage? If we go back a stage we could also ask whether those graduates deserved their university places. A common response to this question might be: it depends on what family advantages they had. Two students may have the same entry qualifications, but if one has a relatively disadvantaged family background, while the other is relatively advantaged, the former might be thought more deserving than the latter. The difference in attitude rests on a distinction between naturally derived and socially derived advantages: natural ability, such as intelligence, is widely considered a legitimate basis for distribution, and any inequality that results from the exercise of intelligence is justified, whereas benefiting from socially inherited advantages, such as an expensive schooling, is regarded as illegitimate. In addition, what a person does with his or her natural abilities is thought morally relevant: people deserve to keep what they have acquired through their own efforts. Of course, this belief in 'meritocracy' – IQ + effort – need not be absolute; most people would support an *unconditional* minimum set of resources.

Before moving on, ask yourself the following questions:

- Should university places be distributed simply on the basis of performance in public examinations, or should other factors, such as socio-economic background, be taken into account?
- How far should the state go in trying to create equality of opportunity?
- Should people with fewer natural abilities get extra state-funded educational resources?

Principles of Equality

The term 'equality' is widely used in political debate, and frequently misunderstood. On the political left, equality is a central value, with socialists and social democrats aiming to bring about if not an equal society, then a more equal society. On the political right, the attempt to create a more equal society is criticised as a drive to uniformity, or a squeezing out of individual initiative. However, closer reflection on the nature of equality reveals a number of things. First, there is no one concept of equality, but rather, as indicated in Figure 3.1, a range of different forms. Second, all the main ideological positions, from right to left, endorse at least one form of equality – formal equality – and most also endorse one or more 'substantive' conceptions of equality. Third, principles of equality are often elliptical, meaning that there is an implicit claim that must be made explicit if we are to assess whether the claim is valid. To explain, since human beings possess more than one attribute or good, it is possible that equality in the possession of one will lead to, or imply, inequality in another. For example, Anne may be able-bodied and John disabled. Each could be given equal amounts of resources, such as healthcare, and so with regard to healthcare they are treated equally, but John's needs are greater, so the equality of healthcare has unequal *effects*. If Anne and John were given resources commensurate with their needs, then they would be being treated equally in one sphere (needs) but unequally in another (resources). The recognition of this plurality of goods, and therefore spheres within which people can be treated equally or unequally, is essential to grasping the complexity of the debate around equality and inequality. What is being distributed – and, therefore, what we are equal or unequal in our possession of – is termed a 'metric'.

The most useful starting point for a discussion of equality is to set out a number of forms of equality, in the shape of a flow chart (Figure 3.1). It is simplified, but the 'flow' of the chart is intended to reflect progressive controversy over different concepts and principles of equality. The first concept – formal equality – is

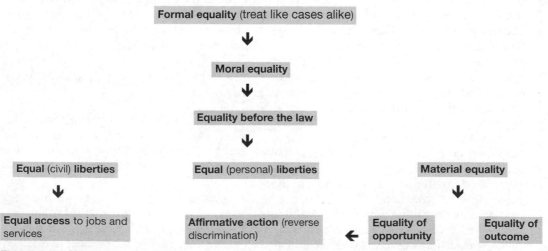

Figure 3.1 Principles of equality

uncontroversial, for it is tautological. Equality of outcome is, arguably, the most controversial. Although this claim is open to dispute, we would also argue that each form presupposes the previous one, so for example equality before the law assumes a belief in moral equality. The point is that you could plausibly stop at equality before the law and reject further principles of equality, but you cannot endorse the idea that people are equal before the law unless you also accept some idea of moral equality.

Each form is discussed in more detail in the course of the chapter, but an initial outline of each will help elucidate the connections between them.

- **Formal equality** To say we should treat like cases alike states nothing more than a tautological truth. If two people are alike in all respects then we would have no reason for discriminating between them; of course, no two people are alike, and the principle is indeed 'formal' – it does not tell us how to treat dissimilar people. Racists do not violate the principle of formal equality, because they argue that racial groups are not 'similar' and so need not, or should not, be treated in the same way.

- **Moral equality** The concept of moral equality is sometimes presented in negative form as a rejection of natural **hierarchy**, or natural inequality. In many societies it is taken for granted that people are, in important respects, deserving of equal consideration. Much discussion in political theory is about the characterisation of moral equality, which, paradoxically, can take the form of *justifying inequality*: that is, if people are morally equal, how do we explain their unequal treatment in terms of the distribution of social goods, such as income? The very idea that such inequality must be justified assumes that people are morally equal – in a society where there is an overwhelming belief in natural inequality, such as, say, a **caste society**, it would simply not occur to those in a higher stratum that they must justify their advantaged position, or that those in a lower stratum should question their subordinate position.

- **Equality before the law** That laws apply equally to those who are subject to them is widely accepted as a foundational belief of many, if not most, societies. It could be argued that this applied even in Hitler's Germany. After the 1935 Nuremburg Laws were passed Jews (as defined by the state) were denied many **rights**, but consistent with 'treating like cases alike' it could be argued that **legal equality** was respected insofar as all members of the class defined by the state as Jews were treated alike: all were equally subject to the laws, despite the laws themselves being discriminatory. However, we argue in the section on Legal Equality that equality before the law is a stronger idea, which implies that there must be compelling reasons for unequal treatment.

- **Equal liberty** A common assumption, especially on the right, is that equality and liberty (freedom) conflict. Certainly, if we were in a situation in which people possessed only 'pure' liberty, that is, we were under no duties to refrain from behaving as we chose, then the exercise of liberty would reflect natural inequalities, including any bad luck that might befall us. But under a state, while our liberty is restricted, the possibility exists for a degree of protection (through 'rights'), such that a space is provided in which we are free to act without the danger of other people interfering in our actions. Once we move from pure liberty to protected liberty an issue of distribution – and, therefore, a trade-off between equality and liberty – arises. Although the state cannot distribute the *exercise of choice*, it can distribute *rights* to do certain things. Of course, even though liberty-protecting rights can be distributed this does not mean that equality and liberty never conflict (we discuss possible conflicts in the section on Equal Liberties).

- **Material equality** The most significant disputes in many societies are connected with the distribution of income, and other tangible material goods, such as education and healthcare. To understand this debate requires a discussion of **class**, because the capacity to acquire material goods is to some extent, and perhaps a very great extent, conditioned by structures that individuals do not control. From birth – and even before birth – a person is set on a course, at each stage of which she has some power to gain or lose material goods, but, arguably, the choices are restricted. Put simply, a person born into a wealthy family has more opportunities than someone with a poor background.

Ch 9: Civil
Disobedience,
pp. 214–17

- **Equal access** If a society places barriers in the way of certain groups acquiring material goods, such as jobs and services, as happened with regard to blacks in the Southern States of the United States until the 1960s, then equal access is denied. On the face of it, guaranteeing equal access may appear closely connected with material equality, but, in fact, it has more to do with equal civic and political rights, or, *liberty*: the liberty to compete for jobs, and buy goods.

- **Equality of opportunity**, unlike equal access, *is* a principle of material equality, and although it commands rhetorical support across the political spectrum, in any reasonably strong version it has significant implications for the role of the state in individual and family life. If a society attempts to guarantee the equal opportunity to acquire, for example, a particular job, then it is going much further than simply removing legal obstacles to getting the job. Realising equal opportunity would require, among other things, substantial spending on education. Indeed, given the huge influence that the family has on a child's prospects, to achieve equal opportunity may entail considerable intervention in family life.

- **Equality of outcome** Critics of equality frequently argue that egalitarians – that is, those who regard equality as a central political principle – want to create a society in which everybody is treated equally irrespective of personal differences, or individual choice. This is a caricature, for it is possible to argue for equality of outcome as a prima facie principle, meaning that we should seek as far as possible to ensure an equal outcome consistent with other political principles. Equality of outcome may also function as a 'proxy' for equality of opportunity: if there are significantly unequal outcomes, then this indicates that there is not an adequate equality of opportunity. This last point leads us into a consideration of affirmative action.

- **Affirmative action** This term originated in the United States and is an umbrella term covering a range of policies intended to address the material deprivations suffered by (especially) black Americans, but also gender inequalities. Although it embraces a wider range of policies, it is often used as a synonym for 'reverse discrimination', or 'positive discrimination'. Examples of reverse discrimination

Exercise

Before discussing these forms of equality in more detail, it is useful to consider a range of attitudes to inequality. Below are listed a number of 'sources' of inequality – that is, characteristics, conditions or events that may result in unequal treatment or unequal relationships. Looking at each in turn, and *considering the views of people you know*, would you say the weight of opinion is for or against each one as a legitimate ground for unequal treatment?

- **Racial characteristics** (however 'race' is defined)

- **Gender**

- **Disability**

- **Intelligence**

- **Social class** into which a person is born

- **Unpredictable bad luck** such as being Involved in an accident

- **Predictable bad luck** such as losing money as the result of a poor investment or career choice.

include the operation of quotas for jobs, or a reduction in entry requirements for college places. Reverse discrimination is best understood as operating somewhere between equality of opportunity and equality of outcome: the principle acts directly on outcomes, but is intended to guarantee equality of opportunity.

Moral Equality

Moral Autonomy and Moral Equality

That people are morally equal is a central belief – often implicit rather than explicit – of societies influenced by the Enlightenment (post-Enlightenment societies). Sometimes people talk of 'natural equality', but this has connotations of natural law – the belief that moral principles have a real existence, transcending time and place. Moral equality can, minimally, be understood as a negative: people should be treated equally because there is no reason to believe in natural inequality. In Chapter 2 it was suggested that in post-Enlightenment societies there was a presumption in favour of liberty, meaning that people should be free to act as they wish unless there was a good reason for limiting that freedom. Parallel to the presumption in favour of liberty, there is also a presumption in favour of equality – people should be treated equally unless there is a strong reason for treating them unequally. But the negative argument does not adequately capture the importance of moral equality: to be morally equal, that is, worthy of equal consideration, implies that you are a certain kind of being – a being to whom reasons, or justifications, can be given. This reflects the roots of the concept of moral equality in the Enlightenment, which challenges authority, and assumes that the human mind is capable of understanding the world. Among the political implications of this philosophical position are, first, that the social world is not 'natural' – inequality must be justified and not dismissed as if it were simply the way of the world. Second, the Enlightenment stresses that human beings are *rational* – they are capable of advancing and understanding arguments, such that justifications for equality, or inequality, are always given to *individual* human beings.

It is a standard starting point of **liberalism** – but also of other ideologies such as **socialism**, **anarchism**, **feminism** and **multiculturalism** – that coercively enforced institutions must be justified to those who are subject to them (although anarchists conclude that coercion cannot be justified); that is, subjects should in some sense consent to those institutions. Since it is unrealistic to think we can reach unanimity on how society should be organised, we must assume a moral standpoint distinct from the standpoints of 'real people'. The most famous recent elaboration of this idea can be found in the work of John Rawls. Rawls asks us to imagine choosing a set of political principles without knowing our identities – that is, we do not know our natural abilities, class, gender, religious and other beliefs, and so on. This denial of knowledge constitutes what Rawls calls the 'veil of ignorance': because the individual does not know his or her identity he or she must, as a matter of reason, put him- or herself in the shoes of each other person, and people are necessarily equal. The idea of equality in Rawls's theory is highly abstract, and the use of the veil itself tells us little about how people should be treated. To generate more concrete principles of equality – that is, principles further down the flow chart – Rawls makes certain claims not implied by the veil of ignorance, and in that sense he goes beyond moral equality; nonetheless, the starting point for Rawls is a situation of moral equality.

Ch 4:
Justice,
pp. 83–9

While Rawls draws strongly egalitarian conclusions from the idea of moral equality, other political theorists, while endorsing the idea of moral equality, derive rather different conclusions. Robert Nozick, in his book *Anarchy, State, and Utopia* (1974), argues that individuals have strong rights to self-ownership, and they enjoy these rights equally, and for that reason there are certain things we cannot do to people, including taxing their legitimate earnings, where **legitimacy** is established by certain principles of justice. We discuss Nozick's theory in more detail in Chapter 4, but the point is that a commitment to moral equality can lead in different directions in terms of whether or not we accept further principles of equality.

Moral Inequality: a Caste Society

We can better understand moral equality by comparing it to a social and political system in which people are assumed to be morally *unequal*. Although there is much debate among historians and anthropologists about its nature, a caste society would appear to be based on natural inequality. The most famous caste system is associated with Hindu society, especially India. Derived from the Portuguese word for lineage (*casta*), caste in Hinduism is based on four principal classes, Brahmans, Kshatriyas, Vaishyas, and Shudras, with the 'untouchables' outside the caste system, and so literally outcastes. From the standpoint of a discussion of moral equality and inequality, the caste system's key feature is that it fuses social position with moral responsibility. The caste into which a person is born is determined by his karmic influences, or behaviour in a previous life.

Each caste has a colour – white for Brahmans, red for Kshatriyas, yellow for Vaishyas, blue for Shudras – each of which may have racial overtones, but as likely has its origins in the association of each colour with a type of occupation, with the Brahman having the right to teach the sacred texts, the Kshatriyas responsible for security and justice, the Vaishyas concerned with trade and land cultivation, with the lowest caste, the Shudras, allocated the most physically demanding work. The outcastes may have developed as a class due to the prohibition on the castes dealing with the killing of animals and animal waste – traditionally, outcaste groups have worked as butchers and tanners, and refuse-collectors, hence the term 'untouchables'. Within the Varna caste system, there operates a *jati* sub-caste system. The Jati was a guild system, regulating employment within each caste – unlike caste, *jati* can be changed with relative ease.

The caste system could be understood to be a means by which evident inequality – in material possessions and social standing – is justified, but it is not justification *to each individual*; if you question your status as a Shudras, then you might be told that your actions in a previous life have determined that status, but there is nothing that you can do *in this life* which can change that status. In this sense, inequality is naturally determined, and caste stands opposed to the Enlightenment ideal of moral autonomy and equality. While caste is a fact of life in India it is explicitly rejected as the basis of citizenship, with the Indian Constitution outlawing caste, and government policies being geared to improving the position of *dalits* ('untouchables' or 'outcastes').

Today, caste discrimination is considered by many to be akin to racism, and India was criticised for refusing a discussion of it at the 2001 UN Conference on racism, held in Durban, South Africa. Caste is, however, an interesting phenomenon and it is worthwhile considering what is objectionable about it. The most obvious is its effects in terms of the treatment of people. One of the most extreme examples of its consequences was the hanging of two teenage lovers from different castes by villagers in 2001 in the province of Uttar Pradesh. But discrimination in employment and services is an everyday occurrence, even if caste is not legally institutionalised in the way that race was in Apartheid South Africa. Another objection – or perhaps observation – is that caste discrimination creates incongruous situations: in large cities, such as Mumbai (Bombay), people from different castes will work alongside one another, and a lower caste person may hold a much superior position. The incongruity of a more skilled and higher-paid person being regarded as inferior in some 'ultimate sense' should force people to consider the validity of caste stratification. Finally, caste, like **race**, is objectionable because the person assigned to a particular caste has no control over his membership of that caste; to believe in natural inequality based on caste (or race) implies a rejection of human autonomy.

With these objections in hand we can, however, ask whether forms of discrimination widely considered to be compatible with moral equality are really so. If caste and race are unacceptable because they are not within the power of individuals to change them, then surely the same can be said of intelligence, and yet intelligence is not only considered an acceptable basis for discrimination, but a laudable one. In the exercise (on p. 63) you were asked to reflect on the attitudes of people you know to different grounds for inequality: racial characteristics; gender; disability; intelligence; class origins; unpredictable bad luck; predictable bad luck. Your conclusions will depend to some extent on your society and culture. In many societies, racial discrimination is rejected as fundamentally incompatible with respect for human autonomy, and it may be thought unacceptable even to pose the question of whether race could be an acceptable ground for unequal treatment (for that reason, we asked you to reflect on other people's attitudes, rather than your own). Racism seems intuitively wrong, and by 'intuition' we mean an immediate judgement, which does not entail or require reasons. Nonetheless, it is important to consider why racism is unacceptable, because the same reasons may lead us, on reflection, to reject those bases for inequality widely accepted as legitimate, such as intelligence.

We suggested that caste was wrong because a person was incapable of changing his caste status, and so to construct a society around caste is to deny human autonomy, or human choice. For many political theorists 'choice' is a central concept in determining which inequalities are acceptable: if you end up in an unequal situation then that is acceptable so long as you are responsible for it. Using the idea of choice, or autonomy, sources of inequality can be grouped: (a) natural endowment – this includes your genetic make-up, and natural abilities, such as intelligence, or good looks, or robust health; (b) socially determined endowment – your class background insofar as this is beyond your control; (c) everyday 'brute' bad luck, such as being disabled as the result of an accident; (d) choice, including predictable bad luck. Ronald Dworkin, a leading US legal and political theorist, argues that choice must be a legitimate basis for inequality: distribution must be choice-sensitive, meaning that (a), (b) and (c) are not acceptable grounds for unequal treatment, while (d) is acceptable (Dworkin, 2000: 287–91). In arguing for this position Dworkin is going much further than moral equality, but the main point is that his argument for those further principles of equality is based on a particular conception of moral autonomy and moral equality: we respect people by not discriminating against them as a result of characteristics beyond their control, but also by holding them responsible for the consequences of their choices. We return to this distinction later in the chapter.

Legal Equality

We need now to move from moral equality to more specific principles of equality, although the concept of moral equality must always be in the background. A starting point for building up a more substantial political theory would be to distinguish the 'core' legal–political institutions from broader socio-economic institutions. In most societies, but especially liberal democratic ones, the core institutions of the state are divided into legislature, executive and judiciary. Put simply, the legislature creates laws, the executive administers powers created through law, and the judiciary interprets and enforces the law. But a social institution is any large-scale, rule-governed activity, and can include the economic organisation of society, such as the basic rules of property ownership, and various services provided by the state that extend beyond simply the creation and implementation of law. We will deal with the wider concept of a social institution later, but in this section we will concentrate on the narrower concept.

As indicated in Figure 3.1, we need to distinguish 'equality before the law' and 'equal civil liberties'. To be equal before the law is to be equally subject to the law, whereas to possess civil liberties is to be in a position to do certain things, such as vote or express an opinion, and obviously we are equal when we possess the same liberties. There is, however, a close relationship between equality before the law and equality of civil liberties, and a historical example will help to illustrate this point. On 15 September 1935 the German Parliament (Reichstag) adopted the so-called 'Nuremberg Laws' governing German citizenship, one of which defined German citizenship (citizenship law, or Reichsbürgergesetz). The law made a distinction between a subject of the state (Staatsangehöriger) and a citizen (Reichsbürger). Article 1 stated that 'a subject of the state is one who belongs to the protective union of the German Reich', while Article 2 stated that 'a citizen of the Reich may be only one who is of German or kindred blood, and who, through his behaviour, shows that he is both desirous and personally fit to serve loyally the German people and the Reich'. Only citizens were to enjoy full, and equal, political rights. The First Supplementary Decree (14 November 1935) classified subjects by 'blood', and denied citizenship to Jews, where Jewishness was defined by the state.

It could be argued that these citizenship laws are compatible with equality before the law, since all subjects are equally subject to the law, despite the fact that the laws are themselves discriminatory (and much the same argument could be applied to the laws of Apartheid South Africa). While on the face of it this argument appears valid, and seems to show how weak both the idea of moral equality and equality before the law are, there are grounds for arguing that Nazi Germany could not maintain that all subjects were equal before the law. US legal theorist Lon Fuller, writing in the early post-war period, observed that Nazi law was not really law at all because it violated certain requirements for any legal system. For Fuller, the essential function of law is to 'achieve **order** through subjecting people's conduct to the guidance of general rules by which they may themselves orient their behaviour' (Fuller, 1965: 657). To fulfil this function law (or 'rules') must satisfy eight conditions:

1. The rules must be expressed in general terms.
2. The rules must be publicly promulgated.
3. The rules must be prospective in effect.
4. The rules must be expressed in understandable terms.
5. The rules must be consistent with one another.
6. The rules must not require conduct beyond the powers of the affected parties.
7. The rules must not be changed so frequently that the subject cannot rely on them.
8. The rules must be administered in a manner consistent with their wording.

Fuller's argument is not uncontroversial, and many legal theorists will reject these rules, but it is plausible to maintain that a condition of a 'law' (so-called) being a law is that it is not arbitrary. Since the first article of the penal code of Nazi Germany asserted that the will of the Führer was the source of all law, it was impossible for subjects to determine what was required of them. Once it is accepted that law cannot be arbitrary then certain conditions follow, including at least a minimal idea of equal basic civil liberties. Chief among the civil, or political, liberties are the right to vote and to hold office; significantly, both these rights were explicitly denied to 'non-citizens' in the Nuremberg Laws (Article 3, First Supplement).

There are other theories of law that do not rest on what Fuller terms an 'internal morality', and which presuppose neither moral equality nor equal liberties. Legal theorist John Austin characterised a 'law' as a general command issued by a 'sovereign' (or its agents). The 'sovereign' is that person, or group of people, who receives 'habitual obedience' from the great majority of the population of a particular territory. So whereas Fuller would argue that (most) Nazi laws were not really laws at all, Austin would have identified Hitler as the sovereign, who, insofar as he commands obedience, issues 'valid' law. This does not mean that his laws were moral: Austin made a sharp distinction between legality and morality. The relationship between morality and legality will be discussed in later chapters, and especially when we turn to the topic of human rights.

Ch 8:
Human Rights,
pp. 185–92

Equal Liberties

As suggested above, the state cannot directly distribute choice, but it can distribute the conditions for choice by granting individuals rights, or 'civil liberties'. In liberal democratic societies the most important rights, or liberties, are freedom of expression, association, movement, and rights to a private life, career choice, a fair trial, vote, and to hold office if qualified. A couple of points are worth noting. First, it is difficult to distribute liberty per se; rather, what is distributed are specific rights-protected liberties. Second, you can have freedom without that freedom being recognised by the state, for no state can exercise complete control. However, when we talk about the distribution of liberty, it is not so much the freedom itself which is being distributed, but rather the *protection* of that liberty – if Sam is guaranteed that he will not be thrown in jail for expressing views critical of the state, but Jane is not given that guarantee, then clearly Sam and Jane are not being treated equally. It is the 'guarantee' – the right to free expression – rather than the expression itself which is up for distribution. The separation between the 'guarantee' (protection of the capacity to choose; right to choose) and the action that is guaranteed does not hold for all liberties. In Figure 3.1 we distinguished between personal and civil liberties; among the latter are rights to participate in the political system. For example, voting – a 'participatory' rather than a 'private' or 'personal' right – is something which is clearly susceptible to *direct* distribution in a way that the freedom to marry whomever you wish (a 'private' right), or not get married, is not (you can, of course, still choose not to vote). Some people can be awarded extra votes than others, or whole groups, such as workers or women, can be denied the vote.

Do Freedom and Equality Conflict?

Freedom (or liberty) necessarily entails choice, and individuals must make choices for themselves. It would follow that the state cannot – and indeed should not – attempt to control individual choice. At best, it can affect opportunities to make choices through the distribution of rights. Does this mean that freedom and equality must necessarily conflict? In addressing this question we need to make a further distinction to the one already made between choice and the capacity, or opportunity, to make choices, so that we have a threefold distinction:

1. Choice, which must be under the control of the individual, and for which the individual can be held responsible.
2. Capacity, or opportunity for choice, which is not under the control of the individual, and for which the individual should not be held responsible.
3. Outcome of the choices of individuals, where outcomes are determined to a large degree by the interactive nature of choice.

Voting illustrates these points. You have a right to vote (2), which you may or may not exercise (1), but even if you exercise that right and vote for a party or a candidate, that choice may be less effective than another person's choice (3). It is less effective if your chosen party or candidate loses, but it might also be less effective in a more subtle way. Imagine that there is just one issue-dimension, say the distribution of wealth, with the left supporting high tax and a high degree of redistribution of wealth, and the right supporting low taxes and a low degree of redistribution. These represent the two extremes and there are various positions in between. Voters are ranged along this axis from left to right. Consider the voter distributions shown in Figures 3.2 and 3.3 (Laver: 112–14).

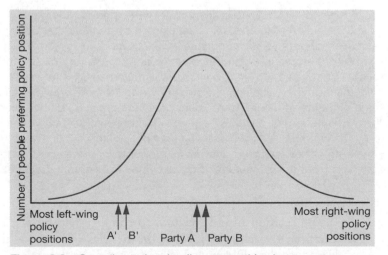

Figure 3.2 One-dimensional policy competition between two parties with votes preferences concentrated in the centre of the policy spectrum. From Laver 1997.

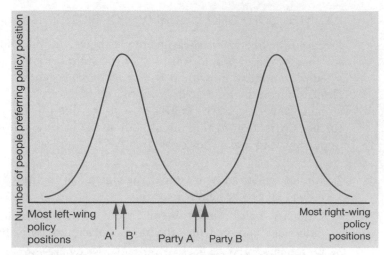

Figure 3.3 One-dimensional policy competition between two parties with votes preferences concentrated in the centre of the policy spectrum.

If there are just two parties then to maximise its vote a party has an incentive to adopt a policy position as close to the median voter as possible. This is the case even under the distribution in Figure 3.3 where the median voter is in a tiny minority. The point is that where you locate yourself relative to other voters will determine how effective your vote is. Equality (or inequality) of outcome is therefore the result of an interaction between the choices of many individuals, and it is impossible to protect freedom of choice and at the same time guarantee equality of outcome.

Swing States

There are 'real-world' illustrations of the power of the median voter, one of which is the conduct of US presidential elections. US presidents are elected by the Electoral College and not directly by the people. Because all but two states operate a 'winner takes all' system election campaigns focus on a small number of states in which the result is likely to be very close, and which therefore might 'swing' either way: even a very narrow victory will guarantee the entire slate of delegates. In the 2004 presidential election the campaign narrowed down to Pennsylvania, Florida and Ohio. Within those states huge amounts of money were spent persuading small numbers of people to switch sides. Voters living in safe states, such as Utah (safe Republican) or New York (safe Democrat) were not pestered by the candidates – for those who hate politics this may have been a relief, but in the long run the interests of key swing groups will take priority over the great majority. There may be 'one person, one vote', but the outcome of using that vote varies greatly, depending on where you live.

The relationship of freedom to equality will be discussed in greater detail in Chapter 4, where the focus is on theories of justice – the aim here is simply to introduce the problem and encourage some reflection on it. At this stage it would be useful to consider two thought experiments (see exercise), the first of which is taken from the work of Robert Nozick, and the second from G.A. Cohen (the work of both theorists is discussed in greater detail in Chapter 4).

Nozick: Marriage Partners

Imagine 26 men and 26 women, one for each letter of the alphabet. Each person wants to marry, and each of the 26 men has the same preference ordering of the women as the others, and likewise each of the 26 women has exactly the same preference ordering of the men. So if we name each person by a letter of the alphabet A, B, C, etc. for the men, and A', B', C', etc. for the women, each man prefers A' to B' and B' to C' and so on, down to the last preference Z'. Likewise, each of the women prefers A to B and B to C, etc., down to Z. That means that all the women want to marry A, and so A has plenty of choice! Likewise, with regard to the men A' has a full range of options. B and B' have one less option, but still a lot of choice, and so on, down to Z and Z' who have no choice but to marry one another (Nozick, 1974: 263–4). **Question:** are Z and Z' denied (a) freedom, and (b) equality?

Cohen: The Locked Room

There are ten of us in a locked room. There is one exit at which there is a huge and heavily locked door. At roughly equal distances from each of us there is a single heavy key (each of us is equally distant from the door). Whoever picks up the key (each is physically able to do so) and with very considerable effort opens the door can leave. But there is a sensor that will register when one person has left, and as soon as he or she leaves the door will slam shut and locked and nobody else will be able to leave – *forever* (Cohen, 1979: 22). **Question:** Are we free to leave?

Let us consider, first, Nozick's example. If we measure equality by the number of marriage partners available then there is an unequal distribution: A and A' have the greatest number of options, and Z and Z' the fewest options. And if freedom is understood as choice, then arguably Z and Z' have no freedom, because they have no choice but to marry each other. But, perhaps, the relevant liberty is determined by the relationship of each person to the *state*: in relation to the state Z and Z' have as many options as A and A'. It is the conjoint choices of individuals that creates an inequality of outcome. Nozick can legitimately maintain that Z and Z' are as free as A and A' because his starting point is the concept of a natural right (to self-ownership); that right will always be held equally regardless of how individuals exercise the right. Nozick's example shows rather more dramatically what we suggested earlier about the differential consequences of voting – each person has a vote, but the effects of exercising that vote vary.

We turn now to Cohen's locked room. If, prior to anyone leaving, a voice from outside asked each in turn 'are you free to leave?' then we would be forced to say 'yes'. If we – plural – were asked whether we were free, the question is more difficult. Collectively, we are not free to leave: *each* is free to leave but *we* are not free to leave. Once again, conditionality is at work, but Cohen draws a different conclusion to that of Nozick from this conditionality. Working with certain Marxist assumptions, Cohen argues that a collectivist political order – one in which there is a much more equal distribution of income – would, in effect, enable more people to leave the room. In 'real-world' terms, that means workers losing their subordinate class position. Unlike Nozick, Cohen is concerned with the choices people actually make, rather than their legal position vis-à-vis the state.

Material Equality

The example of inequality in the outcome of voting preferences illustrated problems of distributing political power, and certainly political power is a major good, but the most involved debates, both in everyday politics and in political theory, concern themselves with the distribution of material goods, such as income, or education, or healthcare. In liberal societies respect for equality before the law and equality of liberties is fairly well embedded in the political culture – while there is controversy over *particular* liberties, the majority of the population expresses support at least for the *principles*. The same cannot be said for principles of material equality. As was suggested in the section on Principles of Equality, while lip-service is paid to equality of opportunity, that term encompasses a great many possible principles of resource allocation, some of which entail radical state intervention in individuals' lives. More often than not, what is being advocated is equal access to jobs and services rather than equality of opportunity.

Equal Access

Equal access is sometimes referred to as 'formal equality of opportunity'. Equal access requires that positions which confer advantages on their holders should be open to all, and that the criteria for award of those positions is 'qualification(s)'. The qualifications required must be publicly acknowledged and intrinsically related to the position. The list of illegitimate grounds for denial of access to a position has gradually expanded, but in, for example, European Union countries, it would include: gender, race, ethnic or national origin, creed, disability, family circumstance, sexual orientation, political belief, and social or economic class. This list, which is not comprehensive, provides prima facie guidance on equal access.

It may be that certain of those characteristics are relevant to a job. For example, the priesthood in the Catholic Church is restricted to men, and normally unmarried, celibate men. Employment in a women's refuge would normally be restricted to women. Legislation outlawing gender discrimination will contain clauses that permit what appears, at first glance, to be discrimination, but which may, in fact, be consistent with gender equality. We argued at the beginning of the chapter that there was a presumption in favour of equal treatment – people should be treated equally unless there were compelling grounds for unequal treatment. The nature of work in a women's refuge obviously provides compelling grounds, consistent with gender equality: since the client group in a refuge is seriously disadvantaged, women employed in the refuge are working towards a more gender-equal society. However, the restriction of the priesthood to men is more problematic and reveals the limits to equal access; this may not be a criticism, for we can say that because equality conflicts with other values, or principles, it necessarily has limits.

The 'compelling reason' for setting aside gender equality in the case of the priesthood is derived from the importance of the equal liberties (or freedoms), among which is freedom of **religion**. Since freedom of religion requires that adherence to a church is voluntary, the church could be said to constitute a private sphere in which consenting adults should be free to act, and that includes being free to discriminate. However this argument, if extended to other spheres of life, would corrode equal access: if churches can discriminate, then why not other employers? It is to block off the claim that firms, universities, shops, sports centres and so on are private spaces in which people should be free to discriminate, that anti-gender-discrimination legislation defines the public sphere widely. Churches are given a special exemption because of the interconnectedness of theological belief with employment: the very nature of the institution requires an all-male priesthood. This contrasts with, say, a restaurant where the customers may have a simple gut preference for eating with people of their 'own kind', and so seek to deny access to ethnic minorities. Nonetheless, there is a legitimate debate to be had over the correct limits between the public and private spheres: if you are renting out your house for a year while you go abroad, should you not be free to choose who occupies the house, where that choice might take the religion or **ethnicity** or marital status or sexual orientation of putative tenants into account? Other people may justifiably condemn your selection criteria, but taking liberty seriously may entail the recognition of a private sphere in which a person is free 'to do wrong'. On the other hand, it might be legitimate to prevent a landlord with a string of properties from applying discriminatory criteria in selecting potential tenants. We are not arguing for a particular line between public and private, but simply identifying a potential limit to the application of the equal access principle.

Ch 2: Freedom, pp. 50–1

Equality of Opportunity

Equal opportunity is a much stronger principle of equality than equal access: as the name suggests, it requires that opportunities for acquiring favourable positions are equalised. This principle is attractive across the political spectrum because it seems to assume a **meritocracy**. The case study introduced at the beginning of this chapter was intended to test intuitive reactions to 'deserved' and 'undeserved' advantages. In Britain there is much popular debate about the social composition of the student bodies in the highest-rated universities. Students educated at fee-paying schools, or at state schools with relatively wealthy 'catchment areas', make up a disproportionately large part of the student intake of these universities. Even on the political right this situation is condemned: the brightest students, rather than the wealthiest students, should get, it is felt, the most desirable university places.

Although politicians disagree about the causes and the solutions to this situation, there is agreement that equal access alone does not ensure a meritocratic outcome. The difficulty is that an 18-year-old student has 18 years of education and socialisation behind her – every day she has been presented with 'opportunities' that a peer may have been denied. Those opportunities will include the emotional support necessary to achieve self-confidence and a sense of self-worth, stimulating conversation that enables her to develop a range of linguistic skills, interesting foreign holidays and activities, the presence of books in the family home, the imposition of a degree of parental discipline sufficient to encourage self-discipline, family networks and contacts, a good diet, and the provision of an adequate workspace. This list could go on, and none of these items relate to formal educational provision. Even parents who do not send their children to fee-paying schools may pay for such things as ballet classes or piano lessons. In short, every day of her life for the previous 18 years she has been given opportunities. To equalise such opportunities would require a very high degree of intervention in family life.

This description of a privileged child may overstate the requirement for an equalisation of opportunity. Perhaps it is not necessary that children have strictly equal opportunities, but rather that each child has a sufficient degree of opportunity to acquire advantageous positions. The idea is that there is a threshold level of opportunity below which a child should not fall. (Although it is not a serious objection to the threshold theory of equal opportunity, there would inevitably be dispute over the correct threshold.)

Another point about equality of opportunity is that the principle presupposes that inequality can be justified, so long as any inequalities are the result of desert. In the case study we distinguished social advantage, native ability (intelligence) and effort. It is a commonly held view that 'IQ + effort' is an appropriate ground for discrimination, and that equal opportunity policies should endeavour to eliminate social advantage as a cause of inequality. But Rawls argues that people no more deserve their native abilities, including their propensity to hard work, than they do those advantages gained from their family and social background (Rawls, 1972: 104). Other theorists, such as Ronald Dworkin and David Miller, argue that Rawls's rejection of desert is inconsistent with other important aspects of his theory, which stress the importance of choice and responsibility (Dworkin, 2000: 287–91; Miller, 1976: 131–55). Nonetheless Dworkin (especially) seeks to eliminate *natural ability* as a justification for inequality, while retaining responsibility for choices made. In this respect both Rawls's and Dworkin's arguments are significantly at variance with popular attitudes. This is an observation rather than a criticism – in Chapter 4 we discuss Rawls's argument in more detail.

Equality of Outcome

Equalisation of outcome seems, on the face of it, neither desirable nor coherent. It is not desirable because it would deny individual choice, and responsibility: if one person chooses a life of leisure and another person chooses a life of hard work why should the state seek to equalise the outcome of those choices? The outcome may not, in fact, be susceptible to equalisation. If income level is the 'metric' subject to distribution, then the outcome can be equalised *for that metric*; but 'welfare' (or 'well-being') is also a relevant metric, and the person living a life of leisure has presumably enjoyed greater well-being than the hard worker, such that the only way the two can enjoy an equal level of well-being is if they had not lived their respective lives of leisure and hard work. The point is that equality is always equality *of something*, and the attempt to equalise along one metric, say income, may result in inequality along another metric. Another difficulty with attempting to achieve equality of outcome is that some goods are 'positional'; for example, an expensive school is valued not simply because it seems to provide better facilities, smaller classes and stronger discipline, but because it is perceived as socially superior, and it can only be superior if there is a limited supply of that type of school. Only a small number of schools can be like Eton in England, or Groton in the United States, such that if there was a substantial increase in public expenditure on schools not every school will be an Eton or a Groton.

Ch 4:
Justice,
pp. 83–9

Despite these objections, equality of outcome can play a role in political debate even if it cannot be made to work as a principle. Rawls justifies inequality by use of the difference principle, but that principle rests on recognising that any inequalities must be to the benefit of the worst off. This argument takes equality of outcome as the baseline against which alternative distributions are to be measured; in effect, Rawls maintains that moral equality could generate equality of outcome, but may also generate inequality of outcome if the worst off consent to that inequality. Equality of outcome has, therefore, a special moral status in Rawls's theory. It should be noted that if Rawls recognised desert as a legitimate source of inequality this tight connection between moral equality and equality of outcome would not hold.

Rawls does not, in fact, defend equality of outcome as a substantive principle. Anne Phillips, though, does defend this principle of equality. Much of Phillips's work has been concerned with political representation, and especially the under-representation of women and ethnic minorities in political institutions, and she takes the case of women in parliament as an example of the need for a principle of equal outcome. The under-representation of women in the British Parliament cannot, she argues, be attributed to lack of ability, or the conscious choice not to enter politics, but must be a consequence of the failure of equal opportunity (Phillips, 2004: 8). Women are not denied equal access to parliamentary representation, and many political parties now have dedicated support for female candidates, which include women's officers, training days, support networks, and the requirement to have at least one woman on every shortlist for candidate selection in a particular constituency. But the only political party that has been successful in increasing female representation in the House of Commons (the elected chamber) has been the British Labour Party, and that success can be attributed to 'all-women' shortlists imposed on local constituencies by the central party. The point being that all-women shortlists guarantee an increase in the number of candidates in Labour-held or winnable seats – the policy acts on outcomes and not on opportunities. The inequality of outcome in the other political parties is an indication that, despite various efforts, equality of opportunity has failed.

Affirmative Action

Affirmative action policies involve an explicit departure from the normal 'equal access' and 'equal opportunity' criteria for awarding a person a favoured position. The normal criteria include: (a) the position is open to all, and (b) selection is by competence, which is measured by qualifications. There are various types of affirmative action policies:

- **Encouragement** The job is advertised in newspapers read by particular communities, such as ethnic minorities.

- **Tie-breaking** If two people are 'equally qualified' then you choose the person from the 'disadvantaged group'. This is the weakest form of affirmative action.
- **Handicapping** An example of this would be requiring higher entry points, or grades, for applicants to university from wealthy backgrounds.
- **Quota system** A certain percentage of jobs must be filled by a particular group – this is usually subject to a requirement of minimum competence.

All-women short lists are a version of the quota system and involve a setting aside of (a), and some critics would argue that it also entails setting aside (b). Affirmative action could, however, be defended on grounds that the evidence of qualification for a position cannot be taken as an accurate indication of a person's competence. To illustrate this point, let us imagine that entry to a good university normally requires 20 points in a school-leaving exam. Person A, from a poor background, scores 17 points, and person B, from a wealthy background, scores 21 points. However, evidence from the performance of previous cohorts of students suggests that '(economically) poor students' with lower entry points achieve a better final result on graduation than 'wealthy students' with higher entry points, and so person A is predicted to do better than B, and therefore 'objectively' is better qualified. Interestingly, this argument is meritocratic, and indeed is a 'technical', rather than a philosophical, objection to other principles of equality: existing evidence of competence is not reliable, so we have to broaden selection criteria to include prospective performance based not on the individual applicant's past behaviour but on the statistical behaviour of students from his 'background'. But distribution is still tied to the actions of individuals.

There are other ways of understanding affirmative action: it may be intended to provide role models; compensate a *group* for past injustices; increase the level of welfare of a disadvantaged group. Some defences are backward-looking, in that they seek to redress something that happened in the past; other defences, such as the one discussed above – prospective student performance – are forward-looking. A common, everyday objection to affirmative action is that it undermines respect and creates resentment: if a person achieves a position through 'positive discrimination' then others may not respect him, while the apparently better-qualified person passed over for the position will resent what seems an unfair selection procedure. This objection, whether or not valid, does identify an important aspect of equality (and inequality): there is an intersubjective dimension to human relationships, such that inequality can result in a lack of respect. Where that inequality seems unconnected to a person's actions – that is, when you end up in an unfavourable position regardless of what you have done – there is a feeling of *resentment* rather than simply disappointment. This suggests that equality should not be understood merely as a mathematical question of who gets what, but is intimately connected to other concepts, such as autonomy, responsibility and well-being.

Summary

We have surveyed a number of principles of equality, and sought to put them into some kind of order. A coherent defence of equality requires a number of things: (a) clear distinctions between different kinds of equality; (b) recognition that any principle of equality must explain what is being equalised, because equality in one sphere (along one 'metric') can result in inequality in another; (c) a scheme for connecting different principles of equality together; (d) an explanation of how equality fits with other political principles, such as freedom and efficiency. One of the tasks of a theory of justice is to connect and order different political values and principles and so the discussion in the next chapter follows directly from this one.

Questions

1. Must freedom and equality conflict?
2. Are there any valid positional goods?
3. Should those of below-average aptitude get more resources than those of above-average aptitude?
4. Should the family be abolished in order to ensure equality of opportunity?

References

Cohen, G. (1979) 'Capitalism, Freedom, and the Proletariat' in A. Ryan (ed.), *The Idea of Freedom* Oxford: Oxford University Press.

Dworkin, R. (2000) *Sovereign Virtue: The Theory and Practice of Equality* London and Cambridge, Mass.: Harvard University Press.

Fuller, L. (1965) 'A Reply to Professors Cohen and Dworkin' *Villanova Law Review*, 655.

Laver, M. (1997) *Private Desires, Political Actions: An Invitation to the Politics of Rational Choice* London: Sage.

Miller, D. (1999) *Principles of Social Justice* Cambridge Mass.: Harvard University Press.

Nozick, R. (1974) *Anarchy, State, and Utopia* Oxford: Blackwell.

Phillips, A. (2004) 'Defending Equality of Outcome' *Journal of Political Philosophy*, 12(1).

Rawls, J. (1972) *A Theory of Justice* Oxford: Clarendon Press.

Further Reading

J. Roland Pennock and John Chapman (eds), *Equality* (New York: Atherton Press, 1967), is a useful collection of essays. Single-authored general works include: Alex Callinicos, *Equality* (Cambridge: Polity Press, 2000); John Rees, *Equality* (New York and London: Praeger, 1971). A longer, and more advanced, work is Larry Temkin, *Inequality* (New York and Oxford: Oxford University Press, 1993). Other interesting single-authored works include Anne Phillips, *Which Equalities Matter?* (Oxford: Polity, 1999) and Matt Cavanagh, *Against Equality of Opportunity* (Oxford: Clarendon, 2002), who challenges traditional assumptions about the nature of meritocracy. Amartya Sen, *Inequality Reexamined* (Oxford: Clarendon, 1992) stresses the importance of the 'equality of what?' question (the importance of identifying 'metrics'). James Fishkin, *Justice, Equal Opportunity, and the Family* (New Haven and London: Yale University Press, 1983) explores the family as a problem for equality. The most important contributions to the equality debate are gathered together in a couple of edited collections: Louis Pojman and Robert Westmoreland (eds), *Equality: Selected Readings*

(New York and London: Oxford University Press, 1997) and in Matthew Clayton and Andrew Williams, *The Ideal of Equality* (Basingstoke: Palgrave, 2000).

Weblinks

A large number of 'equality' sites are maintained by pressure and interest groups, or formal government bodies dedicated to increasing equality. It is interesting to see how the concept is used by these organisations; do not, however, expect sophisticated philosophical discussions. The best sites are those maintained by universities, which provide further links:

- Equality Studies Centre at University College, Dublin (Ireland): http://www.ucd.ie/esc/

- Cardiff University: http://www.cardiff.ac.uk/learn/try/equality/

- Human Rights and Equality Centre, University of Ulster (Northern Ireland): http://www.ulst.ac.uk/hrec/hrec_otherlinks.phtml

Chapter 4

Justice

Introduction

Should people who are intelligent, or good-looking, or naturally charming, be allowed to keep whatever they gain from their exploitation of those natural attributes? Should people be free to pass on their material gains to whoever they choose? If it is a good thing for parents to care about their children, then why should they not be allowed to benefit them? These questions go to the heart of debates about distributive – or 'social' – justice. Distributive justice is concerned with the fair – or 'just' – distribution of resources. In the early modern period, the focus was on property rights as the moral basis for the distribution of resources, and justifications for the state – that is, individuals' obligations to obey the state – were often grounded in the role the state played in protecting those rights. In this chapter we concentrate on contemporary theories of justice, in which private property rights are often regarded as problematic – although one of the three theories discussed is a contemporary restatement and defence of strong private property rights.

Chapter Map

In this chapter we will:

- Discuss an important *liberal egalitarian* theory of justice – that of John Rawls.

- Contrast Rawls's theory with a *libertarian* alternative, advanced by Robert Nozick.

- Consider a major challenge to both theories – that of Gerald Cohen, who argues from a *Marxist* perspective.

- Apply these theories to real-world examples of distributive justice.

A Neet Solution?

Charles Murray, a US social theorist, has observed that Britain is a generation behind the United States in experiencing and addressing the consequences of the development of a social 'underclass', which he dubs the 'neets' – 'not in education, employment or training' (*The Sunday Times*, 27 March 2005). Strongly correlated with single parenthood, Murray claims that attempts in the USA to solve the problem of the neets through state intervention have failed. Pre-school socialisation programmes, 'enrichment programmes' for older children, guaranteed jobs for the unskilled, on-the-job training, schemes to prevent school drop-out have all produced a few 'heart-warming' success stories, but hard statistical data has demonstrated their failure. That the existence of this underclass is, for Americans, a 'dog that no longer barks' can be explained by tough penal policies and an aggressive reclamation of the cities. Streets have been cleared of beggars, schools are de facto socially segregated, graffiti has been cleared from walls, and, most importantly, the prison population has increased to 2 million (Britain would have to imprison 250,000 – compared to the present 80,000 – in order to match that). Murray predicts that by 2020, the slogan 'prison works' will be accepted across large parts of the political spectrum in Britain.

The implications of Murray's 'solution' to social inequality is that those born into the underclass cannot be saved. He accepts this is unfair, because life is a lottery – it is just bad luck to be born into the social underclass. For political theorists this is a crucial issue, and at the heart of the discussion of this chapter.

- Before reading the rest of the chapter, consider whether you agree with Murray's thesis and his solution to the 'problem'. His article can be found here:
http://www.timesonline.co.uk/article/0,,2087-1543363_1,00.html

Theories of Just Distribution

Distributive justice is, as the name suggests, concerned with the just distribution of resources. Despite the mention of penal policy in the above case study, distributive justice must be distinguished from *retributive* justice, which is concerned with how a punishment fits a crime. What might be the basis for the distribution of wealth? Here are some possibilities:

- **Threat advantage** The amount a person earns is the result of that person's relative bargaining power.
- **Need** Everyone should have their needs satisfied – there should be a guaranteed minimum set of resources equivalent to that required to satisfy those needs.
- **Desert** If you work hard and as a consequence increase your earnings relative to others you deserve to keep those additional earnings.
- **Freedom** The pattern of distribution is the result of the choices people make – if you have a product that others *choose* to buy, in buying the product other people have *consented* to the income you gain from selling it, and therefore also to any resulting inequality.
- **Labour** The profit made from the sale of commodities should reflect the contribution that the producer (labourer) makes to the commodity.
- **Maximise utility** We should aim to maximise the overall level of utility in society; 'utility' may be defined as happiness or pleasure or welfare or preference satisfaction.
- **Equality** Resources should be distributed equally.
- **Priority to the worst off** The worst off should be as well off as possible.

Rather than run through all these options we will focus on the work of three thinkers – John Rawls, Robert Nozick and Gerald Cohen. In the course of the discussion comments will be made on all the above options.

How to read:

Rawls's *A Theory of Justice*

Students tend to find Rawls's *A Theory of Justice* a difficult read. Rawls has been criticised as a disorganised writer. However, the book does have a relatively clear structure. It is divided into three parts, nine chapters, and 87 sections. The first part sets out the theory in broad outline, with Chapter 1 a general introduction, Chapter 2 introducing the principles of justice, and Chapter 3 discussing the method by which those principles are derived. If you read nothing else, you should read the first four sections of the book (about 20 pages in total); beyond that the priority should be to read Part One. Part Two discusses the principles in more detail, and Part Three addresses issues relating to moral obligation, and the psychological aspects of adherence to principles of justice. Of the three parts, Rawls himself was least satisfied with the discussion of Part Three, and his later book – *Political Liberalism* (1993) – was, to a significant degree, a revision of it.

John Rawls (1921–2002)

A US academic, he spent most of his working life at Harvard University. Rawls is one of the most important political philosophers of the twentieth century, and his book *A Theory of Justice* (1971) is credited with stimulating a revival in the subject.

There are two 'biographical' points about Rawls directly relevant to our discussion. First, Rawls came from a relatively wealthy family, and had a powerful sense that wealth, or even 'natural assets' such as intelligence, cannot be the basis for a just distribution of resources, for we do not *deserve* our acquired and natural assets. It follows that the wealthy need to justify their wealth. Second, Rawls came from Baltimore (Maryland), which though not part of the Deep South was a Southern State. The sense of the *profound* immorality of slavery informs his work, and it is significant that his two 'heroes' were philosopher Immanuel Kant and President Abraham Lincoln, the former articulating the moral imperative to treat other human beings never merely as means but also as ends, and the latter leading the anti-slavery forces of the North in the American Civil War.

Rawls: an Egalitarian Liberal Theory of Justice

Rawls's book *A Theory of Justice* (first published 1971) had a huge impact on political philosophy. In it he advances a method for making moral decisions about the distribution of resources – not just material resources, but also freedom and political power – and argues that the operation of that method would result in a particular conception of justice, one which is significantly 'redistributivist' (or **egalitarian**).

Rawls locates his work in the social contract tradition of Locke, Rousseau and Kant, and indeed he is credited with reviving this tradition, which had gone into abeyance after about 1800. The 'classical' idea of the contract was that it was the device by which power was legitimated: it is rational from the standpoint of the individual to hand over some (most, all) of the 'rights' he enjoys in the 'state of nature' to a coercive authority. Rawls differs from the classical theorists by taking it for granted that social cooperation under a state is normally a good thing, and so the focus of his theory is not the justification of the state but the distribution of the 'benefits' and 'burdens' of cooperation under a state. The benefits are material goods, personal freedom and political power. The burdens include not only any inequality which may arise, but the fact that principles will be coercively enforced – we are required to obey the state.

Before we set out Rawls's method for choosing 'principles of justice' and discuss what principles would be chosen, two very important points must be made:

1. A theory of justice applies to what Rawls calls the 'basic structure' of society. There is some ambiguity about this concept, but for the purposes of the present discussion we can say the basic structure consists of those institutions that

fundamentally affect a person's life chances. Included would be the structure of the economy – the rules of ownership and exchange – and the provision of services such as health and education, as well as constitutional rights that define how much freedom a person enjoys.

2. While Rawls has been influential on the left of politics, he is a philosopher rather than a politician. What is at issue is the basic structure of society, and not the detailed policy decisions that may be made *within* that basic structure. Furthermore, Rawls is not aiming to persuade merely a majority of people to endorse his theory – he is not fighting an election – but rather offering arguments that no reasonable person could reject: he is aiming for *unanimity*.

The Original Position

Rawls's theory has two parts: an explanation of how we decide what is just, and a discussion of what he believes we would decide is just. We start with the first part. Rawls employs what he terms the original position. The original position is a thought experiment – you are asking a 'what if' question: what if such-and-such were the case? It is not a 'place' – you only 'go into' the original position in a figurative sense. The most important feature of the original position is the veil of ignorance: you *do not* know your class and social position, natural assets and abilities, strength and intelligence, particular psychological characteristics, gender, to which generation you belong, who your family and friends are, and perhaps most controversially of all, your conception of the good – that is, your ideas about what makes life valuable or worth living, such as your religious and philosophical beliefs, but which are not necessarily shared by other people (Rawls, 1972: 12). You do know certain general things about your circumstances. You know you live in a society characterised by moderate scarcity: there are enough resources to satisfy basic needs and leave a significant surplus to be distributed, but that surplus is not sufficient to overcome conflict between people over its distribution. Rawls assumes that people want more rather than less of the benefits generated by cooperation. As well as knowing your society is marked by moderate scarcity you also have a general knowledge of psychology and economics.

Motivation in the Original Position

Rawls attributes to people in the original position a certain psychology, or set of motivations. It is important to stress that Rawls makes these assumptions *for the purposes of his theory*; he does not claim that 'real people' – that is, people who know their identities – have this psychology. In the original position:

- We *all* value certain things – what Rawls terms the (social) primary goods. The primary goods are rights, liberties, powers and opportunities, income and wealth, and the 'bases of self-respect'. The primary goods are valuable to many different ends, so if you choose a career trading in stocks and shares, or, alternatively, living in a self-sufficient community on a remote island you will value these things (93).

- You seek to *maximise* your share of the primary social goods (142).

- You are not a gambler. Rawls tries to avoid assuming a particular attitude to risk; nonetheless, the way the original position is set up would suggest that we would be 'risk averse' (Rawls, 2001: 106–7).
- You are not envious of other people (Rawls, 1971: 143).
- We are mutually disinterested: that is, we are not interested in one another's welfare. You do know, however, that once the veil has been lifted you will have family and friends who you do care about (144–5).
- We live in a 'closed society' – entered at birth and exited at death. Again, this point can easily be misunderstood. We do not know what principles of justice will be chosen – we have not got to that point yet – but it is highly likely that among the principles will be a right to emigrate. The reason Rawls assumes we live our whole lives in one society is that it makes the choice of principles very serious and is a response to an old argument attributed, perhaps unfairly, to the seventeenth-century thinker John Locke, namely, that remaining in a society and using the state's resources – riding along the King's highway – constituted 'tacit consent' to the state. Rawls rejects that argument: for an individual to leave a society and seek asylum elsewhere (or migrate for economic reasons) is such a major step that 'deciding' not to seek asylum (or migrate) cannot be taken to constitute consent to the existing regime. This generates two motivational points: because the choice of principles is a serious one, we would (a) not gamble our interests (a point already made), and (b) we accept the chosen principles will be binding on us once the veil has been lifted – Rawls argues that we experience 'strains of commitment' (145).

It has probably struck you that there is something odd about the motivation of people in the original position. On the one hand, they are purely self-interested – they seek to maximise their individual shares of the primary goods. On the other hand, because they do not know their identities they are *forced* to be impartial, that is, each individual can only advance his or her interests by viewing the choice of principles from the standpoint of each individual. Expressed metaphorically, we have to put ourselves in each other's shoes.

Exercise

Imagine you do not know your age, gender, social class, what you look like, how intelligent you are, your beliefs (religious and philosophical views), who your family and friends are, and so on. The task is to get the best deal for yourself – the biggest income possible. Below is a table setting out a number of income distributions (A, B, C, D). These distributions represent average annual earnings for a whole lifetime (we use dollars in deference to Rawls, but you can choose any currency – it is the distribution that matters, not the absolute amounts). What you have to do is choose one. In making your choice, bear in mind the following:

- Because you do not know your identity you could end up in the top 10 per cent (decile) of earners, or the bottom 10 per cent, or anywhere in between.
- You care only about your own level of income – you are not envious of other people.
- You have got one shot – *whatever you choose is binding on you for the rest of your life*.
- Once you have chosen you will be told your identity.

Table 4.1

Decile	Distribution A	Distribution B	Distribution C	Distribution D
Richest 10%	$210,000	$12,000	$158,000	$105,000
	$105,000	$12,000	$74,000	$61,000
	$61,000	$12,000	$53,000	$49,000
Everybody	$37,000	$12,000	$39,000	$35,000
in between	$29,000	$12,000	$31,000	$28,000
	$21,000	$12,000	$26,000	$25,000
	$16,000	$12,000	$22,000	$21,000
	$10,500	$12,000	$17,500	$18,000
	$5,000	$12,000	$13,000	$16,000
Poorest 10%	$1,000	$12,000	$4,000	$14,000
Average:	$49,550	$12,000	$43,750	$37,200

What would be Chosen in the Original Position?

Now we come to the second part of Rawls's theory: the choice of principles. Agents in the original position are completely free to choose whatever principles they wish, but Rawls does discuss some possible candidates (Rawls, 1972: 124). It should be noted that these are expressed in philosophical language – Rawls does not talk about choosing state socialism or a free market economy (we will say something about Rawls's attitude to socialism and capitalism at the end of the section):

1. Everyone serves my interests – I get what I want [first-person dictatorship].
2. Everyone acts fairly except me [free rider].
3. Everyone is allowed to advance his/her interests as s/he wishes [general egoism].
4. We maximise the aggregate level of goods [classical **utilitarianism**].
5. Option 4 but with a minimum level of goods for each individual.
6. We maximise the average (per capita) level of goods [average utilitarianism].
7. Option 6 but with a minimum level of goods for each individual.
8. Certain ways of life are to be privileged because they have greater intrinsic value [perfectionism].
9. We balance a list of prima facie valid principles, that is, we make an intuitive judgement about the correct trade-off between freedom and equality should they conflict [intuitionism].
10. The two principles of justice [democratic conception].

Rawls argues that we would choose option 10: the democratic conception. Options 1–3 are incoherent. Because you can only have one dictator we would never agree to dictatorship. Option 2 contradicts the strains of commitment, and 3 is unstable. Options 4–7 represent utilitarianism. Utilitarians hold that what we ought to do is maximise the overall *level* of well-being (or 'utility'). They are not concerned with the *distribution* of utility (although options 5 and 7 do give some weight to individuals – they create a 'floor' below which nobody should fall). Classical utilitarianism measures the level of welfare without reference to the number of utility-generating beings (we say 'beings' because non-human animals might generate utility), whereas average utilitarianism divides the level of welfare by the number of utility-generating beings. Compare the following two situations:

(a) 2,000 units of welfare divided by 500 beings;

(b) 1,000 units of welfare divided by 20 beings.

For a classical utilitarian (a) is superior to (b), whereas for an average utilitarian (b) is superior to (a): 50 units versus 4 units.

Perfectionists (option 8) hold that there are certain ways of life worthy of pursuit and the state should aim to bring these ways of life about ('perfect' means to complete, or bring to fruition). This argument does not have great significance for the distribution of income, but it certainly affects what amount of freedom we should have (it relates back to Chapter 2: John Finnis is one kind of perfectionist). Rawls argues that because we are denied knowledge of our particular conceptions of the good we would not opt for perfectionism; we would not, for example, choose to give a particular religion special status. Intuitionism (option 9) entails 'resolving' conflicts of values and interests on an ad hoc, case-by-case basis – we have no method for resolving them. The aim of Rawls's theory is to provide just such a method.

See Ch. 1:
Freedom,
p. 51

The Democratic Conception: the Two Principles of Justice

Rawls argues that agents in the original position would choose the democratic conception. He distinguishes between a special and a general conception, which are versions of the democratic conception. The general conception is: 'all social primary goods . . . are to be distributed equally unless an unequal distribution of any or all of these goods is to the advantage of the least favoured' (Rawls, 1971: 303). Rawls hopes that he can persuade the reader that the general conception would be endorsed even if the special conception, as one version of it, is rejected. The special conception consists of the two principles of justice. As Rawls's original presentation of the two principles was slightly confusing, we will use, in abbreviated form, his revised version from *Justice as Fairness: A Restatement* (Rawls, 2001: 42–3):

1. **Equal liberty**: each person is guaranteed a set of basic liberties.
2a. **Equal opportunity**: there must be equal access to jobs and services under fair equality of opportunity.
2b. **Difference principle**: inequalities are only justified if they benefit the least-advantaged members of society. (Also: just savings principle.)

The first principle is a familiar one – each person has an equal right to free speech, association, conscience, thought, property, a fair trial, to vote, hold political office if qualified and so on. Principle 2a is also familiar – jobs and services should be open to all (equal access), but furthermore society should be so arranged that as far as possible people have an equal *opportunity* to get jobs and gain access to services. 2b – the difference principle – is the novel one, and it is the one we want to discuss.

Rawls maintains that there is a lexical priority of 1 over 2a and 2a over 2b. That means that you cannot sacrifice liberty for economic justice – you must satisfy fully the equal liberty principle before applying the difference principle (Rawls, 1971: 42–3). For example, the greatest source of unequal opportunity is the family – parents favouring their children – but Rawls argues that even though people in the original position are 'mutually disinterested' they do value personal freedom, which includes the freedom to form personal relationships, marry, have a family, and enjoy a 'private sphere' of life. They would, therefore, opt to protect this private sphere even if it resulted in unequal opportunity. Although Rawls's theory does not operate at the detailed level of public policy, he would probably have argued that, for example, outlawing private education contravenes the first principle of justice. On the other hand, he does support high inheritance tax, and that tax not only works directly against privilege but generates resources which can be used to fund an extensive state education system. Lexicality also entails that equal opportunity takes priority over the difference principle. Discrimination in access to jobs might improve the position of the worst off, but it would violate the equal opportunity principle.

Would We Really Choose the Difference Principle?

If you consider the exercise on p. 86, we asked you to choose one of four distributions. Rawls argues that the rational strategy is to choose distribution D. The reasoning behind this is termed 'maximin': *maximum minimorum*, or the *maxi*misation of the *min*imum position. Although Rawls avoids guessing individuals' attitudes to risk, only very risk-averse people would adopt maximin (D) over average utility (C).

It should be said that Rawls does have another argument for D over C, which does not follow from the exercise. The exercise presented a one-off 'time slice' of income, but in the original position we are not choosing a *particular* distribution but a *principle* of distribution, and the principles underlying C and D are quite different: C says 'maximise average expected utility' whereas D says 'maximise the position of the worst off'. There is a 'shifting sands' quality to C: it does not concern itself with any particular group in society, but is concerned only with the average income. It is possible that over time distributions could move quite dramatically and that compared to D the worst-off classes – not just the bottom 10 per cent – could become a lot worse off. D, on the other hand, always gives priority to the worst off.

Let us look at the other two distributions, and the reasoning that might lead to them. Maximax – maximise the maximum – is the reasoning leading to distribution A. This is a very risky strategy. One thing you might have noticed is that per capita income is higher in A than C, and thus one might think that the average utilitarian would opt for A over C. Note, however, we talk of *expected utility*. A maximiser wants to get the highest income possible – everybody, and not just a risk taker, wants to earn $210,000. However, each person knows that she has under distribution A only a 1/10 chance of earning that amount of money; she has a 1/10 chance that she will end up with $1,000 a year. The question is this: does her *desire* for $210,000 outweigh her *aversion* to earning only $1,000? Given certain facts about human psychology – the fact that the utility from an extra amount of income diminishes, the more income you have – she will reason that greater weight should be attached to the avoidance of lower incomes than the enjoyment of higher incomes. So finally we move to B. It is *relativities* that concern someone who opts for B. Rawls argues we are not envious, and therefore we are not concerned with what other people earn, so relativities are unimportant. It might, however, be argued that if one of the primary social goods is self-respect then any inequality will tend to undermine it: there is no easy answer to this, and it does seem that for 'real people' – as against people in the original position – self-worth is (to some extent) attached to income or social status. One possibility would be a trade-off between maximin and the avoidance of extreme inequality, but Rawls would argue that maximin is the best strategy if you were concerned about relativities.

Influences and Impact:

Rawls and Socialism

As suggested at the beginning of this section Rawls was a philosopher rather than a politician; nonetheless it is interesting to consider his relationship to socialism. You will have noted that the list of possible principles that might be chosen in the original position contained rather abstract philosophical positions, such as utilitarianism, perfectionism and intuitionism, and not more concrete economic systems, such as state socialism or free market capitalism. Rawls argued in *A Theory of Justice* that it was largely a technical judgement whether the two principles of justice would best be realised under a socialist or a capitalist system. However, most commentators interpreted Rawls as a 'welfare state capitalist' – the principles would best be realised in a society that combined the free market with a generous redistributive welfare state.

In his last book, *Justice as Fairness: A Restatement* (2001), Rawls indicated that the principles would be very difficult to realise under welfare state capitalism, because under capitalism there is a serious underlying inequality in the distribution of assets, such that transfers from rich to poor always take place *after* production, thus creating a tension between those who are taxed and those who benefit from taxation. Rawls argued for an alternative model, called a 'property-owning democracy' (Rawls: 135–40). In Britain that phrase was adopted by the right, under Prime Minister Margaret Thatcher, but Rawls derives it from economist J.E. Meade, whose theory was quite egalitarian. Meade maintained that inequality must be addressed 'at source', by ensuring that as many people as possible had 'productive assets', and that the state worked to prevent the transmission of privilege. In policy terms, what was required was considerable spending on education – directed particularly at those with less 'natural ability' – and very high inheritance tax.

Robert Nozick (1938–2002)

Like Rawls, Nozick taught most of his working life in the Philosophy Department at Harvard University. Born in Brooklyn, the son of Russian immigrants, he went on to study at the Universities of Columbia and Princeton.

In contrast to his colleague Rawls, his engagement with political philosophy was fairly short lived – after the publication of *Anarchy, State, and Utopia* (1974) he concerned himself with other areas of philosophy, and he appeared to repudiate the claims he made in that book, although without engaging in a sustained self-critique. Nonetheless, despite his move away from political philosophy, the one book he did publish in that area has been enormously influential, and it is the work for which he is best remembered.

Nozick: a Libertarian Theory of Justice

Robert Nozick advanced an alternative to Rawls's egalitarian theory of justice; one that lays stress on the importance of **private property** rights. In his book *Anarchy, State, and Utopia* Nozick seeks to defend the notion of the state against philosophical anarchists, who argue the state can never be justified. But what he defends is a minimal state. A minimal state is a monopoly provider of security services. A more extensive state – one that intervenes in the economy and supplies welfare benefits – cannot be justified. 'Utopia' would be a world in which diverse lifestyles and communities would flourish under the protection of the minimal state.

Nozick's Starting Point: Private Property Rights

The very first line of *Anarchy, State, and Utopia* reads: 'individuals have rights, and there are things no person or group may do to them (without violating their rights)' (Nozick, 1974: ix). Jonathan Wolff argues that Nozick is a 'one-value' political philosopher (Wolff, 1991: 3–4). Other philosophers accept that there is more than one value; for example, they might maintain freedom is important, but so is equality, and since freedom and equality often conflict we need a method for 'resolving' that conflict. Rawls's *two* principles of justice express this idea. Wolff maintains that Nozick's 'one value' is private property, or, more precisely, the *right* to private property. When we use the term property in everyday speech we tend to think of real estate. Everyday usage is not wrong, but political philosophers have a wider conception of private property: it is the legally sanctioned (or morally legitimate) appropriation of things. A *right* is an advantage held against another person – if you have a right, then another person has a duty to do something (or *not* do something: that is, not interfere), so a right is a relationship between people. Bringing together the two concepts – private property and rights – we can say that a right to private property entails the exclusion of other people from the use of something. Nozick's 'entitlement theory' of justice is based on the inviolability of private property rights. There are three parts to the theory:

Part 1: **Just acquisition**
Part 2: **Just transfer**
Part 3: **Rectification**

Just Acquisition – Locke and Nozick

The first question to ask is: how did anybody acquire the right to exclude other people from something? Nozick draws on the work of John Locke (1632–1704) and, specifically, his defence of private property, especially his argument for 'first acquisition'. We have to imagine a historical situation in which nobody owns anything, and then explain (justify) the parcelling up of that which has hitherto been held in common. The standard interpretation of Locke is that he was attempting to reconcile Christianity and capitalism at a time – the seventeenth century – when capitalism was beginning to replace feudalism as the dominant form of economic organisation. Locke began with three Christian premises:

1. God had entrusted the material world to human beings, who were its 'stewards' and thus had a duty to respect it.
2. The implication of 1 is that the world is owned in common by humanity.
3. God as creator had rights to what he created. As God's creatures human beings have a duty to God to preserve themselves.

Capitalism poses a challenge because it was wasteful of natural resources, which violates stewardship. Capitalism implied private ownership and not common ownership, and it threatened to push large numbers of people into poverty and starvation, thus undermining their capacity to fulfil their duty to God to preserve themselves. For example, in seventeenth-century England we begin to see the movement from smallholdings to large estates, with smallholders (serfs) forced to hire out their labour for a daily wage, thus becoming wage labourers. The creation of a class of rural wage labourers presaged the development of an urban working class with the industrialisation of the eighteenth and (especially) the nineteenth centuries. The risks of starvation were significantly greater for the wage labourers than for their earlier counterparts, the serfs.

Christian theology, Locke argued, did not strictly require common ownership, but rather the promotion of the common good, and capitalism, through its capacity to generate wealth, did indeed promote it (Locke, 1988: 291). Locke's starting point for a defence of capitalism is his account of how we go from common ownership to private ownership: if a person mixes his labour with something external to himself then he acquires rights in that thing. Mixing one's labour is sufficient to establish ownership so long as two 'provisos' are satisfied:

- **Sufficiency proviso** There must be 'enough and as good left for others' (288).
- **Spoilage proviso** There must be no wasting away of the product (290).

In practice these two provisos are easily met because of the development of wage labour and money (Locke: 293). Wage labour is premised upon the notion of having property rights in your own body – rights which you cannot alienate, that is, you cannot sell your body – but the product of the use (labour) of your body can be sold, such that your labour becomes a commodity which is hired out.

Wage labour is important for Locke because it enables the buyer of labour to say to the potential seller of labour (wage labourer) that you can acquire sufficient goods to preserve yourself if you sell your labour to me. If you do not, *you* (not me) are violating your duty to God to preserve yourself. Crucially – and of great significance for Marx – that labour does not create rights for the labourer in the product, since the labour which the labourer sells to the buyer is an extension of the buyer's body; Locke argued that 'the turfs my servant has cut are *my* turfs' (289). Wage labour, therefore, satisfies the sufficiency proviso. Money deals with the spoilage proviso – a person's property can be held in this abstract form and thus will not 'spoil', unlike, say, crops, which rot, or animals, who die.

Nozick draws heavily on Locke's acquisition argument, but drops its theological basis. He begins with the assumption of 'self-ownership', that is, you own your body, and all that is associated with it – brain states, genetic make-up and so on, but this is no longer grounded in God's rights as creator. He then adopts Locke's mixed labour device, but he alters the provisos:

- **Sufficiency proviso** Locke was worried that there would come a point in the development of capitalism where some people really did not have enough to survive on, even with the possibility of wage labour. Nozick is not so concerned: so long as everyone is *better off* after appropriation then that appropriation is just (Nozick, 1974: 175–6).
- **Spoilage proviso** Nozick is not worried about 'spoilage', but he does insist that a person cannot acquire a monopoly control over certain goods, such as a water supply (180–1).

Exercise

Imagine a basketball match watched by 3,000 people, each of whom pays $20 to see Chamberlain play, and $8 of that $20 goes directly to Chamberlain (the $8 can be taken to be Chamberlain's marginal value: if he were not playing the organisers would have to sell the tickets at $12). Let us assume that each of the 3,000 spectators and Chamberlain earn $40,000. This is, of course, unrealistic, but it is intended to make a point. We can compare earnings – what Nozick calls 'holdings' – before and after the tickets were bought:

Table 4.2

	Spectators' holdings	Chamberlain's holdings
Before purchase	$40,000 × 3,000	$40,000
After purchase	$39,980 × 3,000	$64,000

Is there any reason why Chamberlain should not keep the $24,000 he has gained as a result of the ticket purchases?

Just Transfer

Just transfer is dependent upon just acquisition, for you cannot justly transfer what you have not justly acquired. Furthermore, acquisition is a very strong idea – it entails full control over the thing that is acquired, including the power to transfer it to another person. Nozick takes the example of Wilt Chamberlain (1936–99), regarded by many to be the greatest basketball player of all time. Consider the exercise on p. 92.

Nozick argues that so long as Chamberlain did not use threats or fraud to acquire each $8 then his additional earning is legitimately his by a simple transfer (161–3). The fact that such transfers will over time create significant inequalities – in the example we went from equality to inequality – is irrelevant, for what matters is that individuals have consented to the transfer. Those who object to such transfers want, in Nozick's words, 'to forbid capitalist acts between consenting adults' (163). To evaluate the force of Nozick's argument we need to compare his theory of justice with the alternatives.

Types of Theory

Nozick divides theories of justice up into two groups – end state and historical (Nozick, 1974: 153–5) – with a sub-division of the second into patterned and unpatterned theories (155–60):

End-state theories These theories are not concerned with what people *do*, but only with the *end result*. Utilitarian theories fall into this category – the aim is to maximise total, or alternatively, average utility. Who gets what under this arrangement is irrelevant: person A may get 25 units and person B 10, and the total is 35 (and average 17.5), but if A got 10 and B 25 the end result would be the same.

Historical theories What people have done (note the past tense) is relevant to the distribution of resources. For example, distribution according to desert, that is, hard work, is a historical principle (actually, 'historical' is a bad label – it would have been better, though less elegant, to talk of *person-regarding* theories, because it is not necessarily what a person has *done* that is relevant – need would be person regarding). Historical theories are further divided into:

- **Patterned** Any principle that involves the phrase 'to each according to _____' (fill in the blank: desert, need, labour and so on) is going to create a pattern (159–60). Nozick includes Rawls's theory as patterned: priority to the worst off (maximin) generates a pattern.
- **Unpatterned** Nozick calls his own theory unpatterned, because whatever distribution exists should be the result of choice. You could argue that this is patterned with the blank filled in as 'choice', but 'choice' is not really the same as desert or need – the latter two provide 'objective' criteria that can be used by a redistributive agency (the state) whereas you choose to do whatever you like.

Individuals may, under Nozick's utopian framework, aim to bring about an end-state or patterned distribution, but what may not happen is that the state *coerce* people into creating that end state or pattern. To appropriate some of Chamberlain's $24,000 is tantamount to forcing him to labour (172).

Nozick and the 'New Right'

Although he was not the prime influence on the 'New Right', which emerged as a powerful political force in the 1980s – that role fell to philosopher Friedrich von Hayek (1899–1992) and economist Milton Friedman (born 1912) – Nozick did have a major impact within the academic community, and perhaps indirectly influenced politicians. Nozick provided powerful philosophical arguments for radically reducing the role of the state and 'setting people free'. Socialists, he argued, are obliged continually to interfere in our lives. Nozick was not, however, a *conservative* if by 'conservative' we mean a position which maintains that the state has a role to play in moulding human behaviour. Conservatives may offer qualified support for the free market, but they fear the consequences of too much freedom. Nozick, as a *libertarian*, argues that freedom is intrinsically good, and so he supported, for example, removing restrictions on recreational drug use and consensual sex.

Rectification

Nozick's comments on the third part of his theory are brief and underdeveloped. If something was acquired or transferred as the result of fraud or theft or force then some mechanism is required for rectifying the situation (Nozick, 1974: 152–3). All that Nozick offers in the way of a theory is the suggestion that counterfactual reasoning be applied: what would be the pattern of holdings if the unjust acquisition/transfer had not taken place? This raises the problem of increased value: if you steal a dollar and make a million dollars as a result, what should you pay back – the dollar or the million dollars? This is a live issue, for unlike Locke, who argued that the United States was 'unowned' prior to European colonisation (Locke, 1988: 299–301), Nozick argues that native Americans had rights to their land and these were violated and thus rectification is required. But Manhattan – whose only trace of native ownership is its name – has increased vastly in value since it was 'acquired' by Europeans: how do we rectify that injustice? Nozick provides no answer.

Cohen: a Marxist Perspective on Distributive Justice

Marx's critique of private property has to be located in his theory of history: human beings have a drive to increase productivity, and this generates two struggles. The first is a struggle against nature, and the second a struggle between human beings. The two are related, for how we organise production will determine how effective we are at using nature to our advantage. Over time the particular structure of organisation – 'mode of production' – changes, but what characterises all modes is a class relationship in which one class exploits another. Exploitation is made possible by the unequal ownership of the two things that enable an increase in production: the means of production, and labour power. The former includes such things as factories and tools, while the latter consists of the skills of labour, both physical and mental. At the time at which Marx was writing – the mid-to-late nineteenth century – capitalism had emerged as the dominant mode of production. For Marx, the key features of capitalism are as follows.

- **Ownership** Under capitalism, in contrast to previous modes of production, every person owns his or her own labour power. However, a minority class – the capitalists, or bourgeoisie – own a monopoly of the means of production, with the consequence that the majority class – the working class, or proletariat – can survive only by selling their labour power to the capitalists.

- **Capital,** which can be defined as an 'expanding source of value', is unequally owned: one class (capitalists, or the bourgeoisie) are in a position to benefit from this expansion of value by virtue of their ownership of the means of production.

- **Exploitation** The true value of labour is not the price it commands in the market (the wage) but the amount of time that goes into the production of the commodity (labour value). The worker does not receive the full value of his product – the difference between the wage and labour value is the amount creamed off by the capitalist. This is what Marx means by exploitation.

- **Use value and exchange value** A distinction is drawn between the value we get from a commodity (use value) and its price (exchange value). Every commodity has a use value, but not everything that has a use value is a commodity. For example, air has a use value but it is not a commodity and hence does not have an exchange value. If pollution became very bad, and everybody had to carry a supply of clean air, and somebody started bottling and selling it, then it would acquire an exchange value in addition to its use value.

- **Markets** Interaction between individuals takes place through the laws of supply and demand. These laws fulfil two functions: (a) to provide information on how much of a particular product should be produced and at what price, and (b) to provide incentives to produce, and these incentives derive from self-interested motivations. Marx argues that the market is not in long-term equilibrium, and is subject to increasingly severe depressions. He further argues that capitalism assumes people are *by nature* selfish; this Marx rejects as an 'ontologisation' of historical experience – that is, turning something transitory into an ahistorical fact.

Marxists have tended not to engage in debate with **liberals** (or **libertarians**), rejecting as they do certain fundamental claims about the nature of human motivation and political epistemology. On human motivation, for example, Rawls maintains that the principles of justice apply to a society characterised by moderate scarcity in which people are in conflict over the distribution of those (moderately) scarce resources. A Marxist would maintain that when production levels reach a certain point – and capitalism is historically useful because it massively increases productivity – we will be in a position to say that there is no longer scarcity and the causes of social conflict will be removed. Regarding political *epistemology* – that is, how we *know* what is just – Marxists maintain that it is only in a post-scarcity situation that we will be able to determine the correct distribution of resources. For reasons too involved to explain here, Gerald Cohen is unusual amongst Marxists in his engagement with liberal (libertarian) thinkers such as Rawls and Nozick. What makes his argument interesting is that he attacks liberals on what they believe to be their strongest ground: freedom.

Biography,
p. 96

Biography | **Gerald Cohen (1941–)**

Born in Canada in 1941, Cohen's Russian-immigrant parents were members of the Communist Party, and up to his teens he attended a Jewish-Communist school.

In his book *If You're An Egalitarian, How Come You're So Rich* (2000), he explains how he gradually distanced himself from the economic determinism of the Communist Party, and without abandoning all Marxist insights saw morality as central to guiding human interaction. His first book, *Karl Marx's Theory of History: A Defence* (1978) was a relatively orthodox defence of Marx, although written in the non-Marxist idiom of what is called 'analytical philosophy'.

In the 1980s he further distanced himself from orthodox Marxism by engaging in a critique of Nozick. In the 1990s he turned his attention to Rawls. He is presently Professor of Social and Political Theory at Oxford University.

Cohen contra Nozick

Cohen does not deny that capitalism gives people freedom to buy and sell labour, but argues that defenders of capitalism make the illegitimate claim that their society is comprehensively free: they falsely equate 'capitalism' with the 'free society'. Cohen maintains that liberals – both 'left-wing' (egalitarian) and 'right-wing' (libertarian) – are wrong. Capitalism does not guarantee the maximum amount of freedom possible. He argues that a moralised definition of freedom is used – the validity of private property rights is taken for granted, such that freedom comes to be defined in terms of private property, and any infringement of it is a reduction of freedom. Cohen provides an example to illustrate his point: Mr Morgan owns a yacht. You want to sail it for one day, returning it without any damage done to it. If you take it you will be violating Morgan's rights, but which situation creates more *freedom*, Morgan's exclusive use of the boat, or your one-day use combined with his 364-days-a-year use (Cohen, 1979: 11–12)?

Cohen argues that for *one day* Mr Morgan is prevented from using his yacht and is forced not to use it – his freedom has indeed been restricted. But Mr Morgan's private property rights prevent you from using the yacht for *365 days* in the year, and force you not to use it (12). Capitalism – the exercise of private property rights – is a complex system of freedom and unfreedom. One could, of course, maintain that the difference between Mr Morgan's use of the yacht and your use of the yacht is precisely that it is *his* yacht; but then we need to justify Mr Morgan's acquisition of the yacht – to say Mr Morgan ought to own the yacht because he does own the yacht is, of course, a circular argument.

A more restricted defence of capitalism is then discussed by Cohen: capitalists do not maintain that their preferred economic system promotes freedom in general, but merely economic freedom. So Mr Morgan's property rights do not restrict your economic freedom, and a capitalist society is better able than any alternative to maximise *economic* freedom (14). To grasp Cohen's response we need to refer back to the important distinction made earlier between use value and exchange value:

(a) If economic freedom is defined as the freedom to *use* goods and services then it restricts freedom whenever it grants it – Mr Morgan's freedom to use his yacht correlates directly to your unfreedom to use it.

(b) If economic freedom is the freedom to buy and sell – that is, exchange products – then this looks better for capitalists. But it is an extremely restricted definition of economic freedom.

Is there then an alternative to capitalism and – crucially – one that increases freedom? Cohen gives a 'homespun' example. Persons A and B are neighbours and each owns a set of household implements, such as a lawnmower, saws, paintbrushes and so on. Each owns what the other lacks. We now imagine a rule is imposed, whereby when A is not using something he owns, B has the right to use it, just so long as he returns it when A needs it. This 'communising rule' will, Cohen maintains, increase 'implement-using' freedom (Cohen, 1979: 16–17).

A capitalist response to this example would be that A and B could increase their implement-using freedom by entering a contract, either a kind of barter, or a money-based relationship. But Cohen's response to this move is to argue that in the example A and B are roughly equal and, therefore, capable of entering a freedom-enhancing contract, but if you generalise across society then that equality does not exist. In fact, there is another response to Cohen, which appeals to efficiency and *indirectly* to freedom: while Cohen's argument is in many ways sound – capitalism entails unfreedom as well as freedom – one has to look at the empirical consequences of different economic systems. Cohen's 'homespun' example does not help because it is a very simple situation in which there are no communication problems. One argument for capitalism is that it avoids an excessively powerful state; it might even be argued that liberalism is the unintended gift of capitalism. The history of socialism has been characterised by an attempt to acquire the advantages of coordination associated with the market, while avoiding the inequalities generated by it.

Cohen contra Rawls

We now to turn to Cohen's response to Rawls. As we have seen, Rawls does not defend unregulated capitalism, and advances a theory of justice that would entail a significant redistribution of income to the worst off. What then is wrong with Rawls? There are three main Marxist objections:

1. Rawls has an incoherent model of human psychology (motivation).
2. Rawls restricts the principles of justice to the basic structure of society, and that conceals exploitation.
3. Rawls rejects self-ownership as morally irrelevant to the distribution of resources. Curiously enough, on this point Cohen sides with the 'right-wing' libertarian Nozick against Rawls.

The first two objections are closely related to one another. If you recall, people in the original position are motivated to maximise their share of the primary goods, but from behind a 'veil of ignorance', meaning that although they are self-interested, they are forced by the way the original position is set up to be impartial. Rational people will, Rawls argues, select the two principles of justice, including the 'difference principle', which entails maximising the position of the worst off (maximin). The original position is intended to 'model' how real people *could* behave. The difficulty is that the theory itself pulls in two different directions: on the one hand Rawls assumes that we – that is, 'we' in the real world, and not in the original position – can develop a commitment to giving priority to the worst off in society, and the difference principle is the structural device by which this is achieved. But how much the worst off *actually receive* will depend on everyday human behaviour. Consider the exercise discussed on p. 86: under maximin the richest 10 per cent get $105,000 and the poorest 10 per cent get $14,000. Imagine you are in the top 10 per cent. What motivations will you have in the 'real world', assuming you endorse Rawls's theory?

(a) You will be committed to giving priority to the worst off and so will regard redistributive income tax as legitimate.
(b) You will be motivated to maximise your income.

These two motivations do not necessarily conflict if we assume – as Rawls does – that inequality generates incentives to produce and thus help the worst off. But if you are really committed to helping the worst off do you not have a moral duty to:

(a) give *directly* – not just through tax – to the poor; and
(b) work to bring about a society in which the poorest earn more than $14,000?

Cohen borrows a slogan from the feminist movement: the 'personal is political' (Cohen, 2000: 122–3). How you behave in your personal life is a political issue. Rawls, along with most liberals, rejects this claim, arguing that the distinction between public and private is essential to a pluralistic society, and that not all aspects of morality should be enforced by the state: while it is right to require people to pay taxes to help the worst off, it is for individuals to decide what they do with their post-tax income. This may not resolve the tension that Cohen identifies between, crudely expressed, public generosity and private avarice, but the onus is on Cohen to explain the role of the state in 'encouraging' private generosity.

This brings us to the second criticism, which relates to the basic structure argument. The rich fulfil their duties to the poor by accepting the legitimacy of taxation, and that taxation is used to fund certain institutions, such as the pre-university education system, money transfers (social security, pensions, etc.) and healthcare. Outside the scope of the original position is a 'private sphere' that includes the family. Rawls accepts that the family is a major source of inequality – the transmission from parent to child of privilege undermines equality of opportunity. But because liberty (the first principle of justice) takes priority over equality (the second principle) there has to be a legally protected private sphere. Not only is the private sphere a source of inequality, it also produces within itself inequality. Here Cohen joins forces with feminist critics of Rawls: families are based on a division of labour, and one loaded against women, but because the recipient of redistribution is the household, and not the individual, there is a class of people – mostly women – who are worse off than that class which Rawls identifies as the 'worst off'.

Cohen argues that what Rawls includes in the basic structure is arbitrary – Rawls cannot give clear criteria for what should or should not be included. He cannot say that the basic structure consists of those institutions which are coercively enforced, that is, we are forced to fund through taxation, because the basic structure is defined *before* we choose the principles of justice, whereas what is coercively enforced is a decision to be made in the original position (Cohen, 2000: 136–7). The basic Marxist point is this: Rawls assumes that human motivations are relatively constant – certainly, people can develop a moral consciousness, but they will remain self-interested. Motivations will always be a mix of self-interest and morality. Marxists reject this, and maintain that social structures determine how people behave.

We come, finally, to the third criticism. Marx argued that the workers do not get the full value of their labour. This argument assumes that there is something a person owns, which generates a moral right to other things: in effect, as a Marxist, Cohen, along with Nozick (who is not a Marxist!), endorses Locke's 'mixed labour' formula. What Cohen rejects is the idea that mixing your labour establishes merely 'first acquisition'. For Locke and Nozick, once the world is divided up into private property the mixed labour formula ceases to be of any use. Cohen argues that a worker *constantly* mixes his or her labour, such that there is a continuous claim on the product. Locke's argument that 'the turfs my servant has cut are *my* turfs' is rejected by Cohen; insofar as the servant (worker) does not get the full value of his labour he is exploited, and the resulting distribution is unjust. Rawls implicitly rejects the notion of self-ownership; that does not mean we do not have rights over our bodies, but rather we have no pre-social rights. The rights we have are the result of a choice made in the original position. This becomes clearer if we look at the concept of desert.

Desert is tied to effort: we get something if we do something. Rawls argues that because we are not responsible for our 'natural endowments' – strength, looks, intelligence, even good character – we cannot claim the product generated by those natural endowments. Under the difference principle one person may earn $210,000 and another $14,000, but not a dime of that $196,000 difference is *justified* by reference to desert. Of course, in *causal terms*, the difference may be attributed, at least in part, to native ability, but that does not *justify* the difference. Rawls goes as far as to say that natural endowments are a social resource to be used for the benefit of the worst off (Rawls, 1972: 179). It is strange that on desert Rawls is the radical, whereas Cohen sides with Nozick. It is true that Nozick does not believe that the rich are rich because they deserve to be rich – Wilt Chamberlain was rich because *other people chose to give him money* to play basketball – but the idea of self-ownership (private property rights) does imply a right to keep the fruit of your labour.

Whether you accept Cohen's argument against Rawls depends to some extent on whether you endorse Marx's labour theory of value. Many people would, however, follow Thomas Nagel in arguing that the value of a product is not the result of the amount of labour which went into it, but rather the other way round: the value of labour is the result of the contribution that labour makes to the product (Nagel, 1991: 99). Ask yourself this: if you have a firm making 'next generation' mobile telephones, which group of workers do you *least* want to lose: the canteen staff? Cleaners? Assembly line workers? Phone designers? Venture capitalists? It could be argued that the last two groups are the most important. The conclusion to be drawn is that if we want to justify an egalitarian distribution of wealth we need what Rawls attempts to offer, which is a moral justification that assumes that many of the poorest will get *more* than that to which their labour 'entitles' them.

Summary

Human beings need to decide how resources are to be distributed, and unless we endorse the anarchist position then the state, which is a coercive entity, will play a role in their distribution. Political theorists disagree about the extent of state involvement in the distribution of resources – Nozick argues for a minimal role, while Rawls – and, implicitly, Cohen – argue for a more extensive role. Underlying the three theories discussed are different conceptions of what it means to be an agent, and of human motivation. Rawls assumes that human beings have mixed motives: they are self-interested but also 'reasonable'. Nozick avoids a discussion of motivation by arguing for a strong conception of human agency – property rights are an extension of self-ownership: so long as we do not violate others' rights, what we do with our rights is for us to decide. Cohen endorses the emphasis on self-ownership, but uses it against Nozick's initial acquisition argument; he also rejects Rawls's motivational assumptions, arguing that we need to change our attitudes and become less acquisitive.

Questions

1. Do people *deserve* to keep the fruits of their labour?
2. If you are as well off as you could possibly be, can you have any grounds for objecting that other people are better off than you?
3. Is taxation 'forced labour'?
4. Should there be an unconditional minimum income for each person?
5. Should the state reward men and women for bringing up children, and doing housework?

References

Cohen, G. A. (1978) *Karl Marx's Theory of History: A Defence* Oxford: Clarendon.

Cohen, G. A. (1979) 'Capitalism, Freedom, and the Proletariat' in Alan Ryan (ed.), *The Idea of Freedom* Oxford: Oxford University Press.

Cohen, G. A. (2000) *If You're An Egalitarian, How Come You're So Rich?* Cambridge, Mass.: Harvard University Press.

Nagel, T. (1991) *Equality and Partiality* New York: Oxford University Press.

Nozick, R. (1974) *Anarchy, State, and Utopia* New York: Basic Books.

Locke, J. (1988) *Two Treatises of Government* (ed. Peter Laslett) Student edn Cambridge: Cambridge University Press.

Rawls, J. (1972) *A Theory of Justice* Oxford: Clarendon Press.

Rawls, J. (1993) *Political Liberalism* New York: Columbia University Press.

Rawls, J. (2001) *Justice as Fairness: A Restatement* Cambridge, Mass.: Harvard University Press.

Wolff, J. (1991) *Robert Nozick: Property, Justice and the Minimal State* Oxford: Polity.

Further Reading

The primary texts are Rawls (1971), Part One; Nozick (1974), Chapter 7; Cohen (1979); Cohen (2000). There are several good commentaries on Rawls, the first of which was Brian Barry, *The Liberal Theory of Justice* (Oxford: Clarendon, 1973); a collection of early essays on Rawls can be found in Norman Daniels (ed.), *Reading Rawls: Critical Studies on Rawls's A Theory of Justice* (Stanford: Stanford University Press, 1989 (first published 1973)); slightly more recent works on Rawls are Chandran Kukathas and Philip Pettit, *Rawls: A Theory of Justice and its Critics* (Cambridge: Polity Press, 1990) and Thomas Pogge, *Realizing Rawls* (Ithaca, New York: Cornell University Press, 1989). There are fewer works on Nozick. The best is Wolff (1991). Others – both collections of essays – are Jeffrey Paul (ed.), *Reading Nozick: Essays on Anarchy, State and Utopia* (Totowa New Jersey: Rowman & Littlefield, 1981) and David Schmidtz (ed.), *Robert Nozick* (Cambridge: Cambridge University Press, 2002).

Weblinks

- The following are useful websites on Rawls:
  http://www.epistemelinks.com/Main/Philosophers.aspx?PhilCode=Rawl
  http://plato.stanford.edu/entries/original-position/
  http://www.policylibrary.com/rawls/

- The following are useful websites on Nozick:
  http://www.epistemelinks.com/Main/Philosophers.aspx?PhilCode=Nozi
  http://dmoz.org/Society/Philosophy/Philosophers/N/Nozick,_Robert/

Chapter 5

Democracy

Introduction

It is very difficult to find anyone who disagrees with democracy these days. Politicians from the extreme left to the extreme right, insist that the politics that they support is democratic in character, so it is no wonder that the term is so confusing. Although fundamentalists may reject the notion of democracy, nobody else does, and whether the ruler is a military dictator, a nationalist demagogue or a liberal, the concept of democracy will be piously invoked in support of an argument.

So in asking what democracy is, we also have to address the question as to why it has become almost obligatory for politicians to claim adherence to the concept.

Chapter Map

In this chapter we will explore the following:

- Democracy has been more and more widely acclaimed from almost all sections of the political spectrum; it has become increasingly confusing as a concept.

- Liberals traditionally opposed democracy, even if the universal assumptions of their theory led their opponents to argue that liberalism was democratic in character.

- Liberals only reluctantly converted to democracy in the nineteenth century, and then only on the assumption that extending the franchise would not undermine the rights of property.

- After World War II politics was seen as the business of a decision-making elite, and participation by the masses was discouraged.

- Democracy involves both direct participation and representation, and representation needs to be based on a sense that the representative can empathise with the problems of her constituents.

- There is a tension between democracy and the concept of the state, and this creates problems for Held's case for a 'cosmopolitan democracy'.

- The question of the state helps to account for the confusions about the polity in ancient Greece, and among conservative critics of liberalism.

- A **relational** view of democracy enables us to tackle the 'tyranny thesis', and to defend the rational kernel of political correctness.

Inside the Voting Booth

Iraqi women stand in a queue at a polling station in Najaf, 30 January 2005.

You are standing in a voting booth, and you notice the people around you. One is a well-known business personality whose photograph you have seen in the local press. He is smartly dressed in an expensive suit, with shiny patent leather shoes. The other person who catches your eye is someone whom you have seen emptying your garbage. She has obviously taken time off work, and is wearing the protective clothing that the council gives to employees who do that particular job. After you have left the booth, and are wandering through the city centre, you notice a person begging. You remind him, after giving him some money, that there is a general election, and he snorts: 'You won't catch me voting: I am not on the voters' register anyway!'

Three different people attract your attention on voting day. A is a wealthy businessman, B is a council employee, and C is a beggar. In law all are equal, and they have equal political rights. Each has a right to cast a secret ballot, but is this sufficient for a system to be called democratic?

Consider the following: how important is it that A has a lot of wealth, B has relatively little, and C is a drug addict who has been disowned by his family and divorced from his wife, and has none? In law they are all equal citizens but, in practice, the amount of social power they have varies dramatically.

Should we take the view that A has worked hard and deserves his success, B has a job that lots of others could do, while C only has himself to blame? Are their differences proof of a free society or evidence that a society is yet to be fully democratic?

A and B want to see the prime minister about an issue that concerns them greatly. Who would you say the PM is likely to see? C has been told to put his life in order: how easy is it for him to become an effective citizen with good health, a reasonable job, and a home of his own?

Democracy and Confusion

The term democracy means rule of the people. But such a concept has created real problems for those who believe that political theory should be value free in character. It is revealing that Dahl in the 1960s preferred to speak of 'polyarchies' rather than democracies, in the hope that the substitute term could appear more 'scientific' in character. For whether democracy in the past has been a good thing or a bad thing, it is difficult to say what democracy is without 'taking sides' in some ongoing debate.

As democracy has become more and more widely praised, it has become more and more difficult to pin it down. John Dunn has noted that 'all states today profess to be democracies because a democracy is what it is virtuous for a state to be' (1979: 11). A term can only be confusing if it is taken to mean contradictory things: majority rule or individual rights; limited government or popular sovereignty; private property as against social ownership. Consider the following: participation versus representation; the collective versus the individual; socialism versus capitalism. All have been defended as being essential to democracy.

It has been argued that the term should be abandoned, and Crick has taken the view that politics needs to be *defended* against democracy not because he is opposed (at least not under all circumstances) to the idea, but because he is in favour of clarity and precision against vagueness and ambiguity. Democracy, he comments, is perhaps 'the most promiscuous word in the world of public affairs' (1982: 56). Bernard Shaw once devoted an entire play – *The Apple Cart* – to the problem. The play tackled the ambiguities of democracy with such flair that it was banned by a nervous Weimar Republic in the 1920s; and in a witty preface Shaw complains that democracy seems to be everywhere and nowhere. It is a long word that we are expected to accept reverently without asking any questions. It seems quite impossible, Shaw protests, for politicians to make speeches about democracy, or for journalists to report them, without obscuring the concept 'in a cloud of humbug' (Hoffman, 1988: 132).

What makes democracy so confusing is that it is a concept subject to almost universal acclaim. But this was not always the position. In the seventeenth century, nobody who was anybody would have called themselves a democrat. As far as landowners, merchants, lawyers and clergymen were concerned – people of 'substance' – democracy was a term of abuse: a bad thing. Even in the nineteenth century, social liberals such as J.S. Mill felt it necessary to defend liberty *against* democracy. It is only after World War I that democracy becomes a respectable term. It is true that Hitler condemned democracy as the political counterpart to economic communism, but Mussolini, the Italian fascist, could declare in a speech in Berlin in 1936 that 'the greatest and most genuine democracies in the world today, are the German and the Italian' (Hoffman, 1988: 133).

The left have generally approved of democracy, but it is possible to find the Russian revolutionary, Trotsky, for example, declaring democracy to be irretrievably bourgeois and counter-revolutionary. A Communist Party secretary declared in Hamburg in 1926 that he would rather burn in 'the fire of **revolution** than perish in the dung-heap of democracy' (Hoffman, 1988: 133). But by the twentieth century attacks on the idea of democracy have become the exception rather than the rule, and with this growing acclaim, the concept has become increasingly confusing.

Crick complains that the term has become a bland synonym for 'All Things Bright and Beautiful', a hurrah word without any specific content (1982: 56). The glow of approval has made it an idea very difficult to pin down.

Democracy and Liberalism

Weldon, the linguistic analyst, has argued that 'democracy', 'capitalism' and 'liberalism' are all alternative names for the same thing (1953: 86). Yet this view has been challenged by a number of theorists. They note that historically liberals were not democrats, even if they were attacked as democrats by conservative critics of liberalism. John Locke, for example, took it for granted that those who could vote were men, merchants and landowners, and the question of universal suffrage (even for men only) is not even raised in his *Two Treatises of Government*. The fact that liberals declared that men were free and equal was taken by conservatives to denote support for democracy, but this was not true!

A hapless King Charles (1600–49) reproached English parliamentarians (who had taken him prisoner) for 'labouring to bring about democracy' (Dunn, 1979: 3). Yet it is clear that Oliver Cromwell (1599–1658) and his puritan gentry did not believe in democracy, and even the left wing of the movement – the Levellers – wished to exclude 'servants' and 'paupers' from the franchise. Cromwellians were alarmed that the egalitarian premises of liberal theory might extend the freedom to smaller property owners to rule (Hoffman, 1988: 154–5). It is true that de Tocqueville (1805–59) writing in the 1840s, could describe the United States of his day as a democracy, but in fact until the 1860s Americans themselves identified democracy at best with one element (the legislature) of the constitution – an element to be checked and balanced by others.

Madison, one of the founders of the US Constitution, had spoken in the *Federalist Papers* of democracies as 'incompatible with personal security or the rights of property', and John Jay, one of the authors of the famous *Papers*, declared that the 'people who own the country should govern it' (Hoffman, 1988: 135). De Tocqueville might describe Jefferson, author of the *Declaration of Independence* (1787) as 'the greatest democrat ever to spring from American democracy' (1966: 249), but in fact Jefferson was a liberal who took the view that voters should be male farmers who owned property. The US political scientist Hofstadter has commented on how modern US folklore has anachronistically assumed that liberalism and democracy are identical (136), and it has missed the point which Crick makes, that there is 'tension as well as harmony' between the two bodies of thought.

Tension – because liberals did not intend the invocation of universal rights to apply to all adults – and *harmony* – because their critics from the right assumed that they did, and their critics from the left felt that if rights were universal in theory, then they should be universal in practice. It is important not to assume that liberal theorists were necessarily democratic in orientation. Rousseau, the eighteenth-century French theorist, felt that democracy was unworkable. It assumed a perfectionism that human nature belied, and was a form of government ever liable to 'civil war and internecine strife' (1968: 113).

De Tocqueville's portrait of the United States is that of a society of radical liberalism, not of democracy: he himself notes the enslavement of blacks and the appropriation of the lands of native Americans. A government publication in the United States could describe democracy even in the 1920s as 'a government of the masses . . . Attitude towards property is communistic – negating property rights . . . Results in demagogism, license, agitation, discontent, anarchy' (Hoffman, 1988: 141). Thus spoke the voice of traditional liberalism!

Biography — Alexis de Tocqueville (1805–59)

Born into a royalist aristocratic family, his father having narrowly escaped execution by the radical French revolutionaries, the Jacobins. De Tocqueville entered government service in 1827 but found it impossible to support the new Orleanist monarchy established in the July Revolution of 1830 or to believe that the old Bourbon monarchy could be restored.

From the spring of 1831 until 1832 he visited the United States with his friend, Gustave de Beaumont, and together they published a book on the American penal system. His *Democracy in America* appeared in two parts – in 1835 and 1840. The book won him international acclaim and after the second part appeared he was elected to the *Académie française.* In the book he argued that democracy requires religion and individualistic customs, and he was struck by the high levels of local participation in the US polity.

In 1835 he visited Ireland, and noted the growing rift between Catholics and Protestants. In 1839 he was elected deputy in Normandy and remained a member of the Chamber until 1848. After the February Revolution of 1848, he was elected to the Constituent Assembly and served on the commission that drew up the republican constitution. He was elected to the new Legislative Assembly in 1849, became its vice-president and, for a few months, was minister for foreign affairs. He was bitterly opposed to Louis Napoleon's coup d'état that ended his political career.

In 1856 he published his unfinished masterpiece, *The Ancient Regime,* in which he characterised the French Revolution as the greatest property transaction in history. He also corresponded with J.S. Mill.

How to read:

De Tocqueville's *Democracy in America*

This is a massive work, usually published in two volumes. The author's preface and introduction in Volume 1 are worth a close read. If you are particularly interested in the political system of the United States, then the earlier chapters are important, but for the critique of democracy, read Chapters 7–9. Chapter 10 contains a breathtaking assessment of the position of blacks and native Americans. In Volume 2 Chapter 8 on equality deserves a careful read and, although the volume is full of fascinating topics such as 'How American Democracy has modified the English Language', Part II can be skim-read with the exception of Chapter 20, which is especially interesting. Part III can be skipped, but Part IV deserves attention and Chapter 6 sets out clearly de Tocqueville's reservations about democracy.

The Problem of Exclusion

Conservative critics could speak of democracy as turning 'natural' hierarchies upside down. In an historic passage, the ancient Greek theorist Plato complains that in a democracy fathers and sons 'change places' and 'there is no distinction between **citizen** and alien and foreigner'. Slaves come to enjoy the same freedom as their owners, 'not to mention the complete equality and liberty in the relations between the sexes generally'. In the end, Plato adds with a flourish, even 'the domestic animals are infected with anarchy' (1955: 336).

It is true that during the fourth and fifth centuries BC an astonishing model of popular rule came to exist in ancient Athens. A popular assembly met some 40 times a year. All citizens were actually paid to attend. All had the right to be heard in debate before decisions were taken, and this assembly had supreme powers of war, peace, making treaties, creating public works, etc. Judges, administrators and members of a 500-strong executive council were chosen, and since they only held office for one or two years this meant that a considerable portion of Athenian citizens had experience of government.

But despite the fact that some have referred to Athenian democracy as 'pure' and 'genuine', it was rooted in **slavery**, patriarchy and chauvinism. Slaves, women and resident aliens had no political rights so that, as has been said, the people in Athens were really 'an exceptionally large and diversified ruling class' (Hoffman, 1988: 145). Not only was Athenian society divided internally, but the payment for jury service, public office and the membership of the executive council, the expensive land settlement programme and the distribution of public funds would not have been possible without the Athenian empire. Democracy was an exclusive idea: the demos – the people with the right to participate in decision making were certainly not all the adults who lived in the society.

But surely all this changed when liberals became converted to the notion of democracy? It is true that after the French Revolution British liberals began to accept the case for universal suffrage, at least among men. But they did so very cautiously and reluctantly, with Macpherson arguing that liberals such as Jeremy Bentham (1748–1832) would have preferred to restrict the vote to those who owned their own houses, but this was no longer acceptable (Macpherson, 1977: 35). James Mill (1773–1836) asserts that all men should have the vote to protect their interests, and then argues that logically these interests could be secured if all women, all men under 40 and the poorest third of the male population over 40 were excluded from the vote. In Macpherson's view, James Mill and Bentham were less than whole-hearted democrats (1977: 39).

The argument between the liberals and the liberals-turned-democrats was over whether the male poor would use their rights to strip the rich of their wealth, or whether they would leave decision making to the middle rank – whom James Mill described as the class in society which gives to science, art and legislation their most 'distinguished ornaments' and is the chief source of all that is 'refined and exalted in human nature'. Both sides of the argument agreed that the business of government is the business of the rich (Hoffman, 1988: 167).

The question of exclusion becomes more subtle as liberals become more enthusiastic about the idea of democracy. T.H. Green and Leonard Hobhouse, two

Biography — Jeremy Bentham (1748–1832)

A brilliant scholar, Bentham entered Queen's College, Oxford, at the age of 12 and was admitted to Lincoln's Inn at the age of 15. Financed by his father, he decided to dedicate his life to writing.

After reading the work of the radical liberal Joseph Priestley, Bentham ceased to be a Tory. In 1776 he wrote *A Fragment on Government*, published anonymously on the basis of his critique of Blackstone. In 1787 he produced a critique of Adam Smith's theory of usury. In 1789 *Introduction to the Principles of Morals and Legislation* was published, where Bentham argued famously that the proper objective of all conduct and legislation is 'the greatest happiness of the greatest number'. In Bentham's view, 'pain and pleasure are the sovereign masters governing man's conduct'. All acts are based on self-interest, it being the business of the law to ensure through painful sanctions that the individual subordinates his own happiness to that of the community. A plan for the reform of the French judicial system won him the honorary citizenship of France, but although he initially welcomed the French Revolution, he attacked the concept of natural right in his *Anarchical Fallacies.*

In 1798 Bentham wrote *Principles of International Law*, in which he argued that universal peace could only be obtained through European unity. He hoped that some form of European parliament would enforce the liberty of the press, free trade, the abandonment of all colonies and a reduction in the money being spent on armaments.

In 1809 he published *Catechism of Reformers,* where he attacked the law of libel as an instrument that could be used against radicals for 'hurting the feelings' of the ruling class. His work was praised and popularised by radical reformers and extracts of his work appeared in the campaigning *Black Dwarf*. When Burdett argued the case for universal suffrage in the House of Commons in 1818, he quoted the work of Bentham in his support.

In 1824 Bentham joined with James Mill to found the *Westminster Review*, the journal of the philosophical radicals.

His most detailed account of his ideas on political democracy appeared in his massive (and unfinished) *Constitutional Code*. Here he made the case for political reform on the grounds that this was the only way to secure the happiness of the majority. He also supported the abolition of the monarchy, the House of Lords and the established church. Women, as well as men, should be given the vote. Government officials should be selected by competitive examination. Politicians and government officials are after all, Bentham argued, the 'servants, not the masters, of the public'.

British social liberals, both supported the idea that women as well as men should have the vote, and by 1928, women were enfranchised. But Green could still take it for granted that men were the head of the family, and Hobhouse argued that women should stay at home and mind the children (Hoffman, 1988: 180). It could be argued that even when women had political and legal equality with men social equality eluded them, and their democratic rights were thereby impaired. This would be vigorously argued by feminists later. Socialists, for their part, continued to contend that even when workers have the vote they do not have the resources to

Biography — **Leonard Trelawney Hobhouse (1864–1929)**

Oxford educated, he was a temporary lecturer at the London School of Economics (LSE) in 1896–7 before becoming a journalist for the *Manchester Guardian* in 1897.

In 1904 he published *Democracy and Reaction* – a book that vigorously attacked imperialism and built upon the opposition he had expressed to the Boer War. He supported the social-reformist policy of the Liberal Party.

He returned to the LSE as a lecturer in 1904. In 1906–7 he became political editor of the short-lived *Tribune,* and in 1907 he was the first Professor of Sociology in a British university. He was pivotal in the establishment and foundation of sociology as an academic discipline and in the refinement of its methodology. All this time he maintained his output in the *Manchester Guardian* and played an active role in developing trade boards.

Strongly influenced by evolutionism, he published *Mind in Evolution* (1901), *Morals in Evolution* (1906) and *Development and Purpose* (1913). His *Liberalism* in 1911 has rightly been described as the best twentieth-century statement of liberal ideals. While Hobhouse saw private property as necessary to the development of the individual personality, he regarded common property as a valuable expression of social life. The state had a paramount role to play in promoting social good, and guarding the moral and spiritual interests of its members. He was a major advocate of the social reforms of the Asquith government.

After World War I he became more pessimistic about freedom and was concerned that a powerful state could undermine the moral autonomy of individuals. In 1922 he published *The Elements of Social Justice.*

exercise their political rights as effectively as those who have wealth, social connections, the 'right' education, etc.

What about international exclusions? Hobhouse argues that 'a democrat cannot be a democrat for his country alone'. Does democracy require support for political rights throughout the world? Hobhouse cannot make up his mind whether to support home rule for the Irish, and he argues that as far as the Crown colonies are concerned, a semi-despotic system is the best that can be devised (Hoffman, 1988: 181). The problem is still relevant. Is US endorsement of democracy compromised by the fact that the government supports regimes such as Kuwait and Saudi Arabia which are not democratic?

The 'Tyranny of the Majority' Thesis

Both J.S. Mill and de Tocqueville raised the problem of democracy as a 'tyranny of the majority'. What is there to prevent a government representing the majority from crushing a minority? Crick endorses what has been called a 'paradox of freedom' – a situation in which an elected leader acts tyrannically towards particular individuals or groups. Crick gives the example of the German elections of 1933 that saw Hitler being appointed chancellor. A more recent example – which Barbara Goodwin raises (1997: 289) – is of the Islamic Salvation Front in Algeria winning an election, but being prevented from governing by the army, on the grounds that the intention of the Front was to install a non-democratic Islamic theocracy.

This resurrects the ancient Greek argument that democracy as the rule of the poor could take the form of a popular despotism. Crick cites the French revolutionary, Robespierre, who speaks of a democratic defence of terror, and Crick comments, in a rather startling passage, that the problem with (**totalitarian**) communists is that they do not merely pretend to be democratic: they 'are democratic' (1982: 60–1; 56).

This leads most commentators to say that democracy must be linked to liberalism so that the term liberal qualifies democracy. A democratic society must respect the rights of minorities as well as majorities. Otherwise, democracy can become dictatorial and oppress individuals by imposing majority tastes and preferences on society as a whole. Built into the US tradition is what one writer has described as a 'neurotic terror of the majority', and new liberals such as Hobhouse argued that checks should be placed upon the British House of Commons to restrain 'a large and headstrong majority' (Hoffman, 1988: 136; 181). Ian Paisley's conception of a 'Protestant state of the Protestant people' may appear democratic, but it certainly did not facilitate participation by the Catholic minority.

The Problem of Participation

Towards the end of World War II the concept of democracy was redefined, in order to bring it into line, so it was argued, with practical realities. Joseph Schumpeter, an Austrian economist and socialist, led the way, contending that the notion of democracy must be stripped of its moral qualities. There is nothing about democracy that makes it desirable. It may be that in authoritarian systems – Schumpeter gives the example of the religious settlement under the military dictatorship of Napoleon I – the wishes of the people are more fully realised than under a democracy (1947: 256).

In Schumpeter's view, democracy is simply a 'political method'. It is an arrangement for reaching political decisions: it is not an end in itself. Since all governments 'discriminate' against some section of the population (in no political system are children allowed to vote, for example), discrimination as such is not undemocratic. It all depends upon how you define the demos, the people. Schumpeter accepts that in contemporary liberal societies all adults should have the right to vote, but this does not mean that they will use this right or participate more directly in the political process. In fact, he argues that it is a good idea if the mass of the population do not participate, since the masses are too irrational, emotional, parochial and 'primitive' to make good decisions.

The typical citizen, he argues, yields to prejudice, impulse and what Schumpeter calls 'dark urges' (1947: 262). It is the politicians who raise the issues that determine people's lives, and who decide these issues. A democracy is more realistically defined as 'a political method' through which politicians are elected by means of a competitive vote. The people do not rule: their role is to elect those who do. Democracy is a system of elected and competing elites.

The 1950s saw a number of studies which argued that politics is a remote, alien and unrewarding activity best left to a relatively small number of professional

Biography — Joseph Alois Schumpeter (1883–1950)

Born in Austria to parents who owned a textile factory, Schumpeter was very familiar with business when he entered the University of Vienna to study economics and law.

He was a student of Friedrich von Wieser and Eugen von Böhm-Bawerk, and as early as 1908 Schumpeter published *Economic Doctrine and Method*. He was only 28 when he wrote his famous *Theory of Economic Development*. In this book he set out many of the ideas that featured in his later work, and he already displayed the broader concerns of the historian and the social scientist. In 1911 Schumpeter took a professorship in economics at the University of Graz, and he served as minister of finance in the Austrian government in 1919.

With the rise of Hitler, Schumpeter left Europe and the University of Bonn where he had been a professor from 1925 until 1932, and emigrated to the United States. In that same year he accepted a permanent position at Harvard, and remained there until his retirement in 1949. His *Business Cycles* appeared in 1939. In 1942 he produced *Capitalism, Socialism and Democracy*, in which

he argues that capitalism will decay not because of its failures, but because of its success. Capitalism would spawn, he believed, a large intellectual class that made its living by attacking the very bourgeois system of private property and freedom so necessary for the intellectual class's existence. Unlike Marx, Schumpeter did not relish the destruction of capitalism. 'If a doctor predicts that his patient will die', he wrote, 'this does not mean that he desires it.'

Capitalism is creatively destructive. The opening of new markets, new methods of production, new products and new types of organisation continually modify the structure of the system, and Schumpeter expressed a preference for monopoly and oligopoly over free competition. But entrepreneurial activity is undermined, not only by those who make it the target of intellectual wrath, but also by the growing bureaucracy and routinisation of large firms.

Schumpeter was president of the American Economic Association in 1948, and his *History of Economic Analysis* was published posthumously in 1954.

activists. Elected leadership should be given a free hand, since 'where the rational citizen seems to abdicate, nevertheless angels seem to tread' (Macpherson, 1977: 92). The model of elitist democracy, as it has sometimes been called, argued the case for a democracy with low participation.

Solutions to the Problem of Low Participation

It could be argued, however, that low participation undermines democracy. How democratic are liberal political systems if, in the United States, for example, the president can be elected with hardly more than half the population exercising their vote? (Although in the 2004 presidential election the percentage of those voting rose to close on 60 per cent.) This means that whatever his majority, he is supported by a minority of the electorate.

In his *Life and Times of Liberal Democracy* Macpherson sets about constructing a participatory model, arguing that somehow participatory democrats have to break the vicious circle between an apathy that leads to inequality (as the poor and vulnerable lose out), and inequality that generates apathy (as the poor and vulnerable feel impotent and irrelevant). Macpherson's argument is an interesting one, because he takes the view that one needs to start with people as they are. Let us assume that the individual is simply a market-oriented consumer who does not feel motivated to vote, or if she votes, does so in order to further her own immediate interests. There are three issues that Macpherson feels work to break this vicious circle.

To consume comfortably and confidently, one needs a relatively decent environment. Going fishing assumes that there are fish to catch and they are safe to eat; swimming can only take place if the sea is not so polluted as to be positively dangerous. A concern about the environment leads the most politically apathetic consumer to contemplate joining an ecological organisation. That is the first loophole.

From a concern with the physical environment, the consumer moves on to the social environment. Inner urban decay, ill-planned housing estates, the ravages of property developers: all these and related issues compel people to become concerned with politics, while insecurity and boredom at the workplace makes it inevitable that there will be involvement in trade union and professional association campaigns for job protection, better pensions etc.

One can add numerous other issues that are forcing people to take a greater concern in the political process. It is crucial not to define politics too narrowly since people participate in all kinds of different ways, and even the person who does not vote may join, say, Amnesty International or Greenpeace in Britain. There is an argument (which we will consider in a moment) for increasing the number of people who vote in parliamentary elections, but it is important to see that democracy requires participation at different levels, and in different ways. The large numbers of people who turned out to protest against the war with Iraq in London showed that a lack of concern with politics can be exaggerated, and the rise of what are usually called the New Social Movements – single issue organisations concerned with peace, the environment, rights of women, etc. – indicate that there is increasing participation, even if some of this participation seems unconventional in character.

There is a growing feeling that 'normal' political processes – in local government, in electing people to parliament – must change in the sense that these institutions need to become more accessible and intelligible to people on the street. In Britain, for example, there is growing interest in schemes to assist voting and voter registration; in reforming legislative chambers; making local government more exciting; introducing devolved and regional government; and other schemes to increase levels of interest and involvement in conventional political processes.

Even if voting is not the only form of democratic participation, it is important and there is, we think, a strong argument for compulsory voting in the United Kingdom. The argument that the citizen has a right not to vote ignores the fact that rights are indissolubly linked to responsibilities, and the act of non-voting harms the interests of society at large. It is true that some may feel that voting is a farce, but the defensible part of this objection – that the voter does not feel that existing parties offer real choice – can easily be met by allowing voters to put their cross in a box which states 'none of the above'. This would signal to politicians the extent to which people were voting negatively through protest.

It is true that the case for compulsory voting would not, taken simply on its own, create a more effective participation. It has to be accompanied by policies that address the inequalities underlying the problem of apathy. A lack of jobs, housing, adequate healthcare, physical and material security remain critical causes of despair and low self-esteem. There is plenty of evidence that mandatory voting raises participation levels and, as Faulks points out, when the Netherlands dropped compulsory voting in 1970, voting turn-out fell by 10 per cent (2001: 24). Italy, Belgium and Australia still compel their citizens to vote. Compulsory voting would encourage people to take an interest in political affairs – become more literate and confident – and it could reduce the time and resources parties use to try and capture the public interest in trivial and sensational ways.

While fines could be imposed upon defaulters, the real sanctions for non-compliance would be moral. Compulsory voting could play an invaluable role in altering our political culture in a socially responsible direction. Faulks quotes Lijphart, who comments that compulsory voting is an extension of universal suffrage (2001: 25). A simple and comprehensive system of voter registration in Britain would also assist people in taking responsibility for governing their own lives, and one can think of numerous devices to facilitate voting. The greater use of postal votes, the extension of time for voting, and a more proportional system would do much to overcome the cynicism that is often expressed at election times. Additionally, we would point to the use of referenda on important issues, and the employment of citizens' juries. In this latter case, a number of citizens, statistically representative of the wider population, discuss particular issues in an intense and deliberative way, and make recommendations based upon questions to relevant experts.

A number of writers have argued that the use of information technology could radically enhance the possibility for direct democracy since as a result of email, the internet, video conferencing, the digitisation of data, two-way computer and television links through cable technology, citizens could remain at home and shape policies rather than rely upon representatives to do so. Clearly such a technology has tremendous potential to empower citizens, and Faulks gives the example of how a citizens' action group used the communications network to raise $150,000 in Santa Monica, California, for the local homeless (1999: 157). Television shows in Britain such as *Pop Idol*, *Big Brother* and *Strictly Come Dancing* already have vast numbers of viewers voting for their chosen 'star': does this indicate the potential for using TV as a medium for giving people greater choice on policies and personalities? Already TV programmes invite viewers to express their views on controversies of the day.

Representational and Direct Democracy

Do we need to make a choice between representational democracy and direct democracy: between situations in which people elect representatives to govern them, or they directly take decisions themselves?

Rousseau, in a famous passage in *The Social Contract*, argues the case for direct involvement, passionately insisting that to be represented is to give up – to alienate – powers that individuals alone can rightfully exercise. Deputies are acceptable since they are merely the agents of the people. Representation, on the other hand, an odious modern idea, involves a form of slavery – a negation of 'will', one's capacity to exert influence (1968: 141). Rousseau's position is generally regarded as untenable. The very notion of representation as a re-presenting of the individual arises from the classical liberal view that citizens are individuals. This is an important and positive idea but, to be democratic, representatives can only act on behalf of those they represent if they understand their problems and way of life.

We do not, therefore, have to make a choice between representational or direct democracy. It is revealing that the argument associated with Edmund Burke (1729–97) – one of the great liberal conservatives – that representatives simply act in what they see (in their infinite wisdom) is the real interest of their constituents, inverts the Rousseauan view that representation is necessarily alienation. Those who have neither the time nor resources to make laws directly need to authorise others to do so on their behalf. Only through a combination of the direct and the indirect – hands-on participation *and* representation – can democratic autonomy be maximised. Of course, there are dangers that representatives will act in an elitist manner: but this is also true of what Rousseau called 'deputies'. Democracy requires accountability, so that people can get decisions made which help them to govern their own lives.

Representation, it should be said, involves empathy – the capacity to put yourself in the position of another – and while it is impossible to actually be another person, it

Ideas and Perspectives:

The 'Mirror' Theory of Representation

It is sometimes argued that representation can only be fair if exact percentages of groups within the population at large are 'reflected' in the composition of representatives. If the population of a particular city (such as Leicester in England) contains, say, 40 per cent of people with black faces, then a mirror theory of representation demands that there should be 40 per cent of representatives who are black. The same is argued about poor people, gays, etc. It is not difficult to see the problem with this notion. Ethnic minorities, as with people in general, are not all the same. Black people in Leicester are divided ethnically, regionally, along class and gender lines, etc. and it would be wrong to assume that one black person is the same as another. A black businessman may not identify with a black trade unionist. It does not follow, therefore, that black representatives will necessarily represent the interests of black constituents, any more than we can assume that women representatives will necessarily represent the interests of women. It is one thing to argue that representatives must have knowledge of (and experience of) the people they represent; quite another that they must represent them in precise numbers.

The mirror theory has a grain of truth in it: representatives should be sensitive to the problems of their constituents, and it helps if a predominantly black constituency, for example, has a black representative. But it has only a *grain* of truth: it is not the whole story. There are an infinity of other factors to consider – gender, class, sexual orientation, etc. We need to distinguish between politically relevant differences and those 'differences' (such as wearing spectacles) that are not normally relevant.

Ch 7: Differen pp. 15(

is necessary to imagine what it is like to be another. Hence, as noted above, accountability is 'the other side' of representation: one without the other descends into either impracticality or elitism. The notion of empathy points to the need for a link between representatives and constituents. Unless representatives are in some sense a reflection of the population at large, it is difficult to see how empathy can take place. Women who have experienced oppression by men (or partners) at first hand are more likely to have insight into the problems women face than men who – however sympathetic they may be – may never have been the recipients of that particular form of discrimination. The same is true with members of ethnic and sexual minorities etc. To have experienced humiliation directly as a disabled person makes one far more sensitive to questions of disability. We need a form of representation that is sensitive to the particular identities and problems of those they represent.

Democracy requires participation, but it would be wrong to assume that this is only possible through direct involvement in political processes. Direct involvement needs to be linked to representation, and it is worth noting that in the ancient Greek polis – often held up as an example of direct democracy – the assembly elected an executive council.

The Argument So Far ...

- Democracy is a particularly confusing concept because nearly everyone claims to subscribe to it.

- In fact this is a relatively recent development. Liberals historically disagreed with democracy, but because liberal theory seemed to apply to everyone this makes it difficult to see who was being excluded. Conservatives accused liberals of wanting to be universally inclusive, just as Plato in ancient Greece accused democrats of wanting to abolish the distinction between citizen and slave.

- Liberals in the nineteenth century reluctantly accepted the need for universal suffrage, although they continued to fear that democracy might express itself as a 'tyranny of the majority'. This fear helps to explain the post-war argument that a realistic view of democracy requires that the people only minimally participate.

- In fact, low participation is something that undermines democracy, and suggestions are offered as to how participation could be increased. But it is important in arguing for more participation that we see democracy as both representative and 'direct'.

Democracy and the State

The problem with much of the analysis of democracy is that it assumes that democracy is a form of the state. Yet it could well be argued that there is a contradiction between the idea of the 'rule of the people' and an institution claiming a monopoly of legitimate force for a particular territory.

This is not to deny that the more liberal the state the better, or that states that have the rule of law, regular elections and universal suffrage are preferable to states which do not. A liberal society has to be the basis for democracy: it is necessary, although not sufficient. Thus to the extent that, for example, Singapore does not allow its citizens to express themselves freely, it is undemocratic.

We want to argue that what makes a liberal society 'insufficient', is that it still needs a state, and the state, it could be suggested, is a repressively hierarchical institution that excludes outsiders and uses **force** to tackle conflicts of interest. Conservatives who complained that democracy is incompatible with the state are right. You cannot be said to govern your own life within the state. When the supreme ruler of the moon was told, as H.G. Wells recalls, that states existed on earth in which everybody rules, he immediately ordered that cooling sprays should be applied to his brows (Hoffman, 1995: 210).

Dahl, in fact, has argued that when individuals are forced to comply with laws, democracy is to that extent compromised (1989: 37). If you vote for a particular party through fear of what might happen to you if you do not, then such a system cannot be called democratic. Liberals have argued that a person cannot be said to act freely if they are threatened with force: yet the logic here points to a position that Dahl does not accept. If force is incompatible with self-rule, then it follows that the state cannot be reconciled with democracy. The use of force against a small number of people – something that no state can avoid – makes the idea of self-government problematic. This is why the notion of democracy as a form of the state is not self-evident, and it could be argued that this assumption weakens David Held's otherwise persuasive case for a 'cosmopolitan democracy'. Held acknowledges that the concept of democracy has changed its geographical and institutional focus over time. Like Dahl (1989: 194), he accepts that the notion of democracy was once confined to the city-state. It then expanded to embrace the nation-state, and it has now become a concept that stands or falls through an acknowledgement of its global character.

Since local, national, regional and global structures and processes all overlap, democracy must take a cosmopolitan form (Held, 1995: 21). Held argues (as, indeed, Dahl does) that people in states are radically affected by activities that occur outside their borders. Whether we think of the movement of interest rates, the profits that accrue to stocks and shares, the spread of AIDS, the movements of refugees and asylum seekers, or the damage to the environment, government is clearly stretching beyond the state.

What obstructs the notion of international democracy, Held argues, is the assumption that states are sovereign, and that international institutions detract from this sovereignty. The position of the United States under the Bush leadership (alarmingly reinforced rather than undermined by the reaction to the appalling events of 11 September 2001) is rooted in the archaic belief that institutions which look beyond the nation-state are a threat to, rather than a necessity for, democratic realities.

The post-war period has seen the development of what Held calls the UN Charter Model (1995: 86). However, although this has made inroads into the concept of state sovereignty (hence the US hostility to the United Nations), it coexists uneasily with what Held calls the 'the model of Westphalia' – the notion that states recognise no superior authority and tackle conflicts by force (1995: 78). A first step forward would involve enhancing the UN model by making a consensus vote in the General Assembly a source of international law, and providing a means of redress of human rights violations in an international court.

The Security Council would be more representative if the veto arrangement was modified, and the problem of double standards addressed – a problem that undermines the UN's prestige in the South (1995: 269). But welcome as these measures would be, they still represent, Held contends, a very thin and partial move towards an international democracy.

Held's full-blown model of cosmopolitan democracy would involve the formation of regional parliaments whose decisions become part of international law. There would be referenda cutting across nations and nation-states, and the establishment of an independent assembly of democratic nations (1995: 279). The logic of this argument implies the explicit erosion of state sovereignty and the use of international legal principles as a way of delimiting the scope and action of private and public organisations. These principles are egalitarian in character and would apply to all civic and political associations.

But how would they be enforced? It is here that Held's commitment to the state as a *permanent* actor on the international scene bedevils his argument. The idea of the state remains but it must, Held contends, be adapted to 'stretch across borders' (1995: 233). While he argues that the principle of 'non-coercive relations' should prevail in the settlement of disputes, the use of force as a weapon of last resort should be employed in the face of attacks to eradicate cosmopolitan law.

Held's assumption is that the existence of this force would be *permanent*. Yet these statist assumptions are in conflict with the aim of seconding this force, that is 'the demilitarisation and transcendence of the war system' (1995: 279). For this is only possible if institutions claiming a monopoly of legitimate force give way to what we have called governments, and the logic of government is, it has been argued above, profoundly different from that of the state. Held contends that we must overcome the **dualisms** between (for example) globalism and cultural diversity; global governance from above and the extension of grass roots organisations from below, constitutionalism and politics. These polarities make it impossible to embed utopia in what Held calls 'the existing pattern of political relations and processes' (1995: 286).

But as challenging as this model is, its incoherence is manifest in Held's continuing belief in the permanence of the state. In an analysis of democracy and autonomy, he argues that the demos must include all adults with the exception of those temporarily visiting a political community, and those who 'beyond a shadow of a doubt' are legitimately disqualified from participation 'due to severe mental incapacity and/or serious records of crime' (1995: 208). Temporary visitors would, it is true, be citizens of other communities. But excluding the mentally incapacitated from citizenship is far from self-evident, and while there may be a tactical argument for excluding serious criminals from voting (although the position on this is changing), the very existence of such a category of intransigent outsiders indicates how far we are from having a democracy.

Held argues that the nation-state would 'wither away' but by this he does *not* mean that the nation-state would disappear. What he suggests is that states would no longer be regarded as the 'sole centres of legitimate power' within their own borders, but would be 'relocated' to and articulated within an overarching global democratic law (1995: 233). Democracy would, it seems, be simultaneously **statist**, supra-statist and sub-statist, but although this is an attractive argument there remains a problem. States, after all, are institutions that claim a monopoly of legitimate force in 'their' particular territory. They are jealous of this asserted monopoly (which lies at the heart of the notion of state sovereignty) and, therefore, cannot coexist equally with other bodies that do not and cannot even claim to exercise a monopoly of legitimate force.

Held seeks to transform the world environment in the interests of self-government and **emancipation**, but he remains prisoner of the liberal view that the state is permanent. As far as Held is concerned, the state merely remains as one of many organisations. Yet the state is incompatible with democracy, and as it gives up its claim to a monopoly of legitimate force it ceases to be a state.

The Ancient Greek Polity and the Problem with Liberalism

The ancient Greek polity was, as noted above, exclusive, and Athenian democracy rested, among other things, upon imperialism. It is revealing that Rousseau as an admirer of the ancient system, is uncertain as to how to respond to its reliance on slavery. On the one hand, he argues fiercely against slavery and takes great exception to Aristotle's comment that there are slaves 'by nature'. On the other hand, he concedes that without slavery democracy in ancient Greece would not have been possible (1968: 52; 142; Hoffman, 1988: 146).

The fact is that ancient Greek democrats took democracy to be a form of the state, although their concept of democracy was mystified by its apparent linkages with the old clan system of tribal times. When Kleisthenes overthrew the oligarchs and forged a new constitution at the end of fifth century BC, the external features of the old system were faithfully reproduced in the arrangements of the new. 'Restoring' the popular assembly, the festivals and the electoral system made it appear as though the people were simply recovering the ancient rights of their old tribal system.

The continuity was deceptive. The new units of the constitution, though tribal in form, were geographical in reality, so that in practice the new democratic constitution actually worked to accelerate the disintegration of the clan system. The development of commerce and industry helped to dissolve away the residues of the old kinship bonds, and introduce a system based on slavery. Morgan, a nineteenth-century US anthropologist, complained that a 'pure democracy' was marred by atrocious slavery (Hoffman, 1988: 147–8), but once we understand that this was a statist form of democracy, then the paradox of popular rule and slavery ceases to be a problem.

Conservatives failed to understand this when they feared that democracy would undermine 'natural' hierarchies. John Cotton, a seventeenth-century divine in New England, spoke of democracy as the meanest and most illogical form of government, since he asked: when the people govern, *over whom* do they rule? Many conservatives overlooked the statist character of classical liberalism. After all, the whole point of the classical liberal concept of the state of nature was to establish the impossibility of life without the state. It is true that classical liberals assumed that humans were 'naturally' free and equal, but they construed these qualities as market-based abstractions, so that inevitably as 'inconveniences' (as Locke politely terms them) set in, the state was required to maintain order.

Rousseau could speak of people leaving the state of nature in order to rush headlong into the chains of the state, but he takes it for granted that the legitimate rule, which forces people to be free, is of course a state.

When King Charles upbraided English liberals for labouring to bring in democracy, and told them that a subject and a sovereign 'are clear different things' (Dunn, 1979: 3), he need not have bothered. Liberals were clearly aware of this distinction. This is why de Tocqueville could describe the United States as a democracy – democracy could be many things, but de Tocqueville never imagined it doing away with the state. Dunn describes democracy as 'the *name* for what we cannot have' – people ruling their own state (1979: 27). But this is because he views the world from the standpoint of a liberal, and he takes it for granted that people cannot govern without an institution claiming a monopoly of legitimate force for a particular territory. One of the delegates of the South German People's Party declared at a conference in 1868 that 'democracy wants to become social democracy, if it honestly wants to become democracy' (Bauman, 1976: 43). It could be argued that the same thing should be said about democracy and the state. Only an institution that looks beyond the claim to exercise a monopoly of legitimate force can call itself a democracy!

Democracy and the Relational Argument

Once we challenge the idea that democracy can be a form of the state, then the argument that the will of the majority may favour arbitrary and repressive rule ceases to be persuasive.

For the point is that majorities cannot repress minorities unless their rule expresses itself in the form of the state. The examples that Crick gives are clearly statist in character, so that the problem is not really with majority rule: it is with the state. For how can we reconcile democracy with an institution claiming a monopoly of legitimate force?

The idea that democracy can express itself as a tyranny of the majority is not only empirically invalid, it is also logically problematic. For it assumes that individuals are completely separate from one another, so that it is possible for one section of the population (the majority) to be free while their opponents (the minority) are oppressed. But this argument is only defensible if we draw a sharp (and non-relational) line between the self and the other. If we embrace a relational approach, then the freedom of each individual depends upon the freedom of the other. As the Zimbabwean greeting puts it, I have slept well, if you have slept well: we may be separate people, but we are also related. It is impossible for a majority to oppress a minority without oppressing itself.

Let me illustrate this logical point with an empirical example. Take the idea that was noted above of Ian Paisley's 'Protestant state for the Protestant people'. Up until 1972, it can be said that in Northern Ireland the Catholic minority were oppressed, and the Protestant majority ascendant. But how free was the majority? What happened if an individual Protestant wished to marry a Catholic, or became sympathetic to their point of view? What happened to Protestants who decided to revere the anti-colonial heritage of Protestants such as Wolfe Tone? How open

Biography   Carl Schmitt (1888–1985)

Born into a Catholic family in Westphalia.

Between 1919 and 1933 he pursued the career of academic jurist, moving from one chair to another. In 1933 he acquired the chair of public law at the University of Berlin. He acted as legal adviser to the national government when it defended itself against a case brought by Prussia in 1932.

From the early 1920s he had been a right-wing critic of the Versailles Peace Settlement and the League of Nations. He was also critical of the political structure of the Weimar Republic. In the 1920s and early 1930s he was closely associated with the Catholic Centre Party and in 1927 he published *The Concept of the Political*. A longer version appeared in 1932 and in 1933 certain alterations were entered into a further edition to make it acceptable to the Nazis. The book only appeared in English in 1976. In the book Schmitt argues that the friend/enemy distinction is a necessary feature of all political communities. Indeed, what defines the 'political' as opposed to other human activities is the intensity of feeling toward friends and enemies, or toward one's own 'kind' and those perceived as hostile outsiders.

From 1929 onwards, Schmitt contended that the president should exercise the emergency power granted him by Article 48 of the Weimar Constitution. He allied himself to General Schleicher. Schleicher resigned after his emergency proposals were rejected by Weimar President Hindenburg. He was assassinated by the Nazis in 1934.

In 1931 and 1932 Schmitt urged Hindenburg to suppress the Nazi Party and to jail its leaders, and he sharply opposed those in the Centre Party who thought the Nazis could be tamed if they were forced to form a coalition government. The Weimar Constitution was overthrown by the Enabling Act of March 1933, and Schmitt joined the National Socialist Party in May of that year. He became director of the University Teachers' Group of the National Socialist League and endorsed the 'leadership principle' propagated by the Nazis. From 1934 he was subjected to attacks from Nazi ideologists and in 1936 he came under investigation from the SS. To ward off these attacks, he began to use racial and biological terminology and defend anti-Semitism, but as pressure continued to mount he retired from public life and devoted himself entirely to scholarly activities.

From September 1945 until May 1947 Schmitt was a prisoner of the US occupational forces in Germany. In the post-war period he continued to write, and despite hostile criticism a volume of his collected works appeared in 1958. His work continued to arouse interest and controversy and he favoured limiting the constitutional changes introduced through the amendment process. In this way he argued that the federal and democratic character of the Bonn constitution could never be altered.

In the 1990s (after Schmitt's death) his books became more influential and a stream of translations and analyses of his work appeared.

could loyalist-minded Protestants be about the partisan character of the police or the electoral malpractices designed to devalue Catholic votes? The point is that in a society in which there is a 'tyranny of the majority' no one is free and thus able to govern their own lives.

Chantal Mouffe, a radical post-structuralist theorist, has argued that democracy leads to the dictatorial rule of the popular will. It embodies the logic of what she calls **identity** or equivalence, whereas liberalism (which she prefers to democracy) respects difference, diversity and individual self-determination (1996: 25). But is this liberal polity a form of the state? On this crucial matter Mouffe is silent, and it is not surprising that her admiration for the pre-war conservative Carl Schmitt places her argument in still more difficulty. While she praises Schmitt for identifying politics with conflict, she is embarrassed by the avowedly statist way in which he interprets conflict (Hoffman, 1998: 60).

For Schmitt, the other is an enemy to be physically eliminated. While Mouffe identifies politics with conflict and difference, she is reluctant to see differences 'settled' in a statist manner through force. She seeks to distinguish between a social agent and the multiplicity of social positions that agents may precariously and temporarily adopt. The pluralism of multiple identities is 'constitutive of modern democracy' and 'precludes any dream of final reconciliation' (1996: 25). But if democracy is a form of the state then it will, indeed, rest upon an oppressive logic of equivalence that suppresses, rather than celebrates, difference.

Ideas and Perspectives:

Democracy and Political Correctness

Political Correctness (PC) swept across US universities in the 1990s and occasioned much controversy. Although it has not made the same impact in British universities, it is often used in conservative discourse as a response to feminist and multiculturalist arguments. The law passed in the British parliament to outlaw fox-hunting – to take a recent example – has been condemned as PC by its opponents.

Political correctness is considered by its critics to be a negation of democracy. There is no doubt that what has given PC its unsavoury reputation is the problem of dogmatism. Feminist and multicultural arguments have been advanced on occasion in an anti-liberal manner that has enabled conservative-minded publicists and thinkers to identify emancipatory causes as being inherently illiberal in character. However, it could be argued that it is counter-productive (and indeed contradictory) to try and advance good causes through intolerance (and even worse harassment and the threat of violence). Emancipation should be liberating – to make it dreary and painful is to crush and distort it.

The cause of anti-racism or the cause of feminism, for example, is not advanced by pushing people into positions for which they are not qualified. The policy of affirmative action – promoting people because they are black or women or belong to a disadvantaged minority – is a risky one that only works at the margins and can easily backfire. The question is always: what is the best and quickest way of making our public and private institutions more representative of the population at large? Given the regrettable fact that elitism and prejudice have existed for so long that some even think they are 'natural' and 'normal', there are no quick and easy solutions – no short-cuts. Would that there were!

The insistence that the right kind of language is used is helpful in so far as it changes people's attitudes and behaviour. But what if it does not? What if people use the 'correct' language but still continue to behave in the old way? Democracy, alas, requires more than a change of language if it is to advance.

Democratic causes are those that empower people. If this is done in a way that commands wide support, we all benefit. Democracy can only advance if it tackles those who are hostile to democracy. PC needs defending both against those who advocate racism, sexism or homophobia, etc. and against those who ruin good causes by acting in an illiberal and unemancipatory manner. The best argument against those who promote good causes in an intemperate and divisive way is to tell them that they are not PC!

The argument that democracy can be tyrannical makes the assumption that individuals and groups can be totally separated from each other. Democracy is conceived of as a Hobbesian Leviathan in majoritarian form (Hoffman, 1995: 202), by which is meant that democracy is analysed in terms of the kind of unrelated individuals that lie at the heart of Hobbes's argument for the state. Once we argue that the mechanisms of government must replace those of the state, then the notion of democracy becomes a way of resolving conflict in a way which acknowledges the identity of the parties to a dispute. It goes beyond the need for an institution claiming a monopoly of legitimate force – the state.

Summary

What makes democracy such a confusing concept is that it has been acclaimed from almost every part of the political spectrum – and is held to stand for contradictory ideals. Contrary to the notion of 'liberal democracy', it is important to remember that before the twentieth century liberals generally opposed democracy even though they were often accused by their conservative opponents of being democratic in character. Although liberalism presented its ideals in universal terms, there were all manner of exclusion clauses in practice. Liberals only reluctantly converted to democracy in the nineteenth century when they felt that extending the franchise would not undermine the rights of property.

The argument has been advanced even since World War II that democracy could mean a 'tyranny of the majority' and that democracy should be 'redefined' to involve a vote for competing elites to make decisions. In fact, increasing political participation is necessary for democracy and the argument for compulsory voting in elections should be taken seriously. It is misleading to argue that democracy involves either direct participation or representation. It involves both. Although representation does not require that those elected 'mirror' the precise proportions of the population, empathy between representative and elector is crucial.

If democracy is to involve self-government, there is a conflict between democracy, on the one hand, and the state, on the other. This is why Held's concept of a 'cosmopolitan democracy' can only be coherently sustained if the international community ceases to be composed of states. The question of the contradiction between democracy and the state has direct relevance for understanding the character and quality of the democracy in ancient Greece. Only by analysing democracy in relation to the state can we develop a relational view that makes it possible to tackle the 'tyranny of the majority' argument effectively.

Questions

1. How democratic are 'liberal democracies'?
2. Is a society more democratic if more people participate in decision making?
3. Can a system be called democratic if it is illiberal in character?

4. Does democracy lead to the 'tyranny of the majority'?
5. Why is democracy such a confusing concept?

References

Bauman, Z. (1976) *Socialism as Utopia* London: George Allen & Unwin.

Crick, B. (1982) *In Defence of Politics* 2nd edn Harmondsworth: Penguin.

Dahl, R. (1989) *Democracy and its Critics* New Haven, Conn.: Yale University Press.

Dunn, J. (1979) *Western Political Theory in the Face of the Future* London: Cambridge University Press.

Faulks, K. (1999) *Political Sociology* Edinburgh: Edinburgh University Press.

Faulks, K. (2001) 'Should Voting be Compulsory?' *Politics Review* 10(3), 24–5.

Goodwin, B. (1997) *Using Political Ideas* 4th edn Chichester, New York and Toronto: John Wiley & Sons.

Held, D. (1995) *Democracy and the Global Order* Cambridge: Polity Press.

Hoffman, J. (1988) *State, Power and Democracy* Brighton: Wheatsheaf Books.

Hoffman, J. (1995) *Beyond the State* Cambridge: Polity Press.

Macpherson, C. B. (1977) *The Life and Times of Liberal Democracy* London, Oxford and New York: Oxford University Press.

Mouffe, C. (1996) 'Radical Democracy or Liberal Democracy' in D. Trend (ed.), *Radical Democracy* New York and London: Routledge, 19–26.

Plato (1955) *The Republic* Harmondsworth: Penguin.

Rousseau, J.-J. (1968) *The Social Contract* Harmondsworth: Penguin.

Schumpeter, J. (1947) *Capitalism, Socialism and Democracy* 2nd edn New York and London: Harper.

Tocqueville, A. de (1966) *Democracy in America* London and Glasgow: Fontana.

Weldon, T. (1953) *The Vocabulary of Politics* Harmondsworth: Penguin.

Further Reading

- Crick's Chapter 3, 'A Defence of Politics Against Democracy' in his *In Defence of Politics* (referenced above) is an absolute must for all interested in the question.

- C.B. Macpherson's *Life and Times of Liberal Democracy* (referenced above) contains a very useful assessment of different 'models'.

- Dahl's *Democracy and its Critics* (referenced above) is clear and comprehensive, and particularly memorable for its critique of majoritarian rule.

- John Dunn has a very thought-provoking chapter on democracy in his *Western Political Theory in the Face of the Future* (referenced above).

- M. Finley, *Democracy Ancient and Modern* London: Chatto and Windus, 1973 has an excellent description of ancient Greek democracy.

- David Held's *Democracy and the Global Order* (referenced above) is very useful for those particularly interested in reworking the concept in the light of international trends.

Weblinks

- For the treatment of democracy in political theory, see:
  http:// www.keele.ac.uk/depts/po/prs.htm or
  http://www.york.ac.uk/services/library/subjects/politint.htm

- For those interested in the direct democracy debate, see:
  http://www.homeusers.prestel.co.uk/rodmell/quest.htm

- David Held's arguments can be seen at:
  http://www.mpi-fg-koeln.mpg.de/pu/workpap/wp97-5/wp97-5.html

Chapter 6

Citizenship

Introduction

Is the term 'citizenship' legal, philosophical, political, social or economic? Or is it a combination of all these dimensions? Does this flexibility make the term so elastic that it is effectively unusable?

The literature on citizenship has burgeoned massively over the past decade, with a journal devoted to the concept; reports on the teaching of the idea to school students; ministerial pronouncements on the subject; and articles and books galore in scholarly and popular publications. There is even a ceremony that has been devised for new citizens! Although the classical concepts of citizenship go back to the ancient Greeks (as we shall see in a moment) and were reworked in classical liberalism, contemporary commentators have sought to develop a concept of citizenship that is much more inclusive than earlier views.

Chapter Map

In this chapter we will discuss:

- The limitations of the ancient Greek concept of citizenship, and the exclusiveness of the liberal view. The abstract character of the liberal view of citizenship, its universal claims to freedom and equality and the inequalities of class.

- Marshall's argument that citizenship, in its modern form, requires social as well as political and legal rights. The rise of the New Right in Britain and the United States and its challenge to the concept of citizenship in the welfare state.

- The barriers that women face to a meaningful citizenship. How and why these barriers prevent women from running their own lives and impoverish their citizenship.

- The case for a basic income as a way of enhancing citizenship.

- Global citizenship as a status that does not contradict citizenship as member of a state. Citizenship as an identity at local, regional and national levels as well. The development of citizenship in the European Union.

- The tension between the state and citizenship, the question of class and citizenship, the case for transforming the market, and the presentation of citizenship as a relational concept.

'Being British': Pride, Passports and Princes

Prince Charles attending citizenship ceremony at Brent Town Hall, 26 February 2004.

In February 2004 19 immigrants received British passports in a ceremony in which they took an oath of allegiance to the Queen as head of state. The Prince of Wales handed out certificates, congratulating those receiving them. 'Being British', declared the Prince, 'is something of a blessing and a privilege for us all'. He hoped that the ceremony added something to the significance of acquiring British citizenship, and 'that it's reinforced your belief, if indeed any reinforcement is required, that you belong here and are very welcome'. He added that 'being a British citizen becomes a great source of pride and comfort for the rest of your life'. *Guardian* journalists in September 2003 found that when they questioned nine British citizens about key aspects of British life, the average score was just 37 per cent. Only a third of the sample could name the Home Secretary and knew what NHS Direct was, about 10 per cent knew what the national minimum wage was, and none knew what the basic rate of income tax was.

- Everyone agrees that British citizens should be able to speak English. But what other duties should someone fulfil in order to become a British citizen? Should they have a basic knowledge about British history, its political institutions and its society?

- Should would-be British citizens have to take an oath of allegiance to the Queen? What if they are republican minded, or feel as Jews, Catholics, Muslims, atheists, Hindus, Sikhs, etc. that the head of the state as an Anglican cannot be said to represent them?

- Should citizens have to vote in elections? Should they be expected to do community service at some stage? Should they receive as citizens a basic income from the government?

- Does citizenship require people to be involved in their locality and region? Should they also be concerned with developments in the European Union? Should they regard themselves as citizens of the world?

Citizenship and Liberalism

The notion of citizenship arises with ancient Greek thinkers (much of the argument here follows Hoffman, 2004). The citizen is traditionally defined as one who has the ability and chance to participate in government (by which is meant the state), but in Aristotle's aristocratic view, citizenship should not only exclude slaves, foreigners and women, but should be restricted to those who are relieved of menial tasks (1962: 111).

We must always bear this in mind when the argument is put for a 'revitalisation' and extension of the Aristotelian ideal of citizenship as the alternation of ruling and being ruled (Voet, 1998: 137). For the positive attributes of ancient Greek theory are undermined by the fact that they express themselves through gender, ethnic and (it should not be forgotten) imperial hierarchies, and we need to challenge the elitist notion of citizenship that the ancient Greeks took for granted.

Even when slavery was apparently rejected by a liberal view of humanity, the concept of citizenship has remained limited and exclusionary. It is revealing that Rousseau insists that the 'real meaning' of citizenship is only respected when the word is used selectively and exclusively (1968: 61). Citizens have property, are national (in their political orientation), and are public and male. Even the classical liberal opposition between citizenship and slavery is weakened by Rousseau's astonishing comment that in unfortunate situations (as in ancient Greece) 'the citizen can be perfectly free only if the slave is absolutely a slave' (1968: 143).

Classical liberalism injects a potential **universalism** into the concept of citizenship by arguing that all individuals are free and equal. Yet the universalism of this concept is undermined by support for **patriarchy**, elitism, colonialism – and as Yeatman has recently reminded us in the case of Locke – by an acceptance of outright slavery (Yeatman, 1994: 62; Hoffman, 1988: 162). Locke not only justifies slavery in his *Two Treatises* but he was a shareholder in a slave-owning company in Virginia. These rather startling facts coexist with the liberal notion of free and equal individuals.

Medieval thinkers, such as the ancient Greeks, have no universal concept of citizenship, because although medieval Christians, for example, had a notion of equality before the Fall, once humans are corrupted by sin ('the mother of servitude'), people divide into citizens and slaves, men and women, etc. in the time-honoured way.

Citizenship and Class

The recent literature on citizenship challenges the liberal concept of citizenship on the grounds that this concept leaves out many categories of people in society. The argument for a broader franchise was essentially an argument for broadening the concept of citizenship so that male workers could enjoy political rights.

Classical liberalism assumed that the individual had property, and some socialists such as Eduard Bernstein saw the notion of citizenship as something that workers could and should aspire to. Marx, on the other hand, appears to be bleakly negative towards the concept of citizenship, arguing that it seems to ignore the realities of a class-divided society. The rights of the citizen, he comments in an oft-cited passage, are simply the rights of the egoistic man (i.e. the property owner), of 'men separated from other men and the community' (Marx and Engels, 1975: 162). Marx's language is not only sexist, but he seems to be saying that citizenship is simply the right to exploit others through the ownership of private property. The possession of citizenship is seen as an anti-social activity.

But his argument is not quite as negative as it sounds. Marx comments that in the possessive individualist society, it is not 'man as *citoyen* but man as *bourgeois* who is considered to be the *essential* and *true* man' (Marx and Engels, 1975: 164). Marx's argument is that citizenship is abstract in so far as it implies an equality of an ideal kind, for this equality is contradicted by the concrete inequalities that exist in the real world. Even if the male worker can vote, how much power does he have over his life if his employer can have him summarily dismissed from this work?

It is important to stress that for Marx, the notion of abstraction does not imply unreality, in the sense that the abstract citizen does not exist. What makes the liberal notion of citizenship abstract is that it *conceals* beneath its benevolent-sounding principles the reality of class. While the *Communist Manifesto* sees the establishment of the 'modern representative State' (Marx and Engels, 1967: 82) as a crucial historical achievement, this state cannot be said to be representative of the community but acts on behalf of the capitalists. The celebrated description of communism as 'an association in which free development of each is the condition for the free development of all' (Marx and Engels, 1967: 105) could be taken, in our view, as a description of citizenship in a classless society.

Marx's concept of abstraction makes it possible to explain why Locke and the classical liberals of the seventeenth and eighteenth centuries could imagine that individuals existed in splendid isolation from one another in a state of nature, while continuing to trade as market partners. The market involves an exchange between individuals that conceals their differing social positions.

Marx's analysis can still be used as a critique of the liberal concept of the citizen, even though the notion of labour as the source of value is contentious. It is clear that how we evaluate goods depends upon the activities of numerous people – managers, workers, supervisors, consumers, entrepreneurs, etc. – and that it would be wrong to suggest that certain categories of people do not contribute to the labour process, and therefore, perhaps, should be 'second-class' citizens. This type of argument simply turns liberalism inside out: it discriminates against the haves in favour of the have-nots, whereas it could be argued that the point is to eliminate the distinction altogether.

Citizenship, Marshall and Social Rights

Liberalism establishes the formal freedom and equality of all members of society itself. Those who have no independent property cannot rest content with legal and political equality but must press on for social equality as well. The Chartists, although campaigners in the nineteenth century for political rights, were fond of saying that the vote is a knife and fork question: the demand for citizenship must be a demand for resources that make individuality not simply a condition to be protected, but a reality to be attained. J.S. Mill presents a developmental view of human nature when he argues that women and workers could become 'individuals'. T.H. Green and Hobhouse, as social liberals, argue the case for more security for workers.

Marshall (1893–1981), a British sociologist, wrote a much-cited essay on *Citizenship and Social Class* in 1950. He presents a classic argument that civil and political rights do not, on their own, create a meaningful citizenship. Social rights are also crucial. For Marshall, 'taming market forces was an essential precondition for a just society' (Marshall and Bottomore, 1992: vi). Marshall is concerned, despite the inadequacies of an argument that have been extensively commented upon, to try and give white male workers a human rather than a purely market identity. He cites with approval the nineteenth-century economist Alfred Marshall's notion of a 'gentleman' in contrast to a mere 'producing machine' (5) and he uses the terms civilisation and citizenship to denote people who are, he argues, 'full members of society' (6). As T.H. (not Alfred!) Marshall sees things, the right to property, as with the right of free speech, is undermined for the poor by a lack of social rights (21).

It is true that Marshall does not see himself as a critic of capitalism. His concern is to make a case for a basic human equality that is not inconsistent with the inequalities that distinguish the various economic levels in a capitalist society, and he even argues that citizenship has become the architect of legitimate social inequality (6–7). But the point is that he does perceive citizenship in tension with capitalism. In a famous passage he sees capitalism and citizenship at war, although (as Bottomore tartly comments), Marshall does not develop this argument (18; 56). It is important not to overlook the extent to which his new liberal reformism unwittingly challenges a class-divided society.

Ch 5: Democracy, pp. 102–24

As a social liberal, Marshall believes that a pragmatic compromise between capitalism and citizenship is possible, even though he can argue that the attitude of mind which inspired reforms such as legal aid grew out of a conception of equality that oversteps the narrow limits of a competitive market economy. Underlying the concept of social welfare is the conception of equal social worth and not merely equal natural rights (24). He notes – as part of his critique - early liberal arguments against universal male suffrage. The political rights of citizenship, unlike civil rights, are a potential danger to the capitalist system, although those cautiously extending them did not realise how great the danger was (1992: 25).

Citizenship has imposed modifications upon the capitalist class system on the grounds that the obligations of contract are brushed aside by an appeal to the rights of citizenship (40–42). In place of the incentive to personal gain is the incentive of public duty – an incentive that corresponds to social rights. Marshall believes that both incentives can be served – capitalism can be reconciled to citizenship since these paradoxes are inherent in our contemporary social system (43).

The preservation of economic inequalities has been made more difficult, Marshall concedes, by the expansion of the status of citizenship. To concede that individuals are citizens is to invite them to challenge the need for class divisions. The great strength of Marshall's argument is that he depicts the drive for social equality as a process that has been taking place for some 250 years (1992: 7). He opens up the prospect of the need to continue progress, given the fact that he later concedes that at the end of the 1970s the welfare state was in a precarious and battered condition (71).

It is certainly true that Marshall ignores the position of women and ethnic minorities, the sectarianism in Northern Ireland, and the peculiar conditions in the immediate post-war period that made a new liberal compromise seem plausible – to conservatives as well as to many social democrats. There were, as Bottomore has noted (58), exceptionally high rates of economic growth, and the deterrent example of the Communist Party states, the self-styled 'real socialism'. Marshall treats capitalism in terms of the income of the rich, rather than the property they own. But our point is that Marshall demonstrates that a concern with the social rights of the citizen challenges the class structure of a capitalist society.

Biography	**Thomas Humphrey Marshall (1893–1981)**

Marshall taught at the London School of Economics from 1925 until his retirement in 1956.

He was originally an economic historian. When he joined the LSE in 1925 it was as an assistant lecturer in social work. He moved to the sociology department in 1929, receiving a readership the following year.

Marshall played a key role in launching the *British Journal of Sociology* in 1949. He edited publications such as *Class Conflict and Social Stratification* and *The Population Problem* in 1938, and this activity played a crucial part in providing the foundations for social class and population studies at the LSE after the war.

He served in the Foreign Office during the war. In 1944 he was appointed Professor of Social Institutions and headed the social science department. From 1949 to 1950 he served as the educational adviser to the British High Commission in Germany, and was appointed Martin White Professor of Sociology in 1954. From 1956 to 1960 he was the director of the social sciences department of UNESCO.

Marshall perceived society as a social system of interrelated activities that allowed the individual free choice. He saw sociology as a discipline to be applied practically – hence his work in social policy and administration, planning, education and equality. He contributed to the development of social policy and administration through research stretching from social policy and the nature of citizenship to social welfare placed within the broader sociological context.

In 1950 he published *Citizenship and Social Class*, a key text in both British sociology and the study of citizenship. His *Social Policy in the Twentieth Century* (1965) provides a clear analysis of the development of welfare policy from 1890 and he argued for the compatibility of modified capitalist enterprise and collectivist social policies, postulating that a free economic market contributed to the enhancement and creation of welfare.

Marshall continued to write after his retirement. Other publications include *Class, Citizenship, and Social Development* (1964) and *The Right to Welfare* (1981).

Citizenship and the New Right

The expansion of social rights, it has been frequently noted, was checked in the mid-1970s, as the capitalist market economy became dominant over the welfare state (Marshall and Bottomore, 1992: 73). New Right or neo-liberal thought seeks to defend individualism and the market against what it sees as menacing inroads created by a post-war consensus around reform. The New Right project, which lasted until the 1990s, is indirectly related to the image of a citizen as a successful entrepreneur who benefits from 'free' market forces.

Ch 4: Justice, pp. 80–101

The argument is that the concept of society is a dangerous abstraction – there are only individuals – but although neo-liberals appear to return to the classical liberal position, gone is the assumption that humans are free and equal individuals. Free, yes, but equal, no. Individuals radically differ according to ability, effort and incentives and, therefore, it is a myth to imagine that they are in any sense equal. New Rightists argue that any attempt to implement distributive or social justice can only undermine the unfettered choices of the free market. 'Nothing', Hayek argues, 'is more damaging to the demand for equal treatment than to base it on so obviously untrue an assumption as that of the factual equality of all men' (1960: 86; see also Heater, 1999: 27). Equality before the law and material equality are seen to be in conflict, and Hayek is in the curious philosophical position of arguing for an 'ideal' or 'moral' equality while denying that any basis for this equality exists in reality.

Both Hayek and Nozick, despite their differences in many theoretical respects, agree that intervention in the market in the name of social justice is anathema. Both link citizenship to inequality. New Right thinkers, in trying to 'roll back the state', seek to confine it to its so-called negative activities – the protection of contracts. Not surprisingly, New Right policies under Thatcher in Britain radically increased the role of the state (in its traditional law and order functions), since weakening the trade unions, cutting welfare benefits and utilising high unemployment as a way of punishing the poor and the protesters involved a radical concentration of state power. Both Thatcher and Hayek share an admiration for General Pinochet, who demonstrated in Chile that enhancing the power of the market may be bad for democracy!

Gray speaks of Hayek 'purifying' classical liberalism of its errors of abstract individualism and rationalism (Faulks, 1998: 61). It could be argued that the New Right supports the weaknesses of classical liberalism without its conceptual strengths. Faulks challenges the argument that the pressure against social rights takes the form of a reassertion of civil rights, since, in practice, Faulks argues that civil rights without social rights are hollow and extremely partial. What is the point of allowing freedom of speech without the provision of education that develops linguistic capacity, or freedom under the law in a system which denies most of the population the resources to secure legal representation?

The notion of freedom as power or capacity is seen by Hayek as 'ominous' and dangerous (1960: 16–17). Hayek supports what he sees as purely negative freedom, but the truth is that negative without positive freedom is an impossible abstraction and a distinction that is alien to the classical liberal tradition. Classical liberal thinkers assumed that (certain) individuals had the capacity to act: what they needed was the right to do so. But Hayek divorces freedom from capacity, and contends that since to be free can involve freedom to be miserable, to be free may mean freedom to starve (1960: 18). No wonder traditional conservatives such as Ian Gilmour see these views as doctrinaire and utopian (1978: 117), and it is revealing that in *The Downing Street Years* Thatcher discusses socialism and 'High Toryism' in the same breath (Faulks, 1998: 79).

The New Right unwittingly demonstrates the indivisibility of rights. Hayek is far from enthusiastic about the exercise of political rights since the mass of the population might be tempted to use their political rights to secure the kind of capacities and power that the free market denies them. In practice, Hayek is an elitist and, as Faulks comments, his version of liberalism is difficult to distinguish from authoritarian **conservatism**. Conflict of a violent kind is simply increased by the creation of vast inequalities, and insofar as the modern United States approximates to the neo-liberal view of citizenship, it is not surprising that this is a society that marginalises its inner city areas and is afflicted by high rates of drug abuse and organised crime (71–2). A Hobbesian Leviathan state, aggravated by the hysteria that has followed the dreadful events of 11 September 2001, reveals the free market as a Hobbesian state of nature without the equality.

Thatcher argues, as Faulks has recalled, that many people fail in society because they are unworthy. 'With such a view, Thatcherism carried to its logical conclusion the abstract and elitist logic of the individualism in neo-liberal political theory' (86). She makes a distinction between *active* and *passive* citizens, and although the coexistence of the free market and strong state seems paradoxical, in fact, as Gilmour has commented, the establishment of a free market state is a 'dictatorial venture' that demands the submission of dissenting institutions and individuals (Faulks, 1998: 89; Gray, 1999: 26).

It would be wrong, however, to see the New Right in purely negative terms. Those who subscribed to New Right ideas sought to free 'individuals' from dependency upon others and often employed sophisticated theories to demonstrate their arguments. The New Right emphasised what is surely an essential ingredient

How to read:

Marshall's *Citizenship and Social Class*

This book usually comes with other essays. These essays are, of course, of interest, but for the purposes of this chapter they can be ignored. Concentrate on *Citizenship and Social Class*: it is a relatively short work. Skim read about half of section 1 until you reach the last couple of pages and then read carefully. Section 2 is important because here Marshall sets out what he considers to be the history of citizenship (at least in Britain) and he deals with the development of civil rights and the problem (as in the Poor Law) when they are divorced from social rights. Section 3 also deserves a careful read since it relates to the extension of political rights. Marshall clears the way for his most important argument noting (in the nineteenth century) the growing interest in the principles of equality and social justice. Section 4 is the most crucial part of his argument, entitled 'Social Rights in the Twentieth Century' and should be read (if necessary, re-read) with great care. Don't worry about the figures from the 1940s – concentrate on the wider points he is making. The 'conclusions' also deserve a read since it is a useful summing up of his argument as a whole.

in citizenship: the need to be independent and think critically for oneself. The challenge is to extend this notion to all inhabitants in society so that the skills of enterprise can be enjoyed widely.

Citizenship and the Case for a Basic Income

As long as social rights are seen as special entitlements for those who have 'failed' they will always be divisive, and reaffirm rather than undermine class differences.

In her assessment of the welfare state, Pateman makes the case for a guaranteed income for everyone (Hoffman, 1995: 205), and the value of this proposal as a citizens' or basic income is that it would be universal. This proposal is also made by New Rightists, who speak of the need for a 'negative income tax'. All would receive this income, regardless of employment status. As Faulks points out (2000: 120), it could decommodify social rights (i.e. take them away from the market), and break with the argument that those who lack capital must work for others. A guaranteed basic income would give people a real choice as to how and in what way they wanted to work, and empower citizens as a whole.

It would enable people to think much more about the 'quality of life' and the ecological consequences of material production. It would enhance a sense of community and individual autonomy, and underpin the social and communal character of wealth creation (Faulks, 2000: 120). It is not difficult to see how a basic income would also dramatically improve the position of women, whose precarious economic position makes them particularly dependent upon men or patriarchal-minded partners. It is true that were this idea taken in abstraction from other policies concerned with reducing inequality (as in the development of a democratic policy for ethnic minorities and movements towards genuinely universal education), then it could be divisive, tying women to domestic duties, and leaving the capitalist labour contract unreformed. But as Faulks comments, 'no one policy can address all possible inequalities' (120).

People seek to work outside the home for social reasons (and not simply economic ones), and a guaranteed income would give people time and resources to be more involved in community-enhancing activities such as lifelong learning, voluntary work and political participation. The argument that universal benefits undermine personal responsibility (Saunders, 1995: 92) seems to us precisely wrong since the assumption that people will only act sensibly if they are threatened with destitution and poverty reflects an elitist disregard for how people actually think.

But what of the cost? Surely a citizens' income is not economically feasible, given the argument that the rich will not tolerate paying higher levels of taxation? The idea of a guaranteed income appears to be a non-starter. There are a number of counter-arguments that should be put:

- A guaranteed income would markedly simplify the difficult and complex tax and benefit system: significant savings could be made here.
- People will pay for universal benefits if they are convinced of the need for them. The widespread support for, say, the British National Health Service as a

provider of universal benefits shows that increasing taxation is much more palatable if people are convinced that it is linked to changes which will really improve their lives. Adair Turner lists some of the collective goods – subsidised public transport, traffic-calming measures, noise abatement baffles and tree screens to make our motorways less intrusive – which he would prefer to (for example) a bigger and more stylish car. 'I would rather pay more tax to get those benefits than have the extra, personal income available to buy more market goods' (2002: 125).

- A guaranteed income is in the interests of all. A basic income would (along with many other egalitarian measures) help to reduce crime and the consumption of drugs, and make society as a whole a more secure and safer place. Would not the rich benefit from such a measure? Capitalism's beneficiaries, Adair Turner argues, should support investment in measures that promote social cohesion, out of their own self-interest (2002: 244). Gray argues that British public opinion wishes to see some goods – basic medical care, schooling, protection from crime – provided to all as a mark of citizenship (1999: 34). Is it not possible that given the right leadership and explanation, this could extend to the kind of economic security provided by a citizens' income?

Of course, it could be argued that a basic income will destroy incentives, just as it was said that a minimum wage would create unemployment, and in the nineteenth century it was contended that a ten-hour day would undermine the labour process. But a government committed to such a dramatic victory of 'the political economy of the working class' (in Marx's celebrated phrase) could find ways of presenting the case for a guaranteed income that would isolate diehard reactionaries.

It is important to stress that while a basic income would do much to increase the quality of citizenship, it would still leave open the question of including people from other countries in a global citizenship. Such an innovation would initially be limited to people of a particular community (Faulks, 2000: 123). It would only really succeed if it was part and parcel of policies that addressed the problem of inequalities between societies.

Citizenship and Women

Are women citizens in modern liberal states? Although women have been citizens in a formal sense in Britain, for example, since 1928 (when they received the vote), there are important senses in which women have yet to obtain real citizenship.

Women, even in developed liberal societies such as Britain, are significantly underrepresented in decision making, and this occurs because of structural and attitudinal factors. The exclusion of women from political processes has been justified by a liberal conception of a public/private divide.

It is true that with Wollstonecraft's *Vindication of the Rights of Woman* (1792), the Enlightenment concepts of freedom and autonomy are extended to women. At the same time Wollstonecraft does not (explicitly at any rate) challenge the division of labour between the sexes or the argument for a male-only franchise. Women, she contends, if they are recognised as rational and autonomous beings, become better wives, mothers and domestic workers as a result – 'in a word, better citizens' (Bryson, 1992: 22–7). Here the term does not imply someone with voting rights, although it does suggest that the citizen is an individual whose activity is both public and private in character. Of course, when Wollstonecraft was writing most men could not vote, and there is some evidence to suggest that Wollstonecraft was in favour of female suffrage, but felt that it was not a demand worth raising at the time she wrote.

Bryson has noted that women find it more difficult to have their voices heard, their priorities acknowledged and their interests met (1994: 16). A recent report documents in detail the underrepresentation of women in all major sectors of decision making in Britain, from Parliament, the Civil Service, the judiciary, the legal profession, the police, local government, health, higher education, the media, public appointments and the corporate sector. For example, the United Kingdom was the fourth lowest in terms of the representation of women in the European Parliament at 24 per cent in 2000; it does better in a relative sense (in 1997) in terms of representation in national parliaments, where it had 18 compared to Denmark's 33 per cent. Only 4.3 per cent of life peers in the House of Lords were women in 2000, while in the most senior grades of the Civil Service 17.2 per cent were women in 1999. Of the High Court Judges in 1999 9 per cent were women, although this is three times as many as women who were Lord Justices! There were 6.4 per cent of chief constables who were women in 2000; 10 years previously there were none (Ross, 2000).

It is true that the representation of women is complex, and it does not follow that women representatives automatically and necessarily represent the interests of women in general. But there is clearly something wrong, as Voet acknowledges, with political institutions that dramatically underrepresent women (1998: 106–8). Citizenship requires both the right and the capacity to participate in political decision making. The real difficulty of women's citizenship is 'the low level of female participation in social and political decision-making' (Voet, 1998: 124; 132).

The public/private divide, as formulated in liberal theory, prevents women from becoming meaningful citizens. It undermines the confidence of women; prejudices men (and some women) against them; puts pressures on leisure time; trivialises and demonises those women who enter public life; and through a host of discriminatory practices that range from the crudely explicit to the subtly implicit, prevents women from taking leadership roles. Women members of the British Parliament still complain that their dress or physical appearance is commented upon in the media, although it would be unthinkable to do the same for men.

It is true that the public/private divide as it operates as a barrier to citizenship is only implicit in liberal societies today. Whereas ancient (by which we mean slave-owning) societies and medieval societies explicitly divided the activities between men and women, under liberalism the public/private divide focuses on the relationship between individuals and the state.

Yuval-Davis (1997) has argued that we should abandon the public/private distinction altogether – a position Voet challenges (1998: 141). It is both possible and necessary to reconstruct the concept of the public and the private so that it ceases to be patriarchal in character. Liberal theory sees freedom, in Crick's words, as 'the privacy of private men from public action' (1982: 18). As Crick's comment (and his revealing use of language) suggests, this is a freedom that extends only to males, since (as MacKinnon puts it) 'men's realm of private freedom is women's realm of collective subordination' (1989: 168). Citizenship requires participation in public arenas. Domestic arrangements are crucial that allow women to be both childbearers (should they wish), and workers outside the home, representatives at local, national and international level, and leaders in bodies that are outside the domestic sphere. This is not to say that women (as with people in general) should not cherish privacy, but the public/private concept needs to be reconstructed (as we have suggested above) so that it empowers rather than degrades and diminishes women.

Women cannot be citizens unless they are treated as equal to men, and by equality we mean not merely sameness but an acknowledgement (indeed a celebration) of difference, not only between women and men but among women themselves.

The involvement of women in contemporary liberal societies as members of the armed and police forces is a necessary condition for women's citizenship because it helps to demystify the argument that only men can bear arms and fight for their country. Deeply embedded in traditionalist notions of citizenship is the idea that only those who go to war for their country can be citizens. It is worth noting, however, that armies in liberal societies will increasingly be used for peacekeeping and even development purposes, so that the notion of soldiers bearing arms is likely to become more and more redundant anyway. But being conscious of the link between patriarchy and war involves rather more than 'opening' up armies to women. It involves a recognition of the link between male domination and violence. Citizenship requires security – not simply in the sense of protection against violence – but in the sense of having the confidence, the capacity and the skills to participate in decision making. What Tickner calls a people-centred notion of security (1995: 192) identifies security as a concept that transcends state boundaries so that people feel at home in their locality, their nation and in the world at large.

It can be argued that the traditional caring role of many women brings an important dimension to citizenship itself. The notion that feminist conceptions of citizenship should be 'thick' (i.e. local and domestic) rather than 'thin' (i.e. public and universalist) rests upon a dichotomy which needs to be overcome. This is why the debate between 'liberals' and 'republicans' is, in our view, an unhelpful one for women (as it is for people in general). Both liberalism and republicanism presuppose that politics is a 'public' activity that rises above social life. Liberals argue for a negative view of the individual who is encouraged to leave public life to the politicians, while republicans stress the need to participate, but both premise their positions on a public/private divide that is patriarchal in essence.

Bubeck (1995: 6) instances Conservative proposals in Britain to extend the notion of good citizenship to participation in voluntary care, protection schemes or neighbourhood policing. These are useful ways of enriching citizen practices for both women and men. But what is problematic is a notion of political participation that ignores the social constraints which traditionally have favoured men and disadvantaged women. The fact that the obligation to care for children and the elderly has fallen upon women as a domestic duty does not make it non-political and private. Bubeck speaks of the existence of 'a general citizen's duty to care'

(1995: 29) and, as she puts it later, the performance of this care needs to be seen as part of what it means, or it implies, to be a member of a political community (1995: 31).

Care should be transformed from what Bubeck calls a 'handicap' of women to a general requirement for all (1992: 34). Providing care should be seen to be as much of an obligation as fighting in a war (1995: 35). But whereas fighting in a war implies a sharp and lethal division between friends and enemies, the provision of care seeks to heal such divisions. The notion of 'conscription' into service that could either exist alongside or be an alternative to the army is an attractive one. A caring service of some kind has an important role to play in developing a citizenship that combats patriarchy and recognises the position of women.

Ch 7: Difference, pp. 156–72

However, we cannot accept Pateman's argument that citizenship itself is a patriarchal category, although it is perfectly true that citizenship traditionally has been constructed in a masculinist image (Mouffe, 1992: 374). Men are different from women, and some women are different from others. Respecting difference is an important part of extending citizenship, so that Mouffe puts the matter in a misleading way when she argues that sexual difference is not a 'pertinent distinction' to a theory of citizenship (1992: 377). Biological differences remain 'relevant' to citizenship even if these should not be used as a justification for discrimination. Differences between men and women no more exclude the latter from citizenship than differences between men can justify exclusion. But it does not follow that these differences cease to be 'pertinent'. We should not, in other words, throw the baby out with the bathwater. One-sided points need to be incorporated – not simply cast aside. Differences between men and women remain relevant but they do not justify restricting citizenship – with all this implies – to either gender.

Global Citizenship

Is citizenship limited to the membership of a particular nation? Writers such as Aron (cited by Heater, 1999: 150) have declared that 'there are no such animals as "European citizens". There are only French, German or Italian citizens'. In this view, citizenship involves the membership of a national or domestic state.

Cosmopolitans argue, however, that the assertion of rights and responsibilities at the global level in no way contradicts loyalties at a regional, national and local level. People, in whatever area of government they are involved, must be respected and empowered, whether they are neighbours in the same block, people of their own nation and region, or members of the other countries in distant parts of the world. One of the most positive features of globalisation is that people meet others of different ethnic and cultural origin and outlook, not only when they travel abroad, but even at the local level. The media (at its best) presents people suffering and developing in other parts of the world as though they were neighbours, so that it becomes increasingly possible to imagine what it is like to be the other. Modern conditions have contributed much to realise Kant's argument that 'a violation of rights in *one* part of the world is felt *everywhere*' (cited by Heater, 1999: 140).

Lister links the notion of 'global citizenship' with a 'multi-layered conception' of citizenship itself (1997: 196), with states acknowledging the importance of human rights and international law. Each layer, if it is democratically constructed, strengthens the other. Global citizenship – a respect for others, a concern for their well-being and a belief that the security of each person depends upon the security of everyone else – does not operate in contradiction with regional, national and local identities. People can see themselves as Glaswegian, Scottish, British and European. Why do they have to make a choice? As Lister puts it, either/or choices lead us into a theoretical and political cul-de-sac (1997: 197). Heater argues that the 'singular concept' of citizenship has burst its bounds (1999: 117) and it is true that dual citizenship (which already exists in some states) represents a much more relaxed view of the question so that a person can exercise state-centred citizenship rights in more than one country. Heater presses the case for a fluid and flexible notion of citizenship, stating that membership of a voluntary association in civil society can qualify a person for citizenship, so that we can legitimately speak of a person as the citizen of a church, a trade union, a club, an environmental group etc. (1999: 121). Heater insists that civil society offers a useful and even superior option to traditional state membership (1999: 121).

It goes without saying that the notion of a world or global citizen cannot prescribe rights and responsibilities with the precision that citizenships set out in written (or indeed unwritten) constitutions can and do. Nor, as Heater shows at some length, is the notion of a world citizen a new one. He gives examples of cosmopolitanism in ancient Greek thought, and quotes the words of the ancient Roman, Marcus Aurelius, that 'where-ever a man lives, he lives as a citizen of the World-City' (1999: 139).

The celebrated Kantian argument for world government is for a loose confederation of states. Heater is sympathetic to the notion of a global citizen, writing that 'a fully-fledged modern world state' might well require 'a transfer of civil allegiance from the state to the universal polity' (1999: 151). He argues that 'political citizenship, so intimately reliant on the possession of the means of force by the state, must remain absorbed in the state as the necessary catalyst for its vitality' (1999: 152). The ideal of cosmopolitan citizenship is the condition in which all human beings have equal recognition as co-legislators within a 'global kingdom of ends' (Linklater, 1999: 56). Soysal even insists that the identity of personhood stressed in human rights discourse takes us beyond both citizenship and the state. Her point is that national and citizenship identities are, in her view, unthinkable without the state (1994: 165).

The Argument So Far . . .

- Citizenship has traditionally been seen as membership of the state.
- This has linked citizenship to *exclusion,* whether of slaves, women or the propertyless.
- The problem of exclusion has been addressed by developing a concept of citizenship that embraces not merely political and legal, but social rights as well. The latter have proved controversial and the New Right has argued that the welfare state creates a 'dependency' that undermines the autonomy of the citizen. The idea of giving all citizens a basic income as of right could, it has been argued, enhance citizenship.

Biography Immanuel Kant (1724–1804)

Born in Königsberg, the capital of East Prussia, the child of poor but devout followers of Lutheran Pietism. Kant's promise was recognised by the Pietist minister Franz Albert Schultz, and he received a free education at the Pietist gymnasium. At 16, Kant entered the University of Königsberg, where he studied mathematics, physics, philosophy, theology and classical Latin literature.

Kant left university in 1746, and his first work was published three years later – *Thoughts on the True Estimation of Living Forces*. Kant then worked as a tutor, serving in households near Königsberg for the next eight years. When he returned to the university in 1755, however, he had several works ready for publication. The first of these was *Universal Natural History and Theory of the Heavens*, a much more successful scientific work than his first. Kant also published two Latin works, which earned him the right to offer lectures at the university as a *Privatdozent* paid directly by his students. The following year Kant published a work on natural philosophy that made him eligible for a salaried professorship, although he was not to receive one until 1770. In these years, Kant also published four essays on earthquakes and winds.

Kant began lecturing in the autumn of 1755. His topics included logic, metaphysics, ethics and physics, and he subsequently added physical geography, anthropology, pedagogy, natural right and even the theory of fortifications. Except for one small essay on optimism (1759), he did not publish again until 1762, when a further four publications earned Kant widespread recognition in Germany. During this period, Kant was deeply struck by the work of Jean-Jacques Rousseau, and he was also acquainted with the philosophy of David Hume.

Kant was appointed Professor of Logic and Metaphysics in Königsberg in 1770. Beginning in 1781, with the first edition of the *Critique of Pure Reason*, Kant unleashed a steady torrent of books. From a politics point of view, the most significant of these include his two essays, 'Idea for a Universal History from a Cosmopolitan Point of View' and 'What is Enlightenment?' in 1784 and *The Groundwork of the Metaphysics of Morals*. In 1793 he wrote the political essay 'On the Common Saying: "That may be right in theory but does not work in practice"', and *Towards Perpetual Peace* appeared in 1795.

Kant retired from lecturing in 1797, at the age of 73, and devoted his remaining years to a work that was to be entitled 'The Transition from the Metaphysical First Principles of Natural Science to Physics', but which was far from complete when Kant ceased working on it in 1803. After a lifetime of hypochondria without any serious illness, Kant gradually lost his eyesight and strength and died in 1804.

- Even in liberal societies where women have acquired political rights, it is arguable that they have been confronted with a number of barriers preventing them from exercising their rights.
- Cosmopolitans argue that citizenship should extend to the world as a whole, so that people are not merely citizens of a particular country, but citizens of the globe.

Citizenship within the European Union

The European Union (EU) is concerned about equalisation and redistributive social policies. Richard Bellamy and Alex Warleigh's edited *Citizenship and Governance in the European Union* (2001) sees the EU and its concept of citizenship as a paradox and a puzzle. Is the Union seeking to establish a new kind of political entity or is it simply another (and larger) version of a state? The EU, this volume argues, has two aspects: one is the market, the other is democracy. Neo-liberals may think of the two as synonymous, but that view is not shared by the contributors to this volume, who point out that citizenship is a political issue that necessarily transcends a market identity.

The argument advanced is that while the current rights of the EU citizen may at present seem somewhat limited, we should be concerned with unanticipated outcomes. Under the provisions of the Maastricht Treaty European citizens have the right to stand and vote in local and European parliamentary elections even if they are not nationals in the states where they reside; they can petition the newly created Ombudsman as well as the European Parliament, and they are entitled to diplomatic protection in third states where one's 'own' state is not represented (2001: 23).

To be sure, the EU was initially conceived as a transnational capitalist society, an economic union that was a free trade area. It could, however, be argued that people such as Jean Monnet had explicitly political objectives right from the start. There is a logic to the EU that extends beyond the purely economic. It may well have been (for example) the *intention* of EU founders to confine sexual equality to the notion of a level playing field constituted by the cost of factors of production, but economic rights require a political and social context to be meaningful. It is the *potential* of EU citizenship that is important. It is this that links a rather passive, state-centred notion to a much more 'active, democratic citizenship' (Bellamy and Warleigh, 2001: 117), a move from a politics of identity – which implies a rather repressive homogeneity – to a politics of affinity that recognises and respects difference.

Citizenship is a 'surprisingly elusive concept' (2001: 143), and the concept is an excellent example of an idea that compels us to think the unthinkable. Indeed, the very notion of citizenship was introduced as an attempt to overcome the 'democratic deficit' – to combat the view that the EU is an alien body and that only nation-states really matter. Undoubtedly there is a 'dualism' at the heart of the concept of EU citizenship. On the one hand, the term is tied to states and markets. On the other hand, the European Court of Justice has interpreted the question of freedom of movement in broad social terms, as a quasi-constitutional entitlement, and not simply as a direct economic imperative. Thus, to take an example, the right to freedom of movement is linked to the right not to be discriminated against by comparison with host-state nationals (2001: 96).

Bellamy and Warleigh (and those who contribute to their volume) acknowledge that current rights of EU citizens are limited, but their point is that once the notion of citizenship is established the anomaly of confining political rights to those who are already citizens of member states, becomes plain. Already, limited rights – like

Biography Jean Monnet (1888–1979)

Born in Cognac, France, Monnet started his professional life as a salesman in his family's cognac business.

During World War I he worked in London in the field of economic cooperation among the Allies and in 1920 was appointed Deputy Secretary-General of the newly established League of Nations. He left the League in 1923 to return to his family business. For the next 15 years he was active in international finance before returning, this time in Washington, to planning economic cooperation between the United Kingdom, France and the United States. It was Monnet who, as France was in retreat before the German advance of June 1940, persuaded Winston Churchill to forward to the French prime minister a draft declaration proclaiming an 'indissoluble union' between France and the United Kingdom.

After the war he was put in charge of the *Commissariat du Plan* responsible for the economic recovery of France. In 1950 he suggested to Robert Schuman, the French foreign minister, the idea of pooling French and German coal and steel production. This led to the establishment of the European Coal and Steel Community (ECSC) with Monnet as the first President of the High Authority (the forerunner of the European Commission).

However, his other great plan of this period, the European Defence Community, came to nothing, and in November 1954 he resigned from the High Authority to devote himself to freelance campaigning on behalf of European unification. He famously commented that national sovereignty was a barrier to peace in Europe, and that 'prosperity and vital social progress will remain elusive until the nations of Europe form a federation'. He was in constant conflict with de Gaulle during the 1960s.

the right to petition the Parliament and refer matters to the Ombudsman – are bestowed on individuals even if they are not members of one of the constituent nation-states, and are therefore not 'citizens'. In Heater's view, the EU is a sophisticated example of a new kind of citizenship: but 'at the moment, to be honest, it is a mere shadow of that potential' (1999: 129).

The European Ombudsman was introduced in 1992 as a result of Spanish enthusiasm for EU citizenship and Danish concern for administrative efficiency. The Ombudsman can deal with a wide range of issues including matters relating to the environment and human rights. Questions of administrative transparency and the use of age limits in employment have been vigorously pursued, and the Ombudsman should not be seen as a 'stand-alone' institution, but one that coexists with courts, tribunals, parliaments and other intermediaries at European, national, regional and local levels.

It is clearly wrong to think that greater rights for European citizens will happen automatically. Those who favour this development will need to struggle for it, arguing that a European identity does not exist in competition with other identities. On the contrary, European institutions have the potential to add to and reinforce national and sub-national governance, although conflict and dialogue exist between these levels.

This requires a movement both upwards and downwards – involving more and more people at every level. The crucial question facing the EU at the moment seems to us to be the status of residents who are currently excluded from EU citizenship. Here, as the Bellamy and Warleigh volume argues, a statist 'nationality' model currently prevails, with ethnic migrants being seen as vulnerable 'subjects' rather than as active and entitled members of the EU. Yet, as is pointed out, Article 25, for example, of the draft Charter of Fundamental Rights does allow residents who are non-citizens to vote and stand for EU elections (Bellamy and Warleigh eds, 2001: 198).

Enlargement of the EU poses another set of challenges. The accession of a state such as Turkey can only broaden the cultural horizons of Europeans, and the problem with Turkey's admission arises around the question of human rights, not because the country is predominantly Muslim in its culture. European citizenship, it could be argued, demonstrates that a citizenship beyond the state is a real possibility.

Does the State Undermine Citizenship?

Citizenship has generally been conceived as membership of the state. Lister comments that 'at its lowest common denominator' we are talking about the relationship 'between individuals and the state' (1997: 3). Voet likewise takes it for granted that citizenship is tied to the state (1998: 9). Oomen argues that the term is meaningless unless it is anchored to the state, so that notions of 'global' or 'world' citizenship cannot be authentic until we have a world or global state. Thus European Union citizenship, he insists, will only become a possibility when the union becomes a multinational federal state (1997: 224). Although Carter is critical of those who reject cosmopolitanism, she takes it for granted that global citizenship requires a global state (2001: 168). Marcus Aurelius is cited by Heater as saying that we are all members of a 'common State' and presenting the 'Universe' as if 'it were a State' (1999: 135).

Yet the case for assuming that being a citizen is only possible if one is a member of a state is contestable. There is, for example, considerable unease among feminist scholars about presenting citizenship as membership of the state. Virginia Held argues that the notion that the state has a monopoly on the legitimate use of force is incompatible with a feminist view as to how society should be organised (1993: 221). Jones sees the nation-state 'as an out-moded political form' (1990: 789) and speaks of the need for a women-friendly polity.

But the question of the state needs to be addressed explicitly. It is not enough to speak, as David Held does, of limiting drastically the influence of the state and market (1995: 224). There has to be a plausible way of looking beyond both institutions, so that an emancipated society becomes possible. It could be argued that the state is actually a barrier to the notion of citizenship, defined here as a set of entitlements which include *everyone*.

Rowan Williams, the Archbishop of Canterbury, delivered a Dimbleby lecture on 19 December 2002, in which he argues – and this was the aspect of his lecture headlined in *The Times* (27 December 2002) – that 'we are witnessing the end of the nation state' (2002: 1). He takes the view that we need to do some hard thinking about what these changes mean for being a citizen. These changes are, he argues, 'irreversible' (2002: 2). Williams's contention is that the nation-state is in decline and is giving way to something he calls the 'market state'. Although he is critical of the latter, he shies away from the argument that the state itself – in all its forms – is the problem.

The notion of citizenship needs to be separated from the state. As we pointed out in Chapter 1, the state is an institution that claims a monopoly of legitimate force for a particular territory: it is a contradictory institution which claims a monopoly it does not and cannot have. This is true both of its claim to have a monopoly of force and a monopoly of legitimacy. This critique of the state challenges the standard view of citizenship as denoting membership of a state. For how can one be a citizen when laws are passed and functionaries exist to manage an institution that is underpinned by, and claims to exercise a monopoly of legitimate force? Even when force is authorised, it still prevents the recipient of this force from exercising rights and duties that are crucial to citizenship, and it means that those against whom such force is not directly exercised live in its shadow. They know that the laws they obey can be 'enforced', so that the absence of fear which is central to citizenship cannot be proven to exist in a society that centres around the state.

It is the role of the state to impose solutions by force when faced with divisions and conflicts of interest that cannot be tackled through arbitration and negotiation. A person who is not free is not a citizen. It may be objected that the state does not simply use force, but claims – in the celebrated definition that is central to our analysis – a monopoly of *legitimate* force. But this is not a convincing argument since legitimacy implies limits, whereas force cannot be limited (however hard authorities might try). Legitimate force is thus a contradiction in terms, and the state, therefore, is an institution that seeks to achieve the impossible. Williams argues that the state can no longer protect citizens, given the existence of intercontinental missile technology (2002: 2), but the state's mechanism for protecting 'its' subjects has always been contradictory and paradoxical.

The Problem of Class

Williams argues that the 'market state' is 'here to stay' (2002: 5), but the nation-state itself has been a 'market state' as long as capitalism and the market have been around. For these systems create divisions of interests that make the interventions of the state necessary.

Hence an inclusive citizenship has to chart a path beyond both the state and capitalism. Class divisions are, however, more complex than classical Marxism has assumed, even though inequality is crucial to the existence of the state since the challenge to the monopoly of the state comes from those who either have too much or too little. Because interests radically conflict, force is necessary to try and sort them out. This is the link between class and the state, and both act as barriers to an inclusive citizenship. Although Marx argues that people are not simply 'individuals' but members of a class, workers also have a gender and national identity, etc., and this materially affects how they relate to others. It is not that the class identity is unimportant: it is merely that it fuses with other identities since these other identities are also a crucial part of the process that organises individuals into a class. If blacks or Catholic Irish in Northern Ireland or northerners in Britain are more likely to be unemployed, their negatively perceived social identity is an integral part of their class status.

It could be argued that membership of a class is a barrier to citizenship. Working-class people often feel that they should not stand for Parliament or take part in politics since they lack the confidence, linguistic skills and education to make decisions. Upper-class people may take it for granted that they and their offspring are 'natural' rulers, and in this way display an insensitivity and lack of understanding of the less well off. Whether class expresses itself in gender or national terms, regional or sexual terms, etc., a society that does not recognise difference in a positive way is a society with a restricted citizenship. By difference, we do not mean division. Divisions prevent people from 'changing places' and having common interests. Common interests make it possible to resolve conflicts in a way that relies upon arbitration, negotiation and compromise, and avoids violence. But how is it possible to overcome class division and capitalism? Marx argues that every historically developed social form is 'in fluid movement' – it has a transient nature (1970: 20). In the third volume of *Capital*, Marx refers to capitalism as a 'self-dissolving contradiction' (1966: 437) in which each step forward is also a step beyond.

The struggle by women to achieve respect and autonomy, the demands by blacks that they should be treated as people and not as a despised racial category, and the insistence by gays that they should be recognised as a legitimate group in society, etc. is as much a blow against the 'free market' as traditional trade union demands for a fairer share of profits. For each time a challenge is successful, the concrete human identities of supposedly abstract individuals is affirmed, and with this challenge the propensity of the market to deal with real people as abstractions is overcome.

Marx is torn between a view of revolution simply as change, and a notion, derived from the 'model' of the French Revolution, of revolution as a dramatic single event. Reforms have a revolutionary significance, and underpin the character of capitalism as 'a self-dissolving contradiction'. Yet it is central both to the dialectical logic of Marx's analysis and to some of his explicit statements that capitalism can be gradually transformed so that, increasingly, a society develops in which freedom and individuality become more and more meaningful.

Citizenship can only develop at the expense of capitalism. Bryan Turner argues that while capitalism promotes early notions of citizenship, it also generates massive inequalities that prevent the achievement of citizenship. He sees a conflict between the redistributive character of citizenship rights and the profit motive of the free market (1986: 38; 24). It is true that he assumes that citizenship should be defined as membership of a state, and he takes a rather abstract view of class which means, as noted above, that he juxtaposes class to gender, ethnicity, etc. in a somewhat mechanistic fashion. Nevertheless, he regards the welfare state as a site of struggle, and he stresses over and over again the contradictory character of capitalism and its fraught relationship with citizenship.

Citizenship, he says, develops as a series of circles or waves (1986: 93). It is radical and socially disruptive, moving through a number of expanding processes, so that social membership becomes increasingly universalistic and open-ended.

Citizenship exists (as he puts it pithily) despite rather than because of capitalist growth (1986: 135; 141). The point is that the argument that citizenship requires a transformation of capitalism can be posed without having to make the case for a dramatic one-off revolution.

A number of 'issues papers' put out by the British Department for International Development point to the fact that the private sector can and must change. Indeed, the argument implies that to speak of capitalist companies simply as 'private' is itself problematic: the largest of these companies can – and need to – be pressurised further along a public road so that they operate according to social and ethical criteria. The reputation and image of companies with prominent interests abroad are tarnished by adverse publicity around issues such as the pollution of the environment, the use of child labour, and the support for regimes that have poor human rights records. Companies should join organisations such as the Ethical Training Initiative (DFID, 2002: 6). It is revealing that some companies speak of a corporate citizenship which shows awareness that production and sales are social processes with political implications. The link between profit and support for ethically acceptable social practices demonstrates that capitalism can be transformed by a whole series of 'victories for the political economy of the working class' – an ongoing process which, arguably, is still in its relatively early stages.

There are no short cuts to the transformation of capitalism. Where the market cannot provide universal service 'autonomously', as it were, it needs to be regulated – and it is through regulation that capitalism is transformed. Adair Turner establishes this interventionist logic when he argues that where market liberalisation (i.e. making people conform to capitalist norms) conflicts with desirable social objectives, 'we should not be afraid to make exceptions' (2002: 174). If citizens desire an efficient and integrated transport service, then this is an objective that must be governmentally provided if the market cannot deliver. Perhaps the exceptions are rather more prolific than Adair Turner – an advocate of socially responsible capitalism – imagines, but it is only through demonstrating that the market cannot deliver that it is possible to transcend the market. Adair Turner is right to argue that the demand for a cleaner environment, safer workplaces, safe food, and the right to be treated with respect in the workplace whatever one's personal characteristics, are just as much 'consumer demands' as the desire for more washing machines, internet usage or more restaurant meals (2002: 187).

Where the market cannot meet these kind of consumer demands, regulation is necessary. The need for public interventions is, Turner argues, increasing as well as changing. This intervention is more explicit in the provision of services that deliver equality of citizenship (2002: 238). Who can disagree with Turner's proposition that we cannot intervene too strongly against inequality in the labour market (2002: 240)? Indeed, for Turner, the key message of 11 September 2001 is the primacy of politics – the need to offset the insecurities and inequalities that capitalism undoubtedly creates (2002: 383). Here, in a nutshell, is the case for transformation.

Transcending the market means that the objectives of the market – freedom of choice, efficiency in delivery – can only be met through regulation and controls. It is not a question of suppressing or rejecting the market but seeking to realise its objectives through invoking standards 'foreign to commodity production'. Adair

Exercise

Imagine that there are five people in a room. One is a well-to-do male financier, the second a female academic, the third a female cleaner, the fourth a male Albanian asylum seeker, and the fifth an unemployed Somalian woman who is an 'illegal' refugee.

The first obviously regards himself as a citizen: he not only votes but dines frequently with cabinet ministers and the permanent secretaries of the Civil Service. The second has useful contacts with the legislature where she is researching into the question of women MPs. The third only occasionally votes but has a passport and travels to Spain for her holidays. The fourth is currently in receipt of modest benefits while his application for asylum is being looked into, while the fifth lives in constant fear that her status will be uncovered and she will be deported.

They are all human beings:

- In what sense can they all be regarded as citizens?

- What kind of programmes can be introduced to help persons four and five?

- What kind of policies will 'encourage' the first person to use his influence to help others?

- Can the second person do more to help? Is the third person really a citizen if she ignores the plight of the less fortunate?

Turner argues that demands for public intervention are going to rise as our markets become freer (2002: 191). Freedom of the market can only be justified when it meets human need: this is the radical difference between suppressing the market and going beyond it.

We are arguing that because markets abstract from differences, at some point they will need to be transcended – but only at the point at which it is clear that they cannot deliver the objectives that a society of citizens requires. Turner takes the view that the market economy has the potential to 'serve the full range of human aspirations' (2002: 290), but he himself acknowledges market failures (as he calls them) in transport policies where there is a bias in favour of mobility and combating environmental degradation (2002: 300). It is these failures that make the case for transformation.

Citizenship as a Relational Concept

Why can some not be citizens while others are subject to force? This argument can only be met if we adopt a 'relational' approach that means that we can only know who we are when we know the position of others. When these others are deprived of their freedom we have no freedom either. Although force particularly harms those who are targeted, the perpetrators of force also lose their autonomy, so that unless everyone is a citizen, then no one is a citizen.

It could be argued that the 'market state', as Williams describes it (2002: 7), promotes an **atomistic** attitude by which we mean an attitude that denies that individuals must be seen in relationship to one another. For example, the critique

Citizenship as a Momentum Concept

Momentum concepts are those that are infinitely progressive and egalitarian: they have no stopping point and cannot be 'realised'. **Static concepts**, by way of contrast, are repressively hierarchical and divisive. The latter must be discarded whereas the former have an historical dynamic that means they must be built upon and continuously transcended. The state, patriarchy and violence are examples of static concepts; freedom, autonomy, individuality, citizenship and emancipation are examples of momentum concepts. De Tocqueville famously formulated democracy as a momentum concept – a concept that has no stopping point. However, his account is marred by static features, such as a traditional notion of God and a fatalist view of 'destiny'. Momentum concepts, as we formulate them, seek to avoid this inconsistency by being infinite in their egalitarian scope. It is crucial to avoid the kind of scepticism and relativism that makes it impossible to identify progress at all.

Citizenship is a momentum concept in three ways:

1. The struggle for citizenship can be developed even by those who seek only limited steps forward and are oblivious of a more wide-ranging agenda.
2. Citizenship involves a process of change that is both revolutionary and evolutionary – it is important we do not privilege one over the other.
3. Citizenship is an ongoing struggle with no stopping point.

It is not that the ends of an inclusive citizenship are not important: it is rather that achieving one element of inclusion (for example the enfranchisement of women) enables us to move to the next (for example the unfair allocation of tasks in the home). People do need to have the right to vote, speak freely and stand for election: but they also need to think about those whose conduct makes it necessary to put them in prison. This is why the case for an inclusive citizenship makes it essential that we look beyond the state.

of patriarchy can be called relational because it argues that men cannot be free while women are subordinated. It is true that in a patriarchal society men enjoy privileges which make them 'victors', but patriarchy oppresses *everyone* (albeit in different ways). Men have begun to realise that patriarchy not only strips them of involvement in childrearing, but subjects them in particular to the violence of war. The idea that our 'right' to exploit or be violent has to be curbed is a problematic use of the term right, since ultimately being exploitative or violent not only harms others, but it also ultimately harms the perpetrator himself. No one, it could be argued, can have a right to harm themselves.

A dramatically unequal world is a world in which large numbers of people will move out of poorer countries in search of a 'better' life. It is in the interest of the 'haves' that they pay attention and work to rectify the deprivations of the 'have nots'. This is what is meant by a relational view of citizenship. Unless everyone is a citizen, then no one is a citizen. It could be argued that if we want to work towards a more inclusive view of citizenship we need to isolate those who are staunchly opposed to extending citizenship whether on misogynist (i.e. anti-female), racist, nationalist grounds or because they are so privileged that they cannot identify with others. The well-being of each depends upon the well-being of all.

Ch 7:
Difference,
pp. 156–72

It is important that we evaluate all differences positively. Although it is likely that the struggle for an inclusive citizenship will be pursued by those who are the victims rather than the beneficiaries of the market and state, people with education and status have a vital part to play in the struggle for emancipation. They may be less subject to prejudice based upon ignorance. In the same way 'outsiders' are more likely to see the need to integrate with the host community in a way that enables people to contribute to (rather than passively accept) dominant norms. The need for self-government affects *everyone* for even the well-to-do are vulnerable to problems in the social and natural environment.

Summary

Ancient Greek notions of citizenship are linked to notions of slavery and imperialism, and liberalism historically has regarded citizenship in an exclusive way. The liberal view of citizenship suffers from being *abstract*, which means that while in theory it offers freedom and equality to all, beneath the abstractions is to be found inequality.

Marshall argues that citizens require social rights as well as political and legal ones, since the latter are seriously weakened if access to material resources is denied. The New Right in Britain and the United States rejected as 'socialistic' the argument for social rights, preferring to define citizenship in marketing rather than in welfare terms. Women are subject to informal pressures in liberal democracies that prevent them from exercising an effective citizenship. It could be argued that individuals would become more independent and involved as citizens if they were in receipt of what has justifiably been called a 'citizens' income'.

Cosmopolitans take the view that it would be wrong to juxtapose involvement at local, regional and national levels with a concern with the world. The European Union has pioneered a concept of citizenship that, although undeveloped, offers a tantalising glimpse of what is possible in the future.

Despite the tendency to define citizenship as membership of the state, it could be argued that the state is actually a barrier to citizenship. As an institution claiming a monopoly of legitimate force, its interventions undermine rather than enhance citizenship. Like the state, the existence of class divisions restricts meaningful citizenship. This point can be underlined when we develop the idea of citizenship as a relational and momentum concept.

Questions

1. Is the notion of global citizenship simply a dream?
2. Is the use of force a barrier to citizenship?
3. Should we extend citizenship to children and animals?

4. Is the liberal view of citizenship satisfactory?
5. Is the view of Marshall as a pioneer of the modern concept of citizenship justified?
6. Does a relational view of citizenship help to assess citizenship in relation to *either* class *or* the state?

References

Aristotle (1962) *The Politics* Harmondsworth: Penguin.

Bellamy, R. and Warleigh, A. (eds) (2001) *Citizenship and Governance in the European Union* London and New York: Continuum.

Bryson, V. (1992) *Feminism and Political Theory* Basingstoke: Macmillan.

Bryson, V. (1994) *Women in British Politics* Huddersfield: Pamphlets in History and Politics, University of Huddersfield.

Bubeck, D. (1995) *A Feminist Approach to Citizenship* Florence: European University Institute.

Carter, A. (2001) *The Political Theory of Global Citizenship* London and New York: Routledge.

Crick, B. (1982) *In Defence of Politics* 2nd edn Harmondsworth: Penguin.

DFID (Department for International Development) (2002) *Issues Paper 3* Kingston upon Thames: DFID Development Policy Forums.

Faulks, K. (1998) *Citizenship in Modern Britain* Edinburgh: Edinburgh University Press.

Faulks, K. (2000) *Citizenship* London and New York: Routledge.

Gilmour, I. (1978) *Inside Right* London, Melbourne and New York: Quartet Books.

Gray, J. (1999) *False Dawn* London: Granta Books.

Hayek, F. (1960) *The Constitution of Liberty* London and Henley: Routledge & Kegan Paul.

Heater, D. (1999) *What is Citizenship?* Cambridge: Polity Press.

Held, D. (1995) *Democracy and the Global Order* Cambridge: Polity Press.

Held, V. (1993) *Feminist Morality* Chicago, Ill. and London: University of Chicago Press.

Hoffman, J. (1988) *State, Power and Democracy* Brighton: Wheatsheaf Books.

Hoffman, J. (1995) *Beyond the State* Cambridge: Polity Press.

Hoffman, J. (2004) *Citizenship Beyond the State* London: Sage.

Jones, K. (1990) 'Citizenship in a Women-Friendly Polity' *Signs* 15(4), 781–812.

Linklater, A. (1999) 'Cosmopolitan Citizenship' in K. Hutchings and R. Dannreuther (eds), *Cosmopolitan Citizenship* Basingstoke: Macmillan, 35–59.

Lister, R. (1997) *Citizenship: Feminist Perspectives* Basingstoke: Macmillan.

MacKinnon, C. (1989) *Toward a Feminist Theory of the State* Cambridge, Mass.: Harvard University Press.

Marshall, T.H. (1950) *Citizenship and Social Class and Other Essays* Cambridge: Cambridge University Press.

Marshall, T. and Bottomore, T. (1992) *Citizenship and Social Class* London: Pluto Press.

Marx, K. (1966) *Capital* vol. 3 Moscow: Progress Publishers.

Marx, K. (1970) *Capital* vol. 1 London: Lawrence & Wishart.

Marx, K. and Engels, F. (1967) *The Communist Manifesto* Harmondsworth: Penguin.

Marx, K. and Engels, F. (1975) *Collected Works* vol. 3 London: Lawrence & Wishart.

Mouffe, C. (1992) 'Feminism, Citizenship and Radical Democratic Politics' in J. Butler and J. Scott (eds), *Feminists Theorize the Political* New York and London: Routledge, 369–84.

Oomens, T. (1997) *Citizenship, Nationality and Ethnicity* Cambridge: Polity Press.

Ross, K. (2000) *Woman at the Top* London: Hansard Society.

Rousseau, J. J. (1968) *The Social Contract* Harmondsworth: Penguin.

Saunders, P. (1995) *Capitalism: A Social Audit* Buckingham: Open University Press.

Soysal, Y. (1994) *The Limits of Citizenship* Chicago, Ill. and London: University of Chicago Press.

Thatcher, M. (1995) *The Downing Street Years* London: HarperCollins.

Tickner, J. (1995) 'Re-visioning Security' in K. Booth and S. Smith (eds), *International Relations Theory Today* Cambridge: Polity Press, 175–97.

Turner, A. (2002) *Just Capital* London: Pan Books.

Turner, B. (1986) *Citizenship and Capitalism* London: Allen & Unwin.

Voet, R. (1998) *Feminism and Citizenship* London, Thousand Oaks Calif. and New Delhi: Sage.

Williams, R. (2002) 'Full text of Dimbleby lecture delivered by the Archbishop of Canterbury', http://www.Guardian.co.uk/religion, 1–9.

Yeatman, A. (1994) *Postmodern Revisionings of the Political* London: Routledge.

Yuval-Davis, N. (1997) 'Women, Citizenship and Difference' *Feminist Review* 57, 4–27.

Further Reading

- Faulks's book (2000, referenced above) is a very useful overview.

- Lister (referenced above) surveys the feminist and citizenship literature with commendable thoroughness.

- *Cosmopolitan Citizenship* (referenced above) is a collection of essays that is worth reading for those concerned about the idea of a global citizen.

- A very interesting critique of the Crick Report on Citizenship Education and much else besides can be found in A. Osler and H. Starkey, 'Citizenship Education and National Identities in France and England: Inclusive or Exclusive?' *Oxford Review of Education* 27(2), 288–305.

- Bryan Turner's *Citizenship and Capitalism* (referenced above) provides a very useful view of the strengths and weaknesses of the Marxist analysis of citizenship.

- Heater's work on citizenship (1999 – referenced above) is very comprehensive.

Weblinks

- For a very useful overview: http://www.citizen21.org.uk/citizenship/index.html

- For material explicitly on being a British citizen:
  http://www.historylearningsite.co.uk/citizenship.htm

- For material on European citizenship, see:
  http://www.whsmith.co.uk/whs/go.asp?breakcontext=y&pagedef=/yso/about.htm

Part 2

New Concepts

In the second part of this book we discuss five concepts: difference, victimhood, human rights, civil disobedience, terrorism. What distinguishes these five concepts from those discussed in Part 1 – state, freedom, equality, justice, democracy, citizenship – is their relatively recent emergence within political theory. Of course the 'classical' ideas themselves have undergone change and much of our discussion in Part 1 focused on contemporary debates, but those debates revolved around 'problems' which emerged in the *earlier* phases of modernity. For example, the problem of state legitimacy and political obligation, the justification of property rights, arguments over the nature of the human agent, conflicts between freedom and equality, and debate about the nature of political authority and collective decision making.

The term 'problem' is used here in a precise, philosophical sense as a 'puzzle' that requires a solution, rather than everyday usage, which roughly defines a 'problem' as a fault, weakness or contradiction. An analogy from the world of music will illustrate what we mean: one of the 'great revolutions' in Western music took place in the first decade of the twentieth century. Although anticipated by nineteenth-century composers, Arnold Schoenberg (1874–1951) is normally credited with the first 'atonal' composition (that is, a work not composed in a key). Schoenberg did not set out to be a musical revolutionary, but rather he sought to save the tonal system. It was recognition that developments within tonality (such as chromaticism) had generated irreparable incoherences which led him to take those developments to their conclusion. In this sense Schoenberg had inherited musical problems – or puzzles – from his predecessors, such as Beethoven, Wagner and Mahler. To some extent political theory can be understood as an attempt to address problems inherited from preceding theorists, and the treatment by contemporary thinkers of classical concepts, or problems, is analogous to Schoenberg's engagement with tonality. The analogy should not be taken too far: music is a relatively self-contained art form, whereas political theory, by its nature, is an engagement with the empirical world, a world it cannot control but which it must interpret.

Political theory can best be thought of as involving two tracks: there is a body of theory, parallel to musical forms, that later theorists engage with and which 'newcomers' to the discipline may find strange and distant from the everyday world of politics, but there is also necessarily an engagement with that world of politics. We would argue that the two tracks are related, for changes in society will eventually work their way through to theoretical reflection. But theorists must also maintain some distance from the world of politics, for otherwise they will be unable to distinguish the merely transitory and parochial from the significant. Without necessarily endorsing his wider philosophy, two observations from Friedrich Hegel are apt here: 'philosophy is time reflected in thought' and the 'the Owl of Minerva begins its flight at dusk'. Political thought must respect the particularity of history but in a way which does not reduce that particularity simply to a series of discrete events, and the Owl of Minerva – that is, understanding – may not emerge, or 'take flight', until we have achieved a necessary perspective on those events.

Engagement with traditional problems of political theory, combined with social and political changes 'external' to the discipline of political theory, but to which political theorists must respond, can generate new problems. It is these new problems that justify separating out the classical and the new ideas. Take the concept of 'difference', which we discuss in Chapter 7: this can be understood either as a development of traditional liberal theorisation of the nature of the human agent, or as a radical shift towards a 'postmodern' perspective on humanity. As a continuation of liberal theory, the concept of difference is linked to identity: when liberals talk about human beings as naturally free and equal, what attributes attach to 'human being'? Do liberals allow for gender or cultural differences between human beings? Respect for identity involves recognising differences within the human subject – differences which mean that we may use different descriptions of ourselves in different situations. If, however, we take the idea of identity as a continually shifting phenomenon to its logical conclusion then we must necessarily empty identity of any 'essentialism'. This means you are what you choose to be and there are no 'grand narratives'. Gayatri Spivak, a literary theorist, argues that she, as a US-educated Asian Indian, cannot claim to speak on behalf of Indian widows, *satis*, who 'choose' to immolate themselves on their dead husband's funeral pyres, because individuals have experiences that cannot be reduced to a single language or 'narrative': feminists who claim there are experiences common to 'women' are not respecting the radical differences which exist between people. Again, without wishing to push the musical analogy too far, postmodernist (or post-structuralist) understandings of identity correspond to Schoenberg's radicalisation of tonal musical forms – the logic of tonality led to atonality, and the logic of difference leads to post-structuralism.

Other concepts discussed in Part 2 are more easily identified as continuous with traditional concepts, but they do, nonetheless, constitute a break with tradition. Consider human rights: early modern natural law theory appears at first sight the progenitor of human rights discourse. The idea that human beings have a moral status as children of God, or are implanted by God with a moral sense, does not seem entirely alien to the contemporary understanding of human rights as standards of behaviour owed to people simply by virtue of their humanity and thus transcending cultural particularity. But the shift from a theological to a secular justification renders the similarity between natural law theory and contemporary human rights theory superficial: human rights are grounded in the idea that the individual human being is a 'self-originating source of valid claims' against others, rather than being part of a natural, or cosmic, order. And the problem to which human rights are supposedly the answer is quite different to the problem to which natural law was a response: human rights functions as a standard for international politics, whereas natural law was intended as a means of rejuvenating Christianity in the context of ecclesiastical corruption.

Civil disobedience and terrorism can also be understood as responses to new problems. Indeed the two concepts dovetail together. Henry Thoreau is widely credited with writing the first work on civil disobedience (in 1849), but it is only after World War II that civil disobedience becomes a significant issue in political theory. We argue that although civil disobedience, that is peaceful but illegal action, is possible in non-liberal societies – Gandhi's campaign against British rule in India being an example – it raises a special problem for a liberal society. Again, we use the word 'problem' in a precise sense, meaning a puzzle that demands a solution. The *puzzle* is this: we have special obligations to obey laws passed through the use of a democratic procedure, but that procedure can generate unjust laws which we have an obligation to disobey. This problem does not exist for a non-democratic society because there is no obligation to obey its laws, even if the laws themselves are 'just'. It follows that in a world where there are no liberal democratic societies civil disobedience will not be a prominent political issue (which is not to say that civil disobedience is not possible in such a world: repressive governments may be met with non-violent resistance). Until the twentieth century there were few, if any, fully liberal democratic societies – the denial of the vote to women ensured this was the case. Early modern theorists could think only in terms of rebellion or revolution, not civil disobedience.

Terrorism is related to civil disobedience, in that in part it is problematic when directed at liberal democratic societies. The differentiation of terrorism as one form of violence among other distinct forms is a consequence of the development of the liberal democratic value of peace: whereas pre-modern societies gloried in violence – think of the esteem attached to 'chivalry' – modern liberal societies stress the importance of peace and order. When liberal democracies use military force they claim to operate within rules of war. Terrorism is characterised as the absence of rules, hence the use of the word 'terror' (unfortunately, the use of an -ism – terrorism – implies it is an ideology rather than a concept, but really it is 'terror' that is the focus of discussion). We argue that the rather clichéd distinction expressed in the statement that 'one person's terrorist is another person's freedom-fighter' is not a useful one, and that the use of terror must be contextualised: against liberal democracies, where there exists a real possibility of political change, terror cannot be justified. In non-liberal societies, or where liberal societies are engaged in proxy wars, it is more difficult to draw a line between the justified and the unjustified employment of terrorist tactics. The point we make here is that the study of terrorism – both empirically in what is called 'terrorology' and ethically in political theory – is a relatively recent phenomenon, emerging under social and political conditions in which the classification of acceptable and unacceptable uses of violence has fundamentally changed.

Chapter 7

Difference

Ch 5:
Democracy

Introduction

In the period since the cold war there has been a substantial amount of interest in the concepts of 'identity and difference'. With the decline of a class analysis of politics writers have felt that the way people see themselves needs to be given much greater emphasis. This is particularly important where someone's identity diverges from the norm, and the fact that a person is black or gay or female or poor is deemed an attribute that needs to be taken into account when assessing the democratic quality of politics. How people see themselves is obviously linked to the way in which they differentiate themselves from others, so that the concept of difference is linked to the notion of identity and they are dealt with as a pair. Difference, it has been said, is 'a magic word of theory and politics radiant with redemptive meanings' (Hughes, 2002: 57).

Chapter Map

This chapter will consider the following:

- A definition of difference: a monolithic and static view of a person's self-awareness is in conflict with democratic norms.

- The postmodern view of 'différance' and its relation to the notion of difference.

- The use of the terms in feminist theory.

- The link between the concept of difference and the premises of liberal theory.

- The implications that difference has for the concepts of democracy and the state.

'A Protestant State for the Protestant People': Difference in Northern Ireland

A new Republican movement mural in West Belfast, 8 April 2004.

People in Northern Ireland have tended, since the founding of the statelet, to identify themselves in political and religious terms. A minority has seen itself as Catholic and Gaelic-Irish (sometimes called 'nationalist'), whereas the majority have identified themselves as Protestant and unionist – the latter term arising because they see themselves as loyal to the British crown and do not favour unification with the Republic of Ireland. These divisions led to Northern Ireland being, in Ian Paisley's rather chilling phrase, a 'Protestant State for the Protestant People', and the repression of the Catholics resulted in the British government in 1972 suspending the local parliament at Stormont (outside Belfast) and imposing direct rule. The Good Friday Agreement signed in 1998 has sought to encourage a new sense of identity and difference. Protestants were to try and understand the vulnerabilities and sensitivities of Catholics, and the nationalist minority were urged to put themselves in the position of unionists who were fearful of a united Ireland. Recent developments have shown the difficulty of this agreement working. A majority of the unionists appear to support Ian Paisley's Democratic Unionist Party, which sees identities in traditional terms, and is hostile to any sharing of power with Irish republicans, who have in the past espoused physical force as a solution to Northern Ireland's problems.

Imagine that you are a unionist who has lost relatives in one of the Provisional Irish Republican Army's (IRA) bombing campaigns. You are understandably suspicious of the fact that Sinn Fein – generally considered to be the political wing of the IRA – has signed the Good Friday Agreement and, as a result, former members of the IRA have taken part in the devolved executive that the Agreement set up and have become ministers.

- Can you change your identity so that you are no longer a 'loyalist who hates Irish republicans', and regard yourself as a 'loyalist who understands where republicans are coming from'?

Now imagine that you are a republican who remembers the stories about parents, uncles and aunts who suffered at the hands of the unionist-minded paramilitary police, the B specials. You were personally traumatised in the late 1960s when loyalist terror gangs set fire to properties owned by nationalists. You detest the unionists and you feel that a united Ireland is only possible through the use of force.

- Can you change your hatred into an attitude of empathy so that you can see why unionists feel so hostile to republicans and identify so passionately with Britain?

Defining Difference

The concept of difference can only be defined when you seek to establish your identity. A person's identity simply arises from how she sees herself (Alibhai-Brown, 2000: 123). Do you define yourself by your nationality – as say a Briton (or Scottish, Welsh or English) or a Norwegian, or a German; do you feel yourself defined by your religion – as a Jew, Christian, Muslim or whatever? Do you identify yourself by your gender, skin colour, religion, class, sexual orientation, etc? Normally the question of identity depends upon context.

If you are travelling outside of the UK, for example, your British nationality will be one you continually assert, whereas in Britain it may be an identity that you invoke much less frequently. If you are visiting a memorial for the victims of the Holocaust, you may feel that it is relevant to assert a Jewish identity; if a colleague is telling you about her sexual problems, then the fact that you are female and, say, gay becomes an identity that you wish to express, even though in other contexts this is an identity which may not require emphasis. A heated argument over the Iraq War may cause you to mention that you come from the Middle East and are a devout Muslim.

It is clear that having an identity only really arises as something of which you are aware when you wish to differentiate yourself from someone else. It is because your nationality is distinctive, or your gender, sexual orientation, religion, etc. is not universally held that your identity comes to the fore. This is why identity is always linked to difference. You are unlikely to assert your identity as a human being unless you are arguing about human rights or discussing the question as to whether animals suffer, since people by definition are human beings, and your human identity is not normally seen as a differentiating factor. This is why difference always implies identity, since to know who you are you must also know who you are not. Understandably people resent their identity being expressed in negative terms. Blacks under apartheid felt aggrieved at being referred to as 'non-whites': an identity that implies a deficiency or lack on the part of those thus labelled. It is said that while 'difference' is endlessly invoked in feminist theory it is often not defined (Hughes, 2002: 57).

The value of asserting identity arises because it is something all people have, even though people who have a dominant identity may think that it is something 'others' have and they do not. The word 'ethnic', for example, is frequently used about those who differ from the dominant norm, as in a situation in which whites in France say that they do not have an ethnic identity: this is something that belongs to others. Feminists feel aggrieved when the word 'man' is used as a synonym for humankind and are not reassured by the argument that 'man' includes women as well. Such identifiers echo earlier assumptions that the only people who really count are males, and therefore it seems appropriate to use 'man' in this all-embracing way.

In fact we all have an identity and we all have more than one. This means that everybody is different from everyone else. A number of crucial questions arise when teasing out the implications of our definition. Are some of our identities more important than others, or does it simply depend upon context? How do we resolve our differences? Do we regard 'others' as enemies that we have to repel, or partners to negotiate with? Under what circumstances do differences become an occasion for violence and war?

The Problem of the Dominant Identity

It is natural that people express an identity which is relevant to a particular context. What is problematic is the 'privileging' of a particular identity so that it becomes one which dominates all others. By this we mean that one identity is deemed dominant over a range of different contexts so that it is seen as far more important than other identities. Thus a nationalist could argue that national identity is more important than **class** or gender identity; a radical feminist would contend that being a woman is more important than being poor; a devout Christian could insist that her religious beliefs 'trump' her identity as a woman or the property she owns.

But why is having a dominant identity a problem? We would argue that if you have a dominant identity then it is more difficult to put yourself in the position of another. You are much more likely to see differences as attributes that threaten you, rather than as a natural part of everyone's identity. You arrange your own identities in strictly hierarchical fashion, so that, for example, the fact that you are a white, heterosexual man seems less important than the fact that you are, for example, Russian. You may be unaware of these other identities or you certainly downgrade them, and hence you are more likely to feel that other people with different identities have something wrong with them. Since you repress or de-emphasise your own different identities you will repress and respond hostilely to the differences of others.

MacKinnon, a radical feminist, argues that difference is a secondary idea – difference, she says, is 'ideational, and abstract and false symmetrical' (1989: 219). This means that asserted differences may be unreal and relatively unimportant. Being a woman is thus more important than being black, a Catholic, lesbian or whatever. This, in our view, makes it difficult to empathise with those who are not women, or who prefer not to identify themselves in gender terms, or who link gender with questions of class, religion, ethnicity etc. Germaine Greer characterises men as women haters and, among the other unsavoury attributes that men have, she sees them as 'doomed to competition and injustice' (1999: 14; 287). But would she take this position if she did not privilege female identity in a way that downgrades all other identities? Surely some men are concerned with justice, while some women extol competition (to echo Greer's example): these facts come to light much more easily if being a woman is regarded as one identity among many, relevant in some contexts but not in others. Having a dominant identity makes toleration of others more difficult.

Proponents of a dominant identity may seek to exclude difference altogether. Gould gives the example of Habermas's notion of the public sphere, where he sees difference as 'something to be gotten past'. 'Diversity may be the original condition of a polyvocal discourse but univocity is its normative principle' (1996: 172). By this Habermas means that differences get in the way of the idea of human freedom and emancipation. Of course, regarding all people as human is important, but so is identifying the differences between them. In fact, the two go together. It is because as, for example, a Christian you see Muslims as human that you feel their differences should be respected and even celebrated. Gould finds it problematic that Habermas takes the view that in the public sphere 'the enhancing role of difference' is downgraded (1996: 173). It is true that differences result in conflict. But we should not regard conflict as necessarily involving violence. Conflict arises from our awareness of difference, and in a non-violent sense is part of agreement. Think about it. How can you have an argument with someone unless you also share certain assumptions?

Biography	**Jürgen Habermas (1929–)**

Between 1956 and 1959 Habermas worked as assistant to Theodor Adorno. In 1964 he was made Professor of Philosophy and Sociology at the University of Frankfurt and in 1971 he became co-director of the newly created Max Planck Institute for the Study of the Conditions of Life in the Scientific-Technical World. Habermas has been a key figure in directing and coordinating various research programmes and has influenced a wide range of empirical and historical studies.

His early work sought a 'reconstruction of historical materialism'. In it Habermas attempted to mobilise all the intellectual resources of the twentieth century in order to redeem the nineteenth-century project of a science of society. In *Knowledge and Human Interests* (1968), his first major work, Habermas promotes the insight that interests inevitably play a role in determining the nature and shape of sociological (and indeed other scientific) investigation. He challenges the claim that science can be ethically neutral and purely technical. Habermas has drawn widely on empirical studies in sociology, anthropology, linguistics and psychology, but always with the aim of providing a modern, up-to-date version of 'human nature' as the basis for the progressive development and evolution of society. Habermas's work is justly claimed – by friend and foe – to be in direct continuity with traditions in social philosophy that stretch back to the beginnings of the Enlightenment.

His *Legitimation Crisis*, written in the early 1970s, argued that capitalism was experiencing severe problems but he declined to identify a social force which would advance an emancipatory solution to these problems. In 1981 he published *The Theory of Communicative Action* in which he maintained that a humane collective life depends on innovative, reciprocal and egalitarian everyday communication. But Habermas is condemned by his postmodern critics for maintaining a connection – however mediated – between questions of legitimation in science and the issue of legitimacy for political institutions. He is accused by Lyotard of presenting a 'grand narrative'. Being singled out for special treatment by postmodernists, Habermas has returned the compliment and is highly critical of what he sees as the irrationalist, nihilist and neo-conservative tendencies within postmodernism. He is deeply suspicious of its extreme scepticism.

Habermas's most sustained and substantial treatment of what he sees as the flaws and dangers of postmodernism is presented in his 12 lectures on *The Philosophical Discourse of Modernity* (1985). Habermas's mentor, Adorno, had held that the logic of modernity itself gave rise to domination. For Habermas, on the other hand, there is no historical necessity for *Zweckrationalität* (instrumental reason) to dominate the modern world.

Everybody has a different point of view, and therefore we should never assume that having things in common – 'sameness' – shuts out difference. Difference, whether of viewpoint, appearance, background, etc. is natural and necessary, and we should avoid thinking of it as problematic. If we do so, we will (even unthinkingly) privilege one identity and, in doing so, assert it as something that dominates others. Of course the idea of encouraging people to articulate their ideas in a public sphere is important but, as Gould asks, what of those who do not or cannot speak in public, 'who from inarticulateness, fear, habit or oppression are removed from participation in public life' (1996: 176)? We should help people to express and defend their differences – not regard difference as something to be ashamed of or to hide. It is true that France has a strong tradition of republicanism. But why should we interpret the separation of church and state in a way that prevents young Muslim women from wearing headscarves? After all, they are not insisting that everyone wears a headscarf: they merely want to display their difference.

Ch 5:
Democracy,
pp. 102–24

The assumption of a dominant identity threatens democracy since democracy requires that *all* seek to govern their own life. If we assume that certain identities are privileged, then those who differ will be excluded, and diversity will be crushed by uniformity.

Postmodernism/Post-structuralism and Difference

Postmodernism or post-structuralism (we will use the terms synonymously) has become influential over the last 15 years. It challenges what it calls modernism, and the tendency of 'modernist' thinkers to see the world in opposites that exclude one another. One of these opposites is privileged, and the other downgraded. Thus, instead of seeing men and women as differences that imply one another – to know what a man is, you need to know what a woman is – modernists tend to regard one as more important than the other. Much of our own argument in this, as in other sections, has drawn upon postmodernist argument, and the rejection of 'dualism' follows from postmodern premises.

Introduction,
pp. xxiii–xxix

Postmodernists have written a good deal about difference, but what makes the postmodern view of difference contentious (in some of its formulations) is that it is often linked to an argument that denies progress, truth and emancipation. Because a person is different, the argument is that it is impossible to understand and sympathise with their view of the world. Difference is seen simply as dividing us, and the unity that makes this difference intelligible is ignored. Using difference in this way makes it impossible, in our view, to acknowledge dissimilarity in a way that shows respect for others and thus strengthens democracy. But many postmodernists are hostile to the idea of 'sameness' or unity, and this leads them to reject the very idea of emancipation – that everyone can govern their own lives albeit with different ideas and identities.

It is argued by Weedon that postmodernism represents a 'position', whereas post-structuralism is merely a method of critique that could be used in the struggle for change (Hughes, 2002: 65). If this is correct, then post-structuralism can avoid the pessimism, scepticism, relativism of which postmodernists are often accused. But whatever term we use, the notion of difference, as presented by Jacques Derrida, contains the idea that we should link dissimilarity with the need to defer meaning. For Derrida, the term 'différance' is a fusion of two senses of the French word 'différer' – to be different and to defer (Abrams, 1999: 57). The significance of a particular phenomenon can never come to rest in an actual 'presence' – by which is meant a language-independent reality. This is a complicated way of saying that we can never understand and empathise with a person's particular attributes, since all meanings are subject to infinite regress. Every phenomenon is different from every other and it is impossible to 'decide' what anything 'really' means. It is true that differences are infinite – try counting a person's differences, the colour of their eyes, their skin, their health, their religion, etc. – and you will soon find that you could go on forever. But each of these differences can only be identified because you yourself are a fellow human and, therefore, have something in common.

The idea that being different makes it impossible to have things in common reflects a sceptical view of the world so that no one can understand anyone else (or even themselves). This kind of scepticism is actually very old, and arises because reality or truth is seen as something that is static and unchanging. Once you discover that the world changes, and that what is here is gone tomorrow, you then deny that reality exists at all. All meanings are deemed arbitrary and purely relative to the language we use. Because meaning cannot be an unchanging absolute truth, it is then argued that it cannot be established at all, but must be 'deferred'. This, of course, makes it impossible to come to a position in which we show respect for diversity and insist that identities are multiple both between and within people. To respect diversity is to link it to something that we all share. If difference is interpreted in a way that excludes what we have in common – 'sameness' – then its real significance cannot be established.

But is this not a rather airy-fairy argument that has no practical importance? Its importance arises from the assumption that we cannot, according to Derrida, distinguish between identities that have validity and those that do not. It is certainly true that differences can be used to discriminate and dominate, and post-structuralists are right to argue that one identity should not be privileged or, as we have said above, treated as dominant. Women, for example, are clearly different from men. But what does this undeniable difference mean? Does it mean that men are entitled to dominate women, and regard themselves as superior? Feminists have been understandably preoccupied with difference because they seek to argue that there is no justification for using differences between men and women as the basis for discrimination and exclusion. Women may be different from men, but in general they are no better and no worse. It does not follow, however, that the differences are all unreal, and that they are arbitrary social 'constructs'. As we argue in 'Ideas and Perspectives' on p. 163, the difference between men and women is *both* constructed socially and naturally based, and it would be wrong to argue that differences would have to be erased before domination ceases.

Post-structuralists sometimes reject what they call 'meta-narratives'. They see these as stories which want to be more than mere stories on the grounds that, in the words of Norris, they claim 'to have achieved an omniscient standpoint beyond and above all other stories that people have told so far' (cited by Hughes, 2002: 65). We all know of 'tall' stories, but these are things people say about themselves that are not true. In fact, all stories are a mixture of truth and falsehood because people are not gods. They are part of history and therefore, however authoritative people sound, future generations will always reveal parts of their story to be inadequate. This is a problem whether the story is about one group of people in particular or about the world as a whole. Why should we assume that 'grand narratives' are absolutely true (in a static and timeless sense) and then reject them? We should never have made this assumption in the first place. An evangelical Christian might, for example, regard the Bible as the source of timeless truth, but this is a fanciful assumption. We do not need to reject it with the same firmness that it is advanced, otherwise we simply turn the assumption inside out. To go beyond the assumption rather than simply invert it we need to see that, like all assumptions, it is a mixture of truth and falsehood.

To argue that differences have no meaning implies that there is no wider realm of reality by which we can distinguish between differences that are (relatively) 'true' and differences which are (relatively) 'false'. It is true that Indian people have darker skins than white Europeans but it is not true that one group is more intelligent than the other. If we make no distinction between beliefs and reality or concepts and objects, then how can we regard some differences as attributes to be

Ideas and Perspectives:

Sex and Gender

A good example of the problem of some post-structuralist treatments of difference is the question of sex and gender. Feminist theory has traditionally distinguished between the two by saying that whereas gender is historical and social, sex is natural and biological. The concern is to challenge the way in which natural biological differences between women and men have been linked to questions of power and domination so that it is argued by defenders of male domination that the biological differences between men and women justify discrimination and exclusion.

Of course, biological questions can be complicated by the fact that identities may overlap so that there are genuinely ambiguous individuals who are both men and women, or who wish to change from one sex to another. But broadly speaking we can argue that there should be gender equality and that biological differences, while 'relevant', have no causative significance in explaining why men may be deemed more powerful than women (Connell, 1987: 82–3; 139–40). The latter is a question of gender rather than sex. It is true that there is a linkage between sex and gender. In sexist societies, gender is reduced to sex so that biological difference is seen as a cause of discrimination, and women and men have different 'memories' based on this treatment. But even in a society where there was gender equality, one could still argue that biological differences would have social implications (Hoffman, 2001: 39). The fact that women give birth to children and are prone, for example, to breast cancer, will necessarily mean that different social patterns of behaviour are relevant to their well-being.

But while it is true that gender and sex are linked, it does not follow that the body is simply created through discourse and has a meaning that, in Shildrick's words, lies 'not in biological fact, but is constructed in and by representation' (1997: 179). Clearly where sex is part of social activity it is gendered and its meaning reflects power relationships and cultural mores. But, as with hunger, sexuality is not wholly divorced from nature, and therefore there is a distinction between sex and gender which arises from the fact that one is a social construct and the other is not. There is certainly a link between sex and gender, but there is also a difference.

Biography | Jacques Derrida (1930–2004)

Born in Algiers of 'assimilated' Sephardic-Jewish parents. He was expelled from school because of growing anti-Semitism. In 1948 he enrolled at the Lycée Gauthier in Algiers to study philosophy, being strongly influenced by Sartre, Kierkegaard and Heidegger.

In 1949–50 he went to France, writing a Master's thesis on the philosophy of Husserl. In June 1956 he married, and became increasingly aware of the difficulties inherent in the encounter between philosophy and literature. In 1957–9 he taught for two years in a school for soldiers' children in Koléa near Algiers as his military service, and took up a teaching post in Paris.

In 1962 he wrote a translation of, and introduction to Edmund Husserl's *The Origin of Geometry*, and 1965 saw him teaching the History of Philosophy at the Ecole Normale Supérieure. He began his association with the journal *Tel Quel*, announcing the arrival of a new critical movement that questioned the claims of positivist literary theory and was influenced by semiology, Marxism, psychoanalysis and the structuralist 'sciences of man'.

In 1967 he published *Speech and Phenomena* (on Husserl), *Of Grammatology* and *Writing and Difference*, and a year later welcomed the student rising in Paris. In 1972 *Positions*, *Dissemination* and *Margins of Philosophy* was published. He divided his time between teaching in Paris and various US universities, including regular visiting appointments at Johns Hopkins and Yale. In 1973 *Speech and Phenomena* was published in English translation. In 1974 *Glas* appeared, Derrida's most 'literary' work to date, in the shape of an

intertextual commentary on Hegel, Genet and the convergence of literature and philosophy. In 1975 he helped found GREPH (Groupe de Recherches sur l'Enseignment Philosophique), set up to examine institutional features of philosophy teaching and to challenge French government proposals to eliminate philosophy from the final-year lycée course.

In 1976 *Of Grammatology* was translated by Gayatri Spivak, with an important introduction. In 1980 *La Carte postale de Socrate à Freud et au-delà* appeared. In 1981 Derrida was arrested and imprisoned in Prague, where he had been running 'clandestine seminars', only to be released as a result of French government intervention. In 1982 he was named A.D. White Professor at Large at Cornell University. *Margins of Philosophy* was translated by Alan Bass, and Derrida appeared in the film *Ghost Dance*.

In 1983 Derrida was invited to play a coordinating role in the International College of Philosophy, a Paris-based communal venture intended to open up philosophy to non-academics, and in 1987 he took up an appointment as regular Visiting Professor at the University of California, Irvine. He published *The Truth in Painting*, and the English translation of *Glas* by John P. Leavey and Richard Rand appeared, together with a companion volume of textual exegesis and commentary.

In 1988 he was awarded the Nietzsche Prize, and his work began to attract massive attention. In 1992 he was awarded an honorary degree at Cambridge University despite bitter opposition. In 1994 he wrote about Freud and Foucault and published his *Spectres of Marx*.

celebrated and some alleged differences as attributes to be challenged? Post-structuralists sometimes reject the very distinction between a theory of knowledge (epistemology) and a theory of being (ontology), which means that it becomes impossible to distinguish genuine differences from false ones.

The truth is relative – different people see the world differently – but it is also absolute – there is a world of reality that enables us to prefer one concept to another. The word 'omniscient' (all knowing) in Norris's argument – that those who put forward meta-narratives subscribe to an omniscient standpoint – is all revealing, since it assumes that if something is not timelessly and purely true then it

Exercise

Three people identify themselves to you. The first is a nationalist who is staunchly opposed to the European Union and what he calls 'rule from Brussels'. The second is a feminist who describes herself as a democrat, black, Norwegian and of Asian origin. The third is a gay man who regards gayness as his main identity since it determines how people treat him, regardless of the fact that he is a man, likes football and lives in Bonn.

Clearly each of these persons has a distinct identity and differs from the others.

• Who has a dominant identity and who has an emancipatory identity?

• Who has a genuine identity and who has a false identity?

cannot be true at all. But, as Sandra Harding (a feminist philosopher) has argued, why should we take the view that, in giving up the idea that there is one static and divinely inspired truth, we must at the same time give up 'trying to tell less false stories'? We can aim to produce less partial and perverse representations about the world 'without having to assert the absolute, complete, universal or eternal advocacy of these representations' (Harding, 1990: 100). But if we reject the whole idea of 'representation' (i.e. that ideas 'represent' or reflect a world external to them), then it becomes impossible to use the term 'difference' critically.

Thus, to return to our example of women and men. They are different, but the differences do not justify discrimination, and this, as far as we can tell, is true. But in saying this, we could hardly deny that deeper insights lie ahead which will certainly alter the way in which this truth is presented. This is why we can say that such an assertion is *both* absolutely *and* relatively true. If it were simply absolutely true, then it would be a statement placed outside of human history. If it were just relatively true, then it would be confined in its scope to the moment we uttered it. By seeing the truth as absolute *and* relative, we are embracing a logic of 'both/and' rather than of 'either/or'.

Some identities are emancipatory, for instance that of a gay person striving for **justice** and recognition in a homophobic society. But some are not. Think, for example, of a gay person seeking medical treatment because they see their sexual differences as 'unnatural' and deviant. If we take the view that the politics of emancipation is itself to be rejected, then how can a discussion of identity and difference be linked to self-development and the self-government of all individuals? Difference ceases to be something we can evaluate (and if it is a real difference, something we can value), and becomes instead a source merely of mystification.

Feminist Theory and Difference

Clearly, the first feminists saw difference as something negative, because it was used to justify discrimination. When Locke or Rousseau spoke of female traits they spoke of differences that prevented women from being heads of households or taking part in politics. The liberal 'public/private' divide was premised on the assumption that women's differences from men made them domestic creatures, suited to the private sphere but not to the public one. Wollstonecraft and J.S. Mill took the universal claims of liberalism which traditionally had applied only to men and argued that women were individuals too – they were just as rational and logical as men – and were therefore entitled to citizenship alongside men.

This notion is held by the Equal Opportunities Commission (EOC), an organisation set up in Britain to monitor and encourage the pursuit of equal opportunities. As far as women are concerned, the EOC seeks a society that 'enables women and men to fulfil their potential, and have their contributions to work and home life equally valued and respected, free from assumptions based on their sex' (Hughes, 2002: 41). In other words, the differences between men and women tend to be disregarded: the emphasis is upon what they have in common. They are equal, *not* different.

Cultural and radical feminists, influential during what may be called second-wave feminism (a feminism that took root in the late 1960s), reversed the earlier assumptions, valuing difference over equality. As Bohan has put it, 'the customary valuation of difference is turned on its head: women's ways of doing are revered, rather than demeaned' (Hughes, 2002: 47). Mothering was seen as the embodiment of virtue, and what was called maternal thinking should, it was argued, be extended to all spheres of public life. This position has led to separatism – not only the physical separation of women and men – but the cultural and intellectual separation as well. The very notion of 'objectivity' is identified as a male value, as is rationality. Adrienne Rich summed up the position succinctly: 'objectivity is male subjectivity'. As Barrett comments, 'men have one reality, women have another, and women's culture can be developed as a separate activity' (1987: 31). Experience is seen as something that differentiates men from women while uniting women against men.

Third-wave feminism – which is a feminism influenced by postmodernism – argues for a notion of difference that extends from differences between women and men to differences among women themselves. Feminism, it is argued, must break from the liberal view that if people are the same then they cannot be different, and if they are different they cannot be the same. On this analysis, the second-wavers merely invert the first-wavers. Instead of arguing that women should be equal to men, they reject equality on the grounds that women are different from men. The feminists who have drawn critically upon postmodernism argue that one should cease to treat equality and difference as 'binary [i.e. exclusive] opposites'. To argue, as Brown does, that we should oppose the notion of gender equality on the grounds that 'equality presupposes sameness or equivalence' (cited in Hoffman, 2001: 41) is to accept uncritically the liberal view that we need to choose between equality and difference, whereas it could be argued that one without the other turns into its polarised opposite.

If we say that because white people are different from black people (as indeed they are, in appearance at least) they are unequal, and to be equal they must be the same, then arguably we violate both equality and difference. Equality is seen as something that suppresses difference – an unattainable goal since every individual is unique – and difference becomes something not to celebrate, but a justification for discrimination, and discrimination mystifies and misrepresents genuine differences. So that unless we link equality with difference we ride roughshod over both. Hartsock (1998: 60) distinguishes between difference as equality and

How to read:

Hughes's *Key Concepts in Feminist Theory and Research*

It is difficult to find a work that deals with the question of difference in a readable fashion, but this has useful and relevant chapters. Skim read the introduction and Chapter 1 but read carefully Chapter 2 on equality and particularly Chapter 3 on difference, which contains a very helpful assessment of post-structuralism and postmodernism, and extends the question of difference into post-colonial theory. Chapter 4 on Choice and Chapter 5 on Care can be skim read. Chapter 6 on Time, though fascinating if one is looking at recent feminism, can be left out here, while Chapter 7 on Experience deserves a close read. Chapter 8 sums up the argument as a whole and should be skim read.

difference as domination. We would go further and argue that when you dominate another you ignore his real differences and exploit a stereotypical and propagandist version of his identity. This is not a real difference but an imaginary one. In other words, unless difference is linked to equality it ceases to be a meaningful category.

Does this mean that women have nothing in common with each other, and therefore feminism itself is concerned with a category – 'women' – that does not exist? It is certainly true that women differ from one another: some are rich and some are poor; some are white and some are black; they have different sexual and linguistic identities, etc. But they also have something in common. They are all subjugated by patriarchally minded men (and women); they are all subject to stereotypes; they all have biological differences that have social implications. This is why we argue, in the discussion on sex and gender, that the idea that differences disappear in an egalitarian society is wrong, because it assumes that equality excludes difference. In fact, each presupposes the other. To suggest that differences must take the form of 'oppressive gender hierarchies' (Hoffman, 2001: 41) is a liberal view that can take either a conservative patriarchal form (men are different from women – therefore they are justified in oppressing them), or a radical feminist form (women are different from men – therefore they should keep themselves apart). Why not argue that men and women are both the same and different? They are all human beings, entitled therefore to human rights and, as with all human beings, each is different from the other.

A feminism that chooses between equality *and* difference ends up unwittingly with a position of domination or separatism. Neither really advances the cause of women's emancipation.

Liberalism and Difference

Liberalism is historically significant because it is based upon what one of us calls elsewhere 'subversive abstractions' (Hoffman, 1988: 150). Liberalism argues that all individuals are free and equal, and it rests its case on these propositions as universal principles. This is subversive because it rejects medieval and authoritarian notions of a natural hierarchy that identifies people as inherently unequal with some explicitly entitled to dominate others. Liberalism ostensibly rejects 'differences' on the grounds that each of us is an individual who is the 'same' as the other.

The problem is of course that while these principles are undeniably subversive they are also *abstract* and, because they are abstract, repressive hierarchies come slithering in through the back door. The abstraction arises because people are seen as property – each individual has property over himself. Why is this abstract?

- It is abstract because it ignores the fact that people only become aware of themselves as individuals *in relation to others*. This means that property is both individual and social – the control that people have over their own bodies and their own objects arises because others cooperate.

- It is abstract because it is one-sided, and therefore ignores all the factors that make people what they are. It is true that individual drive and initiative are among the factors that mould us, but they are not the sole factors. Aspects of our social and natural environment also play their part.

- It is abstract because liberalism assumes that the relations between human and nature (i.e. *human nature*) take the form of an exchange between individuals through the market. This exchange takes away the particular facts of each person's context (whether they are rich or poor; men or women, etc.), and makes it appear that the parties to the exchange are the 'same'.

Why does abstraction allow repressive hierarchies to come slithering through the back door? Treating people as property may mean that they can actually be owned. Hence early liberals agreed with slavery, and Locke constructs an elaborate and thoroughly unconvincing argument to suggest that slaves are individuals who are captives in war – and instead of killing them their owners generously agree to allow them to live (1924: 127–8). Until the twentieth century liberals regarded individuals as men rather than women, since individuals were rational property owners, and women were seen as neither. Although property was supposedly produced by labour, in practice liberals allowed some to work for others. Whole countries could be owned as the property of those who made 'profitable' use of them, so that liberals until relatively recently supported colonialism and imperialism.

What abstraction does is to drive sameness and difference apart. Abstraction suppresses difference so that, because everyone is an 'individual', they are deemed to be all the same. In practice, of course, they are not, and therefore liberalism argues that inequalities are justified because the wealthy are energetic; men are rational; colonialists are 'civilised' etc. Liberalism either suppresses difference in the name of sameness (those who are not 'like us' must be excluded), or it suppresses sameness in the name of difference (because we are different, we are superior and have nothing in common with 'others'). One thing that liberalism cannot do is to celebrate difference, since this would imply that difference is something that is compatible with and in fact indispensable for sameness.

Nozick

Robert Nozick, an extreme liberal, states in his *Anarchy, State, and Utopia*: 'People generally judge themselves by how they fall along the most important dimensions in which they differ from others. People do not gain self-esteem from their common human capacities – self-esteem is based on differentiating characteristics: that's why it's self-esteem.' (Cited by Ramsay, 1997: 94)

Democracy and the State

The analysis of identity and difference has important implications for our view of democracy and the state. If people are to govern their lives, then the differences they have need to be respected, so that they feel comfortable with their identity and able to participate in government.

But what about differences that lead to intolerance and subjugation? Supposing it was argued that only Christians or Muslims could stand for office and vote, form political parties and be regarded as legitimate political actors, what would these differences mean for democracy? A useful guide here is Mill's harm principle. Differences that harm another's interest cannot be regarded as legitimate, and need to be subject to social and legal sanctions. It cannot be accepted that because someone is of a different gender, sexual orientation, religion, etc. they cannot take part in the political process. We have argued above that to treat difference as justification for discrimination is to distort the concept. Recognising difference as part of a person's identity must imply that such difference is compatible with the differences of others.

Ch 2:
Freedom,
pp. 36–55

What happens if a person's apparent difference leads them to harm themselves? It depends, it could be argued, on whether this harm is reversible or not. A person may distinguish herself from another by drinking a substantial amount of alcohol on one particular day, and once she recovers from her hangover she suffers no long-term effects. But what happens if this is part of an addiction to drink that undermines a person's health, so that as a result of repeated drinking such a person cannot take part in political activity? This is a 'difference' that, in our view, is problematic, since it undermines self-development in a way that is potentially irreversible. While it may not be appropriate to employ legal sanctions against people who self-harm in such a way, social pressures are certainly justified since this kind of 'difference' hinders democratic activity. It is a pathology and not really a difference (as we have defined it), and whether it is harm irreversibly inflicted upon others or upon oneself it is problematic for democracy and requires social intervention to arrest it.

Advancing democracy makes it necessary that we distinguish authentic differences from pseudo-differences. Pseudo-differences are those used to justify discrimination and exclusion: we need to act against the latter, preferably through social sanctions, but through the use of physical force if all else fails. It could be argued that we 'discriminate' against children and unqualified people by imposing upon them various restrictions because they are 'different': who would like to be operated upon by someone who has not been properly trained as a surgeon? These are terminological points. In our view, acts to prevent harm do not count as 'discrimination' and therefore we are identifying relevant and thus genuine 'differences'. To refuse to allow a suitably qualified person to be a surgeon would be to exploit a 'pseudo-difference'. A democratic attitude towards difference must concern itself as to whether differences promote self-development or (we would call them pseudo-differences) prevent it.

The state is more contentious because whereas the notion of democracy as self-government is widely accepted (although its implications are not), the state is often seen as unproblematic in character. Yet an institution claiming a monopoly of legitimate force must threaten difference. The use of force to address conflicts of interest means that a person's identity is necessarily disregarded, and they become a thing. This may be the only way to tackle what we have called 'pseudo-differences', that is the assertion of attributes that inflict harm. A person who feels that as a patriot they can attack others, throw bricks through their windows, etc. may need to be restrained through counter-force. Or a person who is different from others, let us say because he is gay, cannot be expected to suffer attacks on his person or his livelihood, and force may have to be employed against those who perpetrate the outrage. The point about force, whether it can be justified or not, is that it suppresses difference and its use by the state exhibits the same problem. Whether it is an attack on defenceless people by an authoritarian state, or a forceful seizure of criminals by a liberal state, the state necessarily crushes difference, since it is impossible to consider a person's attributes comprehensively when using force against them. What we mean by this is the following. Supposing force is used against a man who rapes a woman. The man might be a good gardener, able to repair cars, and very good with computers. None of these attributes are relevant because the man is deemed a rapist, and he must be locked up against his will. The other aspects of his personality are ignored. Such an abstract focus is inevitable when force is used.

Targeting an individual or group through the state makes it impossible to regard their differences positively, as attributes to be celebrated, and this is why states have to draw what postmodernists call 'binary distinctions' – distinctions in which someone wins and someone loses, 'differences' that are perceived in repressively hierarchical terms. The state is an institution that either obliterates or demonises differences. It treats its supporters as the 'same' and its enemies as different, and thus it disrupts the respect for difference that is crucial if people are to govern their own lives. This is why we need to distinguish between state and government. Government seeks to help people help themselves and, therefore, to use their distinct characteristics in a way that contributes towards development.

Ch 1: The State, pp. 12–35

De Tocqueville

De Tocqueville on colonialism as an extinguisher of difference: It is obvious that there are three naturally distinct, one might almost say hostile races. Education, law, origin, and external features too have raised almost insurmountable barriers between them; chance has brought them together on the same soil, but they have mixed without combining, and each follows a separate destiny.

Among these widely different people, the first that attracts attention, and the first in enlightenment, power and happiness is the white man, the European, man par excellence; below him come the Negro and the Indian.

These two unlucky races have neither birth, physique, language in common; only their misfortunes are alike. Both occupy an equally inferior position in the land where they dwell; both suffer the effects of tyranny, and, though their afflictions are different, they have the same people to blame for them.

Seeing what happens in the world, might one not say that the European is to men of other races, what man is to the animals? He makes them serve his convenience, and when he cannot bend them to his will he destroys them . . . It is impossible to destroy men with more respect to the laws of humanity.

Democracy in America 1835/1966: 391; 421

Summary

It is important to clearly define difference, so that we can see that people differentiate themselves in terms of their distinct identity or identities. The problem with 'privileging' a particular identity is that it becomes dominant. The identities of others, or other identities within an individual, are downgraded and ignored, so that it is tempting to suppress these others.

The postmodern or post-structuralist view of 'difference' sometimes sees difference as something that cannot be resolved but must be endlessly 'deferred'. This is based upon a dualistic view of truth that is insupportable.

Feminism initially regarded difference as negative because it was identified with justification for discrimination. Second-wave feminists tended to invert this negativity so that female difference was seen as positive, separating men from women. Recent theorising has, however, sought to emphasise the importance of both sameness and difference. Liberalism is unable to celebrate diversity because its tendency to abstraction treats people as property. Either all are the same or all are different.

The state as an institution that tackles conflicts of interest through force divides people and, therefore, demonises difference and exalts sameness. It is unable to respect identity and thus acts in tension with democracy.

Questions

1. Does a person's identity revolve around one dominant feature?
2. Do you find the concept of 'différance' helpful?
3. Do you agree with the argument that liberalism is unable to handle the concept of difference?
4. What is difference?
5. Does the state facilitate the expression of difference among its inhabitants?

References

Abrams, M. (1999) *A Glossary of Literary Terms* New York and London: Harcourt Brace.
Alibhai-Brown, Y. (2000) *Who Do We Think We Are?* London: Allen Lane.
Barrett, M. (1987) 'The Concept of "Difference"', *Feminist Review* 26, 29–41.
Connell, R. (1987) *Gender and Power* Cambridge: Polity.
Gould, C. (1996) 'Diversity and Democracy: Representing Differences' in S. Benhabib (ed.), *Democracy and Difference* Princeton, NJ: Princeton University Press, 171–86.
Greer, G. (1999) *The Whole Woman* London: Doubleday.
Harding, S. (1990) 'Feminism, Science and Anti-enlightenment Critiques' in L. Nicholson (ed.), *Feminism/Postmodernism* New York and London: Routledge, 83–106.
Hartsock, N. (1998) *The Feminist Standpoint Revisited and Other Essays* Oxford: Westview Press.
Hoffman, J. (1988) *State, Power and Democracy* Brighton: Wheatsheaf Books.
Hoffman, J. (2001) *Gender and Sovereignty* Basingstoke: Palgrave.

Hughes, C. (2002) *Key Concepts in Feminist Theory and Research* London: Sage.

Locke, J. (1924) *Two Treatises on Government* London: Dent.

MacKinnon, C. (1989) *Toward a Feminist Theory of the State* Harvard: Harvard University Press.

Ramsay, M. (1997) *What's Wrong with Liberalism?* London and Washington: Leicester University Press.

Shildrick, M. (1997) *Leaky Bodies and Boundaries* London and New York: Routledge.

Tocqueville, de, A. (1966) *Democracy in America* London: Fontana.

Further Reading

- Carol Gould's 'Diversity and Democracy: Representing Differences' (referenced above) is a very stimulating treatment of the subject, and particularly valuable for its critique of the German philosopher Habermas.

- Barrett's 'The Concept of "Difference"' (referenced above) is a very useful survey of feminist treatments of this question.

- Abrams's *A Glossary of Literary Terms* (referenced above) is a useful book to consult for those who find reading Derrida in the original too daunting.

- Hughes's *Key Concepts in Feminist Theory and Research* (referenced above), discussed in this chapter, has a very valuable chapter on the question of difference.

- Paul du Gay has (along with several others) edited *Identity: a Reader* London: Sage, 2000, which contains valuable excerpts.

Weblinks

- There is a very interesting paper by Barker on Race and Identity and Difference at: http://www.psa.ac.uk/cps/1994/bark.pdf

- For material on post-structuralism and difference, see: http://homepages.gold.ac.uk/psrpsg/reviews/widder.html

Chapter 8

Human Rights

Introduction

A human right is an entitlement to treatment that a person enjoys simply by virtue of being a human being. Human rights are universal, meaning that possession of such rights is not contingent on belonging to a particular state or culture. Although the concept can be traced back to the eighteenth-century Enlightenment – the 'rights of man' – it is only in the twentieth century that a human right became a major concept in political discourse. The widespread ratification by states of the Universal Declaration of Human Rights, which was created in 1948, three years after the end of World War II, has changed world politics; although individuals are frequently denied their human rights, even by states purporting to respect them, the fact of the existence of human rights has shifted international politics from being based simply on nation-states' interest to one based on the recognition that individuals have claims against their own state. But human rights are open to the criticism that they are the product of a particular time and place – post-eighteenth-century Europe, or the West – and their 'imposition' is a form of imperialism. They can also be criticised for elevating individualism above collectivism, and 'negative' rights (to be left alone) above 'positive' rights (to a particular level of resources).

Chapter Map

In this chapter we will:

- Consider the modern discourse of human rights by reference to the Nuremberg trials of Nazi war criminals.

- Study human rights documents, and their philosophical implications.

- Analyse the concept of a right.

- Assess cultural relativist objections to human rights.

- Consider whether human rights can be extended to cover groups, and provide welfare.

Rough Justice?

Saudi Arabia has long been the target of criticism by human rights organisations such as Amnesty International. The country beheads murderers, rapists and drug smugglers. Other punishments include amputation of the right hand for theft, and flogging for selling alcohol. Saudi Arabia has one of the highest rates of execution in the world; beheadings are carried out in public. The condemned are not given notice that the execution will take place and the victim's family are often only informed after the event. Men, women and children are flogged in prisons and in public squares around the country, and there is no upper limit on the number of lashes judges can order.

The Saudi justice system is condemned not just for the perceived brutality of the sentences but also for the inequity of the legal procedures that result in those sentences. Criminal cases are heard by the General Sharia (Islamic Court), and the last stage of judicial review is by the 11-member Supreme Judicial Council. In cases of capital punishment the sentence must be approved by the Royal courts, which interpret the shariah (Islamic law). Many laws are vaguely worded. Prisoners allege that confessions were forced out of them by torture, and that they knew nothing of their case, and could not attend the trials, which are held in secret. Hearings last between five minutes and two hours. Defendants have no right to a lawyer, cannot call witnesses and are denied access to evidence. Wealthy Saudis and Westerners can bribe their way out of custody.

- If Saudi justice was administered fairly – that is, the accused had a lawyer, access to evidence, charges were clearly stated and an appeal was possible – would the punishments themselves be justified?

- Does the fact that, according to media reports, the majority of Saudis support the system of justice on the ground that it deters crime justify it?

- Should the fact that Saudi Arabia signed the United Nations Convention on Torture in 1997 make any difference to whether or not its justice system is valid?

- Does the fact that Saudi law is – it is claimed – based on Islamic law justify its justice system?

Human Rights after Nuremberg

A 'human right' can be defined as an entitlement to treatment a person has simply by virtue of being 'human', and as such human rights must be applicable irrespective of time and place. If we were to say that a person's rights are conditional on her being a citizen of a particular state, or belonging to a particular culture, then the rights would not rest simply on the fact of being a human being, and they would not be universal. This raises a difficulty for human rights discourse. The language of human rights is a modern phenomenon, traceable to the eighteenth-century Enlightenment, but only embodied in legal documents in the twentieth century. This suggests that human rights are culturally specific, that is, the product of a particular time (modern period) and a particular place (Western Europe). For critics of human rights the problem of cultural **relativism** is thought to be fatal – the alleged universalism of human rights simply masks a form of cultural imperialism.

There is no doubt that while human rights are claimed to be universal the widespread use of the concept is a relatively recent phenomenon. It is only with the formulation and signing of the Universal Declaration of Human Rights (hereafter referred to as the 'Declaration') (1948) that respect for human rights has become a significant consideration in domestic and international politics (that does not mean that human rights are, in fact, respected). And alongside the philosophical discourse and political rhetoric there has also developed a body of international human rights law and international legal institutions, such as the International Criminal Court (ICC) in The Hague (Netherlands). So there is a history to human rights. In the course of this chapter we will discuss whether the historicity of human rights undermines the claim made for their universality.

The Declaration was 'adopted and proclaimed' by the General Assembly of the newly formed United Nations on 10 December 1948. It was developed against the background of the war crimes trials known as the Nuremberg trials, which followed the defeat of Germany in May 1945. There were two sets of trials: those of the 'major war criminals', before the International Military Tribunal (1945–6), and those of the 'lesser war criminals' before the US Nuremberg Military Tribunals (1946–49). Among the 'lesser' criminals were medical researchers who had carried out barbaric experiments during the Nazi years (the so-called 'doctors' trial' took place in 1946–47). The Nuremberg process was criticised by some commentators as a series of show trials based on 'victor's justice'; after all, among the indictments were acts that had undoubtedly been carried out by the victorious Allies, such as the blanket bombing of cities. However, Nuremberg is significant for the study of human rights, in part because of its flaws, and in part because it introduced novel concepts. The legally significant features of the Nuremberg process were as follows:

- The indictment, or charges made against the defendants, were created *ex post facto* and were not related to the laws of Germany. The indictment contained four counts (types of charge): (a) conspiracy to wage an aggressive war; (b) planning, preparation and waging of an aggressive war; (c) war crimes, that included, for example, the mistreatment of prisoners of war; (d) crimes against humanity, which included the Holocaust.
- The compulsion defence – 'I was only obeying orders' – was removed.

- The *tu quoque* defence was removed – *ad hominem tu quoque* means 'at the person, you too' and effectively amounts to the defendant saying 'you committed the same crimes, so you have no authority to judge me'.
- The indictment made reference to violations of 'international conventions', but there is no citation of those conventions, with the implication that it was a loose term meaning the 'general standards of criminal law in civilised societies'.

Although the motivation among the leadership of the Allied powers to create the Nuremburg process was largely political, there was a moral consciousness at work, a consciousness that became stronger in later decades. Consequently, Nuremberg posed a problem: on the one hand there was a sense of what can be termed the 'objective wrongness' of what the Nazi regime had done that manifested itself as revulsion at the acts of those on trial. On the other hand, the trials seemed to depend on the creation of *post hoc*, or retroactive, laws. Retroactive laws violate the principle that there can be no crime without an antecedent law: if you do something that is legal at the time of doing it, then you should not be later prosecuted for that act. If retroactive laws are created then power is arbitrary (other 'troubling' aspects of Nuremberg included the rejection of both the *tu quoque* and compulsion defences). There has been considerable debate among legal and political theorists about the retroactivity problem; some theorists argue that German law was suspended at a point during the 1930s, and therefore the laws of Weimar Germany (1918–33) should form part of the basis of the indictment. Other theorists appeal to conventions, such as the prohibition on murder, which all right-thinking human beings, and all properly functioning legal systems, recognise as valid.

The point about Nuremberg is that German law of the Nazi period could not form the basis of the judgment, and so other laws or conventions, not rooted in a particular legal system, had to be used. And Nuremberg is not simply an interesting historical problem, because it has relevance for contemporary debates about human rights: if there are human rights as defined at the beginning of this section, then they are universal, and the universality extends across national boundaries and across times. The Nuremberg problem will not disappear when the last alleged Nazi war criminal has died, for it is fundamentally a philosophical problem: how can there be human rights if there are no laws embodying those rights? But if human rights only exist where there are laws stating those rights, then how can they be universal? The post-Nuremberg codification of human rights in the Declaration and the Genocide Convention (1948) helps to solve a legal problem, but not the political-philosophical one. To explain, the Declaration was (eventually) signed by the governments of most states, and through the force of treaty law human rights have been given legal validity. Had there been such a Declaration in the 1920s to which Germany had signed up, and that was not rescinded by the Hitler regime, then there would have been a clearer legal basis for Nuremberg (there was such a basis for the third count of war crimes: the Geneva Conventions of 1864, 1906 and 1929). However, this does not solve the philosophical problem: if a nation refuses to sign up to any human rights conventions does that mean it is not obliged to respect human rights?

This question – and the distinction between legal and philosophical problems – reveals an ambiguity at the heart of human rights discourse. When we use the term 'human rights' are we referring to a set of legal rights, or to moral rights, or,

Exercise

From what you know of the history of Hitler's regime and World War II consider the following questions:

- What was the underlying motivation for the Nuremburg trials?

- Should we be concerned that many of those on trial had not broken the laws of Nazi Germany (even if they had committed acts of extreme inhumanity)?

- Did it matter to the legitimacy of the trials that with regard to some of the charges the Allies themselves could have been deemed guilty?

perhaps, to some form of political rhetoric that is based on neither legal nor moral grounds? If human rights equate to certain legal rights enjoyed by individuals through international law, then disputes about human rights will take place in a legal framework, by reference to legal documents and judgments. If, however, human rights are moral rights, then disputes are settled by reference to moral concepts and moral arguments. Put simply, as legal rights, human rights are individual entitlements backed up by the force of law; as moral rights, they are individual entitlements supported by the force of argument. As tools of international politics, human rights are intended to secure certain outcomes: a state widely recognised as violating human rights may find itself shunned by other states and, consequently, its interests damaged. Many advocates of human rights rely on a mixture of treaty law and 'shame' to advance their cause. However, the political uses of human rights can generate cynicism. One of the justifications given for the bombing of Serbia in 1999 was that it was an 'exceptional measure to prevent an overwhelming humanitarian catastrophe', namely the mass deportation and killing of Kosovars. Yet the same description could be applied to the situation since 1995 in the province of Chechnya, where Russia has suppressed a breakaway movement, and engaged in a serious violation of human rights. The reasons for action in Kosovo and inaction in Chechnya is, in small part, logistical, but mainly the recognition of realpolitik: Russia has nuclear weapons.

The best approach for further study of the morality, legality and politics of human rights is a consideration of human rights documents, and in the next section we focus on two: the Declaration, and the European Convention on Human Rights.

Human Rights Conventions

Literature on human rights tends to fall into two groups, with limited cross-over between them: human rights law and philosophical discussions of human rights. While respecting the difference between these approaches it is useful for students of political theory to establish the connections between them, because legality and morality are both important in debates about the relationship between the state and citizen. To this end we will look at two human rights documents: the Universal

Declaration of Human Rights (Declaration), and the European Convention on Human Rights (Convention). There are important differences between these two documents, and the aim of our study is to draw out the philosophical and political implications of each document.

Universal Declaration of Human Rights (1948)

The Declaration consists of a Preamble and 30 articles. The Preamble asserts that the 'inherent dignity and of the equal and inalienable rights of all members of the human family is the foundation of **freedom**, justice and peace in the world'. Without specifying the events it acknowledges the 'barbarous acts which have outraged the conscience of mankind', and asserts that human rights must be protected through law.

The 30 articles are reproduced in summary form below. We have grouped them together for purposes of discussion; they are not, in fact, grouped in this way in the Declaration.

Article(s)	
1–2	Human beings should be treated equally, irrespective of personal characteristics or citizenship.
3	Right to life, liberty and security of person.
4–5	Prohibition on slavery, and on torture.
6–11	Equality before the law: equal protection by the state; right to an effective remedy for violation of one's rights; prohibition on arbitrary arrest and detention; right to a fair trial; presumption of innocence until guilt is proven; prohibition on retroactive laws.
12	Prohibition on arbitrary interference in private life.
13–14	Freedom of movement, including emigration; right to asylum in another country.
15	Right to nationality; prohibition on deprivation of nationality.
16	Right to marry; prohibition on forced marriage.
17	Right to own property; prohibition on arbitrary seizure of property.
18–20	Freedom of thought, conscience and religion; freedom of opinion and expression; right to peaceful assembly; prohibition on compulsion to belong to an association.
21	Right to political participation; equal access to public service; 'the will of the people shall be the basis of the authority of the government'.
22–26	Right to social security; right to work, and the free choice of employment; equal pay for equal work; right to 'just and favourable remuneration'; right to join a trade union; right to rest and leisure; right to an 'adequate' standard of living; 'motherhood and childhood are entitled to special care and assistance'; equal protection of children; right to education; right of parents to determine the kind of education their children receive.
27	Right freely to participate in the cultural life of the community.
28	'Everyone is entitled to a social and international order in which the rights and freedoms set forth in this Declaration can be fully realized'.
29	Everyone has duties to his or her community; the exercise of the above rights can only be limited in order to meet the 'just requirements of morality, public order and the general welfare in a democratic society'.
30	Nothing in the Declaration should imply that any state, group or person can engage in actions destructive of any of the rights and freedoms set out in it.

Several important points can be drawn from this document:

1. Although reference is made to the importance of legal protection, the document provides for no legal mechanisms, such as courts, to enforce human rights. And the linguistic style of the document lacks the precision a good legal document should possess.

2. Many of the rights themselves can be grouped: (a) rights that essentially amount to being left alone; (b) rights to participate in the political structure of the country, and to enjoy the protection of its laws; (c) rights to associate with people of your own choosing; (d) social rights, such as employment protection and a minimum level of resources. The first three groups clearly reflect the ethos of a liberal democratic society, whereas the last was a concession to the realities of power politics in the post-war period, where the Soviet Union was keen to stake out a distinct moral position, one that stressed social goods. (We discuss rights to welfare in the final section of this chapter.)

3. The rights are limited by Articles 29 and 30, which talk of the duties of individuals – the reference to the 'requirements of morality' leaves open the possibility that the rights could be interpreted in significantly different ways in different cultures. (We discuss the 'cultural interpretation' of human rights in the section on Relativism versus Universalism.)

European Convention on Human Rights (1950)

The European Convention on Human Rights – officially the Convention for the Protection of Human Rights and Fundamental Freedoms – was adopted in 1950 by the Council of Europe, an international organisation that began with 10 member states and now has 46 (www.coe.int). The Preamble to the Convention makes explicit its relationship to the Declaration by stating as its aim the 'collective enforcement of certain rights stated in the Universal Declaration'. There are, however, several important features that distinguish the Convention from the Declaration. These differences flow from the fact that the Convention is intended as a legal document, whereas the Declaration is a general statement of aspiration:

1. Many of the articles of the Convention are double-headed, meaning that the first part sets out the rights, but the second states a limitation on the right. For example, Article 10 is concerned with freedom of expression, but this is then limited by various considerations, including 'national security', 'public safety', 'protection of health and morals' and the 'protection of reputation'.

2. Section I of the document sets out the rights and freedoms of individuals, but Section II – which is about half the document – is concerned with the powers of the European Court of Human Rights, which was established by the Convention. Part III – 'Miscellaneous Provisions' – deals with various issues relating to the obligations of the contracting states.

3. The Convention has been amended – through 'protocols' – many times since its creation; in most cases this has entailed strengthening, or extending, the rights contained in it. For example, Protocol 6 (1983) restricted the use of the death penalty to times of war or national emergency; Protocol 13 (2002) prohibits the

Exercise

Imagine you are acting (as a lawyer) on behalf of someone (the appellant) making a legal appeal against his or her national government to the European Court of Human Rights. Your task is to construct a case based on the European Convention. Choose one, or more, of the following cases:

- An Irish woman is appealing against the Irish state's ban on abortion.

- A British gay man is appealing against the British state's refusal to enact same-sex partnership laws.

- A French Muslim woman is appealing against the French state's law prohibiting the wearing of 'conspicuous religious dress'.

Once you have constructed a case reverse roles and act as the legal representative of the respective states: your task is to argue that the Convention should not be extended to change the laws of those states.

You may find the European Court of Human Rights' website useful: http://www.echr.coe.int/. Click on 'Basic Texts' for a copy of the Convention.

death penalty in all circumstances. Not all Council members have ratified Protocols 6 and 13: see http://www.worldpolicy.org/globalrights/dp/maps-dp-echr.html.

4. Although there is, unsurprisingly, a strong overlap between the rights contained in both documents, the Convention omits the 'social rights' (Articles 22–26) of the Declaration. Given that the 10 founding members of the Council were all Western European, this is unsurprising. ('Eastern' states joined only after the collapse of state socialism in 1989 – Russia, for example, joined in 1996). For a list of members, see http://en.wikipedia.org.wiki/Council_of_Europe.

Why the Declaration and the Convention are Significant

The Declaration and the Convention are important in what they reveal about the nature and justification of human rights, and in the rest of this chapter we will pursue these further:

1. Human rights privilege certain values over others: there can be no doubt that human rights are individualist, in the sense that the integrity of the individual – her body and mind – and the choices she makes, are the object of protection. Certainly Articles 22–26 of the Declaration stress the social conditions for action, and they raise important questions that we consider in the section on Group Rights and Welfare Rights, but the 'core' human rights are individualist. This raises a couple of questions: do human rights do justice to the full range of values present in liberal democratic societies? Even if they do, can human rights be applied in societies built around a significantly different set of values? These questions are addressed in the next two sections.

2. The differences between the two documents are interesting and important and raise the issue of what happens to the concept of a human right when we try to

apply it in a concrete legal–political situation: must a human right be a legal right? Even if a human right need not be a legal right might it not be that the only human right worth having is one that can be enforced in law? This raises the Nuremberg question: can we have rights that are not recognised in any legal document?

3. Rights will conflict – rights can conflict with one another, and they can conflict with certain duties. A system of rights must, therefore, be compossible, that is, the rights must be mutually possible. Furthermore, rights must be 'actionable', meaning that the fulfilment of the right cannot require impossible actions. To use a slightly silly example, if you have 100 people, and 50 oranges, then you cannot give each person a right to an orange, or, at least, a whole orange. The Convention strives for compossibility and actionability.

We have approached the concept of human rights by looking at actual documents rather than abstract philosophical arguments. However, to test the coherence and validity of human rights it is necessary to move to a more abstract level of discussion. In the following section we consider the concept of a right – that is, any right, not simply a human right – and consider its philosophical implications. Above all, we are concerned with the implication that human rights are individualist, and cannot reflect the full range of values that are present even in a liberal democratic society (we return to this issue in the last section, when we consider (a) group, or cultural rights, and (b) welfare rights). In the section entitled Relativism versus Universalism we extend this objection by considering whether human rights can have validity in non-liberal democratic societies. This entails consideration of what is called the universalism–relativism debate: are there universal moral values, or are such values relative to a particular culture?

What are Rights?

What we want to establish in this section is what the concept of a right presupposes about the nature of the right-holder, and his relationship to other right-holders. In other words, what does a system of rights tell us about the nature of human beings, and their relationship to one another in society? The standard starting point for a discussion of the concept of a right is the scheme set out by legal theorist Wesley Hohfeld.

Categorising Rights: Hohfeld's Scheme

Hohfeld (1923) was not interested in human rights, rather, his aim was to categorise rights as they were used in a domestic legal system, and in particular in his own country, the United States, and other common law countries, such as England (1923). All rights, Hohfeld argued, are relationships: if Jane has a right to something, then there is something that Sam must do, *or refrain from doing*. So the basic idea of a right is an 'advantage' relative to another person, or group of people (that 'group' could be everybody else). Hohfeld argues that there are two kinds of relationship at work in the holding of a right: jural opposition and jural correlation. Since it would unnecessarily complicate the discussion to talk about opposition, we will simplify Hohfeld's scheme and consider only correlation – that is, what other people must do if Jane's right is to be respected. Hohfeld sets out four relationships of correlation, which we can take to be four different types of right (claims, privileges, powers and immunities):

| RIGHT-HOLDER: | Claim | Privilege | Power | Immunity |
| OTHER PEOPLE: | Duty | No-claim | Liability | Disability |

1. **Claim** If Jane possesses a claim (or claim-right) she is in a position legitimately to demand something from another person, or group of people. That other person (or those people) is (are) under a duty to perform the demanded action. For example, if Jane books a flight then she has entered into a contract with the airline company that they will supply a seat on a specified flight – Jane has a claim against the airline company, and were the airline not to supply the seat, Jane could take action in law, which is what is meant by saying that rights are 'actionable'. The claim to the seat was established because Jane exercised another kind of right – a power – when she entered into the contract. However, claims need not be the result of a contract. (We discuss the significance of this later.)

2. **Privilege** (sometimes called a liberty) Of all the four types of right this is the most misunderstood. Some writers prefer to talk of liberty (or freedom), rather than privilege, and argue that the correlative to a liberty is a 'duty not to interfere'. They are partially correct: Hohfeld should have called them liberties, but there is no correlative duty. A liberty simply entails the absence of duty (a 'no-claim'): you are free to do whatever you are not under a duty to do. But that does not mean that other people are under a duty not to interfere in your actions. In fact what are termed fundamental freedoms in human rights documents tend, on closer inspection, to be claims, or powers, or immunities.

3. **Powers** A power entails the ability to create legal relationships. For example, the right to marry is a power that, when exercised, alters your legal relationships: through your actions you alter your legal relationship to the person you marry, and also your relationship to those outside the marriage contract. You cannot marry anyone else unless powers of annulment are first used, and you gain taxation benefits and so alter your relationship to the state. It is through powers that many – but not all – claims are created.

4. **Immunities** To possess an immunity is to be in a position to resist the powers of others. Immunities exist, most often, where there are different levels of legal authority, such as a legislative authority which creates and destroys rights, and a judicial authority that upholds a constitution. The immunities created in a constitution exist to insulate the individual from the powers of the legislature: an immunity *disables* the legislature from exercising powers that would change your legal position. Immunities are often misleadingly referred to as 'fundamental liberties', but must, in fact, be immunities, since liberties are not intrinsically resistant to alteration as a result of legislative action. An example of an immunity would be the 'right to nationality', which amounts to your state being 'disabled' from changing your civil status – put in everyday language, it cannot strip you of your citizenship.

The significance for human rights of Hohfeld's scheme will become clearer when we look at the relationship between the different types of rights, but before doing that it is worth seeing whether we can categorise the rights listed in the Declaration under these headings. In fact, it is very difficult. For example, Article 6 states that 'everyone has the right to recognition everywhere as a person before the law'. That Article is so broad that it could entail a claim against the state, or imply a power to do certain things, or could act as a block on the state changing your legal position, meaning that you possess an immunity. One of the differences between the Declaration and the Convention is that the latter can be more easily broken down in terms of these rights. However, even that document leaves a great deal open about what legal relationships are at work. And we need to know about these relationships to understand the character of human rights, and address the question of whether human rights preclude other important values and principles.

Will Theory versus Benefit Theory

Hohfeld's study was analytical: he wanted to lay out the different forms of rights. He was not interested in explaining the underlying connections between them (he thought claims were 'rights proper', but did not justify this). Since many human rights are, in fact, bundles of Hohfeldian rights, it is important to consider how the Hohfeldian rights connect together. Indeed, as suggested above, the rights contained in human rights documents are very broad in scope, and it may be that different judges will interpret them in very different ways. 'Theories of rights' attempt to connect up the different Hohfeldian rights; some writers assume that a theory must reduce the different Hohfeldian rights to a single right. This is a mistake: what a theory should do is explain the relative importance of each type of right. The two most important theories of rights are benefit theory (also known as interest theory) and will theory (also known as choice theory):

- Benefit theory singles out a claim as the most important kind of right. A right-holder is somebody who benefits, or is intended to benefit, from the performance of a duty. Physical protection would be an example of a claim – you have a *claim* to physical protection, and the state, insofar as it is capable of doing so, has a *duty* to prevent you being physically harmed.
- Will theory singles out powers as primary. A right-holder is someone who is in the position to control the performance of a duty through the exercise of powers. The example of Jane's purchase of a seat on a flight would be an example of powers as primary – to acquire the seat she must exercise a power, and by so doing she acquires a claim.

Benefit theory takes rights to be the way in which *interests* are protected – which is why some theorists prefer the term 'interest theory'. The right-holder need not be in a position to assert his/her/its rights. Will theory stresses *agency*: rights are things we use to control our lives and relationships with other people. Consequently, a will theorist would be much more restrictive about who can have rights. It would be too simplistic to associate benefit/interest theory with the political left, and will theory with the right, but it is the case that those on the left who want to express egalitarian principles in the language of rights will tend to stress interests rather than agency.

The significance of this debate for human rights can be described in terms of depth versus breadth. For a will theorist rights are not broad but they are deep, because if the scope were broadened then rights could be more easily overridden (to 'override' a right is legitimately to set it aside because it conflicts with another, more important, right, or with another principle; the overriding of a right should not be confused with the violation of a right, which is the illegitimate non-recognition of that right). For example, if there is a human right to hold (private) property, but no human right to a minimum level of subsistence, then the property right will not come into conflict with any claim to subsistence. This is not to say that the restriction of human rights to property holding precludes a claim to subsistence, rather it means that the property right 'trumps' the claim to subsistence. On a will theory of human rights, the range of activities and states of being protected by human rights is narrower than on a benefit theory of human rights. Benefit theory permits a greater range of values, but at the price of weakening rights. To summarise the discussion of this section: if the 'rights and freedoms' set out in human rights documents are to be applied to concrete situations then it is necessary to break them down into Hohfeldian rights, which, given that privileges (liberties) are problematic, amounts to three types of right: claims, powers and immunities. The degree to which human rights can encompass the full range of values of a society depends to some extent on which of the Hohfeldian forms is taken to be of primary importance.

Relativism versus Universalism

So far we have talked about the concept of a right and about the historical origins of human rights documents and mechanisms of enforcements. What we have not discussed is the justification of human rights. We assume that the *fact* of law does not necessarily *justify* a law. Once we accept this we are forced to confront the cultural relativism thesis, which can be stated thus:

> Values have to be understood as part of a complex whole; that complex whole is 'culture'. When discussing the universal applicability of 'human rights' we must take into account the impact that they will have on particular cultures. For some cultures those rights express central values, for others they may, with some revision, be compatible with that culture, but for others they may be wholly inappropriate and damaging.

Cultural relativism does not necessarily entail the rejection of morality: the Declaration may be valid for certain cultures. What cultural relativists challenge is the claim to universal application. This raises the question whether a relativist can endorse some form of human rights. One possibility is to distinguish 'state' and 'culture': the Council of Europe is composed of more than 45 states, but it could be argued that there is a single European culture, which has its roots in Christianity (medieval Europe was often referred to as 'Christendom'). Similarly the Islamic world is composed of many states bound together by Islamic culture (it might also be argued that the Arab world, as part of the wider Islamic world, is a distinct culture). If we endorse the distinction between state and culture then it might be possible to talk of trans-national standards of treatment. Those standards would allow a distinction to be made between two types of rejection of human rights: (a) *violation* of culturally accepted human rights by a particular regime; (b) *legitimate rejection* of human rights on cultural grounds. For example, it could be debated whether Saudi Arabian penal policy, such as the amputation of hands, is grounded in Islamic teaching and Arab custom, or whether it simply serves the interests of the Saudi state to have such an apparently draconian form of punishment.

This argument, while plausible, is difficult for a defender of human rights to embrace. As we suggested in the first section of this chapter, human rights are rights that individuals have by virtue of their humanity. The 'cultural argument' makes rights, or any other standard of treatment, contingent on a person's culture. While there may be a role for culture in the justification, formulation and implementation of human rights, the radical 'culturalism' which forms the basis of the cultural relativism thesis is incompatible with a defence of human rights. We need then to consider arguments against cultural relativism or, put another way, arguments for universalism. We set out three types of argument in favour of the universality of human rights – it may be that none of these arguments work, and that we need to return to cultural relativism thesis. The arguments are presented primarily to stimulate reflection on the universalism–relativism debate.

Intuition and Moral Consensus

Jack Donnelly, in his book *Universal Human Rights in Theory and Practice*, defends what he terms weak cultural relativism, which entails strong universalism. Weak cultural relativism assumes that human rights are universally applicable but allows that 'the relativity of human nature, communities and rules checks potential excesses of universalism'. Strong cultural relativism holds that culture is the principal source of the validity of a right or rule, and 'at its furthest extreme, strong cultural relativism accepts a few basic rights with virtually universal application but allows such a wide range of variation that two entirely justifiable sets of rights might overlap only slightly' (Donnelly, 2003: 90).

The looseness of the language of the Declaration Donnelly regards as a strength. The Declaration is a general statement of orienting value, and it is at this level – and only at this level – that a moral consensus exists. For example, Articles 3–12 'are so clearly connected to basic requirements of human dignity, and are stated in sufficiently general terms, that virtually every morally defensible contemporary form of social organization must recognize them' (94). Below we discuss the 'rational entailment' argument, of which there are several versions, but the central idea is that certain standards of treatment can be derived from the conditions which humans require for action, and as such a society cannot deny those standards without also denying the preconditions for its own existence. Donnelly's statement has the appearance of such an argument, but in fact he then goes on to appeal to human intuition. By 'intuition' is meant a strong sense of, or belief in, the rightness or wrongness of something, but without the ability to give a complete explanation of that sense or belief. Donnelly identifies the intuition that people should be treated in a certain way irrespective of their culture by means of a question:

> In twenty years of working with issues of cultural relativism, I have developed a simple test that I pose to sceptical audiences. What rights in the Universal Declaration, I ask, does your society or culture reject? Rarely has a single full right (other than the right to private property) been rejected. (94)

He recalls a visit to Iran in 2001, where he posed the above question to three different audiences. In all three cases discussion moved quickly on to the issue of freedom of religion, and in particular to atheism, and to apostasy by Muslims, which the Declaration permits, but Iran prohibits. Donnelly observed that the discussion was not about freedom of religion, but rather about Western versus Islamic interpretations of that right (we discuss freedom of religion in the final section of this chapter).

Particular human rights are like 'essentially contested concepts' in which there are differing interpretations but strong overlap between them. So long as 'outliers' are few, we can talk about a consensus around human rights. Such 'outliers' would be cultures that do not accept a particular human right. The fact that increasing numbers of states are prepared to sign up to the Declaration, and to later, and more specific, United Nations conventions Donnelly takes to be evidence of a dynamic consensus in favour of human rights. He also observes that when Western states criticise non-Western states for apparently barbaric practices that criticism is sometimes accompanied by a serious lack of self-awareness; in 1994 18-year-old American Michael Fay was convicted by a Singaporean court of vandalising hundreds of thousands of dollars worth of property. He was sentenced to three months in jail, required to pay a fine and, most controversially, was condemned to six strokes of the cane (the cane would leave permanent scars). There was widespread condemnation in the United States. Donnelly tersely observes that President Clinton, while condemning the sentence 'failed to find it even notable that in his own country people are being fried in the electric chair' (99).

To sum up, Donnelly's observations are interesting, but two points are problematic. First, an intuition in favour of human rights at best indicates that there may be something underlying those rights which is, in some sense, universal. But if this is so then it should be possible to move beyond intuition and provide reasons for respecting human rights. Second, the fact that *states* have signed up to human rights conventions does not entail *cultural* agreement: human rights must be recognised as valid by large parts of the populations of states, and not simply by the leadership. In many states the governing elites are disconnected from their peoples, and although states may be considered the main actors with regard to human rights, respect for such rights does depend on popular recognition.

International Hypothetical Contract

The fact that increasing numbers of states are prepared to sign up to human rights conventions does not in itself amount to an argument for the universality of human

Ch 4:
Justice,
pp. 83–9

rights, but it may provide an element in an argument. In Chapters 4 and 7 we discussed the idea of the social contract, which has been a device used by liberal political theorists to justify state power. Our discussion focused on the 'domestic' use of the contract in Rawls's theory of justice. This contrasts with an 'international contract', which is a contract not between individual human beings but between states. We also made a distinction between a quasi-historical contract, whereby we could imagine that people could have agreed contractually to create a state, and the hypothetical contract in which the contractors are 'idealised' and the 'contract' is a thought experiment rather than an imagined historical event.

Interestingly enough, whereas defenders of the historical contract do not claim that there was actually an agreement to enter the state – they claim simply that it was imaginable – international legal institutions can plausibly be described as the product of an agreement between the member states of the international community: agreements to create international institutions. Of course, there is not a single 'moment' of agreement, for the ratification of a convention can take place over decades. Furthermore, there has never been an international agreement to create a single state; such an agreement would constitute the dissolution of all existing states. The closest the international community has come to the creation of a single, multinational global power has been the formation of the United Nations with the commitment by member states to provide military personnel to enforce international law.

The problem of enforcement may be thought a serious deficiency of international law, and one that can only be remedied through the creation of a single state. However, there is a considerable body of international law, such as commercial law, which states respect without recourse to a global enforcement agency. Enforcement, while important, is not the main deficiency evident in a world in which there is no single political and legal agent, for a more significant deficiency is the absence of authoritative determination of the content of the law. Even if all states subscribed to the Declaration, its wording is so general as to require a third-party judgement on its meaning. In practice, the United Nations effectively 'contracts out' the interpretation of human rights to bodies such as the European Court of Human Rights. The general point to make is that a hypothetical international contract differs from a domestic one in that its object is not the creation of a world state that will enforce human rights, but rather it is a device for creating a charter of human rights and associated multinational institutions. States will not then be able to violate human rights on grounds of disagreement about their interpretation, and will have incentives – such as the desire for reputation – to respect them.

Rawls and the International Hypothetical Contract

Ch 4:
Justice,
pp. 80–100

John Rawls extends his theory of 'domestic' justice to the international sphere in his book *The Law of Peoples* (1999). The underlying aim of that book is to outline the just foreign policy of a liberal society: when is intervention in the affairs of another state justified? And what duties do liberal societies have to non-liberal ones? Although that aim is quite narrow, in the course of the book Rawls does present an argument intended to show that non-liberal, non-Western societies can respect human rights. Although he does not use these terms with great precision Rawls makes a distinction between three types of society or 'people':

- **Liberal societies,** such as those which (largely) respect human rights conventions, and the conventions of war.
- **Decent non-liberal societies,** of which there can be several variants, but the one type Rawls discusses possesses a 'decent consultation hierarchy' (hereafter referred to as *decent societies*).
- **Outlaw states** – states that violate the law of peoples, by, for example, waging aggressive wars or engaging in serious violations of human rights. (There are also *burdened societies*, where socio-economic conditions make respect for international law difficult.)

Ch 4:
Justice,
pp. 84–5

Rawls applies the idea of the original position and the veil of ignorance to international law, but there are some significant differences between how these devices are used in Rawls's theory of (domestic) justice, and his law of peoples. These are best summarised as a table:

Domestic justice	Law of peoples
Individual human agents are in the original position.	Representatives of peoples are in the original position.
Agents are denied knowledge of their particular conceptions of the good, e.g. their religious beliefs.	Representatives have knowledge of their conceptions of the good, e.g. the predominant religion of their society.
There is one process whereby principles of justice are selected.	There are two 'runs': (a) liberal societies agree; (b) decent societies agree.

Liberal societies agree among themselves on a 'law of peoples', and then decent societies endorse those same principles. (Rawls argues that liberal democratic societies, by their nature, will tend to respect the human rights of their own peoples and the sovereignty of other peoples – see Democratic Peace.) The law of peoples consists of eight principles: mutual recognition of each people's independence; honouring of agreements; legal equality of peoples; duty of non-intervention (except

Democratic Peace

This is the theory that liberal democracies do not go to war with one another, preferring instead to settle their disputes through negotiation. Immanuel Kant is credited with offering an early version of the theory in his essay 'Perpetual Peace' (published 1795, in Kant, 1996: 317–51), where he argued that 'commerce' (trade) established bonds between peoples, and gave them a material interest in maintaining peace, even where the interests of states conflicted, and, furthermore, the legal traditions of liberal states led them to value arbitration over violence. The Democratic Peace argument was given renewed force with empirical and theoretical studies by Michael Doyle (1997) and Bruce Russett (1993). Doyle studied all wars since 1800 and found no case of two liberal democracies going to war against one another. Obviously, the credibility of the claim depends on how democracy is defined, but the argument is at least plausible.

in the case of dealing with outlaw states and grave violations of human rights); right to self-defence; respect for human rights; respect for the rules of war; duty to assist peoples living under conditions that prevent them from becoming just (liberal) or decent societies. The law requires of liberal societies that they do not seek to change the fundamental character of a decent society.

To understand how a decent society could endorse the law of peoples, and consequently why a liberal society should 'tolerate' a decent society, we need to know the characteristics of the latter. Rawls argues that it is peaceful in that it pursues its interests through trade and diplomacy. The domestic laws of a decent society should be guided by 'common good conception of justice', meaning that while it may not grant the freedoms to individuals enjoyed in a liberal society, in a fundamental sense all citizens are treated equally. There should exist a 'decent consultation hierarchy', which permits the possibility of dissent (the Arab–Islamic concept of Shura would be one example of a consultation hierarchy). Importantly, the common good conception of justice entails respect for human rights, including the right to life, liberty (freedom from slavery and forced labour), personal property and equality before the law. Although a decent society may not permit apostasy and proselytisation, it must accord a degree of religious freedom to minorities, and because that right is limited it must also allow citizens to emigrate. The fundamental philosophical point Rawls makes about human rights is that they should not depend on a particular conception of the human agent as autonomous, but rather 'human rights set a necessary . . . standard for the decency of domestic political and social institutions' (Rawls, 1999: 80).

Human rights fulfil three roles: (a) they are a necessary condition of a regime's legitimacy; (b) they determine the limits of sovereignty – the law of peoples prohibits intervention in the affairs of another state except when that state is violating human rights; (c) they set a limit on the pluralism among peoples. Even if Rawls is correct in arguing that a decent society can respect human rights, are there any grounds for believing that they will do so for reasons other than state interest? Do they respect human rights for the 'right reasons', or because such respect is useful to establishing a reputation in international politics? A similar argument could be applied to the international behaviour of liberal states, but the difference between liberal and non-liberal societies is that human rights are deeply embedded in the culture of the former. Even if the leaders of liberal societies are cynical in their use of human rights rhetoric in international politics – intervening in Kosovo but not Chechnya – they may well (largely) respect human rights in their domestic political systems.

Rational Entailment

The 'rational entailment' argument identifies certain conditions for the existence of social order and from those conditions maintains that there are certain standards of treatment which all societies should respect. The argument can take two forms – empirical and logical. The empirical version observes actual societies and claims that the long-term survival of a society depends on the recognition of human rights. This version has only limited plausibility – many societies function without respect for human rights; it is somewhat more plausible to maintain that human rights-respecting societies are more successful than human rights-violating ones, where success is measured by economic growth and political stability. The logical version does not deny that social life is possible without human rights, but rather that a human rights-violating society cannot justify its own political and legal organisation without falling into contradiction. In Chapter 3 we discussed the citizenship laws of Nazi Germany which effectively stripped Jews of their citizenship and opened the way for serious violation of their human rights – ultimately, the right to life. Legal theorist Lon Fuller argued that Nazi law could not respect certain principles internal to law, such as the prohibition on non-retroactivity. Fuller is not suggesting that Nazi Germany did not 'function', but rather that it could not justify its laws; implicit in Fuller's argument is a belief in human rights, to which he is offering a logical entailment defence. Of course, a society can simply choose not to justify its actions – although that is surprisingly rare – but refusal to engage in the justification process does not undermine the logical entailment argument.

Ch 3: Equality, pp. 67–8

Jürgen Habermas offers the best contemporary statement of logical entailment. Before we get to his defence of human rights against cultural relativism, it is necessary to set out briefly Habermas's rather complex theory of social change. If we define 'culture' as the 'taken-for-granted horizon of expectations', then under conditions of modernity culture is 'threatened' by rationalisation in the form of money (or the market) and bureaucratic power – relations between human beings become consciously instrumental, rather than implicit and 'taken for granted'. There is a diminution of trust. Many theorists, especially in the German philosophical tradition in which Habermas has been formed, are pessimistic about the consequences of modernity. However, Habermas argues that the emphasis on instrumentalisation – or what he calls 'systemic rationality' – ignores the positive achievements of modernity, expressed in 'communicative rationality' (Habermas, 1984: 8–22). The growth in consciousness of human rights is one of the achievements of communicative rationality.

What does Habermas mean by 'communicative action'? People engage in speech acts: person A *promises* to meet person B on Thursday, *requests* B stop smoking, *confesses* to find B's actions distasteful, *predicts* it will rain. Implicit in each speech act is an offer or claim. In the first two cases A is making a claim to normative rightness, in the third case a claim to sincerity, and in the final case a claim to truth. B can contest all three such 'validity claims' (Habermas, 1984: 319–28). The success of each speech act depends upon both parties orienting themselves to principles of reason that are not reducible to individual intentions: in addressing B person A treats her as an end in herself. The validity claims are implicit in all human action, that is, they are universal. This seems a promising basis for defending universal human rights against the challenge of cultural relativism. However, the validity claims are abstract from everyday life, and so to redeem them requires appeal to a stock of culturally specific values. That means the content of human rights is dependent on culture.

One way to address this problem of cultural dependence is to maintain that politics is a dialogue, in which people bring to bear their different cultural perspectives, such that what emerges from the dialogue is something pluralistic yet coherent. For example, Muslims may be criticised by Western feminists for projecting a patriarchal conception of gender relations. By engaging in dialogue Muslims may reform their view of women's rights, but Westerners might also be obliged to recognise the deficiencies in their own understanding of family relations, by, for example, acknowledging the costs entailed in the commodification of sex in a liberal society.

Habermas argues that there is a tradition in Anglophone legal and political theory of conceiving of the state as grounded in the protection of individual 'private' rights – rights derived from the market contract model. Hobbes is the *locus classicus* of this conception of individual–state relations. If we operate with such a theory then it is inevitable that individual rights will be a threat to cultural reproduction; in effect, increasing reliance on rights would be another example of the systemic rationality eroding the lifeworld. We are then left with a choice: either we assert the primacy of individual rights at the expense of cultural interaction, or we maintain the authority of the collective over the individual. Private rights entail the assertion of personal autonomy, but they ignore the other half of the concept of autonomy – public autonomy:

> from a normative point of view, the integrity of the individual legal person cannot be guaranteed without protecting the intersubjectively shared experiences and life contexts in which the person has been socialized and has formed his or her identity. The identity of the individual is interwoven with collective identities and can be stabilized only in a cultural network that cannot be appropriated as private property any more than the mother tongue itself can be. (Habermas, 1994: 129)

The implication of Habermas's argument is that universal human rights are, contrary to Rawls's theory, grounded in human autonomy, but that human autonomy itself has a collective dimension which must take into account cultural interpretations of human rights. Legality is central to the realisation of human rights, and Habermas's theory of law bears some resemblance to Fuller's: law is not reducible to the assertion of will – people are not simply subjects of law – but the formation of law is a discursive process. The legal realisation of human rights will inevitably involve 'local interpretation' – for example, Muslim societies will interpret human rights differently to Western societies – but human beings are bound together through discourse, and discourse presupposes a conception of the human agent as autonomous.

Group Rights and Welfare Rights

In an earlier section (What are Rights?) we raised the problem of the value range of human rights: to what extent can human rights encompass the full range of values in a society? In this final section we address this question by considering two specific kinds of right – group rights and welfare rights.

Group Rights

So far the discussion has implied that it is individual human beings who have human rights. The first question to ask is, can collective entities have rights? At this stage we are not concerned with human rights, but rather with the conceptual issues raised earlier. It is certainly the case that in law, both domestic and international, rights are attributed to collective entities, such as firms or states, for these are individuals in the sense that they have an identifiable – individuated – good which can be secured through rights. Indeed, in English commercial law public limited companies (PLCs) are described as 'artificial persons'. So there is no conceptual problem in talking about collective rights (or group rights); what is at issue is whether a right can be asserted by a group against the state on grounds analogous to those by which individual human beings assert their human rights.

In his book *Multicultural Citizenship* (1995) Will Kymlicka discusses the right to religious freedom, and identifies three elements to this right: (a) freedom to pursue one's (existing) faith (practice); (b) freedom to seek new adherents to that faith (proselytisation); (c) freedom to renounce one's faith (apostasy). He also makes a distinction between internal restrictions and external protections: the former restrict the freedom of individual members of a culture, while the latter protect a (minority) cultural group against the majority culture. Kymlicka argues for the latter against the former. It follows from this that the right to religious freedom must contain all three elements. Traditionally, in Muslim countries only the first element is respected, and the implication of Rawls's argument is that a decent hierarchical society can be said to respect human rights even if it restricts religious freedom to that element. (It should be said that, historically, Muslims have shown much greater tolerance of religious minorities, such as Jews and Christians, than has been the case in Christian Europe with regard to its religious minorities.)

Does Kymlicka's argument amount to a defence of group rights as human rights? Not really, because the right to religious freedom is held by the individual. Those who argue that human rights are 'individualistic' will not be convinced by Kymlicka's understanding of group rights, for there exists a possible conflict between the right and what it seeks to protect: religion. Religion is a collective activity and can only be sustained as a collective activity, but the individual right to freedom of religion implies that as individuals we stand back from a religious community and assess its value for us. It might be, of course, that after reflection we affirm 'our' religious belief, but this implies that only cultures compatible with reflection and revision of belief are capable of recognising the human right to religious freedom.

Welfare Rights

In discussing the Universal Declaration of Human Rights we noted that Articles 22–26 were concerned with 'social rights', and that these rights were dropped from the European Convention. In 1969 the United Nations proclaimed the Declaration on Social Progress and Development, which sets out in more detail principles and objectives for international development. The question is whether it makes sense to talk of welfare rights as human rights, or whether development can only be an aim or aspiration subordinate in moral status to respect for what might be termed the 'negative rights' to be left alone (such rights are not strictly negative for they require action by states).

Defenders of the 'right to development' argue that there are socio-economic conditions to 'negative rights'. To assess this claim we need, first of all, a definition of 'development'. Development could mean either: (a) the right of a *state*, or a *community*, to a certain level of resources, or (b) the right of an *individual* to a certain level of resources. If the individual holds the right (in Hohfeld's language: claim), then who has the corresponding duty: that individual's own state, or rich states, or the international community? If states have the right to development then that would imply that the only relevant issue of wealth distribution is between states, whereas if individuals have the right then the distribution of wealth within a particular state is morally relevant. In fact, it is clear from the 1969 Declaration that the UN took the individual to be the bearer of the right:

> Development is a comprehensive economic, social, cultural and political process, which aims at the constant improvement of the well-being of the entire population and of all its individuals on the basis of their active, free and meaningful participation in the development and in the fair distribution of benefits resulting therefrom.

The human right to development raises a number of philosophical problems. First, as we have argued, rights must be both compossible and actionable, meaning that a set of rights must constitute a coherent whole and they must take a form in which a remedy can be obtained when a person complains that his human rights have been violated. The requirements of development may well result in the setting aside of certain fundamental 'negative' rights, for example, a society that wishes to control urban growth may seek to determine freedom of movement and choice of occupation, so that a problem of compossibility arises. A right to development cannot be actionable in the way that violations of negative rights can be: it is significant that many societies have ratified laws on asylum, and largely respect those laws, but those same societies make it clear that they do not accept economic migrants. Second, the right to development may entail significant intervention in the social, economic and political organisation of other states; certainly, violation of negative rights can justify intervention, but violation of such rights is often clear, whereas the failure of a state to ensure the fair distribution of resources within its boundaries is a much less clear violation, and external intervention may be 'open-ended'.

Summary

The fundamental philosophical debate around human rights is concerned with their alleged 'parochialism': that is, their origins in a particular culture. That something has a history does not, in itself, invalidate its claim to universality, but there is a particular problem about human rights even in those cultures from which they emerged: critics argue that human rights place a great moral weight on individual autonomy to the detriment of other values, such as welfare and community. For defenders of human rights, the increasing spread of human rights discourse indicates a welcome development in humanitarian moral consciousness; for opponents, human rights go hand in hand with the growing power of Western liberalism. We can apply the discussion of this chapter to human rights in Saudi Arabia: against Donnelly, the fact that Saudi Arabia has signed up to human rights conventions guarantees neither that its legal institutions are fair, nor that its punishments are proportional. For Rawls, the Saudi regime would not constitute a 'decent hierarchical people', and for Habermas there is a link between the procedural injustice of the regime and the extremity of its punishments.

Questions

1. Why should states respect human rights?
2. If it can be shown that human rights discourse emerges from a Western tradition does this undermine the claim that they are universal?
3. Is the exercise of human rights compatible with respect for the environment?
4. Is the 'right to welfare' coherent?

References

Convention for the Protection of Human Rights and Fundamental Freedoms (European Convention on Human Rights): http://www.cchr.coe.int/Convention/webConvenENG.pdf.

Donnelly, J. (2003) *Universal Human Rights in Theory and Practice* Ithaca, New York: Cornell University Press.

Doyle, M. (1997) *Ways of War and Peace* New York: Norton.

Habermas, J. (1984) *The Theory of Communicative Action, vol. 1: Reason and the Rationalization of Society* London: Heinemann.

Habermas, J. (1994) 'Struggles for Recognition in the Democratic Constitutional State' in Amy Gutmann (ed.), *Multiculturalism: Examining the Politics of Recognition* Princeton, New Jersey: Princeton University Press.

Hohfeld, W. (1923) *Fundamental Legal Conceptions as Applied in Judicial Reasoning* New Haven, Conn: Yale University Press.

Kant, I. (1996) *Practical Philosophy* (ed. M. Gregor) Cambridge: Cambridge University Press.

Kymlicka, W. (1995) *Multicultural Citizenship: A Liberal Theory of Minority Rights* Oxford: Clarendon Press.

Rawls, J. (1999) *The Law of Peoples* Cambridge, Mass. and London: Harvard University Press.

Russett, B. (1993) *Grasping the Democratic Peace* Princeton, New Jersey: Princeton University Press.

Universal Declaration of Human Rights: http://www.un.org/Overview/rights.html.

Further Reading

It is important to be clear about the nature of *rights* before venturing into a discussion of *human* rights – a good introduction is Peter Jones, *Rights* (Basingstoke: Macmillan, 1994). General discussions of human rights include: Maurice Cranston, *What are Human Rights?* (Taplinger, 1973) and Ellen Frankel Paul *et al.* (eds), *Human Rights* (Oxford: Oxford University Press, 1984). More intellectually demanding are: Alan Gewirth, *Human Rights: Essays on Justification and Applications* (Chicago, Ill: University of Chicago Press, 1982); R.J. Vincent, *Human Rights and International Relations* (Cambridge: Cambridge University Press, 1986). On the issue of cultural relativism read Simon Caney and Peter Jones (eds), *Human Rights and Global Diversity* (London: Frank Cass, 2001); Jane Cowan *et al.* (eds), *Culture and Rights: Anthropological Perspectives* (Cambridge: Cambridge University Press, 2001), and from the above references Donnelly (2003),

Habermas (1994) and Rawls (1999). On collective rights see Judith Baker (ed.), *Group Rights* (Toronto, Ont.: University of Toronto Press, 1994), and on welfare rights see Robin Attfield and Barry Wilkins (eds), *International Justice and the Third World: Studies in the Philosophy of Development* (London: Routledge, 1992).

Weblinks

There are many excellent human rights resources on the web:

- From a more legal perspective:
  http://library.kent.ac.uk/library/lawlinks/human.htm

- The other sites are a mix of theory, law and advocacy:
  Human Rights Resource Center: http://www.hrusa.org/
  Human Rights Education Associates: http://www.hrea.org/
  Human and Constitutional Rights: http://www.hrcr.org/
  Amnesty International: http://www.amnesty.org/
  Human Rights Watch: http://www.hrw.org/

Chapter 9

Civil Disobedience

Introduction

Civil disobedience is the non-violent breaking of a law on moral grounds. While there were theorists of civil disobedience in the nineteenth and early twentieth centuries, and the theory may be applicable to non-democratic societies, this chapter focuses on post-World War II discussion of civil disobedience in a liberal democratic society. Although few people may ever engage in civil disobedience in their lifetimes it is not a peripheral concept, for the justification of civil disobedience touches on the moral basis of majoritarian democracy. Whereas in the pre-modern and early modern periods political theory was concerned with the right to rebel, the fundamental question raised by civil disobedience to a modern audience is this: how is it possible to have a general respect for the rule of law and yet break specific laws?

Chapter Map

In this chapter we will:

- Distinguish **civil disobedience** from legal protest, revolution and 'mere criminality'.

- Discuss whether we have a special obligation to obey democratically agreed laws.

- Analyse one of the most influential philosophical discussions of civil disobedience – that advanced by John Rawls.

- Apply that theoretical discussion to a case study: the Civil Rights Movement in the United States.

- Discuss Martin Luther King's justification of the Civil Rights Movement.

Protest and Survive?

Peace campaigners demonstrating at RAF Greenham Common air base, 12 December 1982.

In 1981 a group of women set off on a march from Cardiff (Wales) to Greenham Common, a British–American airbase located about 60 miles (100 kilometres) west of London, where Cruise Missiles (guided missiles with nuclear warheads) were to be sited. Once there, they established the 'Greenham Common Women's Peace Camp', and for the next two years they attempted to disrupt construction work – which included the building of missile silos – at the base. Despite their efforts the missiles arrived in November 1983. However, the Peace Camp remained for the rest of the decade, and indeed some women continued there until 2000. There were frequent arrests, resulting in fines and, in a few cases, imprisonment. The local council made repeated attempts to evict the protestors. The 1987 Intermediate-range Nuclear Forces (INF) Treaty signed by the United States and the USSR resulted in the removal of the missiles from Greenham Common. By 1991 all the missiles had gone; in 1992 the US Air Force left, soon followed by their British counterparts. The women who remained after 1992 claimed they were now making a symbolic protest against all nuclear weapons. At the heart of the anti-nuclear protests – which took place across Western Europe in the early 1980s – was a belief that if they did not engage in peaceful law-breaking (civil disobedience) then humanity was doomed: the slogan of the British organisation, the Campaign for Nuclear Disarmament (CND) was 'protest and survive', an ironic comment on the title of a 1960s British government guide to citizens on how to survive a nuclear attack: 'Protect and Survive'.

• Were the Greenham Common protestors justified in breaking the law?

Civil Disobedience and Law-breaking

In this chapter we are concerned with justifications for civil disobedience, and naturally it makes sense to start with a definition of 'civil disobedience'. However, as we shall see, definition and justification are closely related, so that a particular definition implies a certain understanding of the role civil disobedience plays in the political system. What we offer here is an initial definition, which will require further clarification: civil disobedience is morally justified law-breaking, *normally* intended to change a particular law or policy. Civil disobedience has then these components: (a) it involves breaking the law – it is not simply legal protest; (b) there are moral reasons justifying the action; (c) the aim is to change a law or policy; it is not intended to bring down an entire political system – civil disobedience is not revolution.

Of all the concepts discussed in this book, civil disobedience is among a relatively small group where theory and practice are closely related, and indeed where some of the most important theorists of the concept have been its practitioners. American Henry David Thoreau (1817–62) is credited with offering the earliest theory of civil disobedience. Thoreau was imprisoned for refusing to pay a tax that was intended to fund what he regarded as an unjust war by the United States against Mexico. In his essay 'Civil Disobedience' (1849), Thoreau argued that an individual had a moral duty to break an unjust law – you should, he suggests, 'let your life be a counter-friction to stop the machine' (Thoreau, 1991: 36). In other words, civil disobedience was intended to obstruct the implementation of immoral policies. Thoreau's argument was highly influential. Mahatma Gandhi (1869–1948) read 'Civil Disobedience' while in prison, and developed both its theory and practice in his struggle against British rule in India. It was also from a prison cell that Martin Luther King, Jr. wrote what became known as the 'Letter from Birmingham City Jail' (1963), a plea to fellow church leaders to accept the legitimacy of non-violent law-breaking in pursuit of equal rights for US citizens. We will discuss King's argument in some detail towards the end of the chapter. Our concern is primarily with the role of civil disobedience in a liberal democratic society, and for that reason we focus on theorists who locate their discussions of civil disobedience within a wider political theory.

Law-breaking

Criminals break laws, and so do people who engage in civil disobedience. How then do we distinguish the civilly disobedient from the merely criminal? In part, the distinction will rest on *how* the law is broken, in part on *why* it is broken. Before discussing the 'how' and the 'why' it is worth reflecting on the questions in the exercise on p. 201.

Reasons for breaking the law fall into four categories, although the fourth is a sub-category of the third:

1. **Individual self-interest** a law is not in the individual's interests.
2. **Group interest** a law is not in the interests of a particular group.
3. **Morality** a law is morally wrong.
4. **Justice** a law is unjust.

Exercise

Consider three cases of law-breaking:

1. Where you have broken a law on grounds of self-interest.

2. Where you have broken a law because you considered the law morally wrong.

3. Where you have broken a law in the process of protesting against something you consider to be morally wrong.

If you have never broken a law on one or all of these grounds, then imagine cases where you might break the law!

Now ask yourself the following questions – taking each of the above cases in turn (paying special attention to the distinction between cases of type 1 and type 2):

• How did you break the law – was it a public act, or did you evade detection?

• Did you feel guilty about breaking the law?

• Did you consider your actions selfish?

• Do you believe you were morally *justified* in breaking the law?

• Were you morally *obliged* to break the law?

• Was the law widely respected – if not, did that make a difference to your attitude?

All defenders of civil disobedience would reject the first category as justifying law-breaking – to break the law simply because it does not suit your interests is to engage in a criminal act. The second category is more complex. Marx argued that it was in the interests of a particular group, the working class, to overthrow the capitalist system and that as a result a classless society would be created. It follows that it is in the long-term interests of *all* human beings that the working class should succeed. But Marx advocated the complete transformation of society – that is, *revolution* – and not merely the removal of certain laws. And there could for Marx be no appeal to morality, for morality is, as are all ideas, the product of existing, capitalist, society.

Civil disobedience, as distinct from revolution, must appeal to moral ideas accessible to those who support the existing laws. The willingness of the civilly disobedient to accept the penalties for their law-breaking assumes that the 'oppressors' can be moved by their actions. Consequently, most theories of civil disobedience rest on the third and fourth categories. But, as we will see, there is an important distinction between breaking a law because you judge it immoral, and breaking it because you believe it is unjust.

Although self-interest is not a justification for civil disobedience, self-interest might well be a motivating factor. For example, the segregation laws operative in the southern states of the United States before the 1960s damaged the interests of *individual* blacks and blacks as a *group*. But this does not invalidate the claims of people such as Martin Luther King, Jr. that he and other blacks were morally justified in breaking the law.

Civil Disobedience and Political Obligation

Although there is debate among political theorists about the kinds of moral reasons that can justify civil disobedience, there is general agreement that civil disobedience implies political obligation. Laws are broken by people who have a respect for the law. To grasp this we need to distinguish political obligation from legal obligation and social obligation:

- **Legal obligation** Laws are by definition obligatory. If you dispute whether you are under a legal obligation to do something, such as pay a certain tax, then the issue can be settled by reference to a statute, or some other publicly stated legal judgment.

- **Political obligation** The question of whether a person has a *moral* obligation to obey the law cannot be settled by pointing to a statute or legal judgment – we need extra-legal arguments to determine whether a moral obligation exists. The term 'political obligation' *normally* means the moral obligation to obey the law (but see the next point).

- **Social obligation** Some political theorists widen the concept of political obligation to include moral obligations not enforced by law. For example, it might be argued that adults in the United Kingdom have a moral obligation to vote; however, while it is a legal requirement to register to vote, it is not a legal requirement to vote. In Australia, in contrast, voting is required by law. We will restrict the term 'political obligation' to the question of obedience to law, so that it does not arise with regard to voting in the United Kingdom, but it does in Australia. (Whether we decide to vote or not may be relevant to political obligation narrowly defined as obedience to law – we discuss this issue below in relation to Peter Singer's argument about participation.)

There are different arguments for political obligation, but one of the most compelling derives from recognising that the state is an attempt to resolve the problem of assurance (the 'Prisoner's Dilemma'): we all gain by cooperation, and cooperation requires that, on occasion, we forgo our immediate self-interest. That creates a dilemma: a person (the **'free-rider'**) is best off if others forgo their self-interest and submit to the state but that person does not, so that he gains the benefits of living under a state without paying the price. The image of the 'free-rider' is the person who breaks the law out of self-interest. However, there are morally motivated free-riders: submission to the state involves not only giving up self-interest but also a degree of moral judgement. It is this which underlies the claim that civil disobedience is only justified if it appeals to certain kinds of moral reasons – reasons shared by (most) fellow citizens.

Civil Disobedience and Democracy

Democracy and Obedience

Civil disobedience plays a special role in democracy, because it not only indicates the moral limits of majority rule, but also forces us to reflect on the justifications *for*

Peter Singer (1946–)

Born in Melbourne, Australia in 1946, Singer is best known for his book *Animal Liberation* (1975), which argues that discrimination on the grounds of species is no more justified than race or gender discrimination. Singer defends a form of utilitarianism. One conclusion he draws is that 'active euthanasia' – which includes what some critics prefer to call infanticide – can be justified. The book under discussion here – *Democracy and Disobedience* – was an early work, and appears somewhat unconnected with his later, better-known works. However, the roots of his utilitarianism can be seen in *Democracy and Disobedience*: each person's views should count equally.

majority rule. For that reason it is important to consider the relationship between civil disobedience and democracy. While many people living in a liberal democracy consider violating the laws of a non-democratic regime to be not only permissible but praiseworthy, they consider it wrong to break democratically agreed laws. Sometimes the objection to civil disobedience in a democracy is revised when people reflect on particular cases, but there remains a core conviction that democracy is special. Peter Singer provides a philosophical defence of this view in his book *Democracy and Disobedience* (1973). Singer uses a very artificial example to illustrate his argument; however, its artificiality helps to bring out the main lines of the argument.

Oxford University is a collegiate university, with most living and teaching centred around the individual colleges. Singer asks us to imagine that each college is equivalent to a state, and the colleges taken together represent the world system of states. The undergraduates in a college form what Singer calls the Association. Students cannot opt out of membership of the Association. A student could transfer to another college at the university, but she would be obliged to join *its* Association. Of course, she could leave the university, but we are to imagine that the whole world is Oxford University, so that short of death there is no possibility of leaving. The Association of each college has been in existence for as long as anybody can remember – if there was ever a point at which it was set up, the records have been lost. The Association charges a subscription from each student, and we can take this to be equivalent to taxation. At this point we come to alternative ways of making decisions on how much to charge and what the money is spent on:

- **The Leader** Some time ago one student who is now the Leader decided that decision making was inefficient, and the decisions arrived at were stupid. He would now make the decisions, albeit guided by the interests of the other students. If anyone objected they would have to fight it out with the Leader's friends, who were the best fighters in the Association.

- **Democracy** Decisions are taken by a majority vote of all members of the Association. At the meetings all members are free to speak, subject to some essential procedural requirements, such as an agreed time limit on speeches. Meetings are conducted fairly, and the votes are calculated correctly. (There is a third model – the 'Senior Member' – but its introduction would unnecessarily complicate the present discussion.)

We assume that under each model decisions have been made without too much dissension – of course, some students will have found themselves on the 'losing side', but they have accepted whatever decisions have been made. However, an issue arises that causes serious dissension. The Association uses some of the subscription money to buy newspapers that are for general use in the common room, and must not be taken away. One day, it is decided that the common room should take a new paper, *The News*. One member of the Association – the Dissenter – objects to this newspaper, arguing that it is racist, and that other members of the Association, less attuned to the paper's bigotry, will be influenced by it to the detriment of the few black students in the college. Consider now the two models:

- **The Leader** The Dissenter asks the Leader to reconsider his decision, but the Leader is unmoved. The Dissenter 'takes things into his own hands' by getting up early each morning and removing the paper before the others have had a chance to read it.
- **Democracy** It had been agreed by majority vote, and after lengthy debate, that the common room would take *The News*. The Dissenter found himself in a minority. At the next and later meetings he attempts to get the decision reversed, but it becomes clear that a majority wants to take the paper. On realising this, the Dissenter behaves in the same way as under the other model: he removes the paper.

With regard to the Dissenter the initial question that Singer poses is not whether he has moral reasons for removing *The News*, but whether the fact that under the Democracy model there are special reasons for not removing it, reasons which do not exist under the Leader model. Participation is the key difference between democratic and non-democratic systems:

> the Dissenter, by voluntarily participating in the vote on the question of whether *The News* should be ordered, understanding that the purpose of the election is to enable the group to reach a decision on this issue, has behaved in such a way as to lead people reasonably to believe that he was accepting the democratic process as a suitable means of settling the issue. (Singer, 1973: 50)

Democratic decision making is a 'fair compromise' between people who have conflicting moral views.

Fair Compromise

Singer distinguishes between 'absolute fairness' and a 'fair compromise'. Fair compromise is fairness *given certain conditions*. To illustrate the distinction between absolute fairness and fair compromise he gives a couple of examples (the second involves a certain amount of gender-stereotyping, but it is Singer's example and not ours!):

- Two people claim a sum of money, and a judge is appointed to adjudicate between them. Although she can be sure only one has a legitimate claim, she cannot establish which one has the claim, and so divides the money up 50/50. This is a fair compromise. An example of an unfair compromise would be to flip a coin.
- A husband and wife argue over who should do night-time baby duties. The husband says he works all day and so should have an unbroken night of sleep, whereas the wife claims she attends to the baby all day, and so should have a break at night. A fair compromise would be to alternate duties. An unfair compromise would be for the wife to do weekday nights, and the husband weekends.

The point about a fair compromise is that a person can still feel that the decision – to split the money, or to alternate baby duties – is 'unfair' in an 'absolute' sense, but that under the circumstances it is fair. As Singer argues with regard to the Dissenter: 'to disobey when there already is a fair compromise in operation is necessarily to deprive others of the say they have under such a compromise. To do this is to leave the others with no remedy but the use of force' (36).

Singer argues that while we cannot consent – either explicitly or tacitly – to the procedure itself, we can consent by our actions to the decisions made under it. Singer borrows a concept from law to express the moral bindingness of participation: estoppel. He quotes an English judge – Lord Birkenhead: 'Where A has by his words or conduct justified B in believing that a certain state of affairs exists, and B has acted upon such belief to his prejudice, A is not permitted to affirm against B that a different state of facts existed at the same time' (51). An everyday, non-legal example would be the British convention of buying a round of drinks in a pub (bar): if four people go to the pub and the first person buys four pints of beer, and then the second person does so, and then the third person likewise, the fourth, who has accepted three pints, can reasonably be expected to buy a round. She has not consented to the rule or convention of buying a round, but her acceptance of the three pints has affected the behaviour of her three friends.

Singer anticipates the objection that the Dissenter can avoid being bound through estoppel simply by not participating in the democratic process. He argues that the notion of a fair compromise generates not only an obligation to accept the decision of the majority, but also to participate in the process: it is not reasonable to sit it out. If you sit it out and then find the decision made is unacceptable you cannot have grounds for refusing to accept the decision, because you were unreasonable in prejudging the decision. People who do not vote can have no complaint against the decisions made by those who do.

Problems with Democracy

Singer's defence of obedience to a democratically agreed law is an 'all things being equal' defence. He does not argue that we should *always* obey such law. Although he does not discuss situations in which civil disobedience is justified, some of the more obvious ones are dealt with below:

(a) In a representative democracy – Singer's example was of a direct one – the elected representatives will not necessarily mirror the social, ethnic and gender composition of the electorate. The fact that elected assemblies often do not mirror their electorates is not in itself a justification for disobedience. However, if it can be shown that a particular group – for example working-class women – has not had its interests communicated then Singer's participation argument is invalidated.

(b) Most voting systems do not take into account the intensity of a person's preferences. A minority may feel *very strongly* about an issue, but they are outvoted by an *apathetic* majority. Civil disobedience can be a means by which not only are views communicated but the *intensity* of those views are made apparent.

(c) Some people find themselves in a permanent minority. This is exacerbated if electoral politics is based on one dominant social characteristic. For example, in Northern Ireland voting is largely along religious lines. In the period 1922–73 there existed a devolved parliament in Northern Ireland with the Protestant Unionists in the majority (although a significant number of Catholics voted for Unionist parties, at least in the early years). The continuous exclusion of Catholics led to the civil rights movement of the 1960s, which was influenced by the US Civil Rights Movement.

(d) Some people are denied the vote. The largest group is children. Their interests are affected by legislation over which they have no control. Civilly disobedient actions undertaken by children are rare but, arguably, groups of adults representing the interests of children could be justified in engaging in civil disobedience on their behalf.

(e) It could be argued that animals have interests and that these are clearly affected by the democratic process. Although nobody would seriously suggest that cats and dogs should be given votes, there might be a duty of care on human beings, and that duty must be articulated. Some notable examples of civil disobedience have been based on concern for animal welfare; in Britain, there has been a long-running campaign against the use of animals in what are seen by some as unnecessary experiments.

(f) The decisions made today will affect future generations. The justification given for some acts of civil disobedience against the building of roads and airports is that fossil fuel emissions exacerbate global warming, which will have catastrophic consequences for future generations.

The implication of the above points is that democracy can on occasion break down, but that it can also be 'fixed'. The more radical challenge lies in the rejection of majority decision making: a person may believe that a law is simply wrong, and no amount of institutional reform can create a situation in which the majority 'makes it right'. For example, defenders of animal experimentation for medical purposes will maintain that they have given due weight to non-human animals as beings worthy of moral respect, but that human beings have greater moral claims. Opponents of such experiments will disagree, and maintain that actions such as breaking into laboratories and releasing animals are justified on moral grounds. It is very difficult to find common ground between these two positions.

We live in a pluralistic society in which there is not only conflict between different individual and group interests, but also between different moral conceptions. The stability and legitimacy of the political system requires some agreement on moral principles. There need not be agreement on all moral issues – after all, liberalism has its roots in the recognition of pluralism – but there must be some agreement. In the next section we reconsider the arguments of Rawls, who does provide an account of that shared morality, but also justifies civil disobedience.

Rawls: Civil Disobedience and Conscientious Refusal

Rawls's discussion of civil disobedience has been highly influential because among writers on civil disobedience. His account is unusual in locating the defence of civil disobedience in a wider political theory. For Rawls the issues raised by civil disobedience go the heart of the moral basis of democracy.

The Context

We discussed Rawls's work in Chapter 4: as the title of his most important work – *A Theory of Justice* (1972) – implies, Rawls sets out a conception of a just society. Most of *A Theory of Justice* is concerned with what Rawls calls ideal theory; that is, he assumes for the purposes of his argument that people comply strictly with the principles to which they have agreed. He departs from this assumption in one relatively short section of the book – the discussion of civil disobedience. It is only in a society where there is partial, rather than strict, compliance with the principles of **justice** that civil disobedience has a role. This is because civil disobedience is an appeal to the majority – to its 'sense of justice'. The majority is being asked to respect principles that it implicitly accepts. In a (fully) just society there would be no need for civil disobedience and in an unjust society there is no sense of justice to which you can appeal.

It may occur to you that Rawls's theory is just that – *his* theory. But what Rawls is trying to do is articulate what he believes is latent in the culture of a liberal democratic society. We do believe that people have rights; that there should be a social minimum (although maybe not the difference principle); those who hold power should be accountable. The aim of a theory of justice is to create a 'model' by which we can analyse those beliefs – we do not just invent principles of justice; this is why the original position is a thought experiment. In a later book, *The Law of Peoples* (1999), Rawls addresses questions of international justice (see Chapter 8: Human Rights). The primary motivation for writing that book was to provide a way of assessing the legitimacy of the foreign policies of liberal democratic societies. This is germane to the present discussion, for civil disobedience has often been directed at what are perceived to be unjust wars.

Obligation to Obey the Law

Rawls begins his discussion with an apparently paradoxical claim: we have a duty to obey unjust laws, but we are also morally entitled, and possibly have a duty, to disobey unjust laws. To understand this we need to consider the structure of Rawls's theory. The principles of justice are chosen from a position in which people are morally equal – the original position. But the chosen principles are fairly general in nature – they do not take the form of constitutional rights, or concrete laws, and *laws* are the object of civil disobedience.

There are several stages between the agreement to principles of justice and the creation of laws, and what happens between these stages is crucial to our understanding of Rawls's argument for civil disobedience. Rawls sets out a four-stage sequence for the production of law:

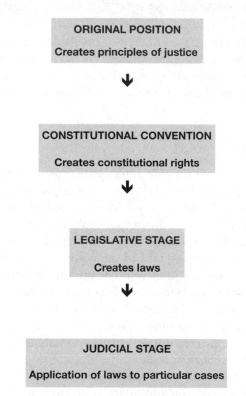

Figure 9.1 Creating law

We are already familiar with the original position. Individuals are required to choose principles of justice behind a veil of ignorance: not only are they denied knowledge of their individual **identities** but also of their particular societies. Rawls argues that rational individuals would choose two principles, which roughly speaking can be summarised as: (1) an equal set of basic liberties, and (2) the guarantee of a social minimum. Once the principles are chosen we need to apply them to real societies. We are to imagine a constitutional convention in which members are denied knowledge of their own identities, but have knowledge of their society. Delegates at the

Ch 4:
Justice,
pp. 84–5

convention are charged with producing a constitution that conforms to the two principles of justice. The convention is imaginary, or hypothetical; although many countries have had something like a constitutional convention – the United States being the obvious example – the exercise can also be applied to a country such as the United Kingdom, which has an uncodified constitution.

Rawls's treatment of the next stage – the legislative – is somewhat unrealistic. He imagines the 'ideal legislator' to be a person who passes statutes that conform to the constitution, but from the standpoint of denial of knowledge of his or her identity. A more realistic view would be that as we move down the sequence of stages the 'veil of ignorance' is progressively lifted, such that at the constitutional stage the delegates know their society but not their individual identities, and at the legislative stage they know both their societies and their identities. If we accept this revision to Rawls's four-stage sequence, then what happens at the legislative stage is a battle for votes, organised by political parties in a majoritarian electoral system. Obviously the danger is that what has been chosen at the first two stages – the principles of justice and the constitution – are jettisoned at the legislative stage in favour of the straightforward clash of competing interests, and the oppression of the minority by the majority. In reality, in a developed liberal democracy this does not happen: politicians usually operate with a sense of justice, and in framing legislation elected representatives quite often ignore the majority of their electorate, and pass laws protective of minority groups. A realistic model of the legislator is a person who is 'cross-pressured': she needs to get elected and re-elected and so cannot ignore the often illiberal views of the electorate, but at the same time she is moved by institutionally embodied principles of justice.

It is at the fourth – judicial – stage that Rawls thinks we have complete knowledge of the facts. This stage entails the application of rules, or laws, to particular cases by judges and administrators, and the following of rules by citizens. The possibility of injustice arises at this stage and therefore also scope for civil disobedience. Given our criticism of Rawls's description of the third – legislative – stage, it would simplify the discussion if we combined the third and fourth stages, and simply called it the legislative stage.

With this sequence of stages now in place we can return to the paradox of conflicting obligations. First, how can we have an obligation to obey unjust laws? At the first stage – the original position – we know that principles of justice must be embodied in a constitution, and constitutions provide the framework for law-making. We also know that people are in conflict with one another, and so laws will never be passed unanimously – there will always be winners and losers. What is required is a decision-making rule that is acceptable to all. It is highly unlikely that anything other than majoritarianism would be chosen in the constitutional convention. The danger is that the majority will sometimes pass unjust laws – laws which, for example, deny equal rights to minority groups. Therefore, we have a conflict:

- The principle of majority rule is effectively endorsed from stage one, which is a standpoint of moral equality, and therefore of justice.
- Majority rule will sometimes generate unjust laws.

If an individual felt entitled and, perhaps, obliged to break every law he deemed unjust, then majoritarian democracy would collapse, and in the process so would the possibility of a just society. The question, or challenge – 'what if everyone did that?' – can always reasonably be asked of someone engaged in civil disobedience.

Rawls argues that the original position argument only works if we assume that we have a moral duty to create and uphold just institutions – this is a 'natural duty' in the sense that it precedes the choice of particular principles of justice. This means: we 'enter' the original position not knowing what principles we will choose, *but committed to respecting whatever principles are chosen*. We do not choose principles but then refuse to live by them.

The natural duty to create and uphold just institutions amounts to respecting the real difficulties of 'operationalising' principles, and so not disobeying every law you think is unjust. On the other hand, upholding justice also means resisting injustice. What civil disobedience then involves is making a judgement not between just and unjust laws but between *different types of unjust laws*. One suggestion Rawls makes for determining the point at which civil disobedience is justified is the degree to which a particular group bears the burden of injustice. If a group finds itself habitually, rather than occasionally, the victim of injustice then there are grounds for civil disobedience. The black community in the southern states of the United States up until the civil rights legislation of the 1960s is an obvious example.

The Nature and Role of Civil Disobedience

Given the fact that in a just society decisions will be made by majority vote – subject to many checks and balances – the possibility of civil disobedience arises for Rawls only in a democratic society:

> At what point does the duty to comply with laws enacted by a legislative majority (or with executive acts supported by such a majority) cease to be binding in view of the right to defend one's liberties and the duty to oppose injustice? This involves the nature and limits of majority rule. For this reason the problem of civil disobedience is a crucial test for any theory of the moral basis of democracy. (Rawls, 1972: 363)

The leading idea behind Rawls's theory of civil disobedience is that in breaking the law *the civilly disobedient are addressing, or appealing to, the sense of justice of the majority*. All the other points that Rawls makes, including the important distinction he makes between civil disobedience and conscientious refusal, lead back to this idea.

Rawls sets out a number of conditions on civil disobedience:

1. **Injustice must be clear** What is unjust is determined by the principles of justice. Of the two, breaches of the first principle – equal liberty – are likely to be much clearer than denial of the second – guarantee of a social minimum (the difference principle). For example, to deny a class of adults the right to vote on grounds of their ethnic or religious identity, or their gender, would be a clear infraction of the first principle. It is not only a clear injustice, but its remedy – granting the equal right to vote – is easy to grasp. On the other hand, significant economic inequality is much less *obviously* unjust, and the solution to the claimed injustice is not apparent.

2. **It involves breaking the law, rather than simply testing it** Some laws are broken in order to force a judicial judgment, but this does not constitute civil disobedience. As we will see this might rule out classifying significant aspects of the struggle against segregation in the southern states as civil disobedience.

3. **It need not involve breaking the law that is the object of civil disobedience** Laws are broken in the process of engaging in civil disobedience, but they need not be the direct object of the civilly disobedient action. For example, in order to protest against an unjust war, you might sit down in the middle of the road, thus violating traffic laws, but it is not the traffic laws that are the target of the action (you will probably accept that it makes sense to have laws which prohibit people sitting down in the road!).

4. **It must be a public act** Civil disobedience is a communicative act – the majority is being given 'fair notice' that a law is unjust. The communicative act consists not simply in the transmission of information – that could be achieved through covert action – but in getting the majority to understand that the civilly disobedient are making an appeal. Indeed, there is a distinction between communicating something to the majority, and *appealing* to it.

5. **It must be non-violent and must not constitute a 'threat'** The reasoning behind this is similar to that behind (4) – the civilly disobedient want the majority to change the law for the right reason, namely because it is unjust and not because they fear the consequences of maintaining the law. Rawls could be criticised for naivety: one group may be genuinely non-violent and non-threatening, but their actions could be unintentionally threatening insofar as they make the majority aware of the existence of other, less peaceful, groups. The shadow of Malcolm X and the Nation of Islam was always behind that of Martin Luther King, Jr. Furthermore, it is not obvious that *non-violent* obstruction undermines the appeal to a sense of justice, and most campaigns have involved the deliberate *inconveniencing* of the majority.

6. **The civilly disobedient accept the penalties for law-breaking** Once again, the reasoning behind this point is that the civilly disobedient are appealing to, rather than threatening, the majority. Willingness to accept the penalties for law-breaking – that is, not resisting arrest – demonstrates sincerity. Such behaviour may embarrass the majority, who must ask themselves whether they really want to punish, often in a draconian fashion, clearly peace-loving people.

7. **Even if laws are seriously unjust, civil disobedience must not threaten the stability of the political system** The thinking behind this requirement is that a situation might arise where there are a number of groups justifiably engaged in civil disobedience, but the conjoint effects of their actions threaten the stability of the political system. In such a situation groups must show restraint. Although it is rather unrealistic, Rawls suggests that civilly disobedient groups might come to an agreement whereby they take it in turns engaging in civil disobedience. One might wonder whether a political system that provokes so much civil disobedience is even 'partially' just, but he may have in mind the United States in the 1960s, when there were civil rights actions *and* anti-Vietnam War actions.

8. **Civil disobedience takes place within 'fidelity to law'** This underwrites the entire project of civil disobedience. The civilly disobedient do not seek to bring down the existing system, but rather they seek to strengthen it by removing

injustice, such that the system will win the loyalty of all citizens. In this sense the civilly disobedient demonstrate fidelity – or faithfulness – to the law.

We round off our outline of Rawls's theory with a discussion of his distinction between civil disobedience and conscientious refusal.

Conscientious Refusal

A distinction can be made between disobedience on general moral grounds, and disobedience on the narrower – but still moral – ground of injustice. Rawls's aim in *A Theory of Justice* was to articulate a morality – a 'theory of justice' – appropriate to the political sphere. That political morality leaves open many other areas of morality. Conscientious refusal may be grounded in that political morality, but it need not be; it may be based on 'religious or other principles at variance with the constitutional order' (Rawls, 1972: 369). The clearest modern example of conscientious refusal is objection to military service, either for general pacifist reasons or because of opposition to a particular war. Rawls argues that such objections cannot be *automatically* accepted, for justice requires on occasion that people be prepared to defend – by force of arms – the political system. However, he concedes that the spirit of pacifism accords with the values underlying a just society – it is rare for nearly just societies to go to war against one another (this is the so-called 'democratic peace argument'). He also argues that an unjust war – a war that violates the laws of peoples – can quite properly be the object of civil disobedience.

Ch 8:
Human Rights,
p. 189

Conscientious refusal cannot be an appeal to the sense of justice of the majority. The danger with conscientious refusal is that it undermines the political order by substituting individual moral judgement for the collective judgement of society. An example would be the refusal to pay taxes that go towards the development and maintenance of nuclear weapons. It is possible that most people are 'nuclear pacifists' – while they might believe that a just war with conventional weapons is possible, the use of nuclear warheads represents a hugely disproportionate response to the aggression of another country. But, among nuclear pacifists, a majority might judge that the *threat* to use – rather than actual use of – nuclear weapons is better than submission to a foreign power. Of course, a nuclear power has to convince the putative enemy country that it really will use the weapons, and so there is an element of subterfuge, as well as risk, behind deterrence theory which seems at odds with the transparency one expects of a just society. Nonetheless, there can be reasonable moral disagreement, such that the will of the majority should prevail.

Another important distinction between civil disobedience and conscientious refusal is that the latter may entail a greater 'introversion' than the former: a significant strand in conscientious refusal is the striving for moral integrity, that is, a feeling that *regardless of the consequences* you cannot support a law or policy. Insofar as conscientious refusal is a form of 'moral purity' it is in tension with civil disobedience, which looks 'outwards' towards the majority, and appeals to it to change. The idea of moral purity is central to Gandhi's *satyagraha*, which means an 'insistence on truth'. Because *satyagraha* is the moral basis of civil disobedience it is often – erroneously – translated as civil disobedience. One final point: conscientious refusal is not incompatible with civil disobedience because an individual might be *motivated* by her non-political moral beliefs, but still attempt to communicate in the language of justice to the majority.

Martin Luther King, Jr. and the Civil Rights Movement

The aim of this final section is to apply the theoretical discussion of the previous section to a case study of civil disobedience: Martin Luther King, Jr. and the Civil Rights Movement in the United States in the 1950s and 1960s. There are several reasons why we have chosen this: (a) it is the most famous example of civil disobedience and the one that influenced Rawls (*A Theory of Justice*, first published in 1971, was written during the period of the Civil Rights Movement); (b) it is now close to 40 years since the main objectives of the movement were achieved, so we can assess its impact – from a Rawlsian perspective this is important, because if civil disobedience is an appeal to the majority to remove injustice *and so strengthen the political system*, then we need to see whether this was as a result of the movement.

Biography	Martin Luther King, Jr. (1929–68)

Born into a family of pastors – his grandfather was the minister at Ebenezer Baptist Church in Atlanta, his father succeeded him, and Martin Luther acted as an assistant minister – he attended segregated public (state) schools in Georgia, going on to graduate with a BA degree (1948) from Morehouse College, and to undertake theological training at the racially mixed Crozer Theological Seminary.

With a fellowship from Crozer he enrolled in graduate studies at Boston University, receiving a doctorate degree in 1955. It was while he was at Boston that he met his future wife Coretta Scott, who, after King's death, wrote an account of their life together: *My Life with Martin Luther King, Jr.* (Scott King, 1970).

In 1954 King became pastor of Dexter Avenue Baptist Church in Montgomery (Alabama) and a member of the executive of the influential National Association for the Advancement of Colored People, and as such spearheaded the bus boycott in Montgomery. During the boycott King was arrested and his house bombed, but the effect was to make King the undisputed leader of the Civil Rights Movement.

In 1957 he was elected President of the Southern Christian Leadership Conference. In the 11 years between 1957 and 1968 King travelled over 6 million miles, spoke over 2,500 times, wrote five books and numerous articles. His most famous speech – the 'I Have a Dream' address – was delivered at the culmination of a march of 250,000 people on Washington DC. He was the youngest man to be awarded the Nobel Peace Prize (1964). On the evening of 4 April 1968, while standing on the balcony of his motel room in Memphis (Tennessee), King was assassinated. Congress passed legislation in 1983 making the third Monday in January 'Martin Luther King Day', a nationwide holiday.

This biography is adapted from that produced when King was awarded the Nobel Peace Prize: http://nobelprize.org/peace/laureates/1964/king-bio.html.

Historical Background to the Civil Rights Movement

The Civil Rights Movement has its roots in the struggle for emancipation from slavery in the nineteenth century. There were sporadic slave revolts before 1860, but it was during the civil war of 1861–5 that the struggle for emancipation become a central focus of US life. During the civil war, the northern and western states of America had remained within the Union, while the 11 southern states formed the Confederacy (the 11 were: Alabama, Arkansas, Florida, Georgia, Louisiana, Mississippi, North Carolina, South Carolina, Tennessee, Texas, Virginia). After President Abraham Lincoln issued the Emancipation Proclamation (1862), slavery became the main issue dividing 'North' (Union) and 'South' (Confederacy). But it is important to stress the constitutional struggle behind the issue of slavery, because this underlay the political debate in the 1950s and 1960s.

The 10th Amendment (the 10th article of the Bill of Rights) guarantees states' rights: 'the powers not delegated to the United States by the Constitution, nor prohibited by it to the States, are reserved to the States respectively, or to the people'. The 'states' rights' argument tended to be used by whichever bloc was in the minority: in the earlier nineteenth century the (minority) anti-slave states of New England asserted states' rights to prohibit the holding of slaves against the majority slave states. When the balance tipped in favour of anti-slavery, the now-minority slave states asserted their rights to maintain a social institution – slavery – which they held to be central to their life and culture.

The Union defeated the Confederacy and in 1866 Congress passed the Civil Rights Act (which followed the 13th Amendment to the Constitution, abolishing slavery), which declared that all persons born in the United States were citizens and so entitled to 'full and equal benefit of the laws'. However, white Southerners, while forced to accept the abolition of slavery, used state power – through the Democratic Party – to deny newly emancipated blacks their voting rights, educational opportunities and other benefits 'of the laws'. The so-called 'Reconstruction' (1865–77) was a failure. So by the beginning of the twentieth century most blacks in the South had lost the right to vote, and there was widespread *legally enforced* segregation of education, transport and other services. In the first half of the twentieth century American blacks were divided over the correct tactics to adopt against discrimination: Booker T. Washington (1856–1915) advocated abandoning politics in favour of economic advancement; W.E.B. Du Bois (1868–1963) founded the National Association for the Advancement of Colored People (NAACP), which demanded full equality in accordance with the US Constitution; after World War I Marcus Garvey (1887–1940) advocated separation from white society, and even emigration to Africa.

The Civil Rights Movement

After World War II – ostensibly a war against racism in which many thousands of black servicemen had fought – the pressure for change increased. We will focus on particular events and tactics, rather than provide a narrative; several of the books (Further Reading) and websites (Weblinks) provide useful timelines.

Discrimination was so widespread – deeply institutionalised – in the South that it is difficult to pinpoint particular laws that were the object of civil disobedience.

However, among the more blatantly discriminatory laws were: the denial of the right to vote (through a wide range of mechanisms); segregated schooling; segregated services, such as seats on buses and places at 'lunch counters'; denial of entry to many facilities, such as libraries, cinemas and swimming pools; denial of places at colleges and universities; illegitimate restrictions on the right to protest; failure on the part of the police to protect blacks against violence from white racists such as the Ku Klux Klan.

Not all the actions of the civil rights activists would fall under the category of 'civil disobedience'. In fact, three strands can be discerned: (a) legal protests and actions, such as the Montgomery bus boycott (although, in fact, such actions soon became 'illegal' as legal devices were deployed against the participants); (b) actions through the courts, using or testing federal law against state law; (c) acts of peaceful law-breaking – that is, civil disobedience – such as refusing to obey police orders to disperse, and sitting at segregated lunch counters, where the proprietors could appeal to state law to enforce segregation. It is extremely important to understand how the Civil Rights Movement took place within a context of constitutional conflict, which mirrored the federal versus states conflict of the nineteenth century. Repeatedly, the federal level attempts to force desegregation on the South. Here are some key examples (federal level in bold):

- 1954: *Brown* v. *Board of Education of Topeka*: **Supreme Court** determines that segregation in public schools is unconstitutional.
- 1957: Nine black students are blocked from entering the formerly all-white Central High School, Little Rock, Arkansas. **Federal troops** sent in to protect the nine.
- 1961: James Meredith becomes first black student to enrol at the University of Mississippi; violence erupts and **President Kennedy** sends in 5,000 **federal troops**.
- 1963: 24th Amendment to the **Constitution** abolishes the poll tax, which had been used to prevent blacks registering to vote.
- 1964: **Congress** passes the Civil Rights Act – the most radical civil rights legislation since the 1866 Civil Rights Act.
- 1965: **Congress** passes the Voting Rights Act.
- 1965: **President Johnson** issues Executive Order 11246, enforcing **affirmative action**.
- 1967: *Loving* v. *Virginia*: **Supreme Court** rules that the prohibition on interracial marriage is unconstitutional.
- 1968: **Congress** passes another Civil Rights Act, this time outlawing discrimination in the sale, rental and financing of housing.

The laws that were the object of civil disobedience were state laws rather than federal laws; in general, the federal level was on the side of the Civil Rights Movement. We now consider some specific actions undertaken by civil rights activists: bus boycotts and freedom rides; sit-ins at lunch counters and other segregated spaces; marches, particularly on electoral registration offices.

Bus Boycotts

In romanticised accounts of the Civil Rights Movement the refusal of Rosa Parks to give up her seat for a white passenger is often taken as the starting point of the

Civil Rights Movement. On 1 December 1955 Parks got on a bus in Montgomery (Alabama), and sat in the fifth row with three other blacks in the 'coloreds' section' of the bus. After a few stops the front four rows filled up, and a white man was left standing; custom dictated that there could not be 'mixed' rows, so all four would be required to move; three of them complied but Parks refused. She was subsequently arrested. Significantly – from the perspective of civil disobedience – the charge was unclear: when a black lawyer tried to find out, the police told him it was 'none of your damn business'. (Legal theorist Lon Fuller argued that valid law must have certain characteristics, among which is clarity.)

Ch 3: Equality, pp. 67–8

It should be said that Parks's action was not entirely spontaneous; the Civil Rights Movement had been looking for a suitable 'victim' to publicise the issue of bus segregation and provoke a widespread boycott, and her action was not really the start of the Movement. There had been previous attempts to bring about a boycott. The boycott was effective, but the authorities then sought legal devices to end it: they required cab drivers to charge a minimum 45 cents per journey (black drivers had been charging 10 cents – the price of a bus ticket; the pro-boycott organisation, the Montgomery Improvement Association (MIA) (headed by Martin Luther King, Jr.), then instituted a 'private taxi' scheme); a very old law prohibiting boycotts was used, and King was arrested; liability insurance on the 'private taxis' was not granted. Eventually a *federal* court decided that such segregation was unconstitutional, and this was confirmed by the Supreme Court.

Freedom Rides

In 1947 the Congress of Racial Equality (CORE) set out to test the Supreme Court's 1946 ruling that segregation on interstate transportation was unconstitutional by sitting in 'whites only' seating. The so-called 'journey of reconciliation' met heavy resistance and was not a success. In 1961 the same strategy was adopted, but this time other court rulings had reinforced the claim for desegregation, and the campaign was better organised: white civil rights activists would sit in 'blacks only' seats and also use blacks only facilities at rest stops, and black civil rights activists would do the reverse on the same buses and at the same stops. They met a great deal of resistance, including mob violence and mass arrests. Ultimately they succeeded in getting the Interstate Commerce Commission to outlaw segregation. From the perspective of Rawls's criteria for civil disobedience, the freedom rides are a grey area: the *political* aim of the action was to shame President Kennedy, who was perceived at the 1960 election to be sympathetic to civil rights, but who on taking office in January 1961 was much cooler about tackling the southern states. The *legal* aim was to test the Supreme Court's 1946 ruling. It is a matter for debate whether *testing* a law constitutes civil disobedience.

Sit-ins

The strategy here was very similar to the freedom rides: groups of black students would challenge segregation by sitting at 'whites only' lunch counters and wait until they were served; once served they moved to the next shop. There was also an element of boycott: the Woolworth's chain had segregated counters in the South, but mixed counters in the North – there was a boycott of New York shops designed to force the company to desegregate its entire chain. At first, the sit-ins met with little resistance – the students were not served, but neither were they harassed. But a white reaction did build up, with white youths attacking the activists, and the police then arresting the (peaceful) activists. A common tactic of the activists was for one group to be ready to take the place of the arrested group, with the consequence that the jails would soon fill up and the machinery of justice grind to a halt. Again, from our perspective this is interesting: Rawls says that civil disobedience must not only be non-violent – and the sit-ins certainly were non-violent – but also non-coercive. Arguably, incapacitating the justice system is coercive. Also, relatedly, and again contra Rawls, the reason why many actions, including the bus boycotts, worked was not because the majority became aware of injustice, but because their interests were damaged – pressure came from bus companies and stores to desegregate.

Electoral Registration Campaigns

The biggest 'flashpoint' was over voter registration. In principle, blacks could vote, but the southern states found numerous ways to make it difficult for them to register as voters: there were few registration offices in black areas; opening hours were highly restricted; potential voters were intimidated with the connivance of the authorities – photographs were taken and employers informed; there was often a tax (poll tax) for registration; there were literacy qualifications (although many blacks were better educated than the officials).

The most famous, or infamous, set of events took place in 1965 at Selma (Alabama). In 1963 just 1 per cent of blacks in Selma were registered to vote. After winning the Nobel Peace Prize (December 1964) King decided that Selma should be the focus of a campaign. After various marches, arrests and considerable violence on the part of the authorities, events came to a head on 7 March 1965 with a march across Edmund Pettus Bridge in Selma (Pettus was a Confederate General) where protestors were met by police and state troopers, who ordered them to disperse. They then attacked the protestors; pictures of their actions were transmitted across the world. What followed was complex, involving decisions such as whether to accept legal injunctions on marches, but eventually the Voting Rights Act (1965) was passed, with the number of registered black voters rising from 23 per cent in 1964 to 61 per cent in 1969. Although it is clear that the Civil Rights Movement affected the general political debate, it is a matter of debate whether *individual* campaigns, such as that at Selma, was causally responsible for *particular* pieces of legislation, such as the Voting Rights Act. We now turn to King's justification of his actions.

Martin Luther King, 'Letter from Birmingham City Jail' (1963)

King's Letter was addressed to fellow – mainly Southern white – clergymen, some of whom had criticised King's campaign of civil disobedience. Given that Rawls argues that civil disobedience is an appeal to the majority, it is important to recognise the *two* audiences King addresses: the clergy are the explicit addressees, but the majority of US citizens are the implicit addressees. Although he does not separate them out we can discern both Christian and secular arguments in the Letter; of course, the great majority of Americans define themselves as Christian, but King communicates awareness that Christian arguments are not sufficient to justify civil disobedience. In setting out King's argument, we follow his narrative of events. Obviously his account should not be treated uncritically, but since our prime concern is with how he justified his actions from his perspective, the veracity of the historical details can be left to historians.

King sets out 'four basic steps' in a campaign of civil disobedience (King, 1991: 69):

1. the collection of facts to determine whether injustice is 'alive';
2. negotiation;
3. self-purification;
4. direct action.

The action that resulted in King's imprisonment – and the occasion for the Letter – were illegal demonstrations in Birmingham, Alabama. These were directed against the 'whites only' and 'no coloreds' signs in shops, the segregated lunch counters, and the deliberate negligence of the police in investigating 18 bombings of black homes and churches over the previous six years. With regard to the first step, there was little doubt that Birmingham had one of the worst records on civil rights in the South.

The next step was to negotiate before engaging in civil disobedience. There were attempts to get the shopkeepers to remove their signs. Promises were made but not honoured. A mayoral election in March 1963 between the reactionary Bull Connor and moderate – but still segregationist – Albert Boutwell resulted in the latter's victory, but because the three-man commission that had run Birmingham, and included Connor, refused to stand down, there was no movement on removal of discrimination. Negotiation had failed. The next step was 'self-purification'. This must be distinguished from what we identified as the 'introversion' that sometimes characterises conscientious refusal. The aim of self-purification is to ascertain whether the protestors will be able to endure violence without reacting violently. To this end, workshops on non-violent protest were held.

Finally, we come to the act of civil disobedience. King argues that one of the aims of civil disobedience is to 'create such a crisis and establish such creative tension that a community which has constantly refused to negotiate is forced to confront the issue' (71). The new Mayor Boutwell might be persuaded that resistance to desegregation was futile. It could be argued – and King was aware of this – that the effectiveness of civil disobedience rests on the existence of a violent alternative to it. Those engaged in civil disobedience need not intend to communicate this message for it to be communicated through their actions. In 1963 the widely perceived 'alternative' to Martin Luther King, Jr. was Malcolm X's Muslim movement (see his biography box). Indeed King cites this movement in his Letter, arguing that if civil rights activists are dismissed as 'rabble rousers' and 'outside agitators' then millions of blacks 'out of frustration and despair, will seek solace and security in black nationalist ideologies, a development that will lead inevitably to a frightening racial nightmare' (77).

Malcolm X (1925–65)

Born Malcolm Little, in Nebraska in 1925, the son of a Baptist minister, Malcolm X – he rejected the 'slave name' Little in favour of X, which denoted his lost African name – became a leading figure in the black separatist movement, a movement that advocated violence to end discrimination, although there is a debate about whether Malcolm X himself ever advocated violence.

While in prison (1946–53) he converted to Islam and joined the Nation of Islam (NOI). He was credited with increasing the NOI's membership from 500 in 1952 to 30,000 in 1963. Disillusioned with NOI, in 1964 he formed the Muslim Mosque and went on pilgrimage to Mecca. His experiences of meeting a wider range of whites persuaded him that integration was possible.

He was assassinated by NOI followers in 1965.

Websites:
http://www.cmgww.com/historic/malcolm/index.htm
http://www.brothermalcolm.net/mxcontent.html
http://www.malcolm-x.org/

Responding to the question how it is possible to obey some laws but disobey others, King argues that there are just laws and unjust laws:

> an unjust law is a human law that is not rooted in eternal and natural law. Any law that uplifts human personality is just. Any law that degrades human personality is unjust. All segregation statutes are unjust because segregation distorts the soul and damages the personality. It gives the segregator a false sense of superiority, and the segregated a false sense of inferiority. (73).

In expanding on this distinction King cites the Christian 'church fathers' Augustine (354–430) and Aquinas (1225–74), Jewish philosopher Martin Buber (1878–1965), and Protestant theologian Paul Tillich (1886–1965). It may appear that King is appealing to a particular moral conception, drawn from Judaism and Christianity, rather than a *political* morality. Three points should be made. First, so long as the underlying appeal extends beyond your own particular conception of what is ultimately valuable, which for King is rooted in Christian teaching, then enlisting Christian (and Jewish) thinkers – Augustine, Aquinas, Buber, Tillich – is legitimate. In effect, King is saying 'I am a Christian, but you do not have to be a Christian to recognise the injustice I describe'. Insofar as we interpret King's argument for civil disobedience to be based on his Christian beliefs it might be thought he is engaged in what Rawls terms conscientious refusal, but conscientious refusal is not incompatible with civil disobedience – a person, such as King, can be motivated by a secular political morality *and* a Christian morality. What would be problematic is to appeal only to a non-political morality. Second, the letter was written to Christian clergy, so the Christian references are unsurprising. Third, King goes on to restate the argument in secular language:

> An unjust law is a code that a majority inflicts on a minority that is not binding on itself. This is difference made legal. On the other hand a just law is a code that a majority compels a minority to follow that it is willing to follow itself. This is sameness made legal. (1991: 74)

He gives a couple of examples, the first of which is problematic. Because the state of Alabama had denied blacks the right to vote they could not be bound by its laws. The danger with this argument is that even if blacks had voted, being in a minority they might have been subject to discriminatory laws. A rather better example is the denial of police permits to demonstrate: King accepts that there should be controls on demonstrations, but objects to the misuse of permits to deny civil rights activists the possibility of peaceful protest, while opponents of civil rights can protest unhindered. (We could also add that peaceful protestors were arrested, while their white attackers were let free; that prisoners were often released into the hands of the Ku Klux Klan; and that the right to choose who to serve in a shop or restaurant was asserted as a right when whites wanted to discriminate, but choosing to boycott buses was deemed illegal.)

King argues that a sign of the good faith of the civil rights activists is that they break the law openly and are willing to accept the penalties for law-breaking. These are, of course, on Rawls's list of conditions for civil disobedience. And finally, as if to underline the stabilising power of civil disobedience, King concludes his Letter with the following statement:

> One day the South will know that when the disinherited children of God sat down at lunch counters they were in reality standing up for the best in the American dream and the most sacred values in our Judeo-Christian heritage, and thusly, carrying our whole nation back to those great wells of democracy which were dug deep by the founding fathers in the formulation of the Constitution and the Declaration of Independence. (1991: 84)

What makes the Civil Rights Movement an important example of civil disobedience is that in philosophical terms it took place in the space between the constitution and lower-level law. This may also, however, raise some definitional difficulties. The most visible aspect of the civil rights struggle was the clash between supporters and opponents of equal rights in the streets, on the buses, and at the 'lunch counters'. But behind that struggle was another: a struggle between federal law and constitutional judgements on the one side, and the southern states on the other. It is notable that when defenders of segregation organised themselves politically – at elections – they adopted the banner of States' Rights: the rights of the states against the president, Congress, and Supreme Court. Civil disobedience was made possible by: (a) the existence of a (basically) just constitution, and (b) the refusal at a lower level of law-making to respect the constitution. It could be argued that what the civil rights activists were doing was appealing, not to the majority of fellow Americans, but to the judiciary; in effect, they were forcing test cases for the legitimacy of state law. On the other hand, it might be maintained that it was through elected representatives in Congress – representatives of 'the majority' – that the great strides forward in civil rights were made. However, the failure of the Civil Rights Movement to change Southerners' attitudes is revealed in the Congressional voting figures for the Civil Rights Act (1964). In the Senate, the Democrats divided 46–21 in favour (69 per cent in favour) and the Republicans were 27–6 in favour (82 per cent). All Southern Democratic Senators voted against. In the House of Representatives, the Democrats divided 152–96 in favour (61 per cent) and the Republicans 138–34 in favour (80 per cent). Of the Southern Democratic Congressman 92 out of 103 (89 per cent) voted against.

Summary

Civil disobedience may seem a marginal political issue, given that most citizens do not engage in it. However, the arguments for and against civil disobedience go to the heart of the moral basis of democracy and, in particular, the only viable form of democracy in a modern society: representative majoritarian democracy. While Rawls's theory of civil disobedience does not really hold up when tested against historical reality it provides a very useful framework within which to assess both the grounds, and the limits, of majoritarian democracy. More generally, the development of the concept of civil disobedience grew out of, but also represents a critique of, early liberal theories of political obligation; civil disobedience implies that human beings should retain a degree of moral autonomy vis-à-vis the state.

Questions

1. Does the fact that a law was passed through a democratic process give us a special reason for obeying it?
2. Can a person who engages in civil disobedience give a coherent answer to the accusation that 'If everybody did that, there would be a collapse in social order'?
3. Is there a valid distinction between civil disobedience and conscientious refusal?
4. Was the American Civil Rights Movement really an example of civil disobedience?

References

King, M.L., Jr. (1991) 'Letter from Birmingham City Jail' in H.A. Bedau (ed.), *Civil Disobedience in Focus* London: Routledge.

Rawls, J. (1972) *A Theory of Justice* Oxford: Clarendon Press.

Rawls, J. (1999) *The Law of Peoples* Cambridge Mass. and London: Harvard University Press.

Scott King, C. (1970) *My Life with Martin Luther King, Jr.* London: Hodder & Stoughton.

Singer, P. (1973) *Democracy and Disobedience* Oxford: Clarendon Press.

Thoreau, D. (1991) 'Civil Disobedience' in H.A. Bedau (ed.), *Civil Disobedience in Focus* London: Routledge.

Further Reading

There is not an extensive literature on civil disobedience (although civil disobedience is often implicitly discussed in the context of political obligation). Nonetheless, the following are useful: H.A. Bedau (1991) contains 'classic' texts on civil disobedience. Another edited collection by Bedau is: H.A. Bedau, *Civil Disobedience: Theory and Practice* (New York: Pegasus, 1969). Two further studies are Chaim Gans, *Philosophical Anarchism and Political Disobedience* (Cambridge: Cambridge University Press, 1992), and Leslie Macfarlane, *Political Disobedience* (London: Macmillan, 1971). For some books on the Civil Rights Movement see: Adam Fairclough, *To Redeem the Soul of America: the Southern Christian Leadership Conference and Martin Luther King, Jr.* (Athens, Geo. and London: University of Georgia Press, 1987); David Garrows, *Protest at Selma: Martin Luther King, Jr., and the Voting Rights Act of 1965* (New Haven, Conn. and London: Yale University Press, 1978): John Salmond, *My Mind Set on Freedom: A History of the Civil Rights Movement, 1954–68* (Chicago, Ill.: Ivan R. Dee, 1997).

Weblinks

Most websites on civil disobedience are activist oriented, but these can be interesting because they provide guidance on carrying out civilly disobedient acts – it is useful to compare this advice with Rawls's checklist:

- ACT-UP (gay rights organisation): http://www.actupny.org/documents/CDdocuments/CDindex.html

- Peace campaigners: http://www.activism.net/peace/nvcdh/

- Animal rights campaigners: http://www.animal-law.org/library/pamphlet.htm

- Fathers4Justice (a British-based group campaigning for fathers' access to their children): http://www.fathers-4-justice.org/

Chapter 10

Terrorism

Introduction

Since 11 September 2001, when the World Trade Center and part of the Pentagon were demolished through terrorist attacks, the question of terrorism has been widely debated in the media and elsewhere.

Just what is terrorism? Can a terrorist be coherently distinguished from a guerrilla or freedom fighter? An analysis of terrorism is particularly important, given the fact that authoritarian regimes may find it convenient to label all manifestations of opposition as 'terrorist' in nature. Why does terrorism arise? And above all, what we can do about it? It is important that we try to understand terrorism not as a way of condoning it but because we will never be able to eradicate terrorism unless we understand it – its sources, its *raison d'être* and its apparent justifications.

Chapter Map

In this chapter we will look at:

- The liberal tradition and **terrorism**. The traditional view of the state as an institution that is not itself terrorist.

- Salmi's distinction between four types of violence, and a critique of Salmi's position. The distinction between political violence and terrorism proper.

- Marx, Lenin and Mao's view of terrorism. The problem of a general theory of terrorism.

- The roots of terrorism.

- The link between terrorism and the state. The problem of US policy towards terrorism.

if these happen to be small societies in which there is little anonymity; between these extremes, terrorism can occur almost anywhere'. He cites Kofi Annan, Secretary-General of the UN, to the effect that the poor suffer enough: why add to their misery by branding them potential terrorists (Laqueur, 2003: 16; 18)? Alongside poverty must be added national and ethnic conflict, although this kind of conflict has not been evident in some countries in which terrorism has occurred. It is useful to distinguish between the 'symptoms' and 'causes' of terrorism (Von Hippel, 2002: 25). No strategy can be successful that simply addresses itself to the symptoms, and ignores the reasons why terrorism arises. Just as it is difficult to define terrorism, it is also difficult to locate terrorism 's roots, but what can be said is that terrorism arises because people cannot 'change places'. This is not because people are different, since we are all different from one another – in terms of our age, occupation, gender, outlook etc. There are a multiplicity of factors involved in an inability to change places: significant disparities in wealth, religious intolerance, bitterness and despair; and the prevalence of a 'blame' culture that helps to convert differences into divisions. When these divisions are not understood, and no realistic strategy exists for overcoming them, we can have terrorism.

The problem with the Laqueur analysis is that it sees terrorism as insoluble. 'It stands to reason', he argues, 'that if all mankind were to live in small countries, preferably in small cities, and if all human beings were well off, there would be less violence, be it crime or terrorism. But there is no reason to assume that violence would disappear altogether' (2003: 15). Lacqueur seeks to argue that terrorism per se is ineradicable. It is clear that no factor, on its own, will do the trick. Removing the problem posed by the state of Israel, eliminating world poverty, tackling repression and injustice, reducing the frustration which inequality engenders, addressing a culture that glorifies war, would clearly help to reduce terrorism. But it would be foolish indeed to imagine that any particular factor, or even taking them together, would eliminate terrorism. The way in which, for example, former colonies had their boundaries drawn – dividing linguistic and ethnic groups in arbitrary fashion – has stored up appalling problems that will take decades to resolve. But why should we assume that terrorism will always exist?

To argue, as Laqueur does, that 'there are no known cures for fanaticism and paranoia' (2003: 10) is to suggest that psychological problems lie outside of social relationships and cause terrorism. We know, for example, that depression and mental illness can arise from problematic family relationships and these are often linked to aggressive, authoritarian and patriarchal attitudes. Psychological problems have their roots in social relationships. To suggest that terrorism will always be with us because it is a complex phenomenon is to generalise from the contemporary world in a way which creates fatalism and despair. The point is that in a world in which poverty, national and ethnic injustices, patriarchal policies and practices were being tackled, people would be better able to 'change places' than they are at the moment. A reduction in terrorism implies logically that terrorism can be eliminated, since there is no evidence that it is part of human nature to murder, maim and destroy for political reasons.

Von Hippel is more positive than Laqueur. She notes that strong authoritarian states – such as Egypt, Algeria and Saudi Arabia – may also provide conditions for terrorism, just as the collapse of states such as the Sudan and Somalia may provide a breeding ground. She concedes that 'sharpening the focus on root causes' can lead to 'politically awkward situations and policy choices'. Nevertheless, these need to be addressed if 'the counterterrorist campaign is to succeed' (Von Hippel, 2002: 38). It is difficult to eradicate terrorism, but the problem is not in principle insoluble.

The Problem of Terror and the State

Ch 1:
The State,
pp. 12–35

We have already cited Hobbes's comment that the state uses terror to maintain order. 'Perhaps it is time', Friedlander argued in 1979, 'to terrorize the terrorists' (1979: 232). It seems to us that built into Weber's definition of the state is an emphasis on the use of violence to settle conflicts of interest, and therefore it can only be plain prejudice to assume that the state cannot or does not use terror against its enemies. Von Hippel concedes that 'no state has a complete monopoly on organized violence' (2002: 30) and as we have pointed out in the chapter on the state, states claim a monopoly which they cannot and do not have.

There is a good deal of confusion in this area. On the one hand, one writer seems to think it necessary to separate terrorism from the monopolistic use of violence claimed by states, and sees terrorism as the work of sub-national groups or non-state entities. On the other hand, he says that during the 1930s terrorism became 'a state monopoly' 'reminding observers that enforcement terrorism has been much more destructive than agitational terrorism' (Gearson, 2002: 11; 15). The reference to 'enforcement terrorism' surely implies that states can and do exercise terror.

Laqueur sees the argument that states use force as a 'red herring', although he concedes that the terrorism exercised by states has caused far more victims than the terrorism exercised by small groups. He gives the example of Nazi Germany and Stalinist Russia (2003: 237), and, it is important to note, even liberal states use force against those who are deemed to break the law. This force can be characterised as terrorism. The terrorism of the liberal state is usually implicit since attempts are made to regulate and limit the use of force by state functionaries. But this terrorism becomes explicit when states (such as the current Israeli state) espouse policies of assassination against their opponents. It is true that there is a difference between the terrorism of small groups and the terrorism of the state (Laqueur, 2003: 237). But the fact remains that while the use of force can under certain circumstances be justified, it can never be legitimate. We may have to use terror against those who will not respond to mere social and moral pressures, in order to create a breathing space in which constructive policies cementing common interests can be employed. In other words, we need to pay careful attention to the context in which terrorism is used. The leader of the Palestinian group Hamas has stated recently that he regretted the death of women and children in suicide bombings, and declared that if the international community supplied his organisation with F-16s and helicopter gunships they would attack the military forces of Israel with those instead.

States, in general, claim a monopoly of *legitimate* force so that the use of force to tackle conflicts of interest has to be authorised, and in liberal states this means (as noted above) that force is legally regulated and formally limited. Two further things can be said about the violence of the state. The first is that it is often a

Ch 1:
The State,
pp. 12–35

response to violence from within the community, and a stateless society is only desirable if social order is secured through what have been called elsewhere governmental sanctions. Where government is relatively weak then a state is important since it seeks, however partially, to secure a monopoly of force. And second, where it is impossible to arbitrate and negotiate around conflicts of interest, the violence of the state is justifiable, although, as argued elsewhere, this must be on the grounds that the use of violence is the only way to provide a breathing space to enable policies to be implemented that will cement common interests. Present violence can only be vindicated if it diminishes future violence.

Nevertheless, the point is that states use terror against terror, violence against violence, and this is a risky and undesirable business. It may be provisionally justified in the sense that under the circumstances there is no other way to create a framework for policies to form common interests. But the elimination of terrorism must address the question of the state: otherwise we normalise and naturalise violence. The belief that the state is permanent may lead to the argument that terrorism is here to stay. If states use violence against individuals, why should this not be described as terrorism?

Schultz, Secretary of State under Reagan (US President 1980–89), argued that terrorism had to be dealt with by force and violence – not by mediation and negotiations, which were seen as a sign of weakness (Chomsky, 2003: 48). We made the point in Chapter 1 that violence is becoming easier and easier to inflict. The same is obviously true of terrorism, as a part of this violence. It is also worth noting that the nature of war itself is changing: as Freedman points out, we have moved over the past century from a situation in which '90 per cent of the casualties of war were combatants to one where 90 per cent are civilians' (2002: 48). The use of violence is becoming more and more costly in character, while becoming easier and easier to inflict.

The Force/Violence Distinction and the Analysis of Terrorism

In characterising the force of the state as violence and thus terrorist, we are not denying the differences that exist between formal and informal terrorism. Indeed a general definition of terrorism presupposes, as argued above, the acknowledgement of serious and significant differences. But simply because two forms of a movement or institution are different, this does not mean that they do not also have something in common.

The argument by Johnston that states use force, whereas criminals and terrorists use violence (1993: 16–17) is unpersuasive, since with the best will in the world it is impossible to limit force. Force by its nature always goes to extremes. State functionaries are not saints: their job – this is particularly true in the case of members of the armed forces – may be to injure and even kill, and it would be naive to think that this is possible in a way which is always proportionate and regulated. The same objection holds for Pettit's argument that it is only when force is used in an arbitrary way that freedom is compromised. He equates the law with the force of the state (1997: 302), but why can we not have laws based upon social sanctions, so that offenders are punished but not in a statist manner? Of course

Ch 1:
The State,
pp. 12–35

this is only possible when people can identify with one another, but these are the kinds of sanctions that are used in everyday life in thousands of institutions which enforce rules and regulations against those who breach them. Pettit's argument is that the use of force only makes you unfree when this force is arbitrary.

But how can force be non-arbitrary? The use of force even when it is regulated and supposedly limited has an irreducibly arbitrary element since you cannot treat a person as a thing (which is what force involves) without an element of arbitrariness. How do you know the way in which the person upon whom the force is inflicted will respond? The perpetrator of force must be ready to act suddenly and unpredictably, so that the notion of arbitrary force is a 'pleonasm', that is force cannot be other than arbitrary. Pettit acknowledges the problem when he concedes that criminal law processes often terrorise the innocent as well as the guilty and in practice, if not ideally, fines and prison sentences can be exposed as domination (1997: 154). It is true that non-arbitrary force is an 'ideal', but it is the kind of ideal that the state can only undermine as an institution claiming a monopoly of force.

Pettit argues that many people, responsive to ordinary norms may not be so responsive if they knew that there was no great sanction attendant on breaking the norms (1997: 154). But this, it could be argued, is wrong. Force, while transitionally necessary in a world where negotiation cannot work, weakens norms, creates resentment and undermines rather than consolidates responsiveness to norms. Pettit takes the view that arbitrary interference involves a high level of uncertainty – there is no predicting when it will strike (1997: 85). This is surely a problem inherent in force itself.

To argue that the goal of the state is the promotion of freedom as non-domination (Pettit, 1997: ix), can only be naive, given the fact that the state as an institution involves arbitrariness and thus domination. Pettit contends that if the welfare and the world-view of the public are taken into account then the act of law or state is not arbitrary (1997: 57). It is certainly true that a 'democratic' state is less arbitrary than an explicitly authoritarian one, but what makes the state inherently arbitrary is its use of force.

In the same way, the political theorist Dagger (1997: 94) does not recognise that forcing a person to be free is not simply a Rousseauian paradox: it is inherent within the state itself. Dagger, as does Pettit, sees dangers in the criminal law but argues that while civic virtue is a positive good, punishment may be a necessary evil (1997: 79). The point is that the state is here to stay. This surely is the nub of the problem. Whether liberalism is accepted (as it is by Dagger) or rejected (by Pettit in favour of republicanism, a view that individuals should participate in politics), terrorism can never be eliminated if we continue to rely upon an institution claiming a monopoly of legitimate force.

Chomsky has spoken of the 'unmentionable but far more extreme terrorism of the powerful against the weak' (2003: 7), but such an analysis is only possible when we see the state as an institutional expression of terrorism itself. It is true that if powerful states would stop participating in terrorism, that would reduce the amount of terrorism in the world by an enormous quantity (2003: 20). Taking the official US government's definition of terrorism – the use of violence to achieve political, religious or other ends through intimidation – are we not entitled to ask whether Israel's invasion of the Lebanon was not a 'text book example' of terrorism thus defined (Chomsky, 2003: 52)?

The Significance of 9/11

Nothing that has been argued so far suggests that force should not be used when innocent civilians are cruelly and heartlessly destroyed as happened on September 11. But the point is that using terror against terrorism is dangerous and can easily be counter-productive, for remember that, according to our critique, the state itself is a terrorist that uses terror against terrorism. This is always a risky business.

Chomsky argues that the current leader of the 'War against Terror' is the only state in the world that has been condemned by the World Court for international terrorism (2003: 50). Friedlander describes terrorism as war and 'combating it is also war' (1979: 237), but might this kind of posture lead to the kind of laws that alienate not only civil libertarians, but citizens generally? Terrorism has been defined in the PATRIOT Act passed in October 2001 in the United States in such a way that it could incorporate simple acts of civil disobedience.

Howard Zinn in his *Terrorism and War* contends that US foreign policy has promoted and provoked terrorism. He cites a Defence Science Board that acknowledges the link between US involvement in international situations and the increase in terrorist attacks (Zinn, 2002: 9). His argument is that if you look at the death and indiscriminate bombing which has occurred then it is impossible to avoid the conclusion that, for example, 'we are terrorizing Afghanistan' (2002: 11). He argues that 'we have to broaden our definition of terrorism, or else we will denounce one terrorism and accept another' (2002: 16). We must allow for the extension of the concept of terrorism to the state itself. He insists that to understand terrorism is not to justify it, and to identify terrorism simply with the fanaticism of individuals is superficial.

Zinn warns that there is a reservoir of possible terrorists among all those people in the world who have suffered as a result of US foreign policy (2002: 17). Not only can a policy of terrorism against terror be counter-productive, but it can also heighten inequalities at home and abroad. The infant mortality rate in the United States is one of the worst in the world and now it is likely to increase (Zinn, 2002: 19). The country spends $350 billion on being a military superpower; yet $101 billion could save 8 million lives in the poorer countries of the world (2002: 18). War ravages civil liberties: even in 1979 it was argued that 'part of the cost of protecting the public against terrorist violence is the reduction of individual rights in a free society' (Friedlander, 2002: 234). But the US public sees anyone who looks Middle Eastern, Arab or Muslim as a potential terrorist. War undermines the pursuit of truth, and encourages domestic imitators. McVeigh, who was a veteran of the Gulf War, described the children he killed in the Oklahoma bombing as 'collateral damage', while the factory bombed in the Sudan on the orders of President Clinton produced not nerve gas, but pharmaceuticals (Zinn, 2002: 21).

Zinn finds that since September 11th an atmosphere has been created in the United States in which it becomes difficult to be critical of US foreign policy (2002: 62). It has been said that the United States now has a national strategy that trumpets freedom in the abstract but subordinates it to counter-terrorism in practice (Daalder *et al.*, 2002: 411). It is difficult to see how the terrorism of the weak can be defeated by the terrorism of the strong. Kurth speaks of 'a dialectical and symbiotic connection, perhaps an escalating and vicious cycle' between Islamic

Ideas and Perspectives:

Terrorism and 9/11

James Hamill, in a recent analysis of the Iraq War, comments that an animosity has been consolidated that 'may contain within it the seeds of a future terrorism' (2003a: 326). The ideological right, he argues, had long held the view that overwhelming force should be deployed regardless of international legal norms, and September 11th legitimised these ideas. They were expressed in a document in September 2002 outlining national strategy, and although attempts to establish a link between Iraq and Bin Laden's al-Qaeda were 'unsuccessful', the policy of dismantling weapons of mass destruction via regime change was pressed (2003a: 328). Iraq provided the old-fashioned, inter-state conflict that made the 'war against terrorism' more concrete and tangible. This strategy document is seen as embodying a 'Bush doctrine' of comparable importance to the 'Truman doctrine' of 1947 that sought 'containment' of the Soviet Union (Kurth, 2002: 404).

Dr Hans Blix, head of the UN Monitoring Commission, has attacked the US and Britain for planning the war well in advance, and contended that they were fabricating evidence against Iraq to legitimise the campaign (Hamill, 2003a: 330). Hamill provides a detailed argument to show that the armed action was in defiance of the UN Charter, and describes the action as 'a war in search of a pretext' (2003b: 9). Hamill's fear is that the launching of an illegal war will foster a climate in which more young people throughout the Arab world will become receptive to the crude anti-Western rhetoric of terror groups (2003b: 100). It will increase rather than diminish the impact of Bin Laden-style extremism, and encourage states to accelerate their own programmes to develop nuclear capability (2003b: 11–13).

Biography   Noam Chomsky (1929–)

Born in Philadelphia, Pennsylvania. His undergraduate and graduate years were spent at the University of Pennsylvania where he received his PhD in linguistics in 1955. During the years 1951 to 1955 Chomsky was a Junior Fellow of the Harvard University Society of Fellows. While a Junior Fellow he completed his doctoral dissertation on 'Transformational Analysis'. The major arguments of the dissertation appeared in *Syntactic Structure* (1957). This formed part of a more extensive work, *The Logical Structure of Linguistic Theory*, which was published in 1975.

Chomsky joined the staff of the Massachusetts Institute of Technology in 1955 and in 1961 was appointed full professor in the Department of Modern Languages and Linguistics. From 1966 to 1976 he held the Ferrari P. Ward Professorship of Modern Languages and Linguistics. In 1976 he was appointed Institute Professor.

In 1958–9 Chomsky was in residence at the Institute for Advanced Study at Princeton, NJ, and in the following years he delivered a number of key memorial lectures. He has received honorary degrees from many universities. He is a Fellow of the American Academy of Arts and Sciences and the National Academy of Science, and has received a number of honours both for his contribution to linguistic theory and his work for peace.

He has visited many countries in South America, the Middle East and Asia, arguing passionately that the United States has caused destruction and misery in its foreign policy. He is particularly concerned with the way in which the media in the United States and Western Europe projects what he sees as a superficial and misleading view of US policy, and he seeks in his campaigning work and writing to develop a radical critique of these policies.

terrorism and US empire (2002: 404). Imaginative policies are needed that seek to address the root causes of terrorism, the poverty, insecurity, lack of self-esteem, injustice, inequality, etc. underlying the frustration and anger which expresses itself in terrorist form. Inverting terrorism cannot eliminate it. As Daalder *et al.* put it pithily, 'unless the United States closes the gap between its words and its deeds, it risks fuelling the very threats that imperil its security' (2002: 411).

Summary

Terrorism uses violence, but the liberal tradition is the first to see violence in the political process as a phenomenon to be condemned. The predominant view is that it is wrong to see the state itself as a terrorist organisation. States may sponsor terrorism, but terrorism is best identified as the use of violence against the state, and terrorists, as those who act on its behalf.

Salmi has distinguished between four types of violence. Only his notion of direct violence involves physical force. The other concepts – indirect violence, repressive violence and alienating violence – use the notion of violence too broadly and fail to make the crucial distinction between violence and the causes of violence. The distinction between political violence and terrorism proper is a crucial one. When people are denied political and legal rights they may resort to political violence. This violence may be problematic (even counter-productive) but it should not be described as terrorism. Terrorism only arises when political violence is directed against liberal states. Those opposing liberalism might be of the left or the right, or take a position that is ideologically ambiguous.

Marx generally identifies capitalist exploitation as 'coercive' (constraining would be a better term) rather than violent in character, and regards violence as justifiable where states deny political rights. Lenin, on the other hand, appears to justify violence even against liberal states. Despite argument to the contrary, terrorism can be defined in general terms even though (as are all movements) it is certainly a variegated and heterogeneous phenomenon. It is only possible to eradicate terrorism if we can analyse its roots, although they may be extremely varied and multiple in character.

States, it could be argued, use terror to tackle conflicts of interest, so that the problem of terrorism is connected to the problem of the state. Without recognising this, counter-terrorist measures (as US policy demonstrates) can make a bad situation even worse.

Questions

1. Is it possible to distinguish between a terrorist and a freedom fighter?
2. What role does the liberal tradition play in defining terrorism?
3. Should we speak of terrorisms rather than terrorism?
4. Is it correct to regard the state itself as a terrorist institution?
5. Do you agree with the argument that the recent war on Iraq has exacerbated rather than reduced the problem of terrorism?

References

Azzam, M. (2003) 'Weapon of the Weak' *The World Today*, August/September.

Bourdieu, P. (1998) *Acts of Resistance* Cambridge: Polity Press.

Bunting, B. (1969) *The Rise of the South African Reich* rev. edn Harmondsworth: Penguin.

Chomsky, N. (2003) *Power and Terror* New York: Seven Stories Press.

Daalder, I., Lindsay, J. and Steinberg, J. (2002) 'Hard Choices: National Security and the War on Terrorism', *Current History* 101 (659) 409–13.

Dagger, R. (1997) *Civic Virtue* Oxford: Oxford University Press.

Fanon, F. (1967) *The Wretched of the Earth* Harmondsworth: Penguin.

Freedman, L. (2002) 'The Coming War on Terrorism' in L. Freedman (ed.), *Superterrorism: Policy Responses* Malden, Mass. and Oxford: Blackwell, 40–56.

Friedlander, R. (1979) 'Coping with Terrorism: What is to be Done?' in Y. Alexander *et al.* (eds), *Terrorism: Theory and Practice* Boulder, Col.: Westview, 231–45.

Gearson, J. (2002) 'The Nature of Modern Terrorism' in L. Freedman (ed.), *Superterrorism: Policy Responses* Malden, Mass. and Oxford: Blackwell, 7–24.

Hamill, J. (2003a) 'The United States, Iraq and International Relations', *Contemporary Review* 282, 326–33.

Hamill, J. (2003b) 'The United States, Iraq and International Relations', *Contemporary Review* 283, 7–15.

Harmon, C. (2000) *Terrorism Today* London: Frank Cass.

Harris, J. (1973–4) 'The Marxist Conception of Violence', *Philosophy and Public Affairs* 3, 192–220.

Hobbes, T. (1968) *The Leviathan* Harmondsworth: Penguin.

Hoffman, J. (1984) *The Gramscian Challenge* Oxford: Basil Blackwell.

Hoffman, J. (1994) *Is Political Violence Ever Justified?* Leicester: Centre for the Study of Public Order, University of Leicester.

Hoffman, J. (1995) *Beyond the State* Cambridge: Polity Press.

Hoffman, J. (1998) *Sovereignty* Buckingham: Open University Press.

Johnston, S. (1993) *Realising the Public World Order* Leicester: Centre for the Study of Public Order, University of Leicester.

Kurth, J. (2002) 'Confronting the Unipolar Moment: The American Empire and Islamic Terrorism', *Current History* 101(659), 414–20.

Laqueur, W. (1987) *The Age of Terrorism* Boston, Mass.: Little, Brown.

Laqueur, W. (2003) *No End to War* New York and London: Continuum.

Lenin, V. (1962) *Collected Works* vol. 10 London: Lawrence & Wishart.

Locke, J. (1924) *Two Treatises of Civil Government* London: Dent.

Marx, K. and Engels, F. (1967) *The Communist Manifesto* Harmondsworth: Penguin.

Marx, K. and Engels, F. (1975) *Collected Works* vol. 3 London: Lawrence & Wishart.

Marx, K. and Engels, F. (1977) *Collected Works* vol. 9 London: Lawrence & Wishart.

Marx, K. and Engels, F. (1978) *Collected Works* vol. 10 London: Lawrence & Wishart.

Miller, D. (1984) 'The Use and Abuse of Political Violence', *Political Studies* 37(3) 401–19.

O'Day, A. (1979) 'Northern Ireland, Terrorism and the British State' in Y. Alexander *et al.* (eds.), *Terrorism: Theory and Practice* Boulder, Col.: Westview, 121–35.

Pettit, P. (1997) *Republicanism* Oxford: Oxford University Press.

Sachs, A. (1991) *The Soft Vengeance of a Freedom Fighter* London: Paladin.

Salmi, J. (1993) *Violence and Democratic Society* London: Zed.

Schram, S. (1967) *Mao Tse-tung* Harmondsworth: Penguin.

Sorel, G. (1961) *Reflections on Violence* New York: Collier.

Volpp, L. (2003) 'The Citizen and the Terrorist' in M. Dudziak (ed.), *September 11 in History* Durham N.C. and London: Duke University Press, 147–62.

Von Hippel, K. (2002) 'The Roots of Terrorism: Probing the Myths' in L. Freedman (ed.), *Superterrorism: Policy Responses* Malden, Mass. and Oxford: Blackwell, 25–39.

Wilkinson, P. (1979) 'Terrorist Movements' in Y. Alexander *et al.* (eds.), *Terrorism: Theory and Practice* Boulder, Col.: Westview, 99–117.

Wilkinson, P. (1986) *Terrorism and the Liberal State* Basingstoke: Macmillan.

Zinn, H. (2002) *Terrorism and War* New York: Seven Stories Press.

Further Reading

- Laqueur's *No End to War* (referenced above) is comprehensive and authoritative. Laqueur has written a huge amount on terrorism, and this is his most recent volume.

- Miller's 'The Use and Abuse of Political Violence' (referenced above) contains some very useful insights into the question.

- Von Hippel's 'The Roots of Terrorism: Probing the Myths' (referenced above) offers a perspective that is both interesting and challenging.

- Hoffman's 'Is Political Violence Ever Justified?' *Social Studies Review,* 4(2) 1988, pp 61–2 is a brief and contentious 'polemic' on the problem.

- Salmi's *Violence and Democratic Society* (referenced above) contains a challenging analysis as to what violence is and how we might identify it.

- Wilkinson's *Terrorism and the Liberal State* (referenced above) provides a very good overview from one of the country's leading academic authorities on the subject.

Weblinks

- For the problem as it is seen in Britain: http://www.homeoffice.gov.uk/terrorism/

- For a detailed source that enables you to visit numerous sites: http://uk.dir.yahoo.com/society_and_culture/crime/types_of_crime/terrorism/

- For a useful survey of terrorism by Halliday, see: http://www.opendemocracy.net/debates/article-2-103-1865.jsp

- For a useful guide to different sources and organisations: http://www.psr.keele.ac.uk/sseal/terror.htm

- For a critique of US reactions to '9/11', see: \http://www.guardian.co.uk/comment/story/0%2C3604%2C1036571%2C00.html

Chapter 11

Victimhood

Introduction

We live in a society in which it has become increasingly common for people to think of themselves as victims. In the United States feminism has sometimes been characterised as 'victim feminism'. We want to argue that 'victimhood' is one of the newer concepts that political thinkers ought to tackle, since it involves the question of the state, conflict resolution and the problem of violence. To espouse victimhood is not the same as being a victim. We will argue that victimhood arises when a person who may be a victim believes that nothing can be done to rectify their situation or expects others to come up with a solution that they cannot conceive themself. Victimhood is a pathology, by which we mean a negative situation that paralyses a person's capacity to act on his own behalf.

Chapter Map

In this chapter we discuss:

- The relationship between victims and violence. The difference between being a victim and espousing victimhood.

- The link between the concept of **victimhood** and the concept of power.

- Women as the victims of victimhood. The question of punishment and legal processes in the analysis of victimhood.

- Victimhood, dualism and emancipation.

- The South African Truth and Reconciliation Commission and the liberal critique of victimhood.

- Contract and victimhood.

- Victimhood and denial.

value of the property itself. In general, it could be argued that violence against property is likely to be counter-productive and set the struggle for democracy back. The cause is invariably overshadowed by the damage caused, and so the content of the protest is lost.

The use of violence in liberal societies is always inclined to be ideologically ambiguous. Laqueur argues with some justification that groups of the extreme 'left' often merge with, and become indistinguishable from, groups of the far right. Anti-Semitism may characterise terrorists who claim emancipation as their objective, and Laqueur poses the question: 'Is Osama bin-Laden a man of the left or right? The question is, of course, absurd' (2003: 8). But why? It is true that the extreme left can merge with the extreme right – but the distinction between left and right is still useful. Anti-liberalism can easily be right wing in character, but it depends upon whether this infringement of liberal values is resorted to as an attempt to emancipate humanity or privilege a particular group. The kind of Islamic fundamentalism that al-Qaeda espouses is right wing, not simply because it is authoritarian but because it opposes (even in the future) democracy, female emancipation, toleration etc. It is impossible to be a left-wing anti-Semite, although one can certainly be critical of the state of Israel and therefore be an anti-Zionist. Anti-Semitism is a particularistic creed (i.e. it does not espouse the freedom of all humans) and can therefore be legitimately characterised as a right-wing doctrine. Ideological ambiguity arises when logically incompatible elements are mixed together and whether something is of the extreme right or the extreme left depends upon the overall judgement we make of the 'mix'.

Is Colonel Qaddafi, the current leader of Libya, a man of the left or right? He is a mixture but his nationalist chauvinism would tend to make him more right than left wing, although we would accept that authoritarian methods can be presented in the name of emancipation. As Harmon notes, Qaddafi's work extolling the virtues of a third way between capitalism and communism was, in the early 1990s, eagerly distributed by the British National Front (Harmon, 2000: 10). The point about terrorism is that the use of violence by the left in conditions of liberal democracy can easily become linked to terrorism of the right, as in the 'critical support' that some Trotskyite groups gave to the Iranian leader Ayatollah Khomeini and the reactionary Taliban.

What are more difficult to categorise are movements such as the IRA that (unlike the Red Brigades of Italy) enjoy a real base of popular support. Why? O'Day warns against the danger of forcing 'Irish terrorism into a strait jacket' (1979: 122). In Northern Ireland, the whole nature of the state has been problematic in liberal terms, and it is difficult, if not impossible, to envisage a minority becoming a majority, because of the nationalist divide. A liberal society can only operate to isolate extremists and advocates of violence if it offers meaningful political rights and the prospect of constitutional change. If this does not occur then we have a classic 'tyranny of the majority' scenario that promotes illiberal values and institutions, as Northern Ireland dramatically demonstrated particularly before 1972 when the police force was partisan and unionists won seats in local elections through manipulating the electoral boundaries. Writing in 1979, O'Day can still speak of the 'deep-seated Catholic grievances' of the nationalist minority in the North (1979: 129). The fact that the Provisional IRA has called a ceasefire with the Good Friday Agreement of 1998, and its political wing has become more preoccupied with simply propagating republican values, suggests that its terrorism was complicated by the popular support it enjoyed and the fact that it did not operate in a conventional liberal state.

O'Day comments that popular support 'may be passive, but it is, nonetheless, real and important' (1979: 124). The 1921 Treaty that partitioned Ireland was seen by republicans as a cynical exercise by the British that created, in the place of the historic nine county Ulster, a six county statelet with a contrived Protestant majority. O'Day speaks of the IRA as having 'enduring appeal'. In O'Day's judgement, much of the Irish activity is 'less properly described as terrorism than a particularly unpleasant form of violence springing directly from the grievances of an oppressed minority or the frustration of the young and unemployed' (1979: 126–27; 132).

Marx on the Problem of Terrorism

We have characterised Marxism as a mixture of post-liberal and anti-liberal views, views that build on liberalism and views which are authoritarian in character. The question of what counts as violence is all important here, since if capitalism itself is seen as a form of violence then Marxists would appear to condone counter-violence even in a liberal society, and this, in our argument, would make Marxism sympathetic to terrorism.

Some argue that, for Marx, death caused by indifference and neglect 'are as much a part of human violence as the violent acts of revolutionaries' (Harris, 1973–4: 192). Now there is no doubt that Marxist violence can be readily justified in conditions where workers either do not have a vote or the franchise is fraudulent. But Harris's argument is questionable. For Marx does not regard the exploitation of labour by capital as violent, and in *Capital* he argues it is 'dull compulsion' of the relations of production that subjects labour to capital. It is not normally violence or force. The *Communist Manifesto* argues that when workers destroyed imported goods, smashed machinery and set factories ablaze, they failed to understand that it is the relations of production that need to be changed, not the instruments of production (Marx and Engels, 1967: 89). Random acts of violence are unhelpful and misguided.

It is true that Marx and Engels in the *Address of the Central Authority to the [Communist] League* speak of the fact that the communists 'must compel the democrats to carry out their present terrorist phrases' encouraging popular revenge against hated individuals or public buildings (Marx and Engels, 1978: 202), but this was said in the throes of violent revolution against an autocratic system and cannot be taken as an endorsement of violence against a liberal state. What makes Marx sceptical about terrorism in general is that it rests upon a belief in an abstract will, not in the maturation of material conditions. This is why he comments in *On the Jewish Question* that the belief that private property can be abolished through the guillotine, as in the reign of terror by the Jacobins, is naive and counter-productive (Marx and Engels, 1975: 156). (The Jacobins were radicals who resorted to terror in the later phases of the French Revolution of 1789.)

The problem of terror arises in Marxism from the belief in the inevitability of revolution. Revolution invariably involves violence, and if such violence is directed against a liberal society it counts as terrorism. Moreover, the idea that the use of violence is purely tactical and arouses no problem of morality ignores the difficulty which violence creates in a liberal society.

The Leninist and Maoist Position on Terrorism

In countries such as Tsarist Russia (1696–1917) the use of violence against particular individuals was deemed counter-productive by the Bolsheviks. Indeed it was labelled terrorism both by its propagators and critics. What made such violence harmful was that it did not advance the cause of anti-Tsarism. Thus the killing of Tsar Alexander II (who had come to power in 1881) created, as Laqueur points out, a backlash and was used to justify more severe policies on behalf of the regime. In the same way, the upsurge of democratic forces that compelled the Tsarist government to introduce a new constitution lost its impact when, as a result of 'terrorist' attacks in 1906, these concessions were withdrawn.

The problem here is that the attacks on particular figures are premised upon a flawed analysis of the political process. Many of the terrorists and champions of political violence, past and present, have been motivated by an anarchist philosophy that extols abstract will-power, and has little regard for broadening and deepening a popular movement opposed to a repressive regime. Marx and Engels condemned the Fenians – the Irish Republican Brotherhood – in London, not because the two revolutionaries did not sympathise with the cause of Irish freedom, but because they felt that blowing up people in London would not strengthen this cause. Even under repressive regimes, where political violence can be justified, terrorist-type violence, the killing of individuals and, worse, civilian bystanders, can be counter-productive and lead to political marginalisation.

What is however problematic is Lenin's view that violence is normally necessary, and raises no ethical dilemmas. To describe the Bolsheviks as the 'Jacobins of contemporary Social Democracy' and to cite with approval Marx's comment that 'French terrorism' involved a settling of accounts with absolutism and feudalism in a 'plebian manner' (Hoffman, 1984: 56) implies that violence is acceptable in, it seems, almost any context. For Lenin, it is an integral part of politics. To define a dictatorship – even the dictatorship of the proletariat – as authority untrammelled by laws and based directly on force (Lenin, 1962: 246), is to condone the use of violence by the post-liberal state and, it would seem, even against the liberal state. Such violence would, in the analysis adopted here, be regarded as terrorism.

Ch 1:
The State,
pp. 12–35

It is surely revealing that Sorel, the French anarcho-syndicalist, at the end of his *Reflections on Violence,* has a hymn of praise to Lenin as a 'true Muscovite' because of his propensity to use violence (Sorel, 1961: 281). Sorel's own rather mystical deification of violence places him closer to the fascists (1961: 23), but it is instructive that he was an admirer of Lenin. Rosa Luxemburg was to express her anxiety over the dictatorial methods and 'rule by terror' that Lenin and Trotsky adopted after the October revolution.

Biography | Georges Sorel (1847–1922)

Born in Cherbourg and, after receiving a private education there, attended the Ecole Polytechnique, where he distinguished himself in mathematics. He entered the Civil Service as an engineer and retired after 25 years, then promptly took up writing, and through innumerable books established his place as a major social critic.

He published nothing before he was 39. In *Le proces de Socrate* (1889) and *La ruin du monde antique* (1894, 1901) he argued that a strong moral structure rested upon a sturdy family, a warrior mentality, and an 'epic state of mind' rooted in myth. He became a socialist in 1892, and in his work on the natural sciences argued that increasingly nature is an artificial construct, and it is absurd to think that an overarching natural science is possible. Workers overcome their own 'natural natures' through acting heroically.

In 1906 he wrote – to give it its title in English – the *Social Foundations of Contemporary Economics* – in which he praised Marx but dismissed his notion of class conflict as 'inevitable' and the argument that life for workers would become increasingly miserable. He was particularly hostile to the idea that violent conflict would come to an end in a higher communist society.

In *The Illusions of Progress* written in 1908 he linked the idea of progress with decadence, and felt that the notion of dialectical progress in Marx's writings would sap the vitality of workers' organisations and subject them to an aristocracy of politicians and state functionaries. He became a syndicalist, taking the view that workers' organisations ought to act through strikes and direct action rather than through conventional political involvement. Myths, he argued, were ideas that steeled people with certainty and moral purpose, and he famously spoke of the 'myth' of the general strike.

He elaborates this point in his *Reflections on Violence* that first appeared in 1908. Here he speaks of the 'social poetry' that sustains moral energy. After 1908 he became pessimistic about the future of the workers' movement, and until 1914 he thought that royalism could provide the moral inspiration needed for action. He showed some sympathy for fascism, and it is said that his passion for revolutionary activity in place of rational discourse made him influential in shaping the direction of fascism, especially in Mussolini's Italy. In his final years he welcomed the Russian Revolution in the hope that it would bring about self-governing workers' councils.

Mao Zedong's notion of guerrilla war draws upon classical Chinese writings and stresses the need to attack an enemy (which is numerically superior) at its weakest points (Schram, 1967: 156). What is new in Mao's formulation is the emphasis upon the need politically to win the confidence of the poor peasantry – a strategy which appears to contradict the notorious Maoist formulation that political power stems from the barrel of a gun. Mao's execution of 'enemies' becomes problematic in terms of the analysis here, when force is unleashed on his political opponents, particularly during the Cultural Revolution, and it is only after the establishment of state power that he can be regarded as a terrorist rather than a freedom fighter.

What we have called the anti-liberal elements within Marxism – in particular the notion of class war and revolution – create support for a political violence that can anxiety eloquently testifies to the fact that violence remains a dangerous process even when it is (justifiably) used against illiberal states, and cannot be called terrorist in character.

Terrorism, Ambiguity and the Liberal State

If political violence can be justified when a state is explicitly authoritarian and denies its opponents any channel of legal change (as in apartheid South Africa), it becomes terrorism when employed against a liberal state. The liberal state, as we have already suggested, is distinctive in its opposition to force or violence as a method of settling conflicts of interest. This is why, under pressure, the liberal state has conceded rights to wider and wider sections of the community, and it promotes in the main a culture of self-reliance and universal freedoms. The opponents of the party in power are entitled to use, as Wilkinson (an academic expert on terrorism) points out, the normal channels of democratic argument, opposition and lobbying through political parties, pressure groups, the media and peaceful protest (Wilkinson, 1979: 40).

Given the fact that the liberal state uses as its legitimating norm the notion that its laws are *authorised*, the use of violence against the liberal state is certain to be counter-productive. Groups such as the June 2nd movement and the Baader Meinhof group grew out of the West German student movement of the 1960s, and were hostile to the liberal state, believing that it merely represented big business. The bombings that they embarked upon succeeded only in provoking the state to tighter security policies with substantial public support. As Harmon points out, the motivating philosophy in the case of violence against liberal societies is often one of anarchism, and violent outrages do not advance, but rather set back, the cause of democracy. The movement against the Vietnam War (1965–73) created, in addition to a legitimate and sensible protest movement, small numbers of terrorists such as the Weathermen, who attacked the officials and property of the state (Harmon, 2000: 6).

Terrible ironies accompany the use of violence in liberal states. Take, for example, attacks by animal rights activists on the directors of companies believed to be involved with testing on animals. These movements justify the most appalling suffering of humans (who are a kind of animal as well), and actions such as these are invariably used by the media to diminish public sympathy for the animal rights cause. Is the destruction of property rather than individuals to be seen as terrorist in nature?

There are two problems here. The first is that the use of violence against property can easily (if unintentionally) harm individuals who are protecting such property, and the illegal nature of the act can have adverse political consequences. We would describe violence against property as 'soft' terrorism since in most circumstances peaceful forms of protest can create a change in opinion and would be more productive. But breaking the law per se does not count as terrorism, and in the movement in Britain against the Poll Tax in the late 1980s widespread public support was created for acts of defiance. The Poll Tax or Community Charge was calculated according to the number of people inhabiting a house rather than the called terrorism, and the Thatcher government was wrong to describe the African National Congress (ANC), which resorted to violence (among other tactics) against the apartheid regime, as terrorist in character. The US government saw the ANC as one of the most notorious terrorist groups at the time. The point is that the ANC only resorted to violence as a response to the actions of a regime that banned the organisation and imprisoned its leaders.

Brian Bunting, a South African who has written widely on the anti-apartheid struggle, has documented in detail the laws passed in the period of 'grand apartheid' under Dr Verwoerd that, among other things, prevented peaceful protest. He cites the comment of Umkhonto we Sizwe (the ANC aligned Spear of the Nation) on its birth in 1961 where it talked about carrying on the struggle for freedom and democracy 'by new methods' that 'are necessary to complement the actions of the established national liberation organizations' (Bunting, 1969: 216). The ANC was no more terrorist than the partisans and liberation movements that fought against the Nazis during World War II. We would therefore disagree with the inclusion of the ANC in Harmon's glossary of terrorist groups (Harmon, 2000: 281). The violence employed by the ANC was regrettable, and it is worth noting that grisly 'neck-lacing' of those seen as regime collaborators (when individuals had old car tyres placed around their necks and these were then set ablaze with petrol) was a practice that the ANC never officially supported. The ANC is better described as a democratic rather than a terrorist movement. Chomsky (2003: 61) speaks of the French partisans using 'terror' against the Vichy regime, but although he intends by this example to expose what he considers to be the hypocrisy of the United States, violence against illiberal systems should not be described in these terms.

Biography,
p. 242

To argue that using political violence against an illiberal state is not terrorist is better than arguing that one can be both terrorist and freedom fighter. This is not to say that the use of political violence in conditions in which it cannot be labelled terrorist is not problematic. We should be careful not to idealise political violence. Movements that resort to violence inevitably commit human rights abuses as well, and anyone who thinks that liberation movements are purely and simply a 'good' thing ought to see how, in contemporary Zimbabwe for example, the use of political violence can leave a legacy of authoritarianism and brutalisation. Reports from human rights groups have noted that in the first half of January 2004 there were 4 deaths, 68 cases of torture and 22 kidnappings, with much of the violence carried out by youths from the ruling ZANU-PF party (http://news.bbc.co.uk/1/hi/world/africa/1780206.stm).

In a moving work, *The Soft Vengeance of a Freedom Fighter* (1991) Sachs, a leading supporter of the ANC, a human rights lawyer and now a judge in South Africa, recalls the anguish he felt when he heard reports that Umkhonto we Sizwe was to target white civilians in the struggle to liberate South Africa. Having lost the sight of one eye and his right arm as the result of a car bomb in Maputo in Mozambique in 1988 (the work of agents of the South African security forces), Sachs feared that a free South Africa might come to consist largely of one-eyed and one-armed people like himself. He was hugely relieved to hear reports that his organisation was not planning to escalate violence in a way that would plunge South Africa 'in an endless Northern Ireland or Lebanon type situation, where action becomes everything and politics gets left behind' (Hoffman, 1994: 22). His produce goods or trade in weapons of war which (again unintentionally) damage the health and environment of others. Salmi's third category relates to what he calls

- *repressive violence* (1993: 20), when people are deprived of their political, civil, social or economic rights, while
- *alienating violence* (1993: 21) – his fourth category – embraces the kind of oppression (ethnic and male chauvinism, racism, hostile acts of homophobia, opposition to AIDS sufferers, etc.) that undermines a person's emotional, cultural and intellectual development. What are we to make of these categories, and their link to the question of terrorism?

It seems to us problematic to characterise direct violence as merely one form of violence among others. For this is the violence that deserves our immediate attention since it prevents people from (even in a formal sense) governing their lives. Salmi estimates that between 1820 and 1970 (after the Napoleonic war through to the Vietnam conflict) some 68 million people died as a consequence of 'direct' violence, and this is the form of violence that, as the public rightly perceives, is the pressing problem (Salmi, 1993: 47). Whereas inaction (as in Salmi's second category) may be categorised as an evil, it cannot be said to constitute violence per se, although it may certainly be the *cause* of violence.

Again, what Salmi calls *repressive* and *alienating violence* may lead to direct violence, but until it does it cannot be called violence (and thus terrorism) as such, although as with the so-called indirect violence of unemployment it certainly harms people and should be condemned. Violence, as we see it, should be restricted to the infliction of deliberate physical harm: a case could certainly be made for incorporating abuse as violence where it leads to physical pain of the kind expressed through depression, etc. But violence becomes too broad a category if it is linked to any kind of pressure that affects someone's 'integrity' if by that is meant their capacity to act in a particular way.

For the same reason we would resist the argument of Bourdieu, a radical French social theorist, that violence can be symbolic or 'structural' (Bourdieu, 1998: 40, 98). Clearly, verbal and other forms of non-physical aggression are *linked* to violence, but we would prefer to distinguish between the causes of violence and violence itself. We will later challenge the notion that the liberal state uses only force and not violence, but we take the view that violence is best defined as the intentional infliction of physical harm.

But although all terrorism is violent, not all violence even against the state is terrorism.

Distinguishing between Political Violence and Terrorism

It is our view that when political violence is used in conditions in which no other form of protest is permissible, then it would be wrong to call it terrorism. Miller argues that 'violence may be permissible in dictatorships and other repressive regimes when it is used to defend human rights, provoke liberal reforms, and achieve other desirable objectives' (Miller, 1984: 406). Such violence should not be

Laqueur, who has written numerous works on the question of terrorism, argues that Iran has sponsored the Hizbullah group in the Lebanon, and it has extended support to Shi'ite groups in Afghanistan and Palestinian groups such as the Islamic Jihad. Iraq under Saddam Hussein, he argues, has been much more cautious in its support for terrorist groups, but it did provide some shelter to the remnants of the Abu Nidal group and the People's Liberation Front for Palestine (Laqueur, 2003: 223–5).

Although we think that there is a strong case for using force and violence as synonyms, Johnston sharply distinguishes the two on the grounds that violence is force that violates some moral or legal norm, so that we can differentiate between, say, police force and criminal violence. He argues that it is important to combine confrontation and conciliation, reason and force in combating violence, and he identifies terrorists as criminals (Johnston, 1993: 16–17). It is true that criminals do not necessarily see themselves as acting politically, whereas terrorists do.

The argument is that because the force of the state is authorised and limited to specific purposes, it cannot be considered 'violent', and therefore the notion of terror and terrorism has to be restricted to those who oppose the state. Miller comments that 'it is a well-entrenched feature of our language that to describe an action as an act of violence is to condemn it forcefully' (Miller, 1984: 403). Wilkinson contends that it is 'sheer obfuscation' to imagine that one can theorise about terrorism in a value-free way (Wilkinson, 1979: 101).

In Miller's view, the force/violence distinction only applies when laws are general; when they are enacted in advance of behaviour they seek to control; when they do not discriminate between persons on irrelevant grounds; and the penalties are standardised and applied impartially (1984: 404). Violence is unpredictable and irregular. It is for this reason that the political theorist Pettit argues that only when force is used in an arbitrary way, is freedom compromised (Pettit, 1997: 302). A non-arbitrary use of force, that is the working of a liberal state, governed by a constitution, does not make you unfree, so Pettit's argument is that the force of a constitutional state does not lead to domination, and therefore should not be regarded as violence.

An Assessment of Salmi

Salmi, a development economist from Morocco, has written an important work entitled *Violence and Democratic Society*. In it he defines violence as an act that threatens a person's physical or psychological integrity (Salmi, 1993: 16), and he distinguishes between four categories of violence.

- *direct* violence involves deliberate attacks that inflict harm (kidnappings, homicide, rape, torture). This would certainly embrace terrorism. But Salmi distinguishes between direct and

- *indirect* violence when, he argues, violence is inflicted unintentionally as in cases of *violence by omission* when, say, inaction contributes to starvation or genocide (as in Roosevelt's failure to intervene in 1942 against Hitler's final solution) (1993: 18). This indirect violence may also take the form of what Salmi calls *mediated* (1993: 19) violence that occurs when individuals or institutions

Liberalism and the Question of Violence

We normally define terrorism as the use of political violence against individuals or the functionaries of the state. But it is clear that violence can be used against the state (and thus individuals) which would not be regarded as terrorism, so that we need to be clear when the use of such violence is regarded as 'terrorist' and when it is not.

Definitions of terrorism necessarily contain reference to acts of violence, and what makes terrorism a negative term is that violence itself is seen as negative. Indeed, it is defined in one recent volume as 'a type of political depravity which unfortunately has become commonplace' (Harmon, 2000: 2). The generalised opposition to violence comes out of the liberal tradition.

In the *Leviathan* written by Thomas Hobbes (1588–1679) there is an emphasis upon avoiding war and establishing a commonwealth based on consent. No covenant can be valid that exposes a person to 'Death, Wounds, and Imprisonment' (Hobbes, 1968: 169). Here is the view that **force** or violence negates freedom, and although Hobbes allows freedom to be consistent with fear and necessity, it cannot be reconciled with force. Indeed, so concerned is Hobbes with the problem of force and the individual's natural right to avoid it, that (unlike Locke) he takes the view that an individual is not bound to fight for the state (Hoffman, 1998: 46).

Locke (1632–1704) likewise argues that only when someone is not under the 'ties of common law of reason', can 'force and violence' be deployed (Locke, 1924: 125). It is true that Locke justifies slavery as a state of war continued between a lawful conqueror and captive (1924: 128), so that even if force can be lawful (a point to which we will return), the liberal tradition sees a conflict between violence and freedom, violence and rights.

The notion of terrorism becomes possible only when violence is seen in negative terms. Whereas pre-modern thought regarded violence as a sign of human empowerment – hence the positive evaluation of the warrior – liberalism argues for a world in which market exchanges are defined as activity that has banished violence. Thus the praise for terrorism, which is offered by Sheikh Azzam, reputedly the teacher of the Saudi terrorist, Osama Bin Laden, cannot be squared with the liberal tradition. The notion that terrorism is some sort of an obligation in the Muslim religion is not only a dubious reading of Islam: it implies a legitimacy for violence which the liberal tradition cannot accept, at least as the criterion of a free person.

It is true that Hobbes refers to the force of the state as 'terror' (Hobbes, 1968: 227), but the use of the term is atypical. It is much more common to refer to the use of force by the state, and terror used by the enemies of a state who resort to what is seen as illegitimate violence.

The State and Terrorism

The liberal tradition often distinguishes between force and violence – and thus force and terrorism. State terrorism refers to states that sponsor terrorism, not the state per se as an organisation that uses terror.

9/11 and its legacy

The World Trade Center burning after the hijacked aircraft hit on 11 September 2001.

Everyone can remember where they were when 11 September happened. There was saturation media coverage, and it was clearly the worst terrorist outrage anyone could recall since World War II. There was a sense of total unreality as a second plane collided with the tower of the World Trade Center not long after the first plane had struck. Thousands of people were already at their desks in both towers, while some 80 chefs, waiters and kitchen porters were working in a restaurant on the 106th floor. Many who worked for firms located in the crash zone were killed instantly. Those on the floors above the collisions were already doomed, their escape routes cut off by fire. And then the news about the Pentagon broke. Overall, the estimated death tolls reached 3,030 with 2,337 injuries. Al-Qaeda was blamed for the atrocities, and there was a sense at the time that this was a truly historic event. Everything that has happened since then, the wars on Afghanistan and Iraq, the passing of anti-terrorist legislation, the establishment of the internment camp at Guantanamo Bay, has confirmed that this was an event with enormous repercussions. It has brought the question of terrorism into everyone's consciousness.

Politicians and ordinary people alike condemned the atrocity. But why did it happen?

- Is the very attempt to understand the events of '9/11' an act of thoughtless condonation, or is understanding crucial to an effective way of responding to the action?

The act was denounced as 'evil'.

- Is this a useful category for characterising terrorist outrages, or is the notion of evil unable to get to grips with the reasons why such an event happened?

What did the terrorist action achieve? Clearly it obtained massive publicity.

- But did it make it easier or more difficult to implement policies that would tackle the causes of the problem?

Human Rights and Victimhood: The South African Truth and Reconciliation Commission (TRC)

Wilson, in his *The Politics of Truth and Reconciliation in South Africa* (2001), evaluates the attempt by the Truth and Reconciliation Commission (TRC) to encourage the forsaking of revenge (2001: xix). The TRC was established in 1995 one year after an African National Congress (ANC) government had been elected to power. Past injustices were to be redressed on the basis of a need for understanding, not vengeance; reparation, not retaliation. The idea of *ubuntu* became a key notion in the immediate post-apartheid order. It was explicitly counterposed to victimisation. Former Archbishop Desmond Tutu, who chaired the commission, took the view that the African understanding of justice is restorative. It sees justice as a force that is concerned not so much to punish but to restore a balance that has been knocked askew (Wilson, 2001: 8–12).

The South African TRC had a wider remit than the Uruguayan or Chilean truth commissions – it could name individuals concerned and grant amnesties. Wilson argues that while the Report of the TRC chronicled acts of a devastating kind, its methods were flawed. It urged reconciliation in a context that meant amnesty for violators of human rights (2001: 97–9).

It brought individual suffering into a public space where it could be collectivised and shared by all (2001: 111). It linked this individual suffering to a national process of liberation, and argued that victims should forgive perpetrators, and abandon any desire for retaliation (2001: 119). The Commission espoused a Christian argument about forgiveness, with Tutu contending that redemption 'liberates the victim' (2001: 120). Punitive retribution was characterised as illegitimate 'mob justice', while loyalties and identities were to be created that had not existed before (2001: 129; 131).

This attempt to avoid victimhood seems admirable, but the problem is that the TRC sought an ethic of forgiveness in the context of past and present savage conflicts of interest, conflicts involving torture, killing and the most grisly forms of repression. As Wilson points out, the white community in South Africa seemed indifferent or plainly hostile to the work of the Commission (2001: 155), and there was insufficient emphasis upon the murderous character of apartheid and the inequalities that it embodied. The right to punish was to be given up in a situation in which the grossest violations of human rights had occurred.

A punitive view of justice was simply dismissed in a situation where it seemed to make sense, and the amnesties granted to state-killers during the apartheid period (who had rather cynically come to the TRC to 'confess') served, in Wilson's view, to deepen rather than reduce polarisation (2001: 161). Cohen notes that South Africans are particularly cynical about the apparent ease with which some of the worst perpetrators have adopted the rhetoric of the 'new South Africa' as if the past never existed (Wilson, 2001: 132). There was a feeling that grievances and pain were not really addressed. Certainly, this was not done by the TRC's grand vision of reconciliation (2001: 171; 175). Little wonder that the TRC proved to be peripheral to the lives of those in townships wracked by revenge killings. Wilson particularly instances the killings that have continued in places like Sharpeville (2001: 187).

Biography

Desmond Tutu (1931–)

Born in Klerksdorp, Transvaal (as it was then). His father was a teacher, and he himself was educated at Johannesburg Bantu High School. After leaving school he trained first as a teacher at Pretoria Bantu Normal College and in 1954 he graduated from the University of South Africa.

After three years as a high school teacher he began to study theology, being ordained as a priest in 1960. The years 1962–6 were devoted to further theological study in Britain leading to a Master of Theology. From 1967 to 1972 he taught theology in South Africa (he was a lecturer in Lesotho between 1970 and 1972) before returning to England for three years as the assistant director of a theological institute in London. He published an African Prayer Book and between 1978 and 1980 he published sermons, press statements, speeches and articles in a volume entitled *Crying in the Wilderness: The Struggle for Justice in South Africa*. He was elected a Fellow of Kings' College in 1978 and in the same year received an honorary doctorate from the General Theological Seminary in the United States. He was involved with the World Council of Churches, attending the Fifth Assembly in Nairobi in 1975 and the Sixth Assembly in Vancouver in 1983.

In 1975 he was appointed Dean of St Mary's Cathedral in Johannesburg, the first black person to hold that position. From 1976 to 1978 he was Bishop of Lesotho, and in 1978 became the first black General Secretary of the South African Council of Churches. Tutu is an honorary doctor of a number of leading universities in the United States, Britain and Germany.

In 1985 to 86 he was Bishop of Johannesburg, becoming Archbishop of Cape Town a year later. In 1985 he was awarded the Nobel Peace Prize in Oslo, Norway for his quest for a non-violent end to apartheid. Under his leadership, the church in South Africa became immersed in the political struggle. He has written widely on the problem of hope and suffering, and contributed to a volume entitled *God at 2000*. He wrote a foreword to Charlene Smith's book on Mandela, and in 1994 he published *The Rainbow People of God: The Making of a Peaceful Revolution*. He co-authored *Reconciliation: The Ubuntu Theology of Desmond Tutu* with Michael Jesse Battle, and wrote *Some Evidence of Things Seen: Children of South Africa* with Paul Alberts and Albie Sachs.

During the investigation of the Truth and Reconciliation Commission that he chaired, he declared that he was 'appalled at the evil we have uncovered'. 'Listening to all the pain and anguish, you take it into yourself in many ways ... maybe one day you will sit down when you think of all those things and you will cry.'

South Africa has one of the world's most liberal constitutions but also one of the highest indexes of socio-economic inequality. It is a society where 50 per cent of the population is classed as living in poverty. The low level of reparations for victims provided by the government and the generous amnesties granted to perpetrators strengthened the view that the TRC's version of human rights violated perceived, everyday principles of justice (Wilson, 2001: 194; 200). Wilson shows, through a detailed analysis, how justice in the township of Boipatong is implemented in a way that emphasises retribution rather than reconciliation. This is seen as creating legitimacy for legal institutions – that such justice can achieve many of the aims of peaceful coexistence sought by advocates of reconciliation and forgiveness (2001: 201). Pure reconciliation was equated by township dwellers with weakness on issues of social order, such as being soft on criminals and apartheid-era murderers. In places like Boipatong where there are local courts, vengeance is regarded as more predictable and routinised (2001: 212).

It is not that the TRC was wrong to address the problem of victimhood with its gory philosophy of an eye for an eye and tooth for a tooth. The case against the notion of victimhood is compelling, and Wilson (like Brown) quotes both Nietzsche and Weber, who identify the desire for punishment with vengeance and an abstract moralism that condemns without attempting to understand (Wilson, 2001: 159). But the TRC in its opposition to local informal courts whose procedures were often arbitrary and which inflicted lashings upon wrongdoers, failed to distinguish between the kind of vengeance which takes the form of unregulated killings and counter-killings, and *retribution*, which, though often motivated by a desire for revenge, dispenses a punitive justice by what Wilson calls 'more institutionalized types of mediation and adjudication' (2001: 162). Without an element of retribution, (even) post-apartheid state legality is often perceived by township residents to be alien to the 'community' (2001: xx).

Wilson concludes with the view that while human rights that stress reconciliation are important, they cannot entirely define the common good of the community as it exists in South Africa today (2001: 224). The problem with the TRC, in other words, was the adoption of an abstract liberal critique of victimhood – not one that takes account of specific circumstances and sees the need to move slowly and gradually beyond the notion of punishment. The point has to be made, as we have argued in Chapter 1, on the state, that transcending the notion of victimhood presupposes a diminution of the kind of dreadful crimes which inevitably give rise to the demand for vengeance. In one of the most violent societies of the world – with a population brutalised by apartheid and hundreds of years of racist oppression – the movement beyond victimhood requires imaginative transitions and multiple stages of a complex and democratic oriented kind. To imagine that abstract invocations of human rights will bring out calmness and forgiveness is simply naive.

Is Contract an Answer to the Problem of Victimhood?

Victimhood arises, it might be argued, because individuals and groups lack a contract between themselves or with the state. The notion of contract represents both the strengths and weaknesses of the liberal tradition. The great strength of contract is that it enshrines a norm of equality and individuality. To enter into a contract with another we have *in some sense* to change places. Ancient and medieval thought has no notion of contract (in the modern sense) because it has no notion of equality and individuality. Hence liberals wax lyrical over the transition from status to contract – from a situation in which people have different roles within a preordained and repressive hierarchy to one in which people supposedly follow their self-interest and freely exchange their goods and services with others.

Would victims be helped if they entered into contracts, symbolically or in reality, with those who were to victimise them? The weakness of contract is that the equality and freedom enshrined in contracts is formal and not real. By this we mean that contracts in themselves do not address the problem of social position and power: they concern themselves with a formal equality that ignores real disparities in wealth, esteem, confidence, education, etc. The labour contract in a capitalist society equalises the position of those who have wealth with those whose situation is such that they must work for another. The marriage contract equalises the position of one partner who has power and resources and (in many cases) another partner who lacks confidence, self-esteem and an ability to break with traditional deference. The prostitution contract (which utopian socialists likened with some justification to the marriage contract) involves an exchange that 'permits' one party to abuse another. Because the equality in this particular contract is so formal as to appear positively fraudulent, most societies outlaw prostitution albeit in hypocritical and one-sided ways.

Just as we need a conception of power that is negative *and* positive, so we need a concept of contract that seeks to translate egalitarian aspirations into an egalitarian reality. The signing of contracts represents a step forward in the sense that both parties seem to recognise themselves in each other. If Israelis and Palestinians could see themselves as contractual partners, that would represent important progress. But if contract is not simply to be a device in which the powerful legitimate their attacks upon the powerless, we need to move beyond the formal and towards the real. This is not to say that we will ever reach a position in which we can say 'everyone is finally equal'. We are only now becoming aware of the way in which mental health and cultural disabilities like dyslexia negatively affect freedom and will-power. The formality involved with the institution of the contract invites us to be aware of (and act to reduce) the gulf between benevolent theory and less than wholly benevolent practice.

This is why the institution of contract is often seen as a solution to the problem of victimisation. In fact, the institution of contract can promote victimhood. If a contract legalises and legitimates exploitation then it is not only compatible with the creation of victims, but it becomes the central device by which people are impoverished and abused in the contemporary world. It is true that the victims of victimhood might reject the very idea of contract on the grounds that because contracts can mask exploitation they are worthless. This makes it all the more crucial that we understand the limitations of the liberal tradition while building upon its strengths. We should neither reject contract nor idealise the idea of contract. The victims of victimhood throw the baby out with the bathwater.

There is an analogy with the question of contract and discourse on human rights. Both are valuable, but both are limited. They abstract from real circumstances, and therefore to understand the problem of victimhood we need to address the context that creates the passivity, resignation and moralism. Dickenson has argued that contractual relations do not have to be unequal and oppressive, though many feminists have thought them to be so (1997: 64). Contracts, she argues, give women authentic subjecthood, but her argument assumes that parties to a contract can be 'genuinely equal' (1997: 174). This is precisely the problem. For the notion of contractual equality involves an abstract attitude that ignores difference.

We prefer Virginia Held's arguments that the notion of humans as contractors is inappropriate for 'morality in general' (1993: 196), that is morality conceived in a concrete fashion, for, as she points out, 'contracts must be embedded in social relations which are non-contractual' (1993: 204). Thus, to take the example used above: a woman who contracts as an 'equal' with a man may have low self-esteem and lack confidence and independent resources. Individualistic liberal conceptions are a useful device as long as we do not overlook the fact that we are abstracting from reality (1993: 219).

Victimhood and Denial

Victimhood – whether of the victim or victimiser – leads to denial. Cohen identifies denial as a personal or collective amnesia, a forgetting of what happened, whether we are talking about genocide and the atrocities that arise from ethnic hatreds, or the perpetration of abuse. In Cohen's view, there is no need to invoke conspiracy or manipulation to understand such cover-up (2001: 12).

Cohen is interested not simply in those who suffer and those who cause this suffering. He is also interested in the response of those who hear about or witness an atrocity and do nothing. Observers, he notes, may share a zone of denial with victims – the refusal to acknowledge a truth which seems too impossible to be true (Cohen, 2001: 14). Bystanders may be similar to perpetrators: they want to believe that they themselves will not become victims of random circumstance and that somehow the victims deserve their fate (2001: 16). When asked about British arms being used in massacres in East Timor, Alan Clark, then British Defence Minister, replied: 'I don't really fill my mind much with what one set of foreigners is doing to another' (Cohen, 2001: 20).

The problem needs to be politically analysed. When a victim seeks to understand their plight critically and rationally, it is then easier for such a person or group to overcome residual denial, self-blame, stigma or passivity, and to seek appropriate intervention. It also becomes correspondingly harder for the offender to offer denials ('She asked for it') that have much chance of being accepted (Cohen, 2001: 52). 'They started it' is the primeval account for private violence. The offender's claim to be the 'real' victim (as in the ethnic cleansing that characterised the break-up of former Yugoslavia) may refer to short-term defence and provocation, but in political atrocities denial of creating victims is likely to be ideologically rooted in historically interminable narratives of blaming the other (2001: 96). The victims, it is said, bring torment on themselves, as in Golda Meir's reproach that Arabs made nice Israeli boys do terrible things to them. A Serb soldier speaks of the Battle of Kosovo (which took place in 1389!) as if it happened the week before. Groups are

Marx

The political state, in relation to civil society, is just as spiritual as is heaven in relation to earth... None of the supposed rights of man ... go beyond the egoistic man, man as he is, as a member of civil society; that is, an individual separated from the community, withdrawn into himself, wholly preoccupied with his private interest, and acting in accordance with his private caprice.

'On the Jewish Question' in Tucker (ed.), *The Marx–Engels Reader* London and New York: Norton, 34; 43.

Victimhood and the State

Victims can espouse victimhood by resorting to the state to 'protect' them. Resort to the law (in a statist sense) becomes a substitute for taking action to tackle the problem in a meaningful way. For in state-centred societies the role of the law is to punish and restrict; it cannot empower and transform.

Brown gives the example of an ordinance in a US city against discrimination in housing on the basis of 'sexual orientation, transsexuality, age, height, weight, personal appearance, physical characteristics, race, color, creed, religion, national origin, ancestry, disability, marital status, sex, or gender' (1995: 65). Such an ordinance, she points out, fails to tackle the problem of poverty and destitution – those who need shelter but cannot afford to obtain it – and assumes in liberal fashion that all have resources. The problem is seen as a formal one – the problem of discrimination. In our view, such an ordinance is not useless but it would be naive to imagine that it empowers those whose differences extend to the ability to buy.

The victims of victimhood see the state as a substitute for empowerment and agency. Of course, people who have suffered may campaign to change the law or influence the state, and such activity will enhance rather than diminish their sense of agency. It is the privatised reliance upon the law and the state to protect and compensate an aggrieved party that signals a manifestation of victimhood. As Brown points out, the state and the law become neutral arbiters of injury (1995: 27).

The state and statist law is taken at face value – they are seen in Hobbesian terms as a substitute (and 'representative') for the will of an individual. The state claims a monopoly of power while the individual has none, and the use of violence by the state against the perpetrator is regarded as a solace to the aggrieved individual.

The notion that the state is 'neutral' and there to defend the powerless individual by punishing their tormentor perpetuates that sense of powerlessness and impotence which is central to the ideology of victimhood. Cohen points out that one of the reasons why 'bystander states' do not intervene when atrocities occur is that they believe that 'the nation-state is not a moral agent with moral responsibilities' (2001: 162) – a prejudice that lies at the heart of Machiavelli's analysis of the modern state.

The argument is that relying upon the state in a passive and uncritical way is problematic. Of course, where the state is pressurised to change its policies so that it promotes solutions that are thoughtful and innovative, then the state can assist in combating victimhood. For example, a parent whose child has been killed by a drunk driver might simply blame the perpetrator and demand a draconian penalty, or in addition the parent might ask the police to remind people who serve alcohol in bars that it is illegal (and irresponsible) to sell alcohol to persons who are driving and who have already had a few drinks. The latter response would still leave the parent (and their child) victims, but it would help the person to resist victimhood.

so enclosed in their 'own circle of self-righteous victimhood' that they cannot learn from anybody outside themselves (Cohen, 2001: 96–7).

Victims are said to be lying and cannot be believed because they have a political interest in discrediting the government. Or 'denial magic' is invoked: the violation is prohibited by the government and so could not have occurred (Cohen, 2001:

105). But not all those who claim to be victims, are necessarily victims. Cohen argues that the notion of repressed memory syndrome (RMS) – often invoked to argue that parents have sexually abused their children – is questionable. The victim, at painful psychic cost, stigmatises the accused (2001: 122).

Victims can also embrace self-denial like the Jews in Germany in the 1930s (Cohen, 2001: 141). Perpetrators, victims and bystanders can, indeed, normalise (in the sense of 'get used to') the most unimaginable horrors. This progressive accommodation may even be essential for atrocities to take place (2001: 188). Victims, as well as perpetrators and bystanders, can suffer a victimhood that leads them to deny suffering and abuse. What makes the concept of victimhood so relevant in today's world is that current versions of identity politics are based on collective identity as *victims*. There is a trend that encourages competition about which group has suffered the most (2001: 290).

The State, Mutuality and Dualism

Cohen argues that the free-market version of globalisation allows a 'post-modern forgetting' to supplement older, more ideological forms. Thus the traditional Turkish denial of the Armenian genocide is supplemented by a discourse of mindless relativism, a mechanical repetition of the idea that every claim must be untrue – there must always be another point of view (Cohen, 2001: 244). In this way, victims, perpetrators and bystanders are encouraged to veil the enormity of the past. But the problem here lies with the state: a relativist version of postmodernism is linked to victimhood because it facilitates a numbing reconciliation to the status quo.

We have argued that victimhood involves a passive acceptance of the violence inflicted by tormentors, or an imaginary solution to the problem that rests in practice upon a belief that the violence is inexplicable and somehow 'natural' in character. Under the influence of victimhood, victims see the world in the same way that tormentors do. They assume that violence is the result of 'fate' – forces over which they have no control – and whereas tormentors appear as the beneficiaries of these beliefs, victims suffer pain and indignity as a consequence. The state, acting as a substitute for the agency of the individual or group, mystifies the mutuality involved in the perpetrator/victim exchange.

Indeed, it is perfectly possible for the victim to become a tormentor. In fact what makes victimhood pathological is that 'victims' easily slip into the position of perpetrators and, since the purveyors of victimhood see violence and suffering as natural and inevitable, they find it impossible to defend themselves except by resorting to the violence from which they have suffered. If the state cannot inflict the violence on their behalf, they do so themselves! Criminals have frequently suffered abuse in their own past, and it is impossible to understand the psychology of tormentors without noting that they too subscribe to the notion of victimhood, even if, in reality, others are the victims, and not themselves. Today's victim easily becomes tomorrow's tormentor, since victimhood rests upon an inversion of a repressive 'relationship', rather than its transcendence. Repression remains: we do not go beyond it.

It is true that perpetrators appear to be dynamic and interventionist, whereas the victims seem passive and fatalistic. But these differences are illusory. The tormentor is no more in control of their destiny than the victim. Indeed, the tormentor seeks to vindicate the violence they inflict upon others, by invoking the status of victim. Nazis saw themselves as the victims of international forces which humiliated Germany; abusive men may have actually suffered abuse themselves, often at the hands of women, and hence see women in general as legitimate targets of their wrath. Unionists in Northern Ireland will recall the horrors of Irish republican violence, and Czechs may justify their hatred of Romanies in terms of the attacks on property that the latter supposedly perpetrate. One cannot understand the extraordinary and tragic acts of violence by the Israeli state against Palestinians without some knowledge of the Jewish experience of the Holocaust.

The ease with which victims and tormentors 'change places' shows that victimhood is a pathology that unites both parties in a deadly and self-destructive embrace. It is true that victims deserve our sympathy in the way that tormentors do not. But victimhood merely perpetuates the violence and suffering involved, whether it is the aggressive violence of the tormentor, or the righteous violence of the victim. In one sense, victims and tormentors *relate* to one another when, under the influence of victimhood, they see the 'other' as inhuman.

But a relationship, as we define it, involves taking responsibility for activity and seeking to understand 'others' in a rational manner. Violence, we would argue, destroys relationships, because through violence people see one another as mere objects, and hence act against the enemy in the same way that they would act against non-human entities. Indeed, part of the discourse of victimhood involves presenting the 'other' as non-human – as objects to be crushed, not as humans to be changed.

A dualism between victims and the 'other' – in our terminology, a division, not a difference – arises with victimhood, and the state employs the language of victimhood to justify its violence. The target of state force is an enemy, evil, inexplicably immoral and thus fully deserving of their fate. The language of abstract moralism ties in with the notion of vengeance: the other must pay for their crimes, she must suffer as the victim has suffered. The state can and does 'victimise' its enemies so that the victims of victimhood are perpetuated in a deadly cycle of violence and counter-violence.

The ideology of 'victimhood' can only be transcended when people have sufficiently cohesive common interests that they can 'change places': the state as the institutionalised expression of victimhood then becomes redundant.

In the last analysis, victimhood expresses itself as a form of self-violence and self-hatred, since the inability to understand why the other has acted in an aggressive way leads to shame and 'guilt'. Wives who are beaten by their husbands may believe that they deserve such violence, since they are worthless individuals who cannot satisfy their partners' 'needs'. As 'wives', they might subscribe to the view that they are naturally disadvantaged by impersonal and inevitable structures which nobody can change.

A relational position, as we have defined it here, involves avoiding the polarising 'either/or' approach associated with modernity and the liberal tradition. Indeed, it is precisely this notion of 'those who are not with us, are against us' which expresses disdain for the 'both/and' logic that lies at the heart of a consistent relational position. A relational view of the world accepts that people are both different and the same, but

'Arbeit Macht Frei'

The gate at Dachau concentration camp bears the infamous motto *Arbeit Macht Frei* (Work Brings Freedom).

Imagine you are in Nazi Germany during World War II. The death camps are at work as part of the so-called 'final solution'. Jews can be heard saying that if they ever get out alive, they will never speak German again, since the German people have inflicted unspeakable horrors upon them. Nazi camp attendants tell themselves that the Jews aren't human and would destroy the Third Reich if they were not exterminated. Residents living outside Dachau see the smoke rising from the camp and can smell the gas, but prefer to believe that it is inorganic rubbish that is being burned and unsanitary clothing purified.

It is clear from this example that the Jews are the victims, the Nazis their tormentors, and the residents unwilling to face the grim truth about what is happening in their neighbourhood.

- How justified is the view that the Nazis represent Germany as a cultural and national identity, although this is the Nazis' ultra-nationalist claim?

- The Nazi camp attendants see the Jews as non-human and a threat to their national identity: why are they unable to see that they and the Jews possess a common humanity?

- The residents sense that something appalling is taking place in their vicinity. Why don't they face reality and do something about it?

- Although each party plays a different and conflicting role, what do the responses we have depicted have in common?

Victims and Violence

In all relationships, power is involved and, therefore, there will be those who are relatively disadvantaged. But the term 'victim' is used to describe a person or group that has been subject to violence or general misfortune. Violence is itself defined as the direct or indirect infliction of physical harm. Victims are people who deserve our sympathy and concern, and although victims of violence are a particular problem, the notion of a victim is wider than this. Men and women who are beaten by their partners are victims; so are people who are attacked by others. In a world in which large numbers of people are killed, maimed or harmed by others, it would be untenable to deny the existence of victims.

By violence we do not simply mean the direct infliction of physical harm by sticks and stones. We also mean the indirect infliction of physical harm which arises from abuse, the kind of insecurity that causes pain and depression, torment of a kind that destroys a person or a people's sense of self-worth. Not all forms of harm stem from violence as we have defined it. It is tempting, but wrong, to identify unemployment, or poverty or destitution as 'structural violence' since violence implies an *intention* to inflict harm. It arises when people cannot change places, and a person or people are treated as *things* or objects by the perpetrator of the violence. Certainly the recipients of violence deserve to be characterised as victims, and this can be the violence of a brigand or the state, since we have argued that violence by the state is still violence however much it may claim legitimacy, authorisation and legality.

Ch 10:
Terrorism,
pp. 224–45

But what of people who suffer? Those who suffer as a result of the unintentional harm inflicted upon them, like poverty or destitution, unemployment or diseases (which may arise through a failure to provide resources or medicine to tackle them), are also victims and they too deserve our sympathy and concern. Honderich has demonstrated the dramatic inequalities that characterise the world today. The worst-off tenth has about 2 or 3 per cent of what there is. In a place like Mozambique the worst-off have this share of what is a very small total, and this affects the distribution of freedom and power, respect and self-respect, health and mortality. The worst-off tenth of the population in Africa have lifetimes of about 30 years (Honderich, 2002: 22; 18).

Clearly we can speak of victims of poverty, starvation and deprivation just as we can speak of victims who are tortured, 'disappear', step on landmines, are thrown into prisons, or are blown to pieces by mechanised instruments of war. We can also speak of people who suffer from ill health (that is not obviously caused through neglect or inequality), such as victims of cancer and heart disease. They are victims because they suffer, and they deserve our compassion.

In short, there is an infinity of categories of people whom we can call victims.

What is Victimhood?

Victimhood is a pathology. It involves the belief that being a victim renders a person or group powerless, a mere object, lacking in agency and thus the capacity to exert independent action. We will argue later that victimhood arises from a mistaken view of power.

Victimhood is seen here as something that is different from the existence of victims. It is true that people need to see themselves as victims (or as having been victims in the past) in order to embrace victimhood, but the two are not the same. Victimhood involves a belief that the violence exerted against an individual or group, or the suffering they experience, is tragically unavoidable. Victimhood induces a righteous inactivity or a futile retaliation that makes a bad situation worse. Where violence is involved it sees this as a product of differences. Hence victimhood is ideological in the sense that it rests upon falsehood, illusion and, above all, a view that the misfortune is 'natural' in the sense that it cannot be changed or ameliorated. Proponents of victimhood argue that the person suffering should simply accept their fate and/or make the perpetrator suffer as they have.

Ch 7:
Difference,
pp. 156–72

Victimhood arises when victims cannot understand why violence has been exerted against them, or why they are in difficult and sometimes degrading circumstances. It is true that the purveyors of victimhood are aware of who is tormenting them where such harm is intentionally inflicted – Jews in the Holocaust camps could point to Nazi soldiers and camp guards; men and women can identify partners who attack them; children are painfully aware that particular adults are abusing them. Oppressed individuals or an oppressed group invariably know who are depriving them of their basic human rights. Moreover, it is obvious to the cancer sufferer what is causing the pain.

But victimhood arises because the knowledge of a person's plight is superficial and thus misleading. Tormentors, for example, are stereotyped, by which we mean they are subject to a process of generalisation that distorts reality. 'Explanations' are offered which suggest that the violence is inexplicable, so that the causality asserted is imaginary and misleading. A person suffering from a disease may believe that it is the will of their creator which causes them pain, and there is nothing which can be done about it.

Jews who are afflicted with victimhood believe that the Nazis are evil because they are Germans. Women assume that men, rather than aggressive partners, are to blame for their oppression; blacks imagine that because their tormentor may be white, whiteness itself creates hostility to black people. This is why we argue that difference should not be seen as the problem. It is true that in many cases tormentors are strikingly different from their victims – but these differences in themselves do not provide a rational explanation for the oppression and discomfort. They do, however, provide a convenient way of 'rationalising' the suffering inflicted. The problem with victimhood is that it is plausible but ultimately misleading. It is tempting for a woman who has been mistreated by male partners to seek a life that shuns men, but this is futile since it assumes that men are inherently aggressive and sexist, and can never change.

Victimhood 'naturalises' the violence and pain that victims suffer, by assuming that such violence and suffering is inevitable and unavoidable. Nothing can be done about it. Hence victimhood paralyses agency in that it promotes a belief that victims are powerless to resist their oppressor in meaningful and realistic ways, or act in ways that might alleviate, if not eradicate, their symptoms. Victimhood, insofar as it espouses resistance, believes that salvation can only come from 'outside' – from a protector who will punish their tormentor, a benevolent spiritual force, or an external agency that rescues the victim who is unable to act on his or her own behalf.

Victimhood and Power

Introduction
to Part 1

Victimhood assumes that power can only be purely negative or purely positive. It is one-sided in its view of human relationships, and victimhood rests upon a polarised and dualistic view of social interaction.

As we pointed out in our first chapter, in pre-modern times (i.e. in slave-owning or medieval societies) power is seen as positive in the sense that it is identified through a person's or group's contribution to the community in which they live. To exercise power is to strengthen relationships with others so that power is identified in communal and relational terms. This notion of power has one major drawback. It ignores the role of the individual – his or her personal interests – and sees power in repressively hierarchical terms. To exercise power is to enact a particular role, and this role is something that is preordained by forces beyond the control of an individual or a group. Power is exercised not by individuals but by priests, lords, men, Christians, Greeks, etc. The community is hierarchically defined internally as well as externally. Men exercise power over women just as lords exercise power over peasants: power is naturalised, and although proponents of positive power argue that such power should be benevolent and sociable, in many cases repression is involved. It is true that slavery can be sustained only as a relationship if slaves accept the rule and role of their masters, but force and domination is crucial to sustaining pre-modern power relationships, even though this repression and force appears nowhere in the concept of power.

A notion of positive power 'on its own' (as it were) can only generate a sense of victimhood since those on the receiving end of 'positive power' may be tempted to regard the violence used against them or the suffering they have to endure as somehow preordained, just as those exercising violence feel that 'nature' has compelled them to act in this way in order to sustain their particular roles. For this reason, the rise of an explicitly theorised concept of negative power represents an important step forward in political theory. The negative view of power is part of the liberal tradition that arises in Europe in the seventeenth century, and takes the view that power is something to be used against nature, other individuals in general, and the state in particular. It is worth noting that what makes the seventeenth-century thinker, Hobbes, a liberal and an exponent of negative power is his view that everyone is first and foremost an individual, and although the state has absolute power over the individual he may refuse to comply with the state where his interest (and in particular his right to life) is threatened.

Power is negative because it is deemed to be an activity *against* others. People no longer enact preordained roles. They behave as individuals and seek to defend their self-interest: this is not immoral or ungodly. Self-interest is deemed 'natural' and in the eyes of Protestantism historically, individualism is in accordance with the creator's wishes. It is not difficult to see that negative power 'on its own' also feeds into the notion of victimhood. The classical liberal tradition seeks to justify action as necessary to an individual's survival, so that victims of violence may see violence and suffering as the result of 'natural' aggressiveness which either must be accepted, or rebutted by becoming a 'natural' aggressor oneself.

In reality, notions of 'roles' and hierarchically defined relationships come in through the back door so that Locke, for example, a seventeenth-century

Exercise

Four people confront you. One is a woman who has been raped; the second is a man suffering from lung cancer; the third is a former soldier who is suffering from severe psychological problems; while the fourth is a homeowner whose house has been burgled by a black intruder.

- The first notes that the man who attacked her has a problem with women that probably goes back to his childhood, although she feels that he should be punished.

- The second feels that the cancer has resulted from the failure of his wife and doctor to take proper care of him.

- The third takes the view that war is a dangerous and unpredictable business and hopes that his children will never have to fight in armies.

- The fourth feels that the burglary demonstrates that black people can never be trusted and should be encouraged to leave the country.

Clearly all four are victims. Which of the four demonstrate attitudes of victimhood?

Introduction,
pp. 2–11

exponent of individual rights, deems men to be naturally stronger than women and therefore the 'natural' leaders of households. Even J.S. Mill in the nineteenth century links his concern with individual development with a belief that Indians, for example, are children who require dictatorial control from paternal Europeans. The problem with the concept of negative power is that it inverts pre-modern notions of positive power: it does not transcend them. Hence, in its one-sided rejection of community and relationships it perpetuates a notion of victimhood. The notion of negative power is classically expounded by Hobbes, who sees power as power *over* another. Power is tied to exclusion, and the body is seen as something that the individual owns as part and parcel of their private property. This notion, although viable as part of a wider theory of power, is untenable on its own. It generates the abstraction, atomism and dualism that the ideology of victimhood requires. Liberalism, it might be said, perfects victimhood by postulating in its classical form the concept of the isolated individual unrelated to anyone else: it cannot transcend it.

Ronai warns that the power dichotomy must not be inverted (Ronai, 1999: 140): the discourse of victim/perpetrator corresponds to naive and one-sided versions of positive and negative power. 'The language of victimhood', she comments, 'is disempowering' (1999: 152). Power is not a static quality that individuals either do or do not possess. It is always negotiated, always provisional, always in motion (Marecek, 1999: 176). It is neither solely positive or simply negative, but *both*.

Are Women Victims?

Radical feminism in particular portrays women as victims of male oppression. Wendy Brown has rightly warned against 'paralyzing recriminations and toxic resentments parading as radical critique' (Brown, 1995: xi). It is not that women do not suffer: victimhood presupposes that they have no guarantees of political redress (1995: xii). Radical feminists 'blame' men and assume that women are impotent or, as we shall see, must rely upon the state and the law as their 'protector'.

Brown identifies victimhood with one-sided attacks on liberalism. She cites Nietzsche's view of freedom as the *will* to assume responsibility for oneself. Contrary to the liberal argument, freedom does not elude power, but involves a power that enhances the individual's capacity to act (Brown, 1995: 25). Victimhood tends to a 'moralising politics' that codifies injury and powerlessness. It seeks not power or emancipation for the victim, but the revenge of punishment so that the perpetrator is hurt as much as the victim. Politics becomes reduced to punishment (1995: 27). In Nietzsche's view, as Brown points out, morality springs from and compensates powerlessness; powerlessness is invested with the Truth, while power inherently distorts (1995: 46). Instead of indulging in recrimination, she argues, we need to engage in struggle.

Central to Brown's argument is the notion of *ressentiment* (revenge) that produces an effect (rage, righteousness) that overwhelms the hurt. It also produces a culprit responsible for the hurt, and a site of revenge to displace the hurt (a place to inflict hurt as the sufferer has been hurt). The late modern liberal subject literally seethes with *ressentiment*. Such an identity becomes 'invested in its own subjection'. Again, she quotes Nietzsche: 'I suffer: someone must be to blame for it' (Brown, 1995: 68–73).

A particular target of her argument is the radical feminist MacKinnon. 'There's no way out', is the most frequent response among students to MacKinnon's work. MacKinnon's account of sexual antagonism is utterly static. Men are depicted as a homogeneous whole that oppresses women, and women are seen as a similarly homogeneous group. What can be done about it? Because MacKinnon sees women as subject to victimhood she eliminates the very dynamic of social change on which Marx, say, counted for emancipatory practice. The oppressed have no inner resources for the development of consciousness or agency. MacKinnon's critique of sexism becomes an implicitly positivist, conservative project. Its 'victims' need protection rather than emancipation. There is an unrelieved past, present and future of domination. Women are relentlessly victimised by their gendered construction. We must curtail and regulate, rather than emancipate. Not freedom, but censorship; more rights to sue for damages, better dead-bolt locks on the doors (Brown, 1995: 92–4). For MacKinnon, the 'solution' is to single out pornography as the essential manifestation of sexism, and to deal with pornography through the proposed ordinances giving women the right to sue for damages. This argument brings to the fore the authoritarian character of MacKinnon's position.

Feminism must find a way that sees women as victims, but avoids victimhood through developing strategies that give women the power and confidence to make inroads into male domination, to act in a way that increases agency and self-determination. A feminist and female therapist interviewed by Marecek declared: 'I think we need to view ourselves as responsible adult human beings who are learning hopefully to make choices and figure things out for ourselves a little better' (Marecek, 1999: 171). Naomi Wolf describes 'victim feminism' as a set of beliefs 'that cast women as beleaguered, fragile, intuitive angels' (Atmore, 1999: 191). Although this is a one-sided presentation of a one-sided position, it is

Friedrich Nietzsche (1844–1900)

Born in Prussia, he was educated at an elite school near Naumburg, and in 1864 became a student of theology and philology at the University of Bonn. In the following year he continued his studies at the University of Leipzig, and in 1869 was appointed Professor of Classical Philology at the University of Basel.

In 1870 he served as a volunteer medical orderly in the Franco-Prussian war, and two years later he published *The Birth of Tragedy* where he argued that tragedy played a central role for the ancient Greeks in maintaining their certainty about life. The book was dedicated to the composer Richard Wagner, and called into question much of the received wisdom about ancient Greece.

However, he broke with Wagner, and in 1879 he resigned from the University. He spent the next ten years of his life in southern Switzerland and northern Italy, and in 1883 he began work on *Thus Spoke Zarathustra*. In 1886 he wrote *Beyond Good and Evil*, and a year later he published *On the Genealogy of Morals*. His argument in the latter centres on the moralities of slave and master but he regards the triumph of slave morality as the internalisation of oppression. In 1888 he wrote *Ecce Homo*, which was published posthumously in April 1908.

He became insane in 1889 and spent the last 11 years of his life in the care of his mother and sister. Although the Nazis made use of his work, they did so fallaciously since Nietzsche opposed nationalism as a futile attempt to prevent the disintegration of the modern state. He did, however, anticipate a war 'such as no-one has ever seen'.

certainly true that the dualistic thinking that underpins this kind of position is contrary to a feminism that takes women seriously.

Dualism, Women and Victimhood

Brown argues that in the case of MacKinnon, a single socially pervasive dualism structures totality, the divide between men and women. Her dualisms and absolutes articulate a profound late modern anxiety (1995: 95). The point has a wider philosophical relevance.

The notion of victimhood presupposes that there is an unbridgeable chasm between friend and enemy, truth and falsehood. Hence it makes a political resolution of conflicts – a resolution based on conciliation and compromise – impossible. The victim not only suffers but, as already noted, the only 'solution' is to make the 'other' suffer as well. Instead of going beyond the notion of a victim, the victor must become a victim if 'justice' is to be secured. It is commonplace to encounter parents whose children have been murdered and who want revenge – the guilty party to be punished as severely as possible. It is an understandable reaction, but it is wholly futile, for how will severe punishment either bring their child back to life or make the perpetrator into a better person? Bitterness prevails over reason, and the dualism between victor and victim remains, albeit in an inverted form.

To transcend victimhood, it is crucial to understand why a person suffers and what can be done about it. It is understandable that when a woman is raped she wants the perpetrator punished, but such a reaction cannot in itself be said to solve the problem, any more than hanging stopped people stealing sheep in the eighteenth century. A culture needs to be developed (and this requires a radical change in the distribution of resources) in which the identity of both parties changes, so that men view women as friends and equals, not as prey and targets. Overcoming dualism is both a philosophical and eminently practical task, for men and women will never be able to change places if the material circumstances of each makes stereotyping seem plausible. Overcoming dualism involves cementing a common interest, so that differences can be resolved through negotiation, and the use of the state becomes redundant.

Ch 1:
The State,
pp. 12–35

The danger with rights for victims, as Brown argues, is that they can entrench a dualism between the ideal and reality, so an unbridgeable chasm between the two exists. Rights mystify as well as provide entitlements. There is a danger that the same device that confers legitimate boundary and privacy can leave the individual to struggle along in a self-blaming and depoliticised universe. Her concern is that asserting rights can mystify the powers that construct, buffet and position the individual (Brown, 1995: 126–8). Asserting rights *can* perpetuate a sense of victimhood.

MacKinnon uses the notion of rights to expose and redress inequalities that arise in liberal societies and are sometimes presented abstractly – as part of 'nature' – which we simply have to accept. Women are wholly identified, as Brown points out, with sexual victimisation (1995: 131). Rights are certainly valuable, but their limitations must be seen. They endow you with an entitlement, but they leave open the question as to how you are going to make this entitlement a reality. 'On their own' they can lead to victimhood, unless the person demanding rights begins to assert a real agency that seeks to realise them as vehicles of emancipation (1995: 133). Gray warns that we should not see rights abstractly: 'as theorems that fall out of theories of law or ethics'. They are judgements about human interests 'whose content shifts over time as threats to human interests change' (2000: 113).

How to read:

Brown's *States of Injury*

This is a valuable book that deals with the theme of this chapter. The preface outlines the arguments to be adopted and deserves a careful read. The introduction can be skim read, but Chapter 2 (Exposures and Hesitations) is important. This contains a useful critique of postmodernism, and material from Nietzsche where Brown identifies Nietzsche's critique of 'slave morality' with what we have called the pathology of victimhood. Chapter 3 (Wounded Attachments) is also important and needs to be digested. Chapter 4 is useful for an understanding of feminism, but in the context of victimhood can be skim read. Chapter 5 is also worth reading carefully and the comments on Marx are of particular interest. Chapter 6 (Liberalism) should be skim read and the last chapter (for purposes here) can be skipped.

How to read:

Sorel's *Reflections on Violence*

This is a classic text that sets out Sorel's support for violence and the myth of the general strike. You need to concentrate on those chapters that deal with Sorel's views of violence in particular (although if you were concerned about his defence of syndicalism – revolutionary trade unionism – you would concentrate on other chapters). You can skip the introductory letter to Daniel Halevy – a French historian – but his 'Introduction to the First Publication' is worth a careful read. Chapter 1 deals with his evaluation of Marxism and socialism and therefore, for purposes of the argument, can be left out. Chapter 2, which deals with what Sorel sees as the pacifist attitudes of the middle classes, deserves a careful read, as does Chapter 3 on 'Prejudices Against Violence'. Note that each chapter contains a brief summary at the top that is worth perusing. Chapter 5 on the 'Political General Strike' can be skipped, but Chapter 6 on the ethics of violence is worth reading carefully. Chapter 7 and Appendix 1 can be skipped, but Appendices 2 and 3 deserve a careful read, since the latter contains Sorel's revealing assessment of Lenin.

become terrorist in character. It is true that Marxism does not support the view (which Frantz Fanon, an Algerian revolutionary, endorsed), that violence is somehow an ennobling and 'cleansing' process. Fanon argues that violence 'frees the native from his inferiority complex and from his despair and inaction; it makes him fearless and restores his self-respect' (Fanon, 1967: 74). This kind of view sees the terrorist as a person without normal relationships: they are wedded to the Struggle or Revolution, not to family and friends. This view is inherent, it could be argued, in violence, and therefore on the surface of things would seem opposed to Marxism's methodology (Marxism speaks of individuals entering into relations with one another). Nevertheless, Marxism does contain aspects that facilitate the use of violence, and thus terrorism, in liberal and socialist societies.

A General Theory of Terrorism?

Laqueur argues that there will perhaps never be an authoritative guide to terrorism because there is not one terrorism, but a variety of terrorisms: what is true for one does not necessarily apply to the others (Laqueur, 2003: 8).

Laqueur is certainly right to stress that terrorism takes many different forms. In the nineteenth century terrorism was linked to struggles for national independence and social justice, and sought to avoid civilian casualties. In the twentieth century this has changed, and the most disturbing feature of what has been called the 'new terrorism' is the way in which no distinction is made between functionaries of a particular regime and ordinary civilians. The IRA tried to give warnings for its attacks; so does ETA (the Basque Euskadi Ta Azkatasuna) – al-Qaeda does not. A recent analysis of the Middle East describes suicide bombing as a 'new terrorism' (Azzam, 2003: 10). A clear distinction, therefore, needs to be made between 'traditional' terrorism that regarded civilian deaths as 'regrettable', and the terrorism of groups such as al-Qaeda which specifically targets ordinary people.

But while distinctions need to be noted, it has to be said that variety is common to all movements and 'isms'. Movements such as socialism and concepts such as democracy are also extremely variegated – terrorism is no different. Laqueur insists that terrorism, 'more perhaps than most concepts', has generated widely divergent interpretations (2003: 232), but there seems to be no reason why this should be so. Of course, it is complicated by the fact that the term has now (mostly) acquired a distinctively pejorative tone but concepts such as democracy have acquired, as we have pointed out, a distinctively positive connotation.

While the search for a 'general theory' needs to be sensitive to difference and variety, it is possible to argue the case for a definition of terrorism while stressing the complexity and heterogeneous nature of the phenomenon. When Laqueur takes the view that 'the search for a scientific, all-comprehensive definition is a futile enterprise' (2003: 238), his problem arises because he assumes that such a definition must be beyond controversy and counter-argument. An impossible demand! He in fact goes on to provide a working definition – 'the systematic use of murder, injury, and destruction, or the threat of such acts for political ends' – which is perfectly acceptable provided we add that such violence is employed in liberal or post-liberal societies. The use of violence to challenge and remove an authoritarian or explicitly anti-liberal regime cannot be called terrorism.

Laqueur also argues that what makes a general theory impossible is the fact that there is not 'one overall explanation' of the roots of terrorism (2003: 22). But this argument rests upon a false juxtaposition between the general and the particular: certainly a theory of terrorism is complex and there are many factors involved. But this is true of all theory. It is a reflection of a complex world, infinite in its particularity. The general can only express itself through the particular, and when we come to present our own 'general theory', it is clear that multiple factors are necessarily involved.

It has been argued that, on the one hand, we should 'perhaps' think of terrorisms rather than terrorism, thus freeing ourselves from the tyranny of the search for an all-embracing and universally acceptable definition. On the other hand, the term 'terrorism' is still used in the singular (Gearson, 2002: 22).

The Roots of Terrorism

There is certainly no simple explanation for terrorism, but finding its roots can only help to provide some guidance on this complex phenomenon. Terrorism is not necessarily to be found in the harshest regimes, since highly efficient dictatorships can make political violence extremely difficult, whereas it is a sad fact of life that regimes that are either democratic or partly democratic have become much more vulnerable to terrorist attack. Regimes that appeared democratic at the outset of terrorist attack may cease to be so – such as the Uruguayan crushing of the Tupamaros – after the threat has been dealt with (Friedlander, 1979: 235).

Laqueur argues that while poverty is a factor it should not be exaggerated: very poor countries may see civil unrest and even civil war, but not terrorism. The followers of terrorism might be poor, whereas the leaderships are wealthy and middle class: 'terrorism rarely occurs in the poorest and richest countries, especially

Index

in a way which enhances the capacity for action and self-determination. Mutuality instead of being negative and self-contradictory becomes positive and empowering.

Victimhood involves an illicit generalisation of the other which makes this positive changing of places impossible. Under the influence of the ideology of victimhood, it is impossible to understand that tormentors not only see themselves as victims, but that an aggressive attitude in one regard may coexist with human or positive attributes in other respects. Nazis, for example, banned smoking (albeit in highly authoritarian fashion) from public places while condoning horrendous experiments on Jews. The project to create a 'purer' world is always dangerous if this 'purity' is seen in abstract and absolutist terms. It is wrong to assume that 'all Germans are Nazis'. Tormentors are not homogeneously evil – they invariably have redeeming features.

None of this means that victims should never use violence or retaliate against tormentors. After all, victims have legitimate self-interests to defend, and they may find it impossible to defend themselves without a protective use of violence. But violence, however provisionally necessary it may be in conditions where people simply cannot change places positively, always destroys relationships. Moreover, violence can easily generate an ideology of victimhood, and this is why it is an extremely dangerous form of activity to undertake or condone.

Freedman puts the point well when he comments that 'victim status is becoming a prized commodity in international politics, because it is a means by which a group with no capacity of its own can acquire powerful external allies' (Freedman, 2002: 48). Not only are these allies usually states, but such an attitude is inherently *statist* in character. Victimhood does disservice to the plight of victims. It perpetuates and aggravates the problems which victims face. Victims, we have argued, are those subject to violence or whose straitened circumstances leaves them prey to exploitation and abuse. Tackling victimhood can only be a long-term process – as we saw in relation to the problems facing a post-apartheid South Africa. It involves the transcendence of dualism, a negative and self-destructive mutuality and, indeed, the state itself.

Summary

Victims are not simply people afflicted by violence; a person can be legitimately called a victim when her life is unintentionally harmed, or she suffers from illness. It is crucial to distinguish between being a victim and espousing victimhood. Victimhood arises when a victim is unable to understand the real causes of his woes and ascribes an imaginary causality to the suffering concerned.

When we approach the question of power in a one-sided way, seeing it either as solely positive or solely negative, then we embrace victimhood itself. Women are often the victims of oppression, but they embrace victimhood when they see this oppression as something that they cannot resist and prevent. A desire simply to punish tormentors and resort to the external sanctions of the law reflects the kind of impotence associated with victimhood.

The temptation to see action in dualistic terms is also a hallmark of victimhood. The notion of rights must be tied to a meaningful action to tackle the problem, otherwise rights themselves can lead to victims espousing victimhood. The South African Truth and Reconciliation Commission sought to tackle the evils of apartheid without creating a sense of victimhood. But it demonstrates the danger of ignoring the particular context in which crimes are committed and how victimhood can only be avoided if resources are provided and legal judgements reached that deal with grievances expressed.

Contract in itself is not an answer to the pathology of victimhood, since contract can unwittingly reinforce, rather than detract from, a sense of victimhood. Contract can play a positive role when its abstract limitations are grasped. Denial is central to victimhood. The tormentor rationalises his wrongdoing, and the bystander finds imaginary reasons for her inactivity. It could be argued that the concept of victimhood is tied to the state as an institution that seeks to justify force by demonising its opponents.

Questions

1. Can one be a victim without espousing victimhood?
2. Is a sense of victimhood inevitable when violence is involved?
3. Should those who victimise others be punished?
4. Can it be said that the person who victimises another is also a victim?
5. Consider the efficacy of the following responses by a victim: (a) resort to state-enforced law; (b) asserting rights that have been trampled upon; (c) acting in concert with others to ensure that the victimisation does not reoccur.

References

Atmore, C. (1999) 'Victims, Backlash and Radical Feminist Theory' in S. Lamb (ed.), *New Versions of Victims* New York and London: New York University Press, 183–211.

Brown, W. (1995) *States of Injury* Princeton, New Jersey: Princeton University Press.

Cohen, S. (2001) *States of Denial* Cambridge: Polity Press.

Dickenson, D. (1997) *Property, Women and Politics* Cambridge: Polity Press.

Freedman, L. (2002) 'The Coming War on Terrorism' in L. Freedman (ed.), *Superterrorism: Policy Responses* Malden, Mass. and Oxford: Blackwell, 40–56.

Gray, J. (2000) *Two Faces of Liberalism* Cambridge: Polity Press.

Held, V. (1993) *Feminist Morality* Chicago, Ill. and London: University of Chicago Press.

Honderich, T. (2002) *After the Terror* Edinburgh: Edinburgh University Press.

Marecek, J. (1999) 'Trauma Talk in Feminist Clinical Practice' in S. Lamb (ed.), *New Versions of Victims* New York and London: New York University Press, 158–82.

Ronai, C.R. (1999) 'In the Line of Sight at *Public Eye: In Search of a Victim*' in S. Lamb (ed.), *New Versions of Victims* New York and London: New York University Press, 139–57.

Wilson, R. (2001) *The Politics of Truth and Reconciliation in South Africa* Cambridge: Cambridge University Press.

Further Reading

- S. Lamb's *New Versions of Victims* (referenced above) is a useful read. Look particularly at the essays by Atmore, Marecek and Ronai.

- Wilson's *The Politics of Truth and Reconciliation in South Africa* (referenced above) is a valuable assessment of the South African Commission.

- Cohen's *States of Denial* (referenced above) contains fascinating material that is relevant to the problem of victimhood.

How to Read,
p. 254

- Wendy Brown's *States of Injury* (referenced above) is a real classic.

- F. Nietzsche, *On the Genealogy of Morals* New York: Vintage, 1969 is worth dipping into.

Weblinks

- There is tantalising reference to a school on the theme of 'beyond victimhood' in: http://www.corrymeela.org/Residential/winter school 99.html

- Questions of power and superiority are dealt from a religious point of view in: http://www.fpireland.org/part1.htm

- Interesting thoughts on the Middle Eastern problem, and its bearing on victimhood: http://www.redress.btinternet.co.uk/thinkpiece.htm

Conclusion

One of the questions that interests students of politics is the relationship between studying politics as an academic discipline and the practice of politics in the world outside. We thought that it might be useful to tackle this question by way of concluding this volume.

Academic Political Theory and Politics

What makes concepts political is that they respond to conflicts that arise in the world of practice. Academic political theory should address itself to the kind of issues that politicians themselves raise, and which are part and parcel of public debate.

It can be problematic to try and treat politics in a purely neutral manner as though it was a study of mere behaviour or an analysis of words. But it does not follow from a critique of what came to be called 'apolitical politics' that academic political theory has no differences from the kind of political theory which appears in party manifestos and in the speeches of politicians.

The fact that academic political theory has something in common with the theory of the publicist and propagandist does not mean that it does not also have something which is different from everyday discourse. Academic political theorists write for individuals who are either academically trained or who are anxious to educate themselves in a systematic and coherent way. Academic political theory is not primarily geared towards convincing an audience of the ideological correctness of its position. Its task is to stimulate rather than persuade, so that rhetoric is curtailed in favour of logic, and sober evidence is offered in place of extravagant emotion. It is not the task of the academic political theorist to exhort people to undertake a particular course of action at a particular time and particular place. Although thinking about a problem is crucial to solving it, this is not the same as actually organising people to implement a solution.

Academic political theory can and should seek to raise the tone of public political debate. Good causes can be strengthened by good arguments, while party positions and publicist writing provide challenging points of reference to make academic political theory more relevant and useful. There is nothing wrong in Thatcher making use of Hayek's work on the free market, even if, in the view of many political theorists, both were mistaken! Academic political theory differs from the theory of the public political world, but it is still *political* in character because, despite these differences, it has common features.

We hope that the mix of classical and new political ideas and ideologies has shown the relevance of theory to political practice, and that when you read the newspaper, see a TV programme or follow the arguments of a text, you will be better placed to make up your own mind as to the wider significance of the positions reported or championed.

Glossary

Abstraction A conceptual and practical process that mystifies and conceals underlying social relationships.

Affirmative action The apparent departure from equal treatment in order to help disadvantaged groups. Affirmative action is also known as reverse discrimination or positive discrimination.

Anarchism A theory that seeks to abolish the state, but adopts statist tools of analysis and hence enjoys no success.

Atomistic An approach that treats individuals and entities in purely discrete terms and ignores the relationships between them.

Authority An exercise of power in which the moral status of the person exercising the power comes to the fore and is seen as legitimate.

Behaviouralism An argument that sees human and natural activity as similar, and hence asks that the study of politics can be presented as a 'natural science'.

Capitalism A system of production that divides society into those who can hire the services of others, and those who are compelled to work for an employer.

Caste society A society in which wealth and other goods are distributed according to some notion of natural inequality.

Citizen A person able to govern their own life. Citizenship is an emancipatory situation towards which we move, but can never actually reach.

Civil disobedience Law-breaking on moral grounds.

Class An identity that divides people based upon economic, social, regional, religious, gender, ethnic and other differences.

Coercion A concept and practice that is close to, but not the same as, force. Coercion involves a threat to use force where this force is credible.

Communitarianism A theory that stresses that all people belong to communities and can only identify themselves in relations with others.

Conflict A clash of interests that can be tackled through violence, but only resolved through non-statist pressures. Conflicts of the latter kind are inevitable and arise from the fact that we are all different from one another.

Consent   Uncoerced acceptance of something, such as state authority.

Conservatism   Conservatism is an ideology that is sceptical about reason: because human beings have limited rational capacities they must rely on tradition to guide them.

Constraint   A natural or social pressure that ensures we do something that we had not intended to do.

Contestability   A concept that points to the fact that an idea is controversial, or can be challenged.

Contractarianism   A stream of liberal thought that imagines the state to be the product of a decision between individuals to agree to submit to it. Contractarianism implies individuals consent to the state.

Culture   The often taken-for-granted web of social relations which encompasses many domains of experience, shapes a person's character, and may provide him or her with a set of values by which to live.

Democracy   A society in which people govern themselves.

Difference   Identifications that separate people and inevitably cause conflict to arise.

Division   Differences that undermine common interests and necessitate the use of force.

Dualism   A gulf between two entities, conceptual or real, that is impossible to cross. It points to a divide rather than a difference.

Ecologism   An ideology centred around 'ecology', stressing the interdependence of all forms of life.

Egalitarianism   A type of political theory that makes equality a fundamental concept.

Emancipation   The capacity of people to act freely, and thus govern their own lives.

Environmentalism   A movement which highlights the importance of preserving the earth's natural resources and guaranteeing a fair share of those resources for future generations. Unlike ecologism it can be combined with many different ideologies.

Equality   Treating 'like cases alike'; different types of equality depend on how we define what is meant by 'like cases' (see legal equality and equality of opportunity).

Equality of opportunity   The equalisation of the opportunity to acquire certain things, or, at least, guaranteeing that each person has a specified chance of acquiring those things.

Ethnicity   The identification of a culture with tangible, visual symbols and signs such as dress, food or religious observance.

Feminism   A theory that works for the emancipation of women.

Force   A pressure that undermines the agency of individuals by physically harming them.

Freedom (or **liberty**)   The absence of constraint, or, alternatively, the existence of choice.

Free-riding Gaining the benefits of cooperation without paying the price. This problem is central to the resolution of the Prisoner's Dilemma.

Genocide The attempt to destroy an entire ethnic or racial group; genocide can take place without mass murder – mass sterilisation is a form of genocide.

Globalisation A linkage between peoples of the globe that enables them to understand and empathise with one another.

Goodness (or **goods, the good**) That which is worth pursuing – 'goods' need not be moral goods: a sharp knife is 'good' for killing people. The 'good' (singular) denotes a view of the world, such as a religion. (*See also* rightness).

Government The resolution of conflicts of interest. It can occur at every level in society; it is inherent in social relationships, and needs to be contrasted with the state.

Harm Damage to somebody or something; normally, damage to a person's fundamental interests.

Hierarchy An asymmetrical linkage that is inherent in relationships. It is normally assumed to be repressive, but it need not be.

Human rights Entitlements to treatment which it is claimed individuals have simply by virtue of being human.

Humanitarian intervention Military intervention in order to prevent the serious violation of human rights.

Identity The sense of belonging to something, or of sharing an attribute, such as religious belief, gender or ethnicity, with other people.

Individual A person who is separate from others but who finds their identity through relating to these others.

Intuition The sense that something is right and wrong, despite the inability to articulate reasons for that view. Much political theory entails appeal to intuitions.

Justice Distributive justice is concerned with the fair distribution of the 'benefits' and 'burdens' of cooperation (retributive justice is a quite separate concept – it is the idea that a punishment should 'fit' a crime).

Law A norm passed by a specific procedure and recognised as binding. A law does not necessarily need force as a sanction.

Legal equality Each person has the right to a fair trial, and sanctions, such as imprisonment, are similar for all people.

Legal moralism The view that the law should be used to enforce moral beliefs or practices – opponents of legal moralism do not reject morality, but argue that non-harmful acts should not be illegal.

Legitimacy Power that has been authorised through an appeal to a wider constituency.

Liberalism An ideology that takes freedom (or liberty) to be a fundamental value; it also regards individuals as naturally equal, although natural equality is, for many liberals, compatible with significant material inequality.

Libertarianism   A form of liberalism that takes private property rights to be of fundamental importance.

Liberty   *See* freedom.

Linguistic analysis   A view that theoretically challenging problems are problems arising from the use of language.

Market   A mechanism that enables exchanges to occur, but in a way which conceals the real power that people possess.

Marxism   A theory whose potential for emancipation is undermined by notions of class war, revolution and dictatorship.

Meritocracy   A society in which wealth, and other goods, are distributed according to innate ability.

Modernism (or **modernity**)   A term that denotes the onset of the liberal period so that modernism is used as a synonym for liberalism.

Momentum concept   A concept that has a potential for freedom and equality, but whose progress is infinite, and therefore can never be realised.

Monopoly   A process or agent that dominates a collectivity demanding ultimate loyalty from its subjects.

Morality   A system of beliefs that emphasises the rightness or wrongness of an activity or process.

Multiculturalism   The existence of a number of cultures in a single political system; alternatively, an ideology which recognises that fact as important or values such diversity.

Nation   A collective, normally territorial, entity which commands allegiance. Some theorists argue that nations are the product of modernity, others claim they are 'primordial' or perennial.

Nationalism   An ideology that takes the nation to be of fundamental value.

Natural   A process that is developmental. What is natural is therefore susceptible to historical change.

Naturalism   A doctrine which treats the natural in a static and ahistorical way. It assumes that what exists at the present can never change.

Neo-conservatism   An American stream of conservatism that stresses natural rights and the importance of resisting what it sees as tyranny.

Order   A stability in the possession of things; security against violence and a trust in others that promises will be kept.

Paternalism   Intervention to restrict a person's freedom on the grounds that it is in his or her interests to do so.

Patriarchal   A static concept and practice that enshrines male domination. Patriarchy need not be pursued by biological men.

Perennialism   A body of theory concerned to explain the rise of the nation. Perennialists claim that nations predate modernity, although nationalism – consciousness of nationhood – is modern.

Political obligation   The moral obligation to obey the state. Many political theorists, especially anarchists, question whether political obligation is possible.

Politics   A public process that involves resolving conflicts of interest. Politics is undermined by force, and is inherent at every level in all societies.

Post-liberalism   A theory that accepts liberalism but goes beyond it, by extending liberal values to all individuals and thus challenging the need for a state.

Postmodernism   A theory that goes beyond modernism and therefore challenges the dualisms and one-sidedness expressed in the modernist tradition.

Power   The capacity to exert pressure on a person or group so that they do something they otherwise would not have done.

Prejudice   Used in a specific sense by conservatives to mean judging the right action by appeal to habit and experience rather than to rational analysis.

Pre-modern   A theory and practice which has yet to obtain the institutions and to support the values of liberalism (or modernism).

Private   The sphere of life in which conflict is imperceptible or embryonic.

Private property   The division of material goods according to which individuals have an entitlement to a certain good and can exclude other people from its use.

Public   The sphere of life in which conflict is manifest and has to be resolved.

Race   A concept used to categorise people according to how they look (phenotypical similarity).

Reconstruction   The reworking of concepts so that an alternative to the status quo is charted.

Relational   An approach that stresses that individuals and collectivities only find their identity in relationships with one another.

Relationship   A linkage that is vitiated by force but whose mutuality is necessarily hierarchical in character and sustained by constraint.

Relativism   The rejection of universalism: moral norms are dependent on a cultural context.

Religion   An organised system of belief and practice centred around an idea of 'holiness' – that is, something outside historical experience.

Revolution   A fundamental transformation of something: revolutions can be social, economic, intellectual and political.

Rightness   That which is obligatory: for example, you should keep your promises. A person can do the right thing for bad reasons, so rightness must be distinguished from goodness.

Rights Individual entitlements to something.

Slavery A term that embraces people who are unfree and are the property of others. Although chattel slavery – the explicit and legal ownership of people – has largely died in the contemporary world, the term can be applied analogously to people who have to work for or are wholly dependent on others.

Socialism An ideology that asserts society is of equal importance to the individual, and it can therefore be regulated publicly in the interests of the individual.

Society A group of people who relate to one another for specific purposes. Societies exist at an infinitely of levels.

Sovereignty The ability to govern one's own life: sovereignty is an absolute concept that can only express itself in particular historical circumstances.

State An institution that claims a monopoly of legitimate force for a particular territory. This claim makes it contradictory and paradoxical.

State sovereignty The claim by supporters of the state that the state has ultimate and final legitimate force over a particular society.

Static concept One that is divisive in character and cannot therefore be reconstructed.

Statism An approach that creates or accepts divisions and thus the need for force to tackle them.

Terrorism The use of political violence in situations in which people have reasonable avenues of peaceful protest.

Toleration The willingness to allow other people to behave in ways of which we disapprove. The first major historical form of political toleration was religious toleration.

Totalitarianism A movement or system that aspires to control every aspect of society in an authoritarian manner. It therefore rejects liberalism and democracy.

Universalism The belief that there are moral codes or values binding on all people, irrespective of culture. The alternative position is cultural or ethical relativism.

Utilitarianism A stream of liberal thought that maintains political institutions should maximise the overall level of utility in society. Utilitarians disagree about the definition of 'utility', but possibilities include pleasure, happiness and preference satisfaction.

Victimhood A belief, usually from victims, that their plight is caused by themselves or others who must be blamed and punished as a substitute for actively seeking the roots of their problem.

Violence A synonym for force.

Will A capacity to exercise choice as an agent.